PAUL *in* ACTS

PAUL *in* ACTS

Stanley E. Porter

LIBRARY OF PAULINE STUDIES

Stanley E. Porter, *General Editor*

Hendrickson Publishers, Inc.
P. O. Box 3473
Peabody, Massachusetts 01961–3473

PAUL IN ACTS, by Stanley E. Porter, is a reprint of THE PAUL OF ACTS: ESSAYS IN LITERARY CRITICISM, RHETORIC, AND THEOLOGY. Wissenschaftliche Untersuchungen zum Neuen Testament 115. Tübingen: J. C. B. Mohr (Paul Siebeck) © 1999. All rights reserved. Hendrickson Publishers' edition reprinted by arrangement with

J. C. B. Mohr (Paul Siebeck), P. O. Box 2040, D–72010 Tübingen

First printing — October 2001

Printed in the United States of America

Cover illustration: Raphael (14v b83–1520), *Paul Preaching at Athens,* 1515–16. Tapestry cartoon. Victoria & Albert Museum, London. Art Resource, N.Y.

Library of Congress Cataloging-in-Publication Data

Porter, Stanley E., 1956–
    [Paul of Acts]
    Paul in Acts / Stanley E. Porter.
      p. cm. — (Library of Pauline studies)
    Originally published: The Paul of Acts. Tübingen : Mohr Siebeck, c1999, in series: Wissenschaftliche Untersuchungen zum Neuen Testament.
    Includes bibliographical references and indexes.
    ISBN 1-56563-613-9 (pbk. : alk. paper)
    1. Paul, the Apostle, Saint. 2. Bible. N.T. Acts—Criticism, interpretation, etc. I. Title. II. Series.

BS2506.3 .P67 2001
226.6'06—dc21

                                                      2001051602

Preface

This volume has been developed and written in much more diverse circumstances than have surrounded any of the other books that I have written. The writing itself has occurred virtually entirely in Europe, though the ideas were first aired publicly mostly in North America. Much of the writing took place in London, England, where I am privileged to be the Professor and Chair of a vibrant and active Centre for Advanced Theological Research and Head of the Department of Theology and Religious Studies. My colleagues, both those younger and those older, are a constant stimulation to do good work, as we share the common purpose of developing and perpetuating a research culture in the finest tradition of British scholarship. One of the most commendable elements of that tradition – and one that Roehampton Institute London safeguards in a highly commendable way – is the openness with which we can discuss various scholarly positions. I have taken advantage of the freedom to re-think many of my stances, some of them reflected in this volume, free from being pulled by stifling critical conformity on the one side, and unreflective confessional orthodoxy on the other. Some of the writing of this volume also occurred in the Protestant Theological Faculty of Charles University in Prague, Czech Republic. As a Visiting Scholar there, I had the opportunity of using the valuable library, and being able to have time to think for uninterrupted periods about many of the issues raised in this book.

Those who have helped in the formulation, refinement and felicitous phrasing (such as there is) of this volume deserve mention, as well. Included are the many attentive auditors who were present when many of the chapters in this volume were first presented at various places and on various occasions spread over three continents. I took particularly full advantage of many opportunities to deliver papers at conferences, especially in North America, in order to develop my ideas on Acts and Paul more completely. Many times there were stimulating and difficult questions asked, as well as healthy conversation afterwards. I wish also to thank two of my research students, Gustavo Martín-Asensio and Matthew Brook O'Donnell, my colleagues Brook W.R. Pearson (who suggested the title for this volume) and Arthur Gibson, and my wife (and closest colleague), Wendy, for reading various versions of this manuscript, and making many well-deserved comments that resulted in serious improvements and refinements.

Lastly, I wish to thank Professor Dr Martin Hengel for his acceptance of this volume into the WUNT Series. He not only provided helpful suggestions for its improvement, but was encouraging of what this monograph is trying to accomplish.

This volume is dedicated to those who suffered, and even died, for their faith and Christian scholarship during the damnable Soviet communist occupation of Central Europe, and especially to those "freedom fighters" of the Protestant Theological Faculty of Charles University, who not only endured but ultimately triumphed.

Stanley E. Porter

Contents

Chapter One

Methods and Assumptions in this Study of the Paul of Acts

The title of this volume, *The Paul of Acts*, is a play on the title of the well-known apocryphal work, the *Acts of Paul*.[1] The play on the title is self-conscious, and descriptive of the project contained within these pages. This is not a tightly-organized monograph that tries to argue a single hypothesis, but a series of studies that focus upon the depiction of Paul in the book of Acts from literary-critical, rhetorical, and theological perspectives, among several others. In a limited sense, this volume is an attempt to provide a "disciplined narrative-critical character study of Paul in Acts," something that Gowler says is "yet to be done."[2] The essays contained within this volume were explicitly written as a result of contemplation of various issues in recent Pauline studies, focused initially upon the Paul of his letters. After having written a number of essays, as well as a monograph, on various dimensions of Paul and his letters,[3] it seemed natural to extend my study and pursue various topics

---

[1] See the recent study of this interesting apocryphal book in J.N. Bremmer (ed.), *The Apocryphal Acts of Paul and Thecla* (Kampen: Kok Pharos, 1996). Cf. R. Brawley, "Paul in Acts: Lucan Apology and Conciliation," in C.H. Talbert (ed.), *Luke–Acts: New Perspectives from the Society of Biblical Literature Seminar* (New York: Crossroad, 1984) 129–147.

[2] D.B. Gowler, *Host, Guest, Enemy, and Friend: Portraits of the Pharisees in Luke and Acts* (ESEC 2; New York: Lang, 1991) 285 n. 209; cf. R.L. Brawley, "Paul in Acts: Aspects of Structure and Characterization," in D.J. Lull (ed.), *Society of Biblical Literature 1988 Seminar Papers* (SBLSP 27; Atlanta: Scholars Press, 1988) 90–105, who commentates on narrative literary devices in pp. 96–103.

[3] The following are what I consider to be the most important works that I have written on Paul and his letters, not including some others mentioned below in this chapter: S.E. Porter, Καταλλάσσω *in Ancient Greek Literature, with Reference to the Pauline Writings* (Estudios de Filología Neotestamentaria 5; Córdoba, Spain: Ediciones El Almendro, 1994); with J.A.D. Weima, *An Annotated Bibliography of 1 and 2 Thessalonians* (NTTS 26; Leiden: Brill, 1998); "The PaulineConcept of Original Sin, in Light of Rabbinic Background," *TynBul* 41.1 (1990) 3–30; "ἴστε γινώσκοντες in Ephesians 5:5: Does Chiasm Solve a Problem?" *ZNW* 81 (1990) 270–276; "Romans 13:1–7 as Pauline Political Rhetoric," *FN* 3 (1990) 115–139; "The Argument of Romans 5: Can a Rhetorical Question Make a Difference?" *JBL* 110 (1991) 655–677; "What Does it Mean to be 'Saved by Childbirth' (1 Timothy 2:15)?" *JSNT* 49 (1993) 87–102; "A Newer Perspective on Paul: Romans 1–8 through the Eyes of Literary

related to Paul in Acts that had suggested themselves. Issues such as the character of Paul as seen in Acts and the letters, the relation of Paul the letterwriter to Paul the speaker, and various dimensions of Paul's theology as seen in Acts and the letters, emerged as suitable for investigation. For that reason, this is not an attempt at a thorough and complete study of all of the various dimensions of how Paul is described and depicted in the book of Acts, to say nothing of it being a study of the book of Acts as a whole. The topics presented are selective ones, but ones that I think address many of the most important issues raised in current scholarship on how Paul appears in the book of Acts, since I believe "that the author of Acts is concerned that his readers should form an adequate estimation of the character of Paul"[4] (my conclusions, however, do not always answer the questions in the way many might have come to expect, according to the critical consensus). To my surprise, once I began writing and putting this volume together, I came to realize that there are not many other books in English that have devoted themselves to studying the Paul of Acts in the way that I do here. Many of these treatments are devoted to various dimensions of the juridical elements of Paul's presence in Acts,[5] usually giving more attention to how these

---

Analysis," in M.D. Carroll R., D.J.A. Clines, and P.R. Davies (eds.), *The Bible in Human Society: Essays in Honour of John Rogerson* (JSOTSup 200; Sheffield: Sheffield Academic Press, 1995) 366–392; "Reconciliation and 2 Cor 5,18–21," in R. Bieringer (ed.), *The Corinthian Correspondence* (BETL 125; Leuven: Leuven University Press/Peeters, 1996) 693–705; "Understanding Pauline Studies: An Assessment of Recent Research," *Themelios* [Part One] 22 (1; 1996) 14–25; [Part Two] 22 (2; 1997) 13–24; "Images of Christ in Paul's Letters," in S.E. Porter, M.A. Hayes, and D. Tombs (eds.), *Images of Christ: Ancient and Modern* (RILP 2; Sheffield: Sheffield Academic Press, 1997) 95–112; with K.D. Clarke, "Canonical-Critical Perspective and the Relationship of Colossians and Ephesians," *Bib* 78 (1997) 57–86; "The Use of the Old Testament in the New Testament: A Brief Comment on Method and Terminology," in C.A. Evans and J.A. Sanders (eds.), *Early Christian Interpretation of the Scriptures of Israel: Investigations and Proposals* (SSEJC 5; JSNTSup 148; Sheffield: Sheffield Academic Press, 1997) 79–96; "Exegesis of the Pauline Letters, including the Deutero-Pauline Letters," in S.E. Porter (ed.), *Handbook to Exegesis of the New Testament* (NTTS 25; Leiden: Brill, 1997) 503–553; with J.T. Reed, "Philippians as a Macro-Chiasm and its Exegetical Significance," *NTS* 44 (1998) 213–231; and "The Rhetorical Scribe: Textual Variants in Romans and their Possible Rhetorical Purpose," in S.E. Porter and D.L. Stamps (eds.), *Rhetoric, Method and the Bible: Essays from the 1998 Florence Conference* (JSNTSup; Sheffield: Sheffield Academic Press, forthcoming). I have also edited, with C.A. Evans, *The Pauline Writings: A Sheffield Reader* (BibSem 34; Sheffield: Sheffield Academic Press, 1995).

[4] C.J.A. Hickling, "The Portrait of Paul in Acts 26," in J. Kremer (ed.), *Les Actes des Apôtres: Traditions, rédaction, théologie* (BETL 48; Gembloux: Duculot; Leuven: Leuven University Press, 1979) 503.

[5] Books that treat certain dimensions of this include H.W. Tajra, *The Trial of St Paul: A Juridical Exegesis of the Second Half of the Acts of the Apostles* (WUNT 2.35; Tübingen:

features relate to the historical context than how they relate to Paul himself. One of these that has proved insightful, with more attention to the narrative and character development than others, is M.-E. Rosenblatt's short *Paul the Accused*.[6] In a narrative-exegetical fashion, she analyzes the book of Acts, especially those passages that are concerned with accusations brought against Paul. Perhaps inevitably, because of the sweep of her topic, her treatment of a given passage is often brief. I have, instead, chosen to treat a smaller number of passages, and discuss them in more detail, without the constraint of focusing on only one theme.

The essays included in this volume have all been researched and written in the last five years, as various new dimensions of the study of the Paul of Acts presented themselves to me as worthy of further exploration. Whereas one of the essays, the earliest, has been previously published, and another is in press at this time,[7] these two chapters have been thoroughly scrutinized and completely re-written in light of the other essays, my continued thinking about the topic, and the most important secondary literature that has appeared since. All of the other essays are published here for the first time.

This series of studies has both fortuitously progressive and decidedly traditional elements to it. The subject matter itself is, it seems to me, one of the more progressive elements. This is not a volume on the theology of Acts, a treatment specifically focused upon the historical Paul as seen in Acts, or a study of ancient rhetoric or epistolography, even though these topics – and others – are introduced in different places and contexts throughout the volume.[8] What this volume intends to be is a depiction of one character, Paul,

---

Mohr–Siebeck, 1989); B. Rapske, *The Book of Acts in its First Century Setting*. III. *The Book of Acts and Paul in Roman Custody* (Grand Rapids: Eerdmans, 1994); J.C. Lentz, Jr, *Luke's Portrait of Paul* (SNTSMS 77; Cambridge: Cambridge University Press, 1993). This is not a complete list, and does not include sections on Paul within larger monographs. A commendable approach to another character in Acts is by F.S. Spencer, *The Portrait of Philip in Acts: A Study of Roles and Relations* (JSNTSup 67; Sheffield: JSOT Press, 1992).

[6] M.-E. Rosenblatt, *Paul the Accused: His Portrait in the Acts of the Apostles* (Collegeville, MN: Liturgical, 1995). One of the important topics discussed in my volume is the "we" passages, a topic of which Rosenblatt takes only short notice (e.g. p. 44).

[7] S.E. Porter, "The 'We' Passages," in D.W.J. Gill and C. Gempf (eds.), *The Book of Acts in its First Century Setting*. II. *The Book of Acts in its Graeco-Roman Setting* (Grand Rapids: Eerdmans, 1994) 545–574, incorporated, with major changes, in this volume as Chapter Two; *idem*, "Paul as Rhetorician *and* Epistolographer?" in S.E. Porter and D.L. Stamps (eds.), *Rhetoric and the Bible: Essays from the 1996 Malibu Conference* (JSNTSup; Sheffield: Sheffield Academic Press, forthcoming 1999), incorporated, with radical expansion, in this volume as Chapter Four.

[8] My major extended treatment of Acts will be published in my commentary on Acts for the New International Greek Testament Commentary Series, edited by I.H. Marshall and

as he is presented and appears in various ways in the book of Acts, sometimes in narrative, sometimes delivering speeches, sometimes traveling. The major material in Acts that provides the basis for discussion of these topics is the "we" passages and Paul's many speeches, and the events that surround these sections.

Without entering into the expansive debate on the topic of literary interpretation of the New Testament,[9] in a sense this is a literary study of the figure of Paul as seen in various ways in the book of Acts.[10] Literary-critical questions – such as those about possible sources used by the author and about the relation of the Paul of Acts to the Paul of the letters – are raised intermittently and at (what I consider to be) crucial junctures. For the most part, however, this series of studies concentrates first and foremost upon how Paul is depicted as a literary character, that is, as a character in Acts. The literary dimensions of this study, therefore, encompass both traditional literary or form criticism, concerned with the study of literary types such as the travel narrative, and modern literary criticism, that is, a phenomenological exposition of a character involved in action (plot). No sustained defense of the methods is offered here. Traditional literary criticism has too long a history to need further discussion of its strengths and weaknesses, as many as those may be.[11] Instead, Chapter Two offers a test of whether a traditional literary-critical method (in conjunction with redaction criticism) can provide a

---

D.A. Hagner (Grand Rapids: Eerdmans; Carlisle: Paternoster), tentatively scheduled to appear in 2004.

[9] For a recent discussion of this topic, see B.W.R. Pearson, "New Testament Literary Criticism," in Porter (ed.), *Handbook to Exegesis of the New Testament*, 241–266; cf. S.E. Porter, "Literary Approaches to the New Testament: From Formalism to Deconstruction and Back," in S.E. Porter and D. Tombs (eds.), *Approaches to New Testament Study* (JSNTSup 120; Sheffield: Sheffield Academic Press, 1995) 77–128. On Acts, see M.A. Powell, *What are They Saying about Acts?* (New York: Paulist, 1991) 96–107. A fairly recent bibliography on the subject is found in M. Minor, *Literary-Critical Approaches to the Bible: An Annotated Bibliography* (West Cornwall, CT: Locust Hill, 1992) 413–420, 450–454. Note that his definition of literary criticism is quite broad and encompassing.

[10] For a discussion and evaluation of literary interpretation of Acts, a helpful, though not entirely convincing, study is F.S. Spencer, "Acts and Modern Literary Approaches," in B.W. Winter and A.D. Clarke (eds.), *The Book of Acts in its First Century Setting*. I. *The Book of Acts in its Ancient Literary Setting* (Grand Rapids: Eerdmans, 1993) 381–414.

[11] For discussion of traditional literary criticism, see D.R. Catchpole, "Source, Form and Redaction Criticism of the New Testament," in Porter (ed.), *Handbook to Exegesis of the New Testament*, 168, 170–175; cf. J. Roloff, *Die Apostelgeschichte* (NTD 5; Berlin: Evangelische Verlags-Anstalt, 1981) 6–10, for a history of discussion of the literary character of Acts. That traditional and modern literary criticism can easily be confused, with what purports to be the latter ending up the former, is seen in J.M. Robinson, "Acts," in R. Alter and F. Kermode (eds.), *The Literary Guide to the Bible* (London: Fontana, 1989) 467–478.

more convincing explanation than other recent methods of analysis in assessing certain phenomena in Acts, in particular the "we" passages, and how they are intertwined in a third-person narrative. (It is in this context that I offer a discussion of the genre of Acts.) This effort is important because of the role that the "we" passages play in revealing the character of Paul in Acts. The attempt to combine theology with form-critical study is also an element not readily found in other treatments of Acts.[12] Once the character of the "we" passages has been described, the theology of the passages, in particular their relationship to the presentation of the character of Paul as he is depicted in these passages, is explored in Chapter Three. The conclusions reached here should provide material for further consideration, since there is found to be some significant differences between the Paul of the "we" passages and the Paul of the rest of Acts. Chapter Four continues this style of exposition, by examining Paul and the Holy Spirit in Acts. This exposition is in terms of how the Holy Spirit and Paul relate to each other in Acts, not treating either independently or as general topics as they occur throughout Acts. This more narrowly circumscribes the subject in terms of the focus of this volume, and, by doing so, introduces a dimension of study that is not usually discussed.

A topic of much recent discussion is the relationship of ancient rhetoric to the study of the Pauline letters.[13] In Chapter Five, I explore this subject from a slightly different angle than is usually employed. Beginning with the basic recognition that the Paul of the letters is an epistolographer and the Paul of Acts is an orator, I address questions raised by this analysis. Included here is brief discussion of the role of speeches in ancient literature, offering my own perspective on the programmatic statement in Thucydides 1.22.1.[14] In this chapter, questions of the relationship between the Paul of Acts and the Paul of the letters are inevitably raised, suggested by the material in Acts as the point of initial comparison. Then, in Chapters Six and Seven, I pursue analysis of the oratorical dimension of Paul's speeches in Acts, dividing the treatment

---

[12] See, for example, H.C. Kee, *Good News to the Ends of the Earth: The Theology of Acts* (London: SCM Press; Philadelphia: Trinity Press International, 1990).

[13] On this topic, see S.E. Porter, "The Theoretical Justification for Application of Rhetorical Categories to Pauline Epistolary Literature," in S.E. Porter and T.H. Olbricht (eds.), *Rhetoric and the New Testament: Essays from the 1992 Heidelberg Conference* (JSNTSup 90; Sheffield: Sheffield Academic Press, 1993) 100–122; *idem,* "Paul of Tarsus and his Letters," in S.E. Porter (ed.), *Handbook of Classical Rhetoric in the Hellenistic Period 330 B.C.–A.D. 400* (Leiden: Brill, 1997) 533–585.

[14] My fuller treatment of this topic is found in S.E. Porter, "Thucydides 1.22.1 and Speeches in Acts: Is There a Thucydidean View?" *NovT* 32 (1990) 121–142; repr. with modifications in *idem, The Greek of the New Testament: Theory and Practice* (SBG 5; New York: Lang, 1996) 173–193.

into expositions of the so-called missionary speeches and of the so-called apologetic speeches. Soards has done much valuable work on the rhetorical dimension of the speeches in Acts.[15] Whereas these two chapters appreciate his work, my approach is different, in that it explores the nature of the speeches in terms of the character of Paul the speechgiver as revealed in Acts, not simply as part of a larger scheme of analysis of all of the speeches in Acts, or simply of all of Paul's speeches. After discussing the character of his missionary and apologetic speeches, I draw some inevitable points of comparison between Paul's approach in the speeches and his approach to similar topics in his letters.

Chapter Eight may well prove to be the most provocative chapter in the volume, not necessarily because of a methodological progressiveness, but because of the nature of the thesis that it advances. In a brief examination of Acts 21, I conclude that there is a distinct possibility that, by the way they behaved, the leaders of the church in Jerusalem in some ways established a context of distrust of Paul, which manipulation indirectly contributed to his arrest. Chapter Nine is placed last so as not to distract from what I have been trying to do in the bulk of the volume – that is, to examine Paul through Acts, and not through his letters. Nevertheless, it seemed almost inevitable that I would finally need to address the major critical questions concerning the relationship between the Paul of Acts and of the letters, which I do through subjecting the major arguments against their close relation to rigorous scrutiny. I was frankly disappointed with the level of precision with which this case has been made, in which assumption often seems to have replaced evidence. Thus, my hope is that, from a methodological standpoint, a contribution of this volume is in its unique drawing together of several areas of recent New Testament studies – including forms of literary criticism, rhetorical criticism and epistolography, as well as theology – in the service of analysis of one dimension of the book of Acts, the depiction of the actions, behavior and beliefs of the Paul of Acts.

There are also a number of elements of this study that will strike the reader as rather traditional. To be straightforward, now that my study is complete (at least for the time being), I am not convinced that there is as great a separation between the Paul of Acts and the Paul of the letters as many have posited. At the least, the arguments that have often been marshalled to establish the differences between the two, when critically scrutinized, do not seem compelling. What differences there are seem to be fully explicable in terms of

---

[15] M.L. Soards, *The Speeches in Acts: Their Conten., Context, and Concerns* (Louisville: Westminster/John Knox, 1994).

Acts and the letters being written by two different authors, with their commonalties pointing to close contact between the two, including the use by the author of Acts (whom I call Luke) of a first-hand source – the "we" passages. In other words, to use the taxonomy of Mattill, my position would probably fall within what he calls the "one-Paul view of historical research."[16] Further, in the rest of the volume, I will often use "Luke" to refer to the author of Luke–Acts, even though the two works are formally anonymous. The conclusion that I have drawn from other study (and do not argue directly in detail, apart from in Chapter Nine) is that the author of Acts was someone much like the traditional figure of Luke (if not Luke himself). It seems to me that, on the basis of historical, literary and theological reasons, that is as reasonable an estimation as any other, and better than most.[17] The difference this makes for analysis in most of the chapters is minimal, however, so even those who categorically reject this analysis should still be able to benefit from much of this volume without this feature obstructing their reading.

Of more personal concern, however, is the methodology of my approach. I believe that there is only limited productive capacity in most literary methods as they are being practiced in New Testament studies today, and my simply invoking and slipping into a phenomenological (or, perhaps, New Critical or formalist) stance without presenting full justification for this approach, some would say, is naive at best, and highly suspect at worst. I am aware of the major critical issues regarding this position, having raised them elsewhere myself,[18] but believe that, nevertheless, the essays stand here on their own without need for justification in this context. Of greater significance, however, is the fact that I have not utilized what I consider to be the next step forward in further New Testament exegetical study, namely, various forms of

---

[16] A.J. Mattill, Jr, "The Value of Acts as a Source for the Study of Paul," in C.H. Talbert (ed.), *Perspectives on Luke–Acts* (Danville, VA: Association of Baptist Professors of Religion, 1978) 76–98, esp. 77–83. Mattill defines the following categories: the One-Paul View of the School of Historical Research, the Two-Paul View of the School of Creative Edification, the Lopsided-Paul View of the School of Restrained Criticism, and the Three-Paul View of the School of Advanced Criticism. According to him, the Two-Paul View is the most dominant.

[17] This subject is discussed in more detail in L.M. McDonald and S.E. Porter, *Early Christianity and its Sacred Literature* (Peabody, MA: Hendrickson, forthcoming 1999) chap. 8; cf. W.G. Kümmel, *Introduction to the New Testament* (trans. H.C. Kee; Nashville: Abingdon: 17th edn, 1975) 147–150 for a brief survey; and the detailed discussion of the historical evidence in C.-J. Thornton, *Der Zeuge des Zeugen: Lukas als Historiker der Paulusreisen* (WUNT 56; Tübingen: Mohr–Siebeck, 1991) 8–81.

[18] See Porter, "Literary Approaches to the New Testament," esp. 97–106.

functional grammatical and sociolinguistically-based discourse analysis.[19] On
the basis of my having explored such methods elsewhere, as well as having
seen the productive results when such methods are creatively employed by
others, I believe that a more rigorous and explicit methodology of text-based
"linguistic criticism" must continue to be developed alongside historically-
based criticism, as is being done in a number of circles.[20] (Elsewhere, I have

---

[19] For some of my explorations in these areas, see S.E. Porter, *Verbal Aspect in the Greek
of the New Testament, with Reference to Tense and Mood* (SBG 1; New York: Lang, 1989);
Idioms of the Greek New Testament (BLG 2; Sheffield: Sheffield Academic Press, 2nd edn,
1994) esp. 298–307; *Studies in the Greek New Testament, passim*; "Studying Ancient
Languages from a Modern Linguistic Perspective: Essential Terms and Terminology," *FN* 2
(1989) 147–172; with J.T. Reed, "Greek Grammar since BDF: A Retrospective and
Prospective Analysis," *FN* 4 (1991) 143–164; "Word Order and Clause Structure in New
Testament Greek: An Unexplored Area of Greek Linguistics Using Philippians as a Test
Case," *FN* 6 (1993) 177–205; "The Date of the Composition of Hebrews and Use of the
Present Tense-Form," in S.E. Porter, P. Joyce, and D.E. Orton (eds.), *Crossing the
Boundaries: Essays on Biblical Interpretation in Honour of Michael D. Goulder* (BIS 8;
Leiden: Brill, 1994) 313–332; "Discourse Analysis and New Testament Studies: An
Introductory Survey," in S.E. Porter and D.A. Carson (eds.), *Discourse Analysis and Other
Topics in Biblical Greek* (JSNTSup 113; Sheffield: Sheffield Academic Press, 1995) 14–35;
"Rhetorical Analysis and Discourse Analysis of the Pauline Corpus," in S.E. Porter and T.H.
Olbricht (eds.), *The Rhetorical Analysis of Scripture: Essays from the 1995 London
Conference* (JSNTSup 146; Sheffield: Sheffield Academic Press, 1997) 249–274; and
"Dialect and Register in the Greek New Testament: Theory," and "Register in the Greek New
Testament: Application with Reference to Mark's Gospel," in M.D. Carroll R. (ed.),
*Rethinking Context, Rereading Texts: Contributions from the Social Sciences to Biblical
Interpretation* (Sheffield: Sheffield Academic Press, forthcoming 1999).

[20] Among others, see, for example, J.T. Reed, *A Discourse Analysis of Philippians:
Method and Rhetoric in the Debate over Literary Integrity* (JSNTSup 136; Sheffield:
Sheffield Academic Press, 1997); *idem*, "Discourse Analysis," in Porter (ed.), *Handbook to
Exegesis of the New Testament*, 189–217; *idem*, "Cohesive Ties in 1 Timothy: In Defense of
the Epistle's Unity," *Neot* 26 (1992) 131–147; *idem*, "To Timothy or Not: A Discourse
Analysis of 1 Timothy," in S.E. Porter and D.A. Carson (eds.), *Biblical Greek Language and
Linguistics: Open Questions in Current Research* (JSNTSup 80; Sheffield: JSOT Press,
1993) 90–118; *idem*, "Discourse Features in New Testament Letters with Special Reference
to the Structure of 1 Timothy," *Journal of Translation and Textlinguistics* 6 (1993) 228–252;
idem, "Modern Linguistics and the New Testament: A Basic Guide to Theory, Terminology,
and Literature," in Porter and Tombs (eds.), *Approaches to New Testament Study*, 222–265;
G. Martín-Asensio, "Hallidayan Functional Grammar as Heir to New Testament Rhetorical
Criticism," in Porter and Stamps (ed.), *Rhetoric and the Bible*; *idem*, "Foregrounding and its
Relevance for Interpretation and Translation, with Acts 27 as a Case Study," in S.E. Porter
and R.S. Hess (eds.), *Translating the Bible: Problems and Prospects* (JSNTSup; Sheffield:
Sheffield Academic Press, forthcoming 1999); and *idem*, "Participant Reference and
Foregrounded Syntax in the Stephen Episode," S.L. Black, "The Historic Present in Matthew:
Beyond Speech Margins," J.T. Reed, "The Cohesiveness of Discourse: Towards a Model of
Linguistic Criteria for Analyzing New Testament Discourse," M.B. O'Donnell, "The Use of
Annotated Corpora for New Testament Discourse Analysis: A Survey of Current Practice and

defined "linguistic criticism"[21] as the utilization of a fully explicated linguistic interpretative framework, rather than simply the adaptation of a highly selective number of insights from modern linguistics that can help the exegete make a particular point.) In that sense, this set of essays may well stand at a turning point in New Testament methodological eras, as New Testament scholars re-assess the methods at their disposal, turning (I hope) to those that offer a more substantial exegetical framework. In other words, I hope that New Testament criticism is moving beyond impressionistic exegesis that makes grammatical and theological statements on the basis of feelings, hunches, the tradition of interpretation alone (especially if it only reflects recent fads), and other undemonstrated (and undemonstrable) assertions. Examination of the most recent New Testament commentaries, including those on Acts, illustrates that we are far from seeing this goal fully realized, however. I have tried to avoid these faults insofar as the confines and boundaries of a traditional methodology allow this, by presenting what seem to me to be substantial arguments, backed wherever possible by quantifiable grammatical analysis and other exegetical considerations. Those looking for comprehensive citation of all the secondary literature in most modern languages will have to look elsewhere, however.[22] I have cited only selective and representative secondary literature, where I think it germane and important, drawing upon a number of commentaries that have captured some of the sense of the narrative of Acts, but never, I hope, as a substitute for an argument.

In writing this volume, I think that I will have succeeded if I have raised a significant number of important interpretative and methodological issues, and prompted revivified and expanded discussion of one of the seminal figures in early Christianity, as he is depicted in the book of Acts.

Future Prospects," and S.E. Porter, "Is Critical Discourse Analysis Critical? An Evaluation Using Philemon as a Test Case," all in S.E. Porter and J.T. Reed (eds.), *Discourse Analysis and the New Testament: Approaches and Results* (JSNTSup; Sheffield: Sheffield Academic Press, forthcoming 1999); as well as some of the essays in Porter and Carson (eds.), *Discourse Analysis and Other Topics in Biblical Greek*, esp. Part I; and S.E. Porter and D.A. Carson (eds.), *Linguistics and the New Testament: Critical Junctures* (JSNTSup; Sheffield: Sheffield Academic Press, forthcoming 1999).

[21] McDonald and Porter, *Early Christianity and its Sacred Literature*, chap. 2. See also R. Fowler, *Linguistic Criticism* (Oxford: Oxford University Press, 1986).

[22] Abundant bibliography is referred to in J. Jervell, *Die Apostelgeschichte* (MeyerK; Göttingen: Vandenhoeck & Ruprecht, 1998) *passim* (which arrived too late for my use in this volume).

Chapter Two

The "We" Passages in Acts as a Source regarding Paul

1. Introduction

The "we" passages in Acts continue to be discussed for their bearing on questions of source and authorship of the book, as well as its historical reliability.[1] The proposals have been several and their variations legion. To summarize, the four major proposals are: (1) they indicate the author's personal presence as an eyewitness (this is the traditional solution), (2) they reflect a diary or literary source, perhaps from the author but more likely from another writer (this is the source-critical solution), (3) they are some form of redacted document, reflecting the author's imaginative editorial manipulation (this is the redaction-critical solution), or (4) they are a literary creation, reflecting the author's creation of a larger fictive narrative work patterned after contemporary literature, or his use of a literary convention for telling of sea voyages in the first-person plural (this is the so-called literary solution).[2]

---

[1] For summaries of past discussion, see J. Dupont, *The Sources of Acts: The Present Position* (trans. K. Pond; London: Darton, Longman & Todd, 1964) esp. 76–112 on "we" and "they" sources, and 113–65 on forms of "itinerary" theories (cf. *idem*, *Études sur les Actes des Apôtres* [LD 45; Paris: Cerf, 1967] 33–40); D. Guthrie, *New Testament Introduction* (Downers Grove, IL: InterVarsity Press, 3rd edn, 1970) 363–377. Dupont (*Sources of Acts*, 166) contends that the quest for sources is probably futile. I am not as pessimistic as he is, as the following argument attempts to show. The recent neglect of the topic in a major Bible dictionary does not bode well for the subject, however. See L.T. Johnson, "Luke–Acts, Book of," *ABD* 4 (1992) 403–420. For general discussion of the history of Acts scholarship, see W.W. Gasque, *A History of the Criticism of the Acts of the Apostles* (BGBE 17; Tübingen: Mohr–Siebeck; Grand Rapids: Eerdmans, 1975); M.C. Parsons and J.B. Tyson (eds.), *Cadbury, Knox, and Talbert: American Contributions to the Study of Acts* (Atlanta: Scholars Press, 1992); and I.H. Marshall, *The Acts of the Apostles* (NTG; Sheffield: JSOT Press, 1992) 84–91.

[2] For summaries of the issues, see especially S.M. Praeder, "The Problem of First Person Narration in Acts," *NovT* 29 (1987) 193–218; C.J. Hemer, *The Book of Acts in the Setting of Hellenistic History* (ed. C. Gempf; WUNT 49; Tübingen: Mohr–Siebeck, 1989; repr. Winona Lake, IN: Eisenbrauns, 1990) 308–334; *idem*, "First Person Narrative in Acts 27–28," *TynBul* 36 (1985) esp. 79–86; C.-J. Thornton, *Der Zeuge des Zeugen: Lukas als Historiker der*

The above proposals run the gamut from a traditional proposal that places the author of Acts himself actually upon the scene of several important episodes in Paul's life, including his sea voyage to Rome, to various literary-redactional proposals that indicate no correlation whatsoever between the author of Acts and any quantifiable historical knowledge regarding the events he purports to report concerning Paul and his companions. The conclusion one draws regarding the "we" passages has implications, therefore, not only for how one estimates some of the literary-historical influences upon creation of the book of Acts and how one sees early Christianity in its Greco-Roman context, but – more specifically – for how one understands the depiction of Paul, especially in Acts, but also in comparison with his letters. In other words, one's interpretation of the origin and function of the "we" passages has implications whether one finds in Acts an accurate depiction of how Christianity – in particular, Paul – responded to travel and missionary endeavor in the Greco-Roman world, whether one finds in Acts a literary work following a different set of conventions, or whether one finds some combination of both.[3] This chapter analyzes the "we" passages in Acts against their Greco-Roman background, subjecting to scrutiny especially the popular views that correlate the "we" passages with various Greek literary traditions, with special attention to the portrait of Paul that emerges. Along the way, evidence is considered regarding the use of the first-person plural in sea voyages in other ancient Greek literature, including that of ancient historical writers. Then, on the basis of a close reading of the "we" passages, a proposal is offered regarding how much can be known, and the attendant level of certainty, with respect to the "we" passages of Acts, and their depiction of Paul. I conclude that the "we" passages were a previously written source used by the author of Acts, probably not originating with him.

Since this chapter attempts to evaluate the "we" passages in terms of their Greco-Roman setting, a number of proposals regarding possible literary parallels are examined in an attempt to establish suitable literary correspondences. Once these literary correspondences are established, then

---

Paulusreisen (WUNT 56; Tübingen: Mohr–Siebeck, 1991) 93–119; and many others cited below. Several commentaries also have important discussions of the issues, including G. Schneider, *Die Apostelgeschichte* (2 vols.; HTKNT 5.1, 2; Freiburg: Herder, 1980, 1982) 1.89–95; and the concise summary in J.B. Polhill, *Acts* (NAC 26; Nashville: Broadman, 1992) 32–39, esp. 36–38; cf. 24; and J.M. Gilchrist, "The Historicity of Paul's Shipwreck," *JSNT* 61 (1996) 30–35.

[3] It is therefore quite surprising that there is no treatment of the "we" passages in J.C. Lentz, Jr, *Luke's Portrait of Paul* (SNTSMS 77; Cambridge: Cambridge University Press, 1993). This study makes little reference to the original ancient sources, one would have thought a necessity in trying to establish the literary character of the book of Acts.

historical comments can be ventured. As will be commented upon below, many exegetes of these passages entertain historical questions far too early in their discussions, before a suitable literary type or genre has been established for these passages. Others assume that they know the historical worth of these passages and then use this supposed knowledge to establish the genre. In either case, fundamental methodological errors are being made, and continue to be promoted. No single proposal has come close to commanding universal assent. The lines regarding these passages unfortunately tend to be drawn according to theological stance, with some scholars opting toward placing these passages into the category of historically reliable witnesses, probably reflecting the first-hand witness of the author, while other scholars opt for placing these passages into the category of some form of literary fiction. One of the great hindrances to settling this debate – besides the normal theological bias that regrettably often obtrudes into exegesis – is the fact that no truly identical literary parallels to these "we" passages have apparently been found in all of ancient Greek literature (see section 2c below, where Robbins's view is discussed). Without new evidence to draw upon, and certainly without exact parallels for comparison, it is all the more incumbent upon the exegete to weigh the suitable literary, contextual, and historical connections carefully.

2. Theories regarding the Literary Character of Acts

In light of these preliminary comments regarding the "we" passages, various alternatives previously mentioned can be usefully evaluated. Space does not permit a discussion of the entire question of the literary genre of Acts.[4] Instead, proposals are evaluated here in terms of their relationship to the question of the "we" passages in Acts. The view to be evaluated first is one that draws upon comparative literary studies and speculates that the "we" passages of Acts are part of a literary strategy by the author. This view takes three major forms in discussion of Acts. Evaluation of these three positions is followed by presentation and critique of redactional and source-critical positions.

---

[4] For recent discussion of the question of genre, see B.W.R. Pearson and S.E. Porter, "The Genres of the New Testament," in S.E. Porter (ed.), *Handbook to Exegesis of the New Testament* (NTTS 25; Leiden: Brill, 1997) 131–166.

a. Acts as Reflecting the Old Testament

A notable literary theory, perpetuated in part because of the difficulty in explaining the "we" passages from a Greco-Roman perspective, attempts to establish correlations between the "we" passages and Old Testament sources, such as Ezra, Daniel, Tobit and *1 Enoch*, on the basis especially of similar shifts in person.[5] This solution, reflecting the tendency in much study of the New Testament to posit Old Testament antecedents for most literary phenomena, is far from convincing, however, and merits little extended discussion. First, there may be precedents of person shifting in the Old Testament books mentioned above, but it cannot be shown that they have influenced the author of Luke–Acts. There are apparently no significant quotations, allusions or parallels to these Old Testament books in the "we" passages of Acts or their surrounding verses.[6] Concerning style, Kurz admits that the "we" passages reflect a more cultivated and Hellenistic style than earlier sections of Acts, which may reflect the Greek Bible. However, similar stylistic patterns of person shifting are found in other Greco-Roman writers, including historians, as discussed below. Secondly, the kind of shifting in person cited in these supposedly parallel passages establishes a relationship among the first-person participants, that is, "I" and "we" (e.g. Ezra 7 in first person singular, ch. 8 in first person plural and ch. 9 in first person singular), a relationship paralleled in many Greco-Roman writers, but not in Acts, where the relationship involves a change of person from third to first, that is, "he/they" and "we." Thirdly, various technical features, such as selection length, etc., are not sufficiently parallel between the Old Testament sections and Acts to prompt direct comparison (e.g. Dan 6:29–10:1 and Acts 16:8–18).[7]

b. Acts as Ancient Romance

A second literary-based proposal argues that the author of the book of Acts uses the "we" passages as one of several literary devices within the larger

---

[5] See, for example, W.S. Kurz, "Narrative Approaches to Luke–Acts," *Bib* 68 (1987) 205–206; J. Wehnert, *Die Wir-Passagen der Apostelgeschichte: Ein lukanisches Stilmittel aus jüdischer Tradition* (GTA 40; Göttingen: Vandenhoeck & Ruprecht, 1989). For a critique, see B.S. Rosner, "Acts and Biblical History," in B.W. Winter and A.D. Clarke (eds.), *The Book of Acts in its First Century Setting*. I. *The Book of Acts in its Ancient Literary Setting* (Grand Rapids: Eerdmans, 1993) 77–78.

[6] See C.A. Evans, *Noncanonical Writings and New Testament Interpretation* (Peabody, MA: Hendrickson, 1992) 201–202.

[7] See Wehnert, *Die Wir-Passagen*, 154–158.

context of the entire book Acts, which is as an example of the ancient romance or novel, a literary form contemporary with Acts.

Before turning to this position, a tangential proposal must be mentioned and assessed. It has been suggested, for example, that the sea voyage of Acts 27–28 contains a literary defense of Paul against divine vengeance, as witnessed by his escape from disaster at sea. It is argued that the scene reflects Attic oratorical conventions and would have served as a possible line of defense in an Athenian court.[8] This theory has little merit, however, not least because there is no indication that this apologetic strategy would have carried any weight in a Roman court, as even Ladouceur, an advocate of this position, admits. More importantly for this chapter, this view does nothing to explain the "we" passages.

The most common current opinion regarding the suitable Greco-Roman literary type or genre for understanding the book of Acts is that it is an example of the ancient romance or novel. Perhaps this hypothesis is understandable in light of the significant interest recently expressed in the topic of the ancient novel, as more and more classicists have rightly come to appreciate the literary accomplishments of popular and later writers of the ancient world, rather than concentrating their attention mostly, if not exclusively, on the most well-known writers of the classical period. In terms of the book of Acts and the New Testament, this hypothesis has perhaps been most prominently argued by Pervo, although he is far from standing alone in representing this position.[9] Drawing upon a number of ostensibly parallel features, Pervo claims that the book of Acts is best categorized by genre as an example of a "historical novel."[10] Actually, he is ambivalent at this point of definition, and creates a literary genre unparalleled by even the ancient texts

---

[8] G.B. Miles and G. Trompf, "Luke and Antiphon: The Theology of Acts 27–28 in the Light of Pagan Beliefs about Divine Retribution, Pollution and Shipwreck," *HTR* 69 (1976) 259–267; and, with modifications, D. Ladouceur, "Hellenistic Preconceptions of Shipwreck and Pollution as a Context for Acts 27–28," *HTR* 73 (1980) 435–449.

[9] R.I. Pervo, *Profit with Delight: The Literary Genre of the Acts of the Apostles* (Philadelphia: Fortress Press, 1987); see also, for example, P. Pokorny, "Die Romfahrt des Paulus und der antike Roman," *ZNW* 64 (1973) 233–244; S.P. Schiering and M.J. Schiering, "The Influence of the Ancient Romances on the Acts of the Apostles," *Classical Bulletin* 54 (1978) 81–88; R. Hock, "The Greek Novel," in D.E. Aune (ed.), *Greco-Roman Literature and the New Testament: Selected Forms and Genres* (SBLSBS 21; Atlanta: Scholars Press, 1988) esp. 138–144; and L. Alexander, "'In Journeyings Often': Voyaging in the Acts of the Apostles and in Greek Romance," in C.M. Tuckett (ed.), *Luke's Literary Achievement: Collected Essays* (JSNTSup 116; Sheffield: JSOT Press, 1995) 17–49; among others. For a recent treatment of the topic, see R.F. Hock *et al.* (eds.), *Ancient Fiction and Early Christian Narrative* (SBL Symposium Series 6; Atlanta: Scholars Press, 1998).

[10] Pervo, *Profit with Delight*, 136.

he cites. Elsewhere, he defines the book of Acts as follows: "Although clearly a theological book and a presentation of history, Acts also seeks to entertain."[11]

This is not the place to offer a thorough critique of Pervo's work,[12] especially since much of it does not have direct relevance for consideration of the "we" passages, but it does have direct bearing on the issue of the Greco-Roman context of Acts. I confine myself to indicating several of the more problematic logical and literary problems. The most telling is perhaps Pervo's failure to identify the book of Acts with either historical writing *or* the ancient novel. Such a mixed genre as he posits does not appear to have been a recognized genre of the Greco-Roman world. Pervo is quick to point out what he sees as parallels in Acts and ancient novels – such as imprisonments, shipwrecks, travel narratives, and various humorous and lighthearted elements – all of which are paralleled in *both* fictional *and* historical texts of the ancient world, but that do not necessarily imply confusion in the use made of them.[13] In the end, however, he wishes to maintain that Luke's primary source, and one that Luke *does* represent despite his literary and theological embellishments, is the history of early Christianity. This results in the supposition of a generic category Acts purportedly follows that is at odds with the ancient literature that Pervo cites as parallel. Despite their purported use of sources (it is arguable whether the novels use sources in anything like the way or manner that Luke does or claims to do), the ancient novels are not, for the most part, trying to be historical novels, but fictive realistic prose narratives.[14] Thus, Pervo actually creates a new and unique genre for the book of Acts, the very thing he is purportedly trying to avoid in his assessment of the book. He must admit as much when he states that one of the features of

---

[11] Pervo, *Profit with Delight*, 86.

[12] For trenchant criticism, see D.E. Aune, *The New Testament in its Literary Environment* (LEC; Philadelphia: Westminster Press, 1987) 79–80; Marshall, *Acts of the Apostles*, 18–21; R. Bauckham, "The *Acts of Paul* as a Sequel to Acts," in Winter and Clarke (eds.), *Acts in its Ancient Literary Setting*, 105–152, esp. 107–116, who attacks the equation between canonical Acts and the Apocryphal Acts of Paul; and Pearson and Porter, "Genres of the New Testament," 142–146.

[13] On the entertainment value of ancient historical literature, see B.L. Ullman, "History and Tragedy," *TAPA* 73 (1942) 250–253; F.W. Walbank, "History and Tragedy," *Historia* 9 (1960) 216–234. On parallels with other literary features of various ancient writers, see E. Plümacher, *Lukas als hellenistischer Schriftsteller: Studien zur Apostelgeschichte* (SUNT 9; Göttingen: Vandenhoeck & Ruprecht, 1972) *passim*.

[14] There are *perhaps* exceptions in Xenophon's *Cyropaedia* and Pseudo-Callisthenes's *Alexander Romance*, because they follow a historical sequence, although they are still fictional.

the ancient novel was that it was predictable in its outcome,[15] something that is far from certain regarding Acts, especially with its abrupt and, in many ways, literarily questionable and unsatisfactory ending. Pervo must minimize other features of Acts, such as the historical preface, because they are not found in ancient novels.[16]

In supposedly establishing the difficulty with seeing Acts as history, Pervo begins by pointing out what he sees as the historical inaccuracies of Acts. He apparently does not recognize that he has moved outside of the form-critical examination in which he purports to engage. He has moved to criteria that have little, if any, bearing at this stage of discussion on whether the book of Acts is, or is not, a historical account.[17] The possible explanations for the supposed historical flaws in Acts are several. For example, Luke could be a

---

[15] Pervo, *Profit with Delight*, 48–50.

[16] See L. Alexander, *The Preface to Luke's Gospel: Literary Convention and Social Context in Luke 1.1–4 and Acts 1.1* (SNTSMS 78; Cambridge: Cambridge University Press, 1993), for the most recent assessment of the evidence, summarized and up-dated in *idem*, "The Preface to Acts and the Historians," in B. Witherington, III (ed.), *History, Literature and Society in the Book of Acts* (Cambridge: Cambridge University Press, 1996) 73–103. See also the still valuable study of K. Lake, "The Preface to Acts and the Composition of Acts," in F.J. Foakes Jackson and K. Lake (eds.), *The Beginnings of Christianity*. Part I. *The Acts of the Apostles*. V. *Additional Notes to the Commentary* (London: Macmillan, 1933) 1–7. Alexander does not appear to recognize the serious criticisms of her position that the Greek of the New Testament reflects the *Zwischenprosa* (pp. 169–172; adopted from L. Rydbeck, *Fachprosa, vermeintliche Volkssprache und Neues Testament: Zur Beurteilung der sprachlichen Niveauunterschiede im nachklassischen Griechisch* [Uppsala: University of Uppsala; Stockholm: Almqvist & Wiksell, 1967] esp. 187–199; these pages have been printed in English translation in S.E. Porter [ed.], *The Language of the New Testament: Classic Essays* [JSNTSup 60; Sheffield: JSOT Press, 1991] 191–204). Three major lines of criticism are whether the very concept of *Fachprosa* as an in-between stratum existed (see E. Pax, "Probleme des neutestamentlichen Griechisch," *Bib* 53 [1972] 560–562), whether access to the *Vulgärsprache* is so difficult through written documents as Alexander and Rydbeck suppose (see H. Kurzová, "Das Griechische im Zeitalter des Hellenismus," in P. Oliva and J. Burian [eds.], *Soziale Probleme im Hellenismus und im römischen Reich* [Prague: n.p., 1973] 218–224), and whether issues of dialect, register and content have been sufficiently addressed (see S.E. Porter, "Thucydides 1.22.1 and Speeches in Acts: Is there a Thucydidean View?" *NovT* 32 [1990] 124–127; *idem, Verbal Aspect in the Greek of the New Testament, with Reference to Tense and Mood* [SBG 1; New York: Lang, 1989] 147–154).

[17] See D.W. Palmer, "Acts and the Ancient Historical Monograph," in Winter and Clarke (eds.), *The Book of Acts in its Ancient Literary Setting*, 3; cf. G.E. Sterling, *Historiography and Self-Definition: Josephos, Luke–Acts and Apologetic Historiography* (NovTSup 64; Leiden: Brill, 1992) 1–19, esp. 2–3; W.C. van Unnik, "Luke's Second Book and the Rules of Hellenistic Historiography," 37–60, and E. Plümacher, "Die Apostelgeschichte als historische Monographie," 457–466, both in J. Kremer (ed.), *Les Actes des Apôtres: Traditions, rédaction, théologie* (BETL 48; Gembloux: Duculot; Leuven: Leuven University Press, 1979).

historian but a bad one, even a very bad one. There were many in the ancient world, but simply because they were bad historians does not mean that they were therefore writing novels. They were simply engaging in bad history writing.[18] Pervo uses Luke's reporting of speeches as an example of bad history writing, but Pervo's criteria for speeches are themselves skewed. Pervo begins with the assumption that recorded speeches in the Greco-Roman world were to be accurate reflections of what was actually said, taking the conservative and, to my mind, still highly questionable view of Thucydides 1.22.1 as purporting to say that speeches were related as they were actually given.[19]

Thinking to have determined the historical inaccuracy of Acts, Pervo then confirms its fictive nature by comparison with Apocryphal Acts.[20] The circular and anachronistic nature of this argument is manifest. He uses texts that are self-evidently derivative in order to assess the primary source. However, these later fictive interpretations of scenes from canonical Acts cannot be used to assess the literary or historical dimensions of Acts itself. This is confirmed by the treatment of canonical Acts even by classicists who consider Apocryphal Acts to fall within the ancient novel tradition. For example, Hägg assumes canonical Acts is a different sort of literature than the Apocryphal Acts of Paul, which he sees as a type of ancient novel.[21] (Pervo himself cites Söder's similar comment, but only to disagree with it.[22]) There is no apparent evidence that anyone in the early Church took canonical Acts as an example of the novel, either.[23]

---

[18] On this issue, see now L. Alexander, "Fact, Fiction and the Genre of Acts," *NTS* 44 (1998) 380–399.

[19] Pervo, *Profit with Delight*, 13 and n. 4; cf. Porter, "Thucydides 1.22.1 and Speeches in Acts," esp. 127–142; P. Satterthwaite, "Acts against the Background of Classical Rhetoric," in Winter and Clarke (eds.), *The Book of Acts in its Ancient Literary Setting*, 355–357; and W.J. McCoy, "In the Shadow of Thucydides," in Witherington (ed.), *History, Literature and Society*, 4–7. Whatever one's view of the statement in Thucydides regarding speeches, one must also establish the relationship between the speeches and the events purportedly reported. On this relationship, see C. Gempf, "Public Speaking and Published Accounts," in Winter and Clarke (eds.), *The Book of Acts in its Ancient Literary Setting*, 259–303, esp. 303.

[20] Others have made similar claims. See, for example, W. Bindemann, "Verkündigter Verkündiger: Das Paulusbild der Wir-Stücke in der Apostelgeschichte: Seine Aufnahme und Bearbeitung durch Lukas," *TLZ* 114 (1989) 705–720.

[21] T. Hägg, *The Novel in Antiquity* (Berkeley: University of California Press, 1983) 154–162; also B.E. Perry, *The Ancient Romances: A Literary-Historical Account of their Origins* (Berkeley: University of California Press, 1967).

[22] Pervo, *Profit with Delight*, 24, citing R. Söder, *Die apokryphen Apostelgeschichten und die romanhafte Literatur der Antike* (Stuttgart: Kohlhammer, 1969) 151.

[23] See M. Parsons, "The Book of Acts as an Ancient Novel," *Int* 43 (1989) 409.

The way Pervo cites the Apocryphal Acts and other texts verges on parallelomania. He is engaging in what appears to be a piling-on of sources that have parallel elements, but are of highly questionable value when analyzed more closely. Most of the supposed similar elements can be paralleled in ancient historians besides novelists, and their use in the ancient novels is not treated in the same way as it is in Acts. The result is an uncontrolled use of purported parallel accounts. For example, not only does Pervo overstate the importance and significance of the shipwreck motif, present in part in the "we" passages, but he gives a distorted view of its relationship to Acts in the ancient novels. He claims to show that the major features of the convention of the shipwreck appear in Acts.[24] In the parallels that he cites from the ancient novelists, however, not one of the sources he cites has all of the features that Acts does. His model of the shipwreck is apparently his own reconstruction of this type, and not one found in ancient literature in the kind of detail that he claims, or that is necessary to establish the validity of the parallel. (One could legitimately ask the further question of how many of these features are "literary" and how many are required simply to relate the account of a shipwreck.) In her study, Praeder, after comparison of ancient sea voyage accounts, concludes that these accounts are quite varied in style and approach, with none of them a true parallel with the accounts in Acts 27–28. She concludes: "Thus the fact that Acts 27:1–8 and 28:11–16 are travelogues is no guarantee of their literary genre, reliability or unreliability, or purpose in Acts 27:1–28:16."[25]

Perhaps most important for this chapter on the "we" passages, however, is the fact that Pervo fails to consider the significance of the use of the first-person plural in any of the passages in which it is found. This includes the passage in Acts 27, a chapter which does figure heavily into his discussion of Acts, since it contains an account of a sea voyage.[26] His only direct reference to the "we" passages in terms of a sea voyage is in an excursus, where he states, apparently as fact, that the conventions of this passage had been established in Homer's *Odyssey* (14.244–258) and were fixed through centuries of imitation, as Robbins has supposedly pointed out (see section c below), the best example being the *Voyage of Hanno*.[27] One can usefully

---

[24] Pervo, *Profit with Delight*, 52 and n. 189.

[25] S.M. Praeder, "Acts 27:1–28:16: Sea Voyages in Ancient Literature and the Theology of Luke–Acts," *CBQ* 46 (1984) 688.

[26] Pervo, *Profit with Delight*, esp. 50–54.

[27] Pervo, *Profit with Delight*, 57 and n. 232; cf. also E. Haenchen, *The Acts of the Apostles: A Commentary* (trans. B. Noble *et al.*; Philadelphia: Westminster Press, 1971 [1965]) 259–261.

speculate why Pervo fails to exploit this supposed convention in Acts. One possible reason for failing to discuss the use of "we" could be the lack of suitable parallels in the novel accounts, evidence that would hurt Pervo's comparison;[28] another reason might be the failure to find a category by which to account for the practice within this kind of historical-fictive writing, since it clearly seems to imply the use of a recognizable source, not simply a historical antecedent. Some have cited passages from Achilles Tatius (2.31.6;[29] 3.1.1; 4.9.6) and Heliodorus (5.17) as illustrating the use of the first-person sea-voyage convention in the ancient novelists. Pervo is probably wise in not suggesting these as parallels, however, since they are not the kind of sustained usage of the "we" convention in narrative that his hypothesis requires, or that is found in the book of Acts. Furthermore, the sea-voyage convention is not established by usage in the *Odyssey*,[30] including the passage cited by Pervo above, or in Vergil's *Aeneid* (3.5), or in any number of other writers sometimes mentioned (see section c below for further discussion).[31] Citation of the *Odyssey* is not surprising, because the entire epic account is formulated around travel, much of it by sea, so almost any use of the first-person plural could be construed as falling within the sea-voyage genre. The majority of the account in the *Odyssey* is not told in the first person, however, as one might expect from the above contention, thus calling into question the origin and even existence of the first-person sea-voyage convention. The obvious differences between the book of Acts and the *Odyssey* further mitigate comparison. One of these differences is the radically different literary genres of these works (poetic epic versus prose historical/fictive narrative), another is the alternation of singular and plural in the *Odyssey*, quite dissimilar to the sustained usage of the first-person plural (without alternation with first-person singular) in Acts, and a third is the lack of identification of the "we" character in Acts, but who is identified in the *Odyssey*, occurring as part of a flashback technique unparalleled in the book of Acts. Thus, the usage of the first-person plural in Acts is without apparent parallel in at least the sources that Pervo has surveyed.

---

[28] Hanno, whom he does use, is a geographer, not a novelist.

[29] But note that the first-person convention begins at 2.31.3, well before the sea voyage.

[30] A number of passages, especially from books 9–12, are often cited, not all of them equally convincing. They exemplify clearly the shift between first-person singular and plural as part of a narrative flashback. See, for example, Homer, *Od.* 9.39 ff., 62 ff., 82 ff., 105 ff., 142, 543 ff., 565–566; 10.16 ff., 28 ff., 56 ff., 77 ff.; 11.23 ff.; 12.8 ff.

[31] See also Lucian, *Varae Historiae* (*True Story*) 1.5–6; Dio Chrysostom 7.2, 10.

c. Acts as Ancient Sea Voyage

Robbins, however, is convinced of the significance of the comparative sources.[32] Robbins's theory is that there are sufficient literary precedents and parallels to indicate that a recognizable ancient convention was that sea voyages be told in the first-person plural, regardless of the author's involvement in the events. Thus, he can dismiss the idea of any sort of historical or first-hand account lying behind these narratives in the book of Acts, because they are merely conventional. Robbins and others have done a tremendous amount of work in marshaling parallels between Acts and other ancient sources, but these sources seem to be unrepresentative and highly selective.[33] There are major problems in the mix of literatures that Robbins cites (Egyptian, Greek and Latin), their temporal range (1800 BC to third century AD) and their variety of literary genres (epic, poetry, prose narrative, oratory, fantasy, autobiography, romance or novel, scientific prose, etc.). Robbins would probably see this as a virtue, since he claims to be establishing a literary genre that is utilized in a range of literatures over the course of centuries. However, the individual accounts are sufficiently distinct (many merely single references in the first-person plural) that attention to individual passages is necessary if any point is to be proven.

If one were to take the literary prefaces of Luke and Acts[34] as the type of preface found in scientific prose, and therefore find the closest parallel to

---

[32] V.K. Robbins, "By Land and By Sea: The We-Passages and Ancient Sea Voyages," in C.H. Talbert (ed.), *Perspectives on Luke–Acts* (Edinburgh: T. & T. Clark, 1978) 215–242; and earlier in his "The We-Passages in Acts and Ancient Sea-Voyages," *BibRes* 20 (1975) 5–18. For a list of most of the possible passages cited, see Praeder, "First Person Narration," 210–211, who also offers a critique (pp. 210–214).

[33] For criticism of Robbins's work in terms of Acts – for example, with regard to the limited usage of the "we" convention in Acts, and lack of its appearance in Acts and other ancient writers when other sea voyages are described – see J.A. Fitzmyer, *Luke the Theologian: Aspects of his Teaching* (New York: Paulist, 1989) 16–22; Kurz, "Narrative Approaches," 216–217; Thornton, *Der Zeuge*, 150 ff. and *passim*; and B. Witherington, III, *The Acts of the Apostles: A Socio–Rhetorical Commentary* (Grand Rapids: Eerdmans, 1998) 640–641.

[34] I take the author of Luke and Acts as the same person, as indicated by the coordinated prefaces, as well as other linguistic, conceptual and historical factors. Besides Alexander, who assumes the identity of the two (*Preface to Luke's Gospel*, 2 n. 1), see H.J. Cadbury, *The Making of Luke–Acts* (New York: Macmillan, 2nd edn, 1958 [1927]; repr. London: SPCK, 1961) esp. 113–126, 213–238; and now I.H. Marshall, "Acts and the 'Former Treatise,'" in Winter and Clarke (eds.), *The Book of Acts in its Ancient Literary Setting*, 163–182; contra M. Parsons and R.I. Pervo, *Rethinking the Unity of Luke and Acts* (Minneapolis: Fortress Press, 1993) *passim*.

Acts in so-called "scientific" writings (as Alexander has argued),[35] there are only two examples cited by Robbins that might constitute legitimate parallels: *Periplus of the Erythraean Sea (Periplus Maris Erythraei)* 20, 57[36] and *Voyage of Hanno (Hannonis Periplus)* 1–3.[37] The existence of only two actual examples gives quite a different impression than the twenty some authors cited by Robbins in his major article. Apart from numbers, there are other interpretative difficulties as well. The *Periplus*, like a number of geographical texts, displays an unstudied and unsystematic use of person, the kind of thing to be expected from a non-literary document.[38] For example, in 20 and 57, the *Periplus* uses first-person plural as a substitute for the impersonal third-person singular in describing the course one (or "we") would sail in a particular circumstance – not an actual voyage but a recommended course.[39] The few instances cited here are unlike the usage in Acts, and trivial in number and importance for establishing a literary genre.

Hanno's voyage, cited by Pervo and relied upon heavily by Robbins as one of his three most important examples, is more straightforward than their presentations of it might lead one to believe.[40] The use of third person at the beginning of the document (ἔδοξε…πλεῖν…καὶ ἔπλευσε) is reflective of the conventions of the scientific preface that Alexander has studied in detail.[41] In her description, she shows that these prefaces can be isolated from the ensuing text, and that these prefaces have their own style and literary characteristics, including often the use of the third-person or first-person singular.[42] This describes Hanno's account quite accurately. The preface (1), which consists of a declaration by the Carthaginians regarding the sailing task of Hanno, is followed by a description of the voyage that the author undertook (2–18), conveyed throughout the rest of the work, as one might expect, in the first-person plural (ἐπλεύσαμεν). Müller's edition understands

---

[35] Alexander, *Preface to Luke's Gospel*, esp. chap. 6. For criticism of Alexander's assessment of prefaces, see Palmer, "Acts and the Ancient Historical Monograph," 21–26.

[36] K. Müller (ed.), *Geographici Graeci Minores (GGM)* (Paris: Didot, 1855–1861; repr. 1882) 1.273, 299.

[37] *GGM* 1.1–14.

[38] Similar phenomena are found in Scylax, *Periplus Maris Interni* 40, 100 (*GGM* 1.39, 273), Agathemerus, *Geographiae Informatio* 20 (*GGM* 2.481), *Compendium of Geography* 4.5 (*GGM* 2.495). So Hemer, "First Person Narrative," 85 and n. 11.

[39] See Praeder, "First Person Narration," 213 n. 65, who describes the first-person usage as referring to habitual or recommended practices. She also lists examples of first-person plural usage in *Periplus* 26, 29 and 48.

[40] See Hemer, "First Person Narrative," 82–83.

[41] See Alexander, *Preface to Luke's Gospel*, 125–136, esp. 237.

[42] Alexander, *Preface to Luke's Gospel*, esp. 101.

the text that way and prints it as such, with a break between the preface and body of the text. This has implications for Robbins's analysis, however. If this were a valid parallel, just as this account in Hanno purports to be the record of an actual voyage by the narrator, are we to take the "we" passages in Acts as the same kind of record? This is not what Robbins apparently has in mind. And neither are the literary proportions in Hanno's account at all comparable with what we find in Acts, where there are several smaller first-person plural sections embedded within an essentially third-person narrative, not a first-person plural narrative prefaced by a short third-person programmatic description. There is the further difficulty that Hanno's account is probably a translation from a Punic source, which does call into question its validity for indicating a Greek literary tradition. A major difficulty with Alexander's original analysis of the prefaces to Luke–Acts, as she herself has admitted, is that her contention that Acts is scientific prose is essentially concerned with the linguistic and not the content level of analysis.[43] The book of Acts, in so far as its literary structure and content are concerned, is not paralleled in the scientific literature she has in mind, thus probably calling into question the suitability of Robbins's two alleged examples as generic parallels.

If one were to take the prefaces of Luke and Acts as reflecting the type of preface found with historical accounts in the Greco-Roman world,[44] and to compare Acts with these extra-biblical examples, Robbins's parallels would, I believe, still remain unconvincing and perhaps unrepresentative. He does not cite any Greek historian of the time who reflects a parallel usage of the "we" convention found in Acts, apart from the highly fragmentary *Episodes from the Third Syrian War* (see below). He does cite Caesar's *Gallic Wars* (*Bellum Gallicum*) 5.11–13 as evidencing a shift from third-person to first-person technique, but this is in a passage that has nothing to do with a sea voyage; in

---

[43] See L. Alexander, "Luke's Preface in the Context of Greek Preface-Writing," *NovT* 28 (1986) 69 (this view was found in her original doctoral thesis [pp. 130–150], of which this article is a brief summary, and of which her monograph is a published revision). Alexander apparently felt the full force of her argument, modifying her position in her *Preface to Luke's Gospel*, 200–210, esp. 200; cf. *idem*, "Preface to Acts," 101. She goes further in her attempt at a corrective in "Marathon or Jericho? Reading Acts in Dialogue with Biblical and Greek Historiography," in D.J.A. Clines and S.D. Moore (eds.), *Auguries* (JSOTSup 269: Sheffield: Sheffield Academic Press, 1998) 92–125. See also Sterling, *Historiography and Self-Definition*, 340.

[44] To my mind, this is a much more plausible and convincing conclusion in light of the developed historical prefatory tradition from Thucydides to well beyond the time of the New Testament, including such authors as Josephus. As merely one example, see D. Earl, "Prologue-Form in Ancient Historiography," *ANRW* 1.2 (Berlin: de Gruyter, 1972) 842–856.

fact, it is not even in narrative, but recounts meteorological observations, as Barrett has pointed out.[45] Robbins's only other example comes from Josephus's *Life* 3.14–16, but this example hardly proves his case, since it contains an expected and legitimate alternation between first-person singular and plural within the context of an acknowledged historical account: "I reached Rome...for our ship foundered..." In responding to Robbins's citation of the similar *Od.* 9.39–41 (see section b above), Barrett says regarding the use of first person in this kind of account, "It is simply that in any vehicle larger than a bicycle there may well be a number of passengers who become, for a time, a community. 'I left Durham on the 14.55, and we reached London on time.' So *we* did."[46]

Regarding the *Episodes from the Third Syrian War* (Robbins's title), this is a fragmentary papyrus containing a narrative account of several episodes in the conflict in c. 246 BC between the Ptolemies and the Seleucids.[47] It appears that Robbins has moved beyond the evidence – the four column text is so fragmentary that one must work from a text missing the first half of every line of the first and third columns (the third is worse than the first), and thus without a continuous sense. It appears that "we" is used for the Ptolemies, whose spokesman is narrating the account, and "they" is used for the Seleucids. It is true that for the most part the "we" portion is located on the sea and the "they" portion on the land, but this is not maintained consistently, since at one place "they" is used of what happened by sea (col. 2, lines 2–3). The pronouns are apparently used to designate the participants, not to indicate the literary location or convention. Besides the difficulty with consistency, this example is not a parallel instance with what is found in Acts, which consistently maintains the use of "we" in blocks of material, not apparently to specify the participants (since the participants are never listed), but as a marking device for a portion of narrative. Acts does not use "we" and "they" as group markers the way this papyrus narrative does. An admitted difficulty for any analysis of the book of Acts, it must be conceded, is that there is apparently no significant parallel yet found in any major Greek historian, including the earlier classical authors and the later Oxyrhynchus

---

[45] C.K. Barrett, "Paul Shipwrecked," in B.P. Thompson (ed.), *Scripture: Meaning and Method* (Festschrift A.T. Hanson; Hull: Hull University Press, 1987) 53–54.

[46] Barrett, "Paul Shipwrecked," 53. The same kind of pattern can be argued regarding the shift in person in Ezra 7–9 (see section a above). Note also that even a bicycle can have two seats.

[47] L. Mitteis and U. Wilcken (eds.), *Grundzüge und Chrestomathie der Papyruskunde*, II.1 (Leipzig: Teubner, 1912) 1–7, no. 1. See Hemer, "First Person Narrative," 83.

historian, that evidences a similar use of the anonymous first person plural embedded within a third-person narrative.

Robbins concludes his list of parallels considered significant with an example from the *Antiochene Acts of Ignatius* (*Acta Martyrii Ignatii*). However, this text is of questionable relevance to the entire discussion, since it is significantly later in date of composition than the book of Acts and composite in origin. One interesting correlation with the book of Acts, however, is the apparent random beginning and ending of the "we" section during a sea voyage, and the extension of it beyond the end of the sea voyage. Lightfoot sees this as a method by which Ignatius is singled out from his companions, including the narrator, possibly, though not necessarily, including authentic tradition regarding Ignatius.[48] This, of course, does nothing to support Robbins's hypothesis regarding the use of "we" to indicate a convention for telling of sea voyages. Robbins's proposal does not seem to me to provide the means of solving the difficulty of the "we" passages in Acts. To the contrary, he does not seem to have established the existence of an ancient literary form used to relate sea voyages, and certainly has not yet demonstrated that it is relevant for discussion of Acts. To be sure, he has gathered a wealth of material that uses the first-person plural at various points, but one must be cautious not to be seduced by an uncontrolled use of items that have only superficial similarity. The literary genres are not similar enough to constitute parallels, the instances of first-person usage are often incomparable because they are too brief or are first-hand accounts by the actual authors or reflect a flashback technique, and there is not the kind of straightforward equation with the sea voyage that would be necessary to establish this as an ancient literary type.

d. The "We" Passages as Redactional Additions

If a particular literary type or genre does not answer the question of what the author of the book of Acts is doing in these "we" sections, others have suggested that the use of "we" is a self-conscious part of the author's redactional strategy. The suggestion is sometimes made that the author has created the "we" sections as a means of providing ostensible documentation or footnotes for the account, without actually or necessarily drawing upon any such historical or even literary sources.[49] As Conzelmann and Lindemann

---

[48] J.B. Lightfoot, *The Apostolic Fathers* (2 vols.; London: Macmillan, 2nd edn, 1889; repr. Peabody, MA: Hendrickson, 1989) 2.II.389–390.

[49] Hemer (*Book of Acts*, 316–317, 319–321) differentiates a redactional view that sees some source behind the use of "we" and a pseudonymous or purely fictive creation. That kind of differentiation – though useful and often found in studies of Acts – is not necessary here,

state bluntly and boldly, "the 'we' sections are meant to create the impression of an eyewitness account, although this is actually not the case."[50] In other words, the use of the "we" convention is to create a literary fiction of first-hand witness, either in support of a supposed source or as if one were an actual eyewitness, but neither is actually the case. This theory has taken many different forms in the hands of different redaction critics. For example, some propose that these sections were created from third-person reports and stories, a third-person itinerary, a story of a sea voyage including a storm and shipwreck, a first-person model for such a story, or simply from no source at all.[51]

In many ways, this is the least satisfactory and least probable of the proposed solutions. The fundamental problem is that it is difficult to establish that such a convention would have been recognized by the ancients, in light of there failing to be suitable ancient literary parallels. There are other problems as well. First of all, the redaction-critical solution seems to assume that the redacted sources, if they existed at all, were false or fictitious, or at the least something very different from the form in which they appear in Acts. This assumption is something that can be established only with more extra-textual evidence than exists, since no suitable literary parallel has been found

---

since the point is that the use of the convention of the first-person plural is a product of the author, whether or not a source lay behind this literary technique. In any case, any original source has been radically changed so as to be virtually unrecognizable.

[50] H. Conzelmann and A. Lindemann, *Interpreting the New Testament: An Introduction to the Principles and Methods of N.T. Exegesis* (trans. S.S. Schatzmann; Peabody, MA: Hendrickson, 1988) 241; cf. also H. Conzelmann, *Die Apostelgeschichte* (HNT 7; Tübingen: Mohr–Siebeck, 1963) 5–6 and *ad loc.*; W. Marxsen, *Introduction to the New Testament: An Approach to its Problems* (Philadelphia: Fortress Press, 1968) 168; Schneider, *Die Apostelgeschichte*, 1.92–93; G. Lüdemann, *Early Christianity according to the Traditions in Acts: A Commentary* (trans. J. Bowden; Minneapolis: Fortress Press, 1987) *passim*; among many others. The view probably stems from M. Dibelius, *Studies in the Acts of the Apostles* (ed. H. Greeven; trans. M. Ling; London: SCM Press, 1956) 204–206 and *passim*. For other literary solutions, see R.C. Tannehill, *The Narrative Unity of Luke–Acts: A Literary Interpretation.* II. *The Acts of the Apostles* (FFNT; Minneapolis: Fortress Press, 1990) 246–247, 264, 330, 335; W.S. Kurz, *Reading Luke–Acts: Dynamics of Biblical Narrative* (Louisville: Westminster/John Knox, 1993) chap. 7.

[51] See Praeder, "First Person Narration," 194–195, for a summary of the proposals, and 194–206 for detailed criticism. The itinerary theory is most closely associated with Dibelius, *Studies in the Acts of the Apostles, passim*; E. Norden, *Agnostos Theos: Untersuchungen zur Formengeschichte Religiöser Rede* (Stuttgart: Teubner, 1913; repr. Darmstadt: Wissenschaftliche Buchgesellschaft, 1956) 313–327. This theory has been refuted by G. Schille, *Die Apostelgeschichte des Lukas* (THNT 5; Berlin: Evangelische Verlags-Anstalt, 1983) 337–338, following his "Die Fragwürdigkeit eines Itinerars der Paulusreisen," *TLZ* 84 (1959) 165–174; as well as Conzelmann, *Die Apostelgeschichte*, 5–6; Haenchen, *Acts*, 84–86.

for comparison. This view has transformed a literary-historical question (i.e. concerning the relation between the "we" passages and the book of Acts in terms of apparent historical deductions to be drawn from this relationship) into a purely literary one (i.e. concerning the literary relations among a non-historical or non-existent source, the "we" passages and the book of Acts), but one that cannot be solved simply from the literary evidence available, apart from unquantifiable assertions. Any possible, *even if tentative*, solution must begin from the "we" passages – not from hypothetical sources.

Secondly, if one must assess the use of the "we" convention on the basis of simply its appearance in the text (arguments from probability aside, at this point), one must ask the question of why it is that the redactor only used the "we" convention in a few later sections, rather than interspersing it throughout the narrative or using it at crucial points where substantiation would have enhanced the narrative. Conzelmann and Lindemann suggest that Acts 27–28 is particularly interesting in this regard, since "This sea voyage is the only description of a genuine journey in Acts."[52] The implication is that the author may well have drawn upon an existing narrative of a shipwreck and then later interpolated the Pauline scenes, since, the authors contend, the Pauline scenes are separable from the rest of the narrative.[53] Of course, Conzelmann and Lindemann's view that chs. 27–28 are the only "genuine journey" in Acts reveals their bias regarding the historical reliability of the rest of the account and any possible sources behind it; but, more importantly, it answers a literary question regarding the use of "we" by appealing to historical evidence that is simply unavailable. This analysis also begs the further question of why it is that the "we" convention is also used in Acts 16, 20 and 21, as they recognize that it is.

Thirdly, one might further ask what textual indicators point to this occurring in the narrative, when the author gives no further clues. Some sort of identification would be useful in light of the fact that no other commensurate literary parallel has been established. Such logical difficulties indicate that one must begin with the book of Acts itself, rather than unsubstantiated assertion or speculation. The author of Acts makes no apparent or obvious attempts to correlate location and the use of the "we" convention, to identify the participants included in the reference to "we" (Paul is not even consistently associated with this group; see section 3 below), or even to give some indication of the relation of "we" to the usual

---

[52] Conzelmann and Lindemann, *Interpreting the New Testament*, 241.
[53] Lüdemann, *Early Christianity*, 14, 257, 259, following J. Wellhausen, *Noten zur Apostelgeschichte* (Berlin: Teubner, 1907) 1–21.

use of the third person in the narrative. This causes the "we" passages to appear *prima facie* as independent literary units that have been introduced into the narrative. One might reasonably assume that when something resembling a source is cited that, in fact, a source *is* being cited. This should be the basis of further investigation until it can be established otherwise, rather than the ingenuous assumption that the audience would recognize the convention of falsely claiming first-hand acquaintance. Besides, if the audience knew that this artificial literary convention were being used, it would appear unnecessary for the convention in fact to have to be used! Thus, the very reason for it disappears, unless the author is attempting to deceive his audience into thinking that he was a first-hand witness. This suggests the problem of pseudonymity, but that issue should not be introduced here, especially since neither Acts nor the "we" passages name their author or source.[54]

3. The "We" Passages as an Independent Source regarding Paul

At the end of this critical assessment of these literary theories, it can be tentatively concluded that a suitable literary explanation for this phenomenon has not yet been found, whether in terms of placing the book of Acts into the category of ancient romance or novel, or seeing the "we" passages as derived from some pre-established literary convention for relating a sea voyage, or positing redactional creation of the first-person plural narrative. The failure of these proposals is not to say that the book of Acts is in every way unique in ancient literature, however. Of course, ancient historical narratives are told predominantly in the third person, with many of them including participation by the author, often using the first-person singular or even plural.[55] But what distinguishes these historical works is the fact that it is clear that the author or narrator is identified with the first-person singular reference, or is a member of the group indicated by the first-person plural, an identification distinctly missing in Acts. In fact, apart from the prologue, with the singular, and the

---

[54] See Hemer, *Book of Acts*, 320. On some of the implications of pseudonymity, see S.E. Porter, "Pauline Authorship and the Pastoral Epistles: Implications for Canon," *BBR* 5 (1995) esp. 113–123.

[55] As thorough a survey of this literature as is to be found is made by Thornton, *Der Zeuge*, 152–184.

plural "we" passages, Acts does not use the first person as a narrative stance, something found relatively frequently in ancient Greek historians.[56]

What distinguishes the "we" passages of Acts is their sudden appearance, with no introduction or preparation by the narrator or author, and their equally sudden disappearance. Some take the use of the "we" convention as an indication of the first-hand witness of the author, but this abrupt appearance and disappearance within units of narrative arguably points away from the author being easily equated with the "we" voice of these passages, and toward the conscious incorporation and indication of a source. The basis for this conclusion is that the literary feature that distinguishes the "we" passages is their use of the first-person plural in the mouth of the narrator, without previous preparation or introduction of this convention. In these passages, there is a proportionate use of the oblique cases of the first-person plural personal pronoun, but only three instances of the first-person nominative plural, all in the traditionally labeled second passage (Acts 20:6, 13; 21:7). This means that, for the most part, first-person plural verbs convey the first-person plural reference simply by means of the verb ending, not by an overly abundant use of the personal pronoun.[57]

a. Defining the "We" Passages

To gain a more precise understanding of what is being done in these sections, especially as it helps to define the depiction of Paul, a closer look at the individual passages is necessary (the reconstructed Greek text of the "we" passages is printed in the Excursus at the end of this chapter). The first extends from Acts 16:10 to 16:17.[58] Acts 16:10 is not a sea voyage, but

---

[56] See Praeder, "First Person Narration," 208–209; Thornton, *Der Zeuge*, 148–197. Thus several other proposals with regard to establishing the Greco-Roman context of the "we" passages are not germane at this point. See E. Plümacher, "Wirklichkeitserfahrung und Geschichtsschreibung bei Lukas: Erwägungen zu den Wir-Stücken der Apostelgeschichte," *ZNW* 68 (1977) 2–22, but who admits (pp. 14–15) that there is no exact parallel from ancient Greek literature to the convention in Acts (and use of the "we" convention within Acts itself is inconsistent, since there are sailing voyages in Acts 13–14 and 18 without the "we" convention); and Aune, *New Testament in its Literary Environment*, 122–124, esp. 124.

[57] On monolectic verb structure in Greek, and the concept of person, see S.E. Porter, *Idioms of the Greek New Testament* (BLG 2; Sheffield: JSOT Press, 2nd edn, 1994) 293, 76–77.

[58] There is a textual variant in D at Acts 11:28 that indicates use of the first-person plural in a genitive absolute construction. In the *UBSGNT*[4], the reading of the text as printed (i.e. without the variant) indicates a certainty of "A." This text-critical discussion is not contained in the previous editions. On this variant, in terms of the "we" passages, see M. Wilcox, *The Semitisms of Acts* (Oxford: Clarendon Press, 1965) 129. The textual traditions of Acts fall outside my purview. For recent discussion, see W.A. Strange, *The Problem of the Text of*

begins implicitly in Troas, where Paul has the vision of the man of Macedonia. The first use of the first-person plural that distinguishes the "we" passage is introduced simply by the first-person plural verb, ἐζητήσαμεν ("sought").[59] There is no specification or indication of who the "we" might be, apart from thinking that it might include Paul, Silas and Timothy, and quite possibly the narrator (see Acts 16:1 ff.).[60] In Acts 16:11–12a, the sea voyage from Troas to Philippi is narrated. Although some commentators treat 16:1–10 and vv. 11 ff. as separate units,[61] this is probably unwise, since it splits up the clearly unified "we" passage. The use of the first-person plural continues after the sea voyage, even though the travelers are in Philippi for a while. It is in the midst of Paul's Philippian encounter with the fortune-telling slave girl that the first-person narrative abruptly changes back to third person. However, it is worth noting that, in v. 17, the last verse using "we" in this first section, there is a palpable separation of Paul from "us." Several scholars dispute the significance of this differentiation,[62] but its presence here and in other "we" passages is worth noting, since the distinction is probably not necessary for the narrative, and the "we" convention could have been extended to include the entire group. Plümacher believes that this differentiation is consistent with these "we" passages, in which Paul is the

---

Acts (SNTSMS 71; Cambridge: Cambridge University Press, 1992). If the first-person plural could be proved to belong at 11:28, of course the entire argument in this chapter and in many other treatments of the "we" passages would have to be re-assessed. Parenthetically, I have often wondered about the validity of including A readings in the printed Greek edition, unless there is something more to them than meets the eye, in which case, it raises the question of whether they should be rated as A, especially by the revised definition of the criteria (see *UBSGNT*[4], p. 3*). On larger issues raised by the revised criteria for assessing variants in the UBS editions, see K.D. Clarke, *Textual Optimism: A Critique of the United Bible Societies' Greek New Testament* (JSNTSup 138; Sheffield: Sheffield Academic Press, 1997) esp. 70–153.

[59] Lüdemann (*Early Christianity*, 177) asks whether the ἡμῖν ("us") of Acts 16:9 in the paraphrase of the man of Macedonia is attached in some way to use of the first-person plural in v. 10.

[60] See F.F. Bruce, *The Acts of the Apostles* (Grand Rapids: Eerdmans, 3rd edn, 1990 [2nd edn, 1952]) 356; contra Haenchen, *Acts*, 490, and Schneider, *Die Apostelgeschichte*, 2.208, who both think the "we" includes only the first three mentioned (Haenchen disputes a "we" source). See Chapter Three for further discussion of the identity of the "we."

[61] See, for example, R. Pesch, *Die Apostelgeschichte* (2 vols.; EKK 5.1, 2; Solothurn: Benziger; Neukirchen-Vluyn: Neukirchener, 1995 [2nd edn], 1986) 2.95–106, among many others.

[62] Bruce, *Acts*, 360; Hemer, "First Person Narrative," 81–82; and Praeder, "First Person Narration," 196.

focus of attention.[63] In this instance, Paul is the one who is intending to respond to the slave girl, and he is singled out here for reference apart from "us." This is a noteworthy distinction in a passage in which the first-person plural is used of other events, even though the episode was probably instigated by Paul (e.g. v. 13, where it says that "we" spoke with the women, but, in v. 14, the woman Lydia comes to hear what was being said by Paul). The passage from 16:10–17 usefully serves as a model of what one might expect in a section that makes consistent use of the first-person plural in the narrative conveyance. The "we" section breaks off while Paul is still in Philippi (in fact it breaks off mid-episode, with the slave girl speaking!), and does not correspond exactly to Paul's arrival or departure. At every place where the narrator refers to the people with Paul (and often, apparently, Paul with the group), he uses the first-person plural, until the narrative clearly takes up a consistently maintained third-person stance.

The next "we" passage is frequently said to extend from Acts 20:5 to 21:18,[64] although a number of scholars divide it into two sections, 20:5–15 and 21:1–18.[65] There are several problems with the traditional analysis of this as a single passage, however, which are related to the consistency of the narrative voice. Instead, it seems most likely that there are not one but two "we" passages here. The "we" section resumes in 20:5, even though the action focusing on "us" does not begin until v. 6.[66] The narrative identifies (see v. 4) some who go on ahead and wait at Troas, while an unidentified group called "we," who were in Philippi,[67] set sail (v. 6) for Troas (vv. 7–12, although with no first-person plural references in vv. 9–12), where they stayed until they sailed for Miletus (vv. 13–15).

---

[63] Plümacher, "Wirklichkeitserfahrung und Geschichtsschreibung bei Lukas," 13–14; cf. H.J. Cadbury, "'We' and 'I' Passages in Luke–Acts," *NTS* 3 (1957) 128.

[64] See, for example, F.S. Spencer, *The Portrait of Philip in Acts: A Study of Roles and Relations* (JSNTSup 67; Sheffield: JSOT Press, 1992) 247, but who bases his decision on other than linguistic criteria. He appears to change his mind in *Acts* (Readings; Sheffield: Sheffield Academic Press, 1997) 191–197. J. Munck (*The Acts of the Apostles* [AB 31; rev. W.F. Albright and C.S. Mann; Garden City, NY: Doubleday, 1967] xliii) believes that the "we" source can be inferred from Acts 20:1 to the end of ch. 28, even though "we" is not used throughout.

[65] See, for example, Aune, *New Testament in its Literary Environment*, 123 (he claims that the first passage is Acts 20:3–15, but this must be an error).

[66] See Lüdemann, *Early Christianity*, 221.

[67] Bruce (*Acts*, 40) takes it that the "we" figure (for him, Luke) was left in Philippi and now rejoins the group. This is the traditional view, still followed by many. Cf. Haenchen, *Acts*, 581–582, who debates who the "we" here are. The suggestions are several, none clearly proved.

The passage extending from Acts 20:5 to 21:18 has several noteworthy alternations in the composition of those identified by the first-person plural. The first occurs at 20:7, where Paul is seen to be discussing with the people, and 20:11, where it says that "Paul left (ἐξῆλθεν)," leaving the first-person plural group to make its way without Paul to Assos, where they picked him up (v. 14), and the group was reunited once more. These are apparently two more instances where Paul is distinguished from "us."[68] A more sizable break occurs at the speech that Paul gives to the Ephesian elders, which interrupts the flow of the narrative in the sense that there is a palpable and lengthy hiatus in the use of the first-person plural. This has prompted some scholars to posit that the speech to the Ephesian elders has been inserted within the first-person narrative.[69] The last use of the first-person plural by the narrator occurs in 20:15, where it is said that "we" arrived in Miletus. The "we" convention does not resume until 21:1, with the speech to the Ephesian elders in between. Once the speech ends in 20:35, there are several occasions in vv. 36–38 where the third person is used, but where one might have expected the first-person plural, if the convention were being maintained.[70] Thus, one should probably specify that 20:5–15 is the second "we" passage.

The section from Acts 21:1 to 21:18 consistently maintains the use of first-person plural and constitutes the third "we" passage.[71] The section opens with the group still in Miletus, although they soon depart for Jerusalem by means of a sea voyage to Caesarea (vv. 1–8),[72] followed by a journey on land to Jerusalem (vv. 9–18). In vv. 11–14, there is again a division between Paul and the others of the group referred to by "we," made plausible in light of Agabus's prophecy and the members of the group trying to convince Paul not to go to Jerusalem. Verse 15 resumes the inclusive use of "we," which continues until arrival in Jerusalem. Then, in v. 18, the section closes with a distinction made between Paul and "us," with the "us" seen as accompanying Paul to see James (on Acts 21:17–26, see Chapter Eight below). It is arguable

---

[68] Contra Lüdemann, *Early Christianity*, 221–222, who takes them as seams that indicate redaction.

[69] For example, E. Haenchen, "The Book of Acts as Source Material for the History of Early Christianity," in L.E. Keck and J.L. Martyn (eds.), *Studies in Luke–Acts* (Philadelphia: Fortress Press, 1966) 272; L.R. Donelson, "Cult Histories and the Sources of Acts," *Bib* 68 (1987) 11–19; and many others.

[70] Contra Dupont, *Sources of Acts*, 76 n. 1, who claims there was no opportunity to indicate use of the "we" convention.

[71] Conzelmann and Lindemann, *Interpreting the New Testament*, 240.

[72] Kurz ("Narrative Approaches," 218) notes the expanding and contracting "we" in Acts 21:5–6, which sometimes includes everyone (v. 6) and sometimes distinguishes between "we" and "they" (v. 6); see *idem*, *Reading Luke–Acts*, 114–117, for further examples.

that this distinction between Paul and the others is not completely necessary at this point in light of their common adventures, except that this is the style of the narrator of the "we" passages.

The final "we" section (of the traditional three or four – see above) is usually said to extend from Acts 27:1 to 28:16.[73] This section, however, should also be divided into two smaller "we" passages. Thus, the fourth "we" passage extends from 27:1–29. In the intervening narrative period in Acts, Paul has been moved from Jerusalem to Caesarea in light of the plot against his life. This section begins chronologically in Caesarea, and is comprised essentially of one sea voyage. It is worth noting, however, that, just as with all of the other "we" sections, at the very beginning of the section there is no explicit indicator of place in 27:1, simply the reference to the intention to sail to Rome from the port of Adramyttium in v. 2.[74] The first-person plural stance is maintained throughout, and ends in v. 29, when the boat is perilously close to being wrecked on Malta. Within this section, Paul is singled out twice in relation to the rest of the "we" group. First, he tries to give advice to the centurion, but this advice is rejected (v. 11), and then he gives a speech of encouragement in vv. 21–26, to which no one is recorded as responding. From 27:30–44, there is only one use of the first-person plural, at v. 37, with ἤμεθα ("we were"), an incidental and (apparently) trivial use of an inclusive first person ("we" includes everyone on board the ship), very similar to that found in some of the texts cited above (see sections 2b and c).[75] There are several other places where one might have expected the first-person plural to be used in its conventional way in order to maintain narrative continuity. Although the beginning of the pericope could justify the third person in reference to the soldiers, the major portion arguably requires first person – at least vv. 33, 35, probably 36, and 38, in light of vv. 37, 42, 43, and 44. It is within this section (27:30–44), which should probably not be included within the "we" section, that the troublesome episode of Paul's advice being accepted by the centurion is found (vv. 31–36).

Even though the group of fellow travelers has been mentioned in the narrative, the first-person plural is not used again until Acts 28:1, where it resumes with the shipwrecked group on the island of Malta. After a lengthy

---

[73] For example, Schneider, *Die Apostelgeschichte*, 1.94; Witherington, *Acts*, 480; among many others.

[74] Acts 27:1 reads "when it was decided that we would sail for Italy," maintaining the same tone of control of the situation by the "we" group as found in 21:1–18 (contra Bruce, *Acts*, 511, who disputes these two passages being placed together in this way). The Western textual tradition "corrects" 27:1 to state that the governor decided to send Paul to Rome.

[75] This characterization reflects Hemer, *Book of Acts*, 319 n. 29.

stay on Malta, where Paul is distinguished from the others in his group on
several occasions (vv. 3–6, 8),[76] the group sails to Puteoli, and then travels by
land to Rome. Here Paul is again distinguished from the group, being allowed
to stay on his own (v. 16). Cadbury claims that this separation is not like the
previous ones, since the guard is still there,[77] but this distinction probably
indicates that Paul is separated from "us." The section 28:1–16 consistently
uses the "we" narrative convention, except in those few places where Paul is
distinguished, and should be considered the fifth "we" section of Acts.

b. Implications of the "We" Passages

The above description gives grounds for pursuing the following implications
with regard to the "we" passages in their literary context. I will assume the
findings from the discussion of the literary proposals above, including the fact
that there has not been found any comparable literary parallel that explains
this usage. This leaves the onerous task of reasoning through the possible
alternatives regarding this usage from the evidence of the text itself and from
what we can reasonably argue on the basis of these textual phenomena. There
are several conclusions that can be drawn from these data.

1. *Context*. These passages are less formidable in their context in the book
of Acts than the standard description of their parameters indicates. Rather
than covering the entire section, for example, from Acts 27:1 to the end of
ch. 28, or at the least to 28:16, including the troublesome section at the end of
ch. 27, these sections are much more modest in length. Even though the "we"
convention begins and ends abruptly, the passages are otherwise well
integrated stylistically into the rest of the book (see below). They have been
logically and literarily incorporated into the flow of the text of Acts,
interwoven with other material in third-person narrative format. The
transition, for example, at 16:10, moves from the first-person plural of the
message of the man of Macedonia (v. 9) to the "we" section.

2. *Form*. Each of these units follows a standard pattern with four major
features to it, and thus has form-critical implications. Each begins mid-event
at a particular locale, such as Troas, Philippi, Miletus, Jerusalem–Caesarea or
Malta, even though each place usually must be inferred from the context as
continuing the narrative flow, since an explicit statement of location is
usually not made or does not occur until later. Each contains a record of at
least one sea voyage, as well as often a land voyage or at least a significant

---

[76] Cf. Conzelmann, *Die Apostelgeschichte*, 147, who thinks that Acts 28:9–10 shows that
the "we" passage is not that of an eyewitness (*Augenzeugenbericht*).

[77] Cadbury, "'We,'" 129.

stay on land (the exception is the fourth passage, Acts 27:1–29).[78] Each
arrives at a destination that is the point of departure for the next "we" section,
no matter what intervenes between the two sections, and thus illustrates
topographical connection throughout.[79] Thus, the first section (16:10–17)
ends in Philippi, the point of departure for the next section (20:5–15), which
ends in Miletus, the point of departure for the next section (21:1–18), which
ends in Jerusalem, even though the major point of arrival in the travel is
Caesarea.[80] The overall narrative establishes the point of departure for the
next section (27:1–29) as Caesarea. Even though Caesarea is not specifically
mentioned, the ordering of the narrative, with its sailing course, and the "we"
passage indicate that this is where the voyage began. The sea voyage of 27:1–
29 ends in Malta, the point of departure for the final section (28:1–16), which
ends in Italy and, specifically, Rome. Each section, although it consistently
utilizes the "we" convention, also at some point distinguishes Paul from the
rest of the group. On the basis of these four unifying form-critical features, it
appears compelling to me that what we have in the "we" sections is a separate
and distinct literary source utilized by the author of Acts, a continuous and
coherent, independent "we" source focusing on Paul and his missionary
travels.[81] This view is to be distinguished from other source-critical views
(currently out of fashion in redaction-critical and literary circles) that say that
the author of Luke–Acts used a "we" source, by seeing it as a continuous and
originally undivided source which the author has taken over, not excerpted
from notes, a diary or a travelogue. The continuous source was then
incorporated into the text of Acts. This position also claims that the "we"
passages can be used as a reliable guide to establishing sources, without
necessarily making an explicit claim about their historical reliability or
authorship.

Lüdemann argues against a definable source because "we" appears
abruptly, the passages fit the context without tension, and the author of Acts
could have redacted the "we" references,[82] but these objections are
contradictory. The abruptness of the use of "we" in fact causes the kind of

---

[78] Cf. Pesch, *Die Apostelgeschichte*, 1.48.

[79] See Schneider, *Die Apostelgeschichte*, 1.89.

[80] See Bruce, *Acts*, 40.

[81] See K. Lake and H.J. Cadbury, *The Beginnings of Christianity*. Part I. *The Acts of the Apostles*. IV. *English Translation and Commentary* (ed. F.J. Foakes Jackson and K. Lake; London: Macmillan, 1933) 193; W.G. Kümmel, *Introduction to the New Testament* (trans. H.C. Kee; Nashville: Abingdon, 17th edn, 1975) 174–188, esp. 177. Cf. Haenchen, *Acts*, 87, who indicates that most source-critical views argue for much larger sources than the "we" passages.

[82] Lüdemann, *Early Christianity*, 26.

tension in the context that demands explanation. Luke could have redacted the "we," but a clear motivation for this has not been established (see the section above on redaction criticism, and below). The factors cited above point to an explicit use of a continuous, integral source.[83]

3. *Literary Style*. The question of literary style must be considered, and this involves several of its facets. The first is with regard to the vocabulary and syntax of the "we" sections. It was argued by Harnack, and has since then been commonly accepted, that the literary style of the "we" passages resembles that of the rest of Acts, apart from the use of the first-person plural.[84] It is true that for the most part these sections literarily resemble the style of the rest of Acts, so far as lexicon and syntax are concerned (apart from an abundance of *hapax legomena*, which should not, however, be neglected – see below). One must ask, however, how significant this conclusion is for disproving an independent "we" source. Lüdemann calls these findings into question, pointing out that classical methods of literary criticism are not always germane for Acts, since none of its sources is preserved in the same way that the Gospels' are (Luke and Matthew using Mark, for example). Furthermore, regarding the use of vocabulary statistics to show that the "we" passages simply originated from the same author as that of Acts, Lüdemann does not accept that sufficient criteria for calculating and using lexical and syntactical data have been developed.[85] Harnack admits that

---

[83] Contra Dibelius, *Studies in the Acts of the Apostles, passim*; Conzelmann, *Die Apostelgeschichte*, 5–6. Most scholars, though mentioning a "we" source, do not believe that it can be established.

[84] See A. Harnack, *Luke the Physician: The Author of the Third Gospel and the Acts of the Apostles* (trans. J.R. Wilkinson; London: Williams & Norgate, 2nd edn, 1909) 26–120, who also cites many who preceded him; *idem, The Acts of the Apostles* (trans. J.R. Wilkinson; London: Williams & Norgate, 1909) 162–202; *idem, Neue Untersuchungen zur Apostelgeschichte und zur Abfassungszeit der synoptischen Evangelien* (Leipzig: Hinrichs, 1911) 1–21; and J.C. Hawkins, *Horae Synopticae: Contributions to the Study of the Synoptic Problem* (Oxford: Clarendon Press, 2nd edn, 1909) 182–189. Cf. H.J. Cadbury, *The Style and Literary Method of Luke* (Cambridge, MA: Harvard University Press, 1920; repr. New York: Klaus, 1969) 1–39 on language and style; J.M. Watt, *Code-Switching in Luke and Acts* (Berkeley Insights in Linguistics and Semiotics 31; New York: Lang, 1997); Wilcox, *Semitisms of Acts*, 60, who graphically charts that there are three sections of Acts that, by his calculations, have no Septuagintalisms: Acts 14:23b–16:8, 19:2–29:9, and 24:15–26:9, all overlapping with "we" passages.

[85] Lüdemann, *Early Christianity*, 9. Lüdemann apparently is referring to the fact that the sample passages are far shorter than is thought necessary to calculate these kinds of statistics. Work in stylistics requires a far larger corpus than is available in the Greek New Testament. See A. Ellegård, *A Statistical Method for Determining Authorship* (Gothenburg Studies in English 13; Göteborg: University of Göteborg, 1962) esp. 13–14; M.B. O'Donnell, "Linguistic Fingerprints or Style by Numbers? An Evaluation of the Use of Statistics for New

there are 111 *hapax legomena* in the "we" passages, that is, words that are not in Luke or Acts (162 that are not in Acts). The "we" passages have a disproportionately high number of *hapax legomena* (approximately two and a half times that of the rest of Acts), as Harnack tries to explain away.[86] There is a further difficulty, suggested by Lüdemann. Even though there may be lexical and syntactical coherence between the "we" passages and the rest of Acts, one cannot overlook the fact that the author of Luke–Acts is open about his use of sources, which implies editing. The author admits as much in Luke 1:1–4, and this has been quantified in the traditional explanation of Synoptic source theory with Markan priority (and even with a theory of Matthean priority), and is further demonstrable, if not for sources at least for editing, in the three accounts of Paul's conversion (Acts 9, 22, 26).[87] Harnack observes this in the Gospel of Luke, noting that, in passages where Luke is dependent upon Mark, introductory καί ("and") may be the only evident proof of Luke's dependence, the narrative otherwise having been re-written in Luke's own style.[88] It is quantifiable from other historians of the ancient world as well that it was common to reshape sources so that the original source was covered over by the author's own style.[89]

There are several other literary features related to the "we" passages that ought to be considered, however. One is the detail regarding Philippi provided in Acts 16:11–12, a level of detail not elsewhere provided in Acts, as Hemer admits.[90] The theory of a "we" source minimizes the difficulty

[86] Harnack, *Luke the Physician*, 84–85. The figures need to be adjusted in light of my re-assessment of the length of the "we" passages (my total number of verses is 82, as opposed to Harnack's 97), but the point is not significantly different, and the ratios should be roughly commensurate. This would, in fact, constitute an argument for Luke not writing the source; contra Gilchrist, "Historicity," 34 n. 20.

[87] See B. Witherington, III, "Editing the Good News: Some Synoptic Lessons for the Study of Acts," in Witherington (ed.), *Literature, History and Society*, 324–347.

[88] Harnack, *Luke the Physician*, 93.

[89] M. Hengel, *Between Jesus and Paul* (trans. J. Bowden: London: SCM Press, 1983) 4, 135 n. 17. He cites Livy, Dionysius of Halicarnassus, Philo and especially Josephus, where it is quantifiable how he used the Septuagint, 1 Ezra, *Letter of Aristeas*, 1 Maccabees. On this topic, see Cadbury, *Making of Luke–Acts*, 169–183, where he discusses Josephus and his use of predecessors; and F.G. Downing, "Redaction Criticism: Josephus' *Antiquities* and the Synoptic Gospels (I, II)," *JSNT* 8 (1980) 46–65; 9 (1980) 29–48 (Downing's two chapters are reprinted in S.E. Porter and C.A. Evans [eds.], *New Testament Interpretation and Methods: A Sheffield Reader* [BibSem 45; Sheffield: Sheffield Academic Press, 1997] 161–179, 180–199).

[90] Hemer, *Book of Acts*, 346–347; cf. Fitzmyer, *Luke the Theologian*, 4–5.

regarding how it is that the "we" narrator separated from the group at Philippi in ch. 16 and did not rejoin it until ch. 20, again at Philippi, if the "we" sections are seen to come from a literary source (apparently knowledgeable about Philippi) intercalated into Acts, or into which other events have been interpolated.[91] There was not necessarily a passage of time (as depicted between Acts 16:18 and 20:5) so far as the author of the source was concerned. Another feature is the description of travel details for those other than Paul, as in 20:13–14. The most distinguishing features must not be minimized, however, and these include the four-part organizational pattern cited above and, of course, the use of the first-person plural convention. That this first-person plural is not to be minimized is confirmed simply by virtue of the fact that no one has otherwise explained its usage here in Acts any better than on the basis that it is what it appears to be – indication of the use of a source, an apparent fact that cannot be ignored.[92]

4. *Use of "We."* The implications of the use of "we" must be further considered. The range of opinion, as noted above, has run the gamut from suggesting that this usage indicates use of Luke's own diary, a travelogue or notes, to an entirely artificial literary convention, and many points in between. In light of the Lukan intention to provide an orderly account as expressed in the prologue to the Gospel (Luke 1:1–4), in conjunction with that of Acts (1:1), it is surprising that the use of the first person is found only in the later chapters of Acts, and at only these specific points. The literary abilities of the author of Luke–Acts cannot be overlooked, including, for example, his attention to Septuagintal style, and his utilization of more heavily Semitic language in the opening chapters of the Gospel and the first half of Acts.[93] What strikes most readers about these stylistic features is the consistency and plausibility of these literary conventions, as suitably reflecting the nature of the speakers and events. For example, the opening chapters of Acts, focusing upon Jerusalem, may have more of a Semitic feel to them,[94] reflected in some linguistic usage. If the "we" passages originated

---

[91] Haenchen, "Book of Acts," 272.

[92] Cf. Cadbury, "'We,'" 129, who points out that Harnack never answered the question of why the author or editor purportedly maintained a consistent style, except for the continued use of "we."

[93] On Lukan style, see J.A. Fitzmyer, *The Gospel according to Luke* (2 vols.; AB 28, 28A; Garden City, NY: Doubleday, 1981, 1985) 1.107–128, where bibliography is cited; and the still valuable, J. de Zwaan, "The Use of the Greek Language in Acts," in F.J. Foakes Jackson and K. Lake (eds.), *The Beginnings of Christianity*. Part I. *The Acts of the Apostles*. II. *Prolegomena II: Criticism* (London: Macmillan, 1922) 30–65.

[94] Caution is needed with regard to defining and unduly stressing Semitic influence upon the Greek of the New Testament, however. See Porter, *Verbal Aspect*, 111–156.

with the author of Luke–Acts, it is only logical to suggest that he would not have maintained this convention as he has done. A more likely way for him to have handled it, if it did reflect his first-hand acquaintance, was to indicate some sort of equation of himself with this group, or, at least, to let it be seen that the switch in person was motivated by an autobiographical purpose.

The proposal that the author has simply imported with little refinement his notes or travelogue is mitigated by several factors. These include, first, the fact that the shipwreck of Acts 27 could have resulted in any documents being lost or ruined (to say nothing of the cost and transportation problems connected with carting papyrus around)[95] and, secondly and more

---

[95] A.D. Nock, "The Book of Acts" (Review of M. Dibelius, *Aufsätze zur Apostelgeschichte, Gnomon* 25 [1953] 499 and n. 3), reprinted in his *Essays on Religion and the Ancient World* (ed. Z. Stewart; 2 vols.; Cambridge, MA: Harvard University Press, 1972) 2.823 and n. 12. In S.E. Porter, "The 'We' Passages," in D.W.J. Gill and C. Gempf (eds.), *The Book of Acts in its First Century Setting. II. The Book of Acts in its Graeco-Roman Setting* (Grand Rapids: Eerdmans, 1994) 571 n. 81, a further comment was added to this note, apparently by the editors and unbeknownst to me, concerning my doubting the plausibility of any papyrus (Lukan or otherwise) surviving Paul's shipwreck. This supplemented note referred to B. Rapske, "Acts, Travel and Shipwreck," in Gill and Gempf (eds.), *The Book of Acts in its Graeco-Roman Setting*, 34 n. 151, where he includes this account as an argument for the plausibility of the papyrus documents surviving possible inundation: "Even in the chaos of sudden seaboard disaster, there is at least some chance of preserving important personal articles. When dumped overboard because of crowding in his own ship, Caesar, for example, 'plunged into the sea, and after swimming for two hundred paces, got away to the nearest ship, holding up his left hand all the way, so as not to wet some papers which he was carrying, and dragging his cloak after him with his teeth, to keep the enemy from getting it as a trophy'" (Suetonius, *Caesar* 64 LCL).

There are several issues raised here. First is the virtual impossibility of performing such a swimming maneuver as it is suggested that Caesar did. Secondly, this incredible account is perhaps understandable in light of the tendencies of Suetonius, an ancient biographer two hundred years removed from the event and known for taking a favorable (and unhistorical) view of his subjects, and presenting often dubious accounts (see C.W. Fornara, *History in Ancient Greece and Rome* [Berkeley: University of California Press, 1983] 186). Thirdly, what we know of papyrus does not bode well for its surviving a shipwreck. Papyrus was sometimes treated with cedar oil, but this was to protect it against insects. Papyrus was often put in a wrapper, or stored in a chest (see F.G. Kenyon, *The Palaeography of Greek Papyri* [Oxford: Clarendon Press, 1899] 24). This raises further questions, however. Would there have been fully waterproof containers (such as a jar with a cork lid, sealed with tar or wax), would Luke have had one with him, would the papyrus have been in the container at the time of the wreck, and would Luke have been able to secure them in the container in time? Grain being transported in ships often had a sample taken out and placed in a leather pouch as a test of its quality at the time of shipment (G. Rickman, *The Corn Supply of Ancient Rome* [Oxford: Clarendon Press, 1980] 121–122). Since papyrus reacts to water much as a modern newspaper does when it gets wet, documents meant to be permanent, such as an attestation to citizenship, were written on wood for ordinary citizens (bronze for soldiers) (see A.N. Sherwin-White, *The Roman Citizenship* [Oxford: Clarendon Press, 2nd edn, 1973] 315–316).

importantly, what is seen to be the generally consistent syntax (and less so, lexis) of these sections in comparison with the rest of his material.[96] The consistent syntax argues for writing of the source by the author near the time of composition of the book (which minimizes the need for the "we" convention as reflecting first-hand acquaintance at some earlier time now past), but the use of the "we" convention argues for an earlier writing (and makes it more difficult to explain the consistency of style). These factors point away from simple importation and toward self-conscious utilization by the author of Acts.

If the author of Luke–Acts incorporated the "we" material to the extent that he appears to have done, why was the first-person convention maintained? The use of "we" continues to be a nagging problem for most explanations of the "we" convention. The best explanation is, therefore, that the author draws upon an earlier source concentrating upon Paul that has been redacted. The use of the first-person narrative technique must be taken seriously. It may well be that the author of Luke–Acts has included his own eyewitness narrative,[97] but I believe that a better explanation is that these

---

But to keep the papyri free from damage, the contents of a container would have had to be kept completely dry, otherwise the papyrus would have gotten damp and possibly even begun to mold, and certainly would have lost its lettering to the backside of the page against it on a scroll or single sheet (C.R. Gregory, *Canon and Text of the New Testament* [Edinburgh: T. & T. Clark, 1907] 305). (When papyrus was re-used, it was washed with a sponge to prepare a clean surface; see I. Gallo, *Greek and Latin Papyrology* [Classical Handbook 1; London: Institute of Classical Studies, 1986] 10.) Whether Caesar had his papers in a protective case or not, he obviously was greatly concerned that they not get wet, or they would be ruined. Thus, I believe it very likely that papyrus documents carried by the travelers of Acts 27 would not have survived inundation. I wish to thank Dr Bernhard Palme of the Papyrussammlung of the Österreichische Nationalbibliothek for his discussion of this issue with me, and his very helpful insights.

[96] The issue of the syntax and style of the "we" passages within the larger context of Acts requires further linguistic examination. Here the concept of consistent syntax is being accepted from the earlier discussion noted above in order to argue the position being advocated here.

[97] This is the traditional view, and is well represented by, for example, W.M. Ramsay, *The Church in the Roman Empire before A.D. 70* (London: Hodder & Stoughton, 4th edn, 1895) 6–8, among several other works; R.B. Rackham, *The Acts of the Apostles* (London: Methuen, 8th edn, 1919) xli–xlii; Bruce, *Acts*, 41; Munck, *Acts*, xiii; M. Hengel, *Acts and the History of Earliest Christianity* (trans. J. Bowden; London: SCM Press, 1979) 66; R. Jewett, *Dating Paul's Life* (London: SCM Press, 1979) 15; W. Neil, *The Acts of the Apostles* (NCB; London: Marshall, Morgan, Scott, 1973) 22–25; Fitzmyer, *Luke*, 1.35–53; *idem*, *Luke the Theologian*, 1–26, esp. 3–7, 11–16; I.H. Marshall, *The Acts of the Apostles* (TNTC; Grand Rapids: Eerdmans, 1980) 39; Hemer, *Book of Acts*, 321; Kurz, *Reading Luke–Acts*, 111–124, esp. 123; Thornton, *Der Zeuge*, 272–340, esp. 272–280; Gilchrist, "Historicity," 36–50; J. Jervell, *The Theology of the Acts of the Apostles* (New Testament Theology; Cambridge:

sections seem to have come from an author other than the author of Luke–Acts,[98] who provided valuable information regarding Paul and his companions. Like others, this source has been, for the most part, integrated into the warp and woof of the book of Acts, as the lexical and especially syntactical studies have apparently indicated, but without losing several essential features that identify this source, including the use of the first-person narrative technique and the four-part literary structuring around a sea voyage. Apparently the "we" source was at one time a continuous independent narrative, either which has been separated and subtly dispersed at several places in the narrative of Acts,[99] or into which various supplementary Pauline episodes have been interposed, such as Paul's speech to the Ephesian elders at Miletus, events in Jerusalem, and the stay at Malta. The lack of use of the first-person plural nominative pronoun to mark significant beginning and ending points in the first-person narrative points away from the author utilizing his own material, whether written by him for the occasion or taken from a previously written source, since he does not apparently believe that he has the freedom to heighten the effect of the source material, or to eliminate tell-tale signs of its being used ("we"). It cannot be substantiated on the basis of what is found in Acts whether the writer of the "we" source was himself an eyewitness or first-hand witness[100] to the events narrated, although on the basis of the use of the first-person narrative convention in other writers it is plausible, and in fact likely, to think that such was the case.[101] Neither can it be substantiated whether this source itself is the product of earlier compilation and composition, although to see it this way is the tendency of much recent criticism.[102] It can be speculated that the author of Luke–Acts'

Cambridge University Press, 1996) 1–10, esp. 2–3; *idem*, "The Future of the Past: Luke's Vision of Salvation History and its Bearing on his Writing of History," in Witherington (ed.), *History, Literature and Society*, esp. 117; and Witherington, *Acts*, 485.

[98] Kümmel, *Introduction*, esp. 177; C.K. Barrett, *Luke the Historian in Recent Study* (London: Epworth, 1961) 22.

[99] A possible parallel might be the way that material found in Matthew 5–7 is distributed in several places in Luke's Gospel (e.g. Luke 6, 8, 11, 12, 13, 14, 16 *passim*).

[100] Alexander (*Preface to Luke's Gospel*, esp. 120–123) points out that the more likely understanding of αὐτόπται is "first-hand witness" (which may or may not include being an eyewitness, but knowing those who were), not necessarily "eyewitness."

[101] Cf. Thornton, *Der Zeuge*, 84 ff.

[102] Lüdemann, *Early Christianity*, *passim*; Praeder, "First Person Narration," 198, who contends that failure to identify the "we," to explain their relationship to their being witnesses or to Paul, and to explain their significance, all argue against their being eyewitnesses. It must be admitted that much source and redaction criticism of individual sub-units within the "we" passages is highly speculative and subject to the same criticisms as noted above. Despite many useful insights, there are some very weak arguments. For example, Lüdemann

use of such a source (if it is not by the author himself, a possibility that cannot be entirely dismissed) indicates either significant gaps in his own knowledge at this point or special regard for this "we" source leading to its consequent incorporation. The apparently unmotivated utilization of the source at various places, as well as the freedom allowed the source in discussing travel when Paul was not present (e.g. Acts 20:13–14), perhaps pushes the balance toward, at the least, a source that the author of Luke–Acts considered reliable, providing a suitable framework for much of the detail of these several episodes, especially as they relate to Paul.

4. Conclusion

Neither biblical nor extra-biblical literary evidence, especially as it is presented in alternative theories regarding the Greco-Roman literary affinities of Acts, is sufficient to explain the use of the first-person plural narrative convention in the so-called "we" passages in Acts. These theories have helped to focus and refine analysis of the book of Acts itself, but it is to Acts that one must go in order to push forward discussion. A fresh analysis of the evidence of the passages in their contexts points to the author of Luke–Acts utilizing a previously written "we" source, probably (although not certainly) not one originating with the author himself. Although there is some indication that the integrity with which the text is handled in light of the author's programmatic statement in Luke 1:1–4 could point to an eyewitness or first-hand witness, this cannot be determined with certainty. More likely is the conclusion that the author of Acts has utilized a continuous, independent source, probably discovered in the course of his investigation of the events of early Christianity. The source was thought to have merit for the narrative, although this does not necessitate it being an eyewitness. There are many interesting questions regarding the authorship, original context, place and time of origin of this source, but information is lacking to push this examination much further by simply exploring these issues. Once this source has been identified, as I believe that I have done, the next stage of investigation is to study this "we" source in an effort to get a better understanding of the events which it purports to represent, with attention to

---

(p. 231) cites Acts 21:17 as a redactional seam, because, although Paul and his fellow travelers are clearly in Jerusalem (v. 16), they are said to "re-enter" in v. 17. Actually, the genitive absolute construction uses γενομένων, in Luke not a verb of motion but of existence. Lüdemann has apparently created his own redactional problem that he cannot solve.

the perspective and theology of the "we" passages, especially as it reveals the character and behavior of Paul.

Excursus: The "We" Source of Acts[103]

16.10 ὡς δὲ τὸ ὅραμα εἶδεν, εὐθέως ἐζητήσαμεν ἐξελθεῖν εἰς Μακεδονίαν συμβιβάζοντες ὅτι προσκέκληται ἡμᾶς ὁ θεὸς εὐαγγελίσασθαι αὐτούς. 16.11 ἀναχθέντες δὲ ἀπὸ Τρῳάδος εὐθυδρομήσαμεν εἰς Σαμοθράκην, τῇ δὲ ἐπιούσῃ εἰς Νέαν Πόλιν 16.12 κἀκεῖθεν εἰς Φιλίππους, ἥτις ἐστὶν πρώτης μερίδος τῆς Μακεδονίας πόλις, κολωνία. ἦμεν δὲ ἐν ταύτῃ τῇ πόλει διατρίβοντες ἡμέρας τινάς. 16.13 τῇ τε ἡμέρᾳ τῶν σαββάτων ἐξήλθομεν ἔξω τῆς πύλης παρὰ ποταμὸν οὗ ἐνομίζομεν προσευχὴν εἶναι, καὶ καθίσαντες ἐλαλοῦμεν ταῖς συνελθούσαις γυναιξίν. 16.14 καί τις γυνὴ ὀνόματι Λυδία, πορφυρόπωλις πόλεως Θυατείρων σεβομένη τὸν θεόν, ἤκουεν, ἧς ὁ κύριος διήνοιξεν τὴν καρδίαν προσέχειν τοῖς λαλουμένοις ὑπὸ τοῦ Παύλου. 16.15 ὡς δὲ ἐβαπτίσθη καὶ ὁ οἶκος αὐτῆς, παρεκάλεσεν λέγουσα,/εἰ κεκρίκατέ με πιστὴν τῷ κυρίῳ εἶναι, εἰσελθόντες εἰς τὸν οἶκόν μου μένετε· καὶ παρεβιάσατο ἡμᾶς. 16.16 ἐγένετο δὲ πορευομένων ἡμῶν εἰς τὴν προσευχὴν παιδίσκην τινὰ ἔχουσαν πνεῦμα πύθωνα ὑπαντῆσαι ἡμῖν, ἥτις ἐργασίαν πολλὴν παρεῖχεν τοῖς κυρίοις αὐτῆς μαντευομένη. 16.17 αὕτη κατακολουθοῦσα τῷ Παύλῳ καὶ ἡμῖν ἔκραζεν... 20.5 οὗτοι δὲ προελθόντες ἔμενον ἡμᾶς ἐν Τρῳάδι, 20.6 ἡμεῖς δὲ ἐξεπλεύσαμεν μετὰ τὰς ἡμέρας τῶν ἀζύμων ἀπὸ Φιλίππων καὶ ἤλθομεν πρὸς αὐτοὺς εἰς τὴν Τρῳάδα ἄχρι ἡμερῶν πέντε, ὅπου διετρίψαμεν ἡμέρας ἑπτά. 20.7 ἐν δὲ τῇ μιᾷ τῶν σαββάτων συνηγμένων ἡμῶν κλάσαι ἄρτον, ὁ Παῦλος διελέγετο αὐτοῖς μέλλων ἐξιέναι τῇ ἐπαύριον, παρέτεινέν τε τὸν λόγον μέχρι μεσονυκτίου. 20.8 ἦσαν δὲ λαμπάδες ἱκαναὶ ἐν τῷ ὑπερῴῳ οὗ ἦμεν συνηγμένοι. 20.9 καθεζόμενος δέ τις νεανίας ὀνόματι Εὔτυχος ἐπὶ τῆς θυρίδος, καταφερόμενος ὕπνῳ βαθεῖ διαλεγομένου τοῦ Παύλου ἐπὶ πλεῖον, κατενεχθεὶς ἀπὸ τοῦ ὕπνου ἔπεσεν ἀπὸ τοῦ τριστέγου κάτω καὶ ἤρθη νεκρός. 20.10 καταβὰς δὲ ὁ Παῦλος ἐπέπεσεν αὐτῷ καὶ συμπεριλαβὼν εἶπεν, μὴ θορυβεῖσθε, ἡ γὰρ ψυχὴ αὐτοῦ

---

[103] This reconstruction of the "we" source provides a guide to what at least part of this source may have looked like (the part that Luke used), without engaging in form-critical assessment of all of its possible changed wording or of what may have been deleted. In that sense, this text is meant to be indicative, rather than definitive. For a somewhat similar reconstruction, see Harnack, *Neue Untersuchungen*, 3–9, but who, however, simply prints the four "we" passages as they are usually offered, without seeing them as a single, connected narrative.

ἐν αὐτῷ ἐστιν. 20.11 ἀναβὰς δὲ καὶ κλάσας τὸν ἄρτον καὶ γευσάμενος ἐφ'
ἱκανόν τε ὁμιλήσας ἄχρι αὐγῆς, οὕτως ἐξῆλθεν. 20.12 ἤγαγον δὲ τὸν
παῖδα ζῶντα καὶ παρεκλήθησαν οὐ μετρίως. 20.13 ἡμεῖς δὲ προελθόντες
ἐπὶ τὸ πλοῖον ἀνήχθημεν ἐπὶ τὴν Ἄσσον ἐκεῖθεν μέλλοντες ἀναλαμβάνειν
τὸν Παῦλον· οὕτως γὰρ διατεταγμένος ἦν μέλλων αὐτὸς πεζεύειν. 20.14
ὡς δὲ συνέβαλλεν ἡμῖν εἰς τὴν Ἄσσον, ἀναλαβόντες αὐτὸν ἤλθομεν εἰς
Μιτυλήνην, 20.15 κἀκεῖθεν ἀποπλεύσαντες τῇ ἐπιούσῃ κατηντήσαμεν
ἄντικρυς Χίου, τῇ δὲ ἑτέρᾳ παρεβάλομεν εἰς Σάμον, τῇ δὲ ἐχομένῃ
ἤλθομεν εἰς Μίλητον. 21.1 ὡς δὲ ἐγένετο ἀναχθῆναι ἡμᾶς ἀποσπασθέντας
ἀπ' αὐτῶν, εὐθυδρομήσαντες ἤλθομεν εἰς τὴν Κῶ, τῇ δὲ ἑξῆς εἰς τὴν
Ῥόδον κἀκεῖθεν εἰς Πάταρα· 21.2 καὶ εὑρόντες πλοῖον διαπερῶν εἰς
Φοινίκην ἐπιβάντες ἀνήχθημεν. 21.3 ἀναφάναντες δὲ τὴν Κύπρον καὶ
καταλιπόντες αὐτὴν εὐώνυμον ἐπλέομεν εἰς Συρίαν καὶ κατήλθομεν εἰς
Τύρον· ἐκεῖσε γὰρ τὸ πλοῖον ἦν ἀποφορτιζόμενον τὸν γόμον. 21.4
ἀνευρόντες δὲ τοὺς μαθητὰς ἐπεμείναμεν αὐτοῦ ἡμέρας ἑπτά, οἵτινες τῷ
Παύλῳ ἔλεγον διὰ τοῦ πνεύματος μὴ ἐπιβαίνειν εἰς Ἱεροσόλυμα 21.5 ὅτε
δὲ ἐγένετο ἡμᾶς ἐξαρτίσαι τὰς ἡμέρας, ἐξελθόντες ἐπορευόμεθα
προπεμπόντων ἡμᾶς πάντων σὺν γυναιξὶ καὶ τέκνοις ἕως ἔξω τῆς πόλεως,
καὶ θέντες τὰ γόνατα ἐπὶ τὸν αἰγιαλὸν προσευξάμενοι 21.6
ἀπησπασάμεθα ἀλλήλους καὶ ἀνέβημεν εἰς τὸ πλοῖον, ἐκεῖνοι δὲ
ὑπέστρεψαν εἰς τὰ ἴδια. 21.7 ἡμεῖς δὲ τὸν πλοῦν διανύσαντες ἀπὸ Τύρου
κατηντήσαμεν εἰς Πτολεμαΐδα καὶ ἀσπασάμενοι τοὺς ἀδελφοὺς
ἐμείναμεν ἡμέραν μίαν παρ' αὐτοῖς. 21.8 τῇ δὲ ἐπαύριον ἐξελθόντες
ἤλθομεν εἰς Καισάρειαν καὶ εἰσελθόντες εἰς τὸν οἶκον Φιλίππου τοῦ
εὐαγγελιστοῦ, ὄντος ἐκ τῶν ἑπτά, ἐμείναμεν παρ' αὐτῷ. 21.9 τούτῳ δὲ
ἦσαν θυγατέρες τέσσαρες παρθένοι προφητεύουσαι. 21.10 ἐπιμενόντων δὲ
ἡμέρας πλείους κατῆλθέν τις ἀπὸ τῆς Ἰουδαίας προφήτης ὀνόματι
Ἅγαβος, 21.11 καὶ ἐλθὼν πρὸς ἡμᾶς καὶ ἄρας τὴν ζώνην τοῦ Παύλου,
δήσας ἑαυτοῦ τοὺς πόδας καὶ τὰς χεῖρας εἶπεν, τάδε λέγει τὸ πνεῦμα τὸ
ἅγιον, τὸν ἄνδρα οὗ ἐστιν ἡ ζώνη αὕτη, οὕτως δήσουσιν ἐν Ἱερουσαλὴμ οἱ
Ἰουδαῖοι καὶ παραδώσουσιν εἰς χεῖρας ἐθνῶν. 21.12 ὡς δὲ ἠκούσαμεν
ταῦτα, παρεκαλοῦμεν ἡμεῖς τε καὶ οἱ ἐντόπιοι τοῦ μὴ ἀναβαίνειν αὐτὸν
εἰς Ἱερουσαλήμ. 21.13 τότε ἀπεκρίθη ὁ Παῦλος, τί ποιεῖτε κλαίοντες καὶ
συνθρύπτοντές μου τὴν καρδίαν; ἐγὼ γὰρ οὐ μόνον δεθῆναι ἀλλὰ καὶ
ἀποθανεῖν εἰς Ἱερουσαλὴμ ἑτοίμως ἔχω ὑπὲρ τοῦ ὀνόματος τοῦ κυρίου
Ἰησοῦ. 21.14 μὴ πειθομένου δὲ αὐτοῦ ἡσυχάσαμεν εἰπόντες, τοῦ κυρίου τὸ
θέλημα γινέσθω. 21.15 μετὰ δὲ τὰς ἡμέρας ταύτας ἐπισκευασάμενοι
ἀνεβαίνομεν εἰς Ἱεροσόλυμα· 21.16 συνῆλθον δὲ καὶ τῶν μαθητῶν ἀπὸ
Καισαρείας σὺν ἡμῖν, ἄγοντες παρ' ᾧ ξενισθῶμεν Μνάσωνί τινι Κυπρίῳ,
ἀρχαίῳ μαθητῇ. 21.17 γενομένων δὲ ἡμῶν εἰς Ἱεροσόλυμα ἀσμένως

ἀπεδέξαντο ἡμᾶς οἱ ἀδελφοί. 21.18 τῇ δὲ ἐπιούσῃ εἰσῄει ὁ Παῦλος σὺν
ἡμῖν πρὸς Ἰάκωβον, πάντες τε παρεγένοντο οἱ πρεσβύτεροι. 27.1 ὡς δὲ
ἐκρίθη τοῦ ἀποπλεῖν ἡμᾶς εἰς τὴν Ἰταλίαν, παρεδίδουν τόν τε Παῦλον καί
τινας ἑτέρους δεσμώτας ἑκατοντάρχῃ ὀνόματι Ἰουλίῳ σπείρης
Σεβαστῆς. 27.2 ἐπιβάντες δὲ πλοίῳ Ἀδραμυττηνῷ μέλλοντι πλεῖν εἰς
τοὺς κατὰ τὴν Ἀσίαν τόπους ἀνήχθημεν ὄντος σὺν ἡμῖν Ἀριστάρχου
Μακεδόνος Θεσσαλονικέως. 27.3 τῇ τε ἑτέρᾳ κατήχθημεν εἰς Σιδῶνα,
φιλανθρώπως τε ὁ Ἰούλιος τῷ Παύλῳ χρησάμενος ἐπέτρεψεν πρὸς τοὺς
φίλους πορευθέντι ἐπιμελείας τυχεῖν. 27.4 κἀκεῖθεν ἀναχθέντες
ὑπεπλεύσαμεν τὴν Κύπρον διὰ τὸ τοὺς ἀνέμους εἶναι ἐναντίους, 27.5 τό
τε πέλαγος τὸ κατὰ τὴν Κιλικίαν καὶ Παμφυλίαν διαπλεύσαντες
κατήλθομεν εἰς Μύρα τῆς Λυκίας. 27.6 κἀκεῖ εὑρὼν ὁ ἑκατοντάρχης
πλοῖον Ἀλεξανδρῖνον πλέον εἰς τὴν Ἰταλίαν ἐνεβίβασεν ἡμᾶς εἰς αὐτό.
27.7 ἐν ἱκαναῖς δὲ ἡμέραις βραδυπλοοῦντες καὶ μόλις γενόμενοι κατὰ τὴν
Κνίδον, μὴ προσεῶντος ἡμᾶς τοῦ ἀνέμου ὑπεπλεύσαμεν τὴν Κρήτην κατὰ
Σαλμώνην, 27.8 μόλις τε παραλεγόμενοι αὐτὴν ἤλθομεν εἰς τόπον τινὰ
καλούμενον Καλοὺς Λιμένας ᾧ ἐγγὺς πόλις ἦν Λασαία. 27.9 ἱκανοῦ δὲ
χρόνου διαγενομένου καὶ ὄντος ἤδη ἐπισφαλοῦς τοῦ πλοὸς διὰ τὸ καὶ τὴν
νηστείαν ἤδη παρεληλυθέναι παρῄνει ὁ Παῦλος 27.10 λέγων αὐτοῖς,
ἄνδρες, θεωρῶ ὅτι μετὰ ὕβρεως καὶ πολλῆς ζημίας οὐ μόνον τοῦ φορτίου
καὶ τοῦ πλοίου ἀλλὰ καὶ τῶν ψυχῶν ἡμῶν μέλλειν ἔσεσθαι τὸν πλοῦν. 27.11
ὁ δὲ ἑκατοντάρχης τῷ κυβερνήτῃ καὶ τῷ ναυκλήρῳ μᾶλλον ἐπείθετο ἢ τοῖς
ὑπὸ Παύλου λεγομένοις. 27.12 ἀνευθέτου δὲ τοῦ λιμένος ὑπάρχοντος πρὸς
παραχειμασίαν οἱ πλείονες ἔθεντο βουλὴν ἀναχθῆναι ἐκεῖθεν, εἴ πως
δύναιντο καταντήσαντες εἰς Φοίνικα παραχειμάσαι λιμένα τῆς Κρήτης
βλέποντα κατὰ λίβα καὶ κατὰ χῶρον. 27.13 ὑποπνεύσαντος δὲ νότου
δόξαντες τῆς προθέσεως κεκρατηκέναι, ἄραντες ἆσσον παρελέγοντο τὴν
Κρήτην. 27.14 μετ' οὐ πολὺ δὲ ἔβαλεν κατ' αὐτῆς ἄνεμος τυφωνικὸς ὁ
καλούμενος Εὐρακύλων· 27.15 συναρπασθέντος δὲ τοῦ πλοίου καὶ μὴ
δυναμένου ἀντοφθαλμεῖν τῷ ἀνέμῳ ἐπιδόντες ἐφερόμεθα. 27.16 νησίον δέ
τι ὑποδραμόντες καλούμενον Καῦδα ἰσχύσαμεν μόλις περικρατεῖς
γενέσθαι τῆς σκάφης, 27.17 ἣν ἄραντες βοηθείαις ἐχρῶντο ὑποζωννύντες
τὸ πλοῖον, φοβούμενοί τε μὴ εἰς τὴν Σύρτιν ἐκπέσωσιν, χαλάσαντες τὸ
σκεῦος, οὕτως ἐφέροντο. 27.18 σφοδρῶς δὲ χειμαζομένων ἡμῶν τῇ ἑξῆς
ἐκβολὴν ἐποιοῦντο 27.19 καὶ τῇ τρίτῃ αὐτόχειρες τὴν σκευὴν τοῦ πλοίου
ἔρριψαν. 27.20 μήτε δὲ ἡλίου μήτε ἄστρων ἐπιφαινόντων ἐπὶ πλείονας
ἡμέρας, χειμῶνός τε οὐκ ὀλίγου ἐπικειμένου, λοιπὸν περιῃρεῖτο ἐλπὶς
πᾶσα τοῦ σῴζεσθαι ἡμᾶς. 27.21 πολλῆς τε ἀσιτίας ὑπαρχούσης τότε
σταθεὶς ὁ Παῦλος ἐν μέσῳ αὐτῶν εἶπεν, ἔδει μέν, ὦ ἄνδρες,
πειθαρχήσαντάς μοι μὴ ἀνάγεσθαι ἀπὸ τῆς Κρήτης κερδῆσαί τε τὴν ὕβριν

ταύτην καὶ τὴν ζημίαν. 27.22 καὶ τὰ νῦν παραινῶ ὑμᾶς εὐθυμεῖν· ἀποβολὴ
γὰρ ψυχῆς οὐδεμία ἔσται ἐξ ὑμῶν πλὴν τοῦ πλοίου. 27.23 παρέστη γάρ μοι
ταύτῃ τῇ νυκτὶ τοῦ θεοῦ, οὗ εἰμι ἐγώ ᾧ καὶ λατρεύω, ἄγγελος 27.24 λέγων,
μὴ φοβοῦ, Παῦλε, Καίσαρί σε δεῖ παραστῆναι, καὶ ἰδοὺ κεχάρισταί σοι ὁ
θεὸς πάντας τοὺς πλέοντας μετὰ σοῦ. 27.25 διὸ εὐθυμεῖτε, ἄνδρες·
πιστεύω γὰρ τῷ θεῷ ὅτι οὕτως ἔσται καθ' ὃν τρόπον λελάληταί μοι. 27.26
εἰς νῆσον δέ τινα δεῖ ἡμᾶς ἐκπεσεῖν. 27.27 ὡς δὲ τεσσαρεσκαιδεκάτη νὺξ
ἐγένετο διαφερομένων ἡμῶν ἐν τῷ Ἀδρίᾳ, κατὰ μέσον τῆς νυκτὸς
ὑπενόουν οἱ ναῦται προσάγειν τινὰ αὐτοῖς χώραν. 27.28 καὶ βολίσαντες
εὗρον ὀργυιὰς εἴκοσι, βραχὺ δὲ διαστήσαντες καὶ πάλιν βολίσαντες εὗρον
ὀργυιὰς δεκαπέντε· 27.29 φοβούμενοί τε μή που κατὰ τραχεῖς τόπους
ἐκπέσωμεν, ἐκ πρύμνης ῥίψαντες ἀγκύρας τέσσαρας ηὔχοντο ἡμέραν
γενέσθαι. 28.1 καὶ διασωθέντες τότε ἐπέγνωμεν ὅτι Μελίτη ἡ νῆσος
καλεῖται. 28.2 οἵ τε βάρβαροι παρεῖχον οὐ τὴν τυχοῦσαν φιλανθρωπίαν
ἡμῖν, ἅψαντες γὰρ πυρὰν προσελάβοντο πάντας ἡμᾶς διὰ τὸν ὑετὸν τὸν
ἐφεστῶτα καὶ διὰ τὸ ψῦχος. 28.3 συστρέψαντος δὲ τοῦ Παύλου φρυγάνων
τι πλῆθος καὶ ἐπιθέντος ἐπὶ τὴν πυράν, ἔχιδνα ἀπὸ τῆς θέρμης ἐξελθοῦσα
καθῆψεν τῆς χειρὸς αὐτοῦ. 28.4 ὡς δὲ εἶδον οἱ βάρβαροι κρεμάμενον τὸ
θηρίον ἐκ τῆς χειρὸς αὐτοῦ, πρὸς ἀλλήλους ἔλεγον, πάντως φονεύς ἐστιν ὁ
ἄνθρωπος οὗτος ὃν διασωθέντα ἐκ τῆς θαλάσσης ἡ δίκη ζῆν οὐκ εἴασεν.
28.5 ὁ μὲν οὖν ἀποτινάξας τὸ θηρίον εἰς τὸ πῦρ ἔπαθεν οὐδὲν κακόν, 28.6
οἱ δὲ προσεδόκων αὐτὸν μέλλειν πίμπρασθαι ἢ καταπίπτειν ἄφνω νεκρόν.
ἐπὶ πολὺ δὲ αὐτῶν προσδοκώντων καὶ θεωρούντων μηδὲν ἄτοπον εἰς αὐτὸν
γινόμενον μεταβαλόμενοι ἔλεγον αὐτὸν εἶναι θεόν. 28.7 ἐν δὲ τοῖς περὶ
τὸν τόπον ἐκεῖνον ὑπῆρχεν χωρία τῷ πρώτῳ τῆς νήσου ὀνόματι Ποπλίῳ,
ὃς ἀναδεξάμενος ἡμᾶς τρεῖς ἡμέρας φιλοφρόνως ἐξένισεν. 28.8 ἐγένετο
δὲ τὸν πατέρα τοῦ Ποπλίου πυρετοῖς καὶ δυσεντερίῳ συνεχόμενον
κατακεῖσθαι, πρὸς ὃν ὁ Παῦλος εἰσελθὼν καὶ προσευξάμενος ἐπιθεὶς τὰς
χεῖρας αὐτῷ ἰάσατο αὐτόν. 28.9 τούτου δὲ γενομένου καὶ οἱ λοιποὶ οἱ ἐν
τῇ νήσῳ ἔχοντες ἀσθενείας προσήρχοντο καὶ ἐθεραπεύοντο, 28.10 οἳ καὶ
πολλαῖς τιμαῖς ἐτίμησαν ἡμᾶς καὶ ἀναγομένοις ἐπέθεντο τὰ πρὸς τὰς
χρείας. 28.11 μετὰ δὲ τρεῖς μῆνας ἀνήχθημεν ἐν πλοίῳ παρακεχειμακότι
ἐν τῇ νήσῳ, Ἀλεξανδρίνῳ, παρασήμῳ Διοσκούροις. 28.12 καὶ καταχθέντες
εἰς Συρακούσας ἐπεμείναμεν ἡμέρας τρεῖς, 28.13 ὅθεν περιελόντες
κατηντήσαμεν εἰς Ῥήγιον. καὶ μετὰ μίαν ἡμέραν ἐπιγενομένου νότου
δευτεραῖοι ἤλθομεν εἰς Ποτιόλους, 28.14 οὗ εὑρόντες ἀδελφοὺς
παρεκλήθημεν παρ' αὐτοῖς ἐπιμεῖναι ἡμέρας ἑπτά· καὶ οὕτως εἰς τὴν
Ῥώμην ἤλθαμεν. 28.15 κἀκεῖθεν οἱ ἀδελφοὶ ἀκούσαντες τὰ περὶ ἡμῶν
ἦλθαν εἰς ἀπάντησιν ἡμῖν ἄχρι Ἀππίου Φόρου καὶ Τριῶν Ταβερνῶν, οὓς
ἰδὼν ὁ Παῦλος εὐχαριστήσας τῷ θεῷ ἔλαβε θάρσος. 28.16 ὅτε δὲ

εἰσήλθομεν εἰς Ῥώμην, ἐπετράπη τῷ Παύλῳ μένειν καθ' ἑαυτὸν σὺν τῷ φυλάσσοντι αὐτὸν στρατιώτῃ.

Chapter Three

The Theology and Perspective of the "We" Passages in Acts and the Portrait of Paul

1. Introduction

In the previous chapter, I established that the "we" passages in Acts constitute a continuous, independent source utilized by the author of Luke–Acts. The author has apparently intercalated this narrative "we" source throughout his own narrative, or perhaps, better still, used this "we" narrative as the basis or framework for part of his larger narrative account of the early Church, especially the second part concerned with Paul. The five "we" passages, when extracted from Acts and connected together (Acts 16:10–17; 20:5–15; 21:1–18; 27:1–29; 28:1–16),[1] form an 82 verse land- and sea-travel narrative that takes Paul and his companions from Troas to Rome (see the Excursus to Chapter Two for a reconstruction of this source). The significant indicators in the text of this source material are several, including the use of the first-person plural and the consistent connection of place locations (Troas to Philippi, Philippi to Miletus, Miletus to Jerusalem, Jerusalem–Caesarea to Malta, and Malta to Rome).[2] This chapter develops the implications of these findings in two directions. First, since this constitutes a continuous source, probably (though not necessarily) originating with someone other than the author of Luke–Acts, and possibly, though not necessarily, originating with an eyewitness or at least a first-hand witness, it is worth attempting to reconstruct the theology and perspective of this source. This chapter will focus upon the author's narrative orientation as revealed through the continuous narrative itself. The second dimension of this chapter is to explore the theological and related reasons for Luke's selection of these passages, shifting focus from the passages themselves (assuming there must have been something in this source that

---

[1] Not all divide the sources this way, with most only finding four "we" passages. They usually combine the fourth and the fifth (e.g. G. Schneider, *Die Apostelgeschichte* [2 vols.; HTKNT 5.1, 2; Freiburg: Herder, 1980, 1982] 1.93). For discussion, see Chapter Two, "The 'We' Passages in Acts as a Source regarding Paul," especially section 3.

[2] See Schneider, *Die Apostelgeschichte*, 1.89.

interested Luke) to how they relate to Luke and his varied interests, especially his attempts to depict Paul. The questions to be asked are why, from a theological and perspectival standpoint, Luke was attracted to and used this source, how his own theology and perspectives are exemplified in or even enhanced or influenced by his use of it, and what this source reveals about the character and thought of Paul in the rest of Acts.

2. The Theology and Character of the "We" Source

Several preliminary observations can be drawn from what remains of the "we" author's writings. Before examining the theology and perspective of the source, two caveats must be registered, however. The first is that, although it would be desirable to have some definitive idea of who the actual writer of this source was – and this desire may well have helped to push some scholars either toward or away from seeing the author of Acts as the author – barring discovery of some now unknown (and almost unimaginable) source, any speculation along such lines must remain that, speculation. This limitation has not stopped many scholars from such unbridled hypothesis, however.[3] Some of the many people accredited with authorship of the "we" passages, besides Luke himself, are: Timothy, Barnabas, Titus, Silas, even Mark, or an unnamed disciple of Paul. A reasonable case can be made for several of them on the basis of how they appear in the surrounding contexts, or in distinction to others mentioned. But how can any of these be substantiated? They cannot, despite the best of intentions. This probably makes any analysis of the "we" passages a little more speculative than it would be if an author could be found, since it is disconnected from any recognizable companion of Paul, and hence from a specific authorial context. Nevertheless, this limitation does not prevent us from making some useful observations on the text. After all, we know so very little about most of Paul's companions anyway, that to have merely a name may well still tell us next to nothing. We may not know the actual author, but we do have a very good idea of some of the parameters of his knowledge, and possibly of some of his experiences. It is what we *can* determine that I wish to explore in more detail.

---

[3] See J. Wehnert, *Die Wir-Passagen der Apostelgeschichte: Ein lukanisches Stilmittel aus jüdischer Tradition* (Göttingen: Vandenhoeck & Ruprecht, 1989) 130–136; J. Dupont, *The Sources of Acts: The Present Position* (trans. K. Pond; London: Darton, Longman & Todd, 1964) 79–80; C.-J. Thornton, *Der Zeuge des Zeugen: Lukas als Historiker der Paulusreisen* (WUNT 56; Tübingen: Mohr–Siebeck, 1991) 312–313.

Here the second caveat must be mentioned. Although the 82 verses that make up the "we" passage demonstrate a significant amount of internal coherence and connectedness,[4] especially as attention is paid to the locations mentioned, there is no firm way to establish the exact length and content of the original narrative. The account, as the author of Luke–Acts records it, begins *in medias res*, with no formal introductions or conclusions of any sort. It is recognizable mostly because of the use of "we," and the "we" passage picking up the thread of the narrative. This means that there is no specification of who exactly constitutes the group called "we." In fact, the constituency of this group may very well shift in the course of the narrative, but this alteration is not always made clear. This factor also means that there is no indication of what it is that they have experienced together before, although it seems that they have been together for at least enough time that they are willing to accept Paul's vision (Acts 16:10) as sufficient reason for leaving immediately, and, along with him, interpreting this as God's call. It also means that there is no indication from the author of the "we" passages how the story, at least as he knew it, turns out in the end. Like Acts itself, which ends with Paul imprisoned, having been held under arrest for two years, the final "we" passage ends even more abruptly (28:16), with Paul living by himself with a Roman guard to watch him. In some ways, it is arguable that this ending may have been the termination of the "we" account, since it seems to be a suitable and final conclusion, or at least as suitable and final as the conclusion of the book of Acts. But this simply cannot be proved. It is just as likely that the author of the "we" account knew something more about Paul that Luke did not want to include. A reasonable conclusion in light of these features of structure is that Luke has cited only a portion of the entire account, even if that portion was a relatively large one. But what has he left out? Would that require an adjustment in our estimation of the author's perspective, especially on Paul? We shall never know the answer to these and similar questions, since we must deal with the text as we have reconstructed it, deduced from its current literary context.

The first part of this chapter, then, deals with the theology and perspective of the author of the "we" passages, before turning to Luke's reasons for using the source. Regarding the "we" passages, Walaskay has noted that scholars have seen little of theological interest in these sections, especially with their sea

---

[4] I have not here attempted a discourse analysis of the "we" passages as a single source, but such an investigation is warranted.

voyages.[5] This neglect unfortunately continues, even in recent treatments of the book of Acts.[6] When the "we" passages are isolated and examined, however, there are four major issues that are worth mentioning and explicating in some detail. (a) The first perspective of the author of the "we" passages is in terms of the understated way in which he depicts how divine guidance is given and received, and how the missionary endeavor, while focusing upon Paul, is not devoted exclusively to him. (b) The second perspective to note is that the author of the "we" passages reflects very much a Hellenistic perspective, tending to minimize any distinctive importance of the Jews as other than simply part of the larger Greco-Roman world. (c) The third is the way in which Paul is depicted, not as a brilliant orator, but rather as a man of understated competence. (d) And the fourth is the way in which Paul is not depicted as a miracle worker or man of magic. It is best to see each of these in contrast to the way similar kinds of episodes to these are depicted in the rest of Acts. When this is done, the distinctive perspective of the "we" passages becomes more evident, especially in the way that the character of Paul is depicted. There have been few, if any, significant analyses of the "we" passages from these kinds of source- or literary- (and redaction-)critical perspectives.[7] Perhaps one of the reasons for the neglect is that these passages have often been directly linked with the author of Luke–Acts, and consequently have been included within discussion of the book of Acts as a whole (see Chapter Two for more detailed discussion of the possible relations of the "we" passages to the author of Acts). Perhaps these passages have been seen as indicating a particular literary style or form utilized in Acts (see Chapter Two for discussion of the options regarding the genre of the book of Acts), or perhaps it is because they have been seen to

---

[5] P.W. Walaskay, *"And so We Came to Rome"*: *The Political Perspective of St Luke* (SNTSMS 49; Cambridge: Cambridge University Press, 1983) 60.

[6] See, for example, H.C. Kee, *Good News to the Ends of the Earth: The Theology of Acts* (London: SCM Press; Philadelphia: Trinity Press International, 1990), who apparently does not differentiate the "we" passages in discussing the theology of Acts; L.T. Johnson, *The Acts of the Apostles* (SP 5; Collegeville, MN: Liturgical, 1992), who, in an insightful commentary on the book, states in his interpretation of Acts 16:11–24, "In fact, the presence of these first person passages seems to have little impact on the development or meaning of the story, and this commentary will not take up the issue again until we examine Paul's sea voyage in ch. 27" (p. 297); J.T. Squires, *The Plan of God in Luke–Acts* (SNTSMS 76; Cambridge: Cambridge University Press, 1993), who does treat this topic in other sections, however, such as Acts 17 (see below Chapters Five and Six); C.H. Talbert, *Reading Acts* (New York: Crossroad, 1997) 148. I hope to be able to show otherwise in this chapter.

[7] See Dupont, *Sources of Acts*, 77.

be "uninteresting" on their own.[8] Whatever the reason, I think that there is much more to these passages than has often been appreciated.

a. Understated Depiction of Divine Guidance

The first characteristic of the "we" passages for consideration is that the author of the passages depicts, in an understated fashion, the way divine guidance is given and received, and shows how the missionary endeavor, while focusing upon Paul, is not devoted exclusively to him. The "we" passages begin with a very simple and straightforward story of divine guidance through a vision. To be more specific, the first "we" passage does not actually depict the vision (found in Acts 16:9), but takes up the narrative that is in response to it. In fact, in none of the purported visions or divine communications in the "we" passages is God (or Christ) quoted directly; either an angel is said to have spoken or God's words are quoted secondhand (unlike, for example, 18:9–10, where God is directly quoted when he speaks to Paul). The reference in 16:10 to Paul having seen a vision perhaps implies that v. 9 should be included in the source, but since there is not the use of the first-person plural, this cannot be certain.[9] The vision directs Paul to Macedonia, the stated destination. The vision is taken in a matter-of-fact way as having indicated that God has called Paul and his companions to preach the gospel to the Macedonians. Nothing in the vision says that God inspired it, perhaps reflecting the Old Testament idea that visionary experiences were assumed to be divine in origin, or, even more convincingly, possibly indicating the common Greco-Roman belief in divine signs as things that could not be ignored.[10]

Besides the lack of depiction of direct communication with God, this visionary communication is in significant contrast to other instances of divine guidance in Acts. The most spectacular is probably the episode at Pentecost, in which there are sounds of violent winds, what seem to be tongues of fire, and

---

[8] M. Hengel, *Acts and the History of Earliest Christianity* (trans. J. Bowden; London: SCM Press, 1979) 66. Hengel thinks that the "we" passages were Luke's personal account, and that Luke's personal experiences were uninteresting. But contrast F.S. Spencer, *Acts* (Readings; Sheffield: Sheffield Academic Press, 1997) 162–163, who emphasizes their interest for and involvement of the reader. It is obvious that more explicit criteria are needed to make judgments such as these.

[9] See J. Rius-Camps, *Comentari als Fets dels Apòstols*. III. *"Fins als confins de la terra": Primera i segona fases de la missió al paganisme (Ac 13,1–18,23)* (Collectània Sant Pacià; Barcelona: Facultat de Teologia de Catalunya/Herder, 1995) 214, who recognizes that divergences in the recensions are accentuated at this point.

[10] See R.M. Ogilvie, *The Romans and their Gods in the Age of Augustus* (London: Chatto & Windus, 1969) 9–23. Cf. J.B. Polhill, *Acts* (NAC 26; Nashville: Broadman, 1992) 346, for a recounting of other speculation on the vision.

speaking in various languages before a huge crowd (Acts 2:2–4). Even Paul's own conversion in Acts is depicted in all three instances as a spectacular event of divine intervention, including flashing lights, direct divine messages and strong physical effects (9:3–9; 22:6–11; 26:13–18).[11] Peter also receives a message regarding reception of the Gentiles by means of a vision, but one that has not only an extended message but a divine graphic object lesson as well (10:9–20).

Although Paul is clearly the major figure in this initial episode of the "we" passages, having seen the vision, it is the entire group that responds to it by preparing to leave. Perhaps even more noteworthily, it appears to be the entire group that concludes that God has called them, according to the narrator: "God had called us to preach the gospel" (Acts 16:10). The author of the "we" source does not hesitate to show that others accompanied Paul in this effort. In fact, the author goes further and frequently distinguishes Paul from his companions, treating all of the participants as integral to the narrative. The result is that, while Paul continues to be the figure of greatest importance, he is seen in relation to others who work with him, sometimes directly accompanying him but, at other times, in contrast to him, even though involved in the same events. For example, in 16:17, Paul is separated from "us" when the slave girl continues to follow. Several scholars dispute whether this differentiation is significant,[12] but the fact that the distinction is made here and in other "we" passages is worth noting, since reference to Paul as separate from "us" is not required by the narrative, and the "we" convention could apparently have been extended to include the entire group. Plümacher claims that this differentiation is consistent with the "we" passages,[13] since Paul constitutes the focus of attention. In this passage, Paul, since he is the one who intends to respond to the slave girl, is singled out for reference apart from "us." This clear distinction of participants occurs in a passage where first-person plural reference has also been used with events that Paul probably instigated (e.g. v. 13). There may be even more to it than this, however, since the words "the rest of us" are not necessary to the narrative. It may be that the author is drawing attention to this

---

[11] See D. Marguerat, "Saul's Conversion (Acts 9, 22, 26) and the Multiplication of Narrative in Acts," in C.M. Tuckett (ed.), *Luke's Literary Achievement: Collected Essays* (JSNTSup 116; Sheffield: JSOT Press, 1995) 127–155.

[12] F.F. Bruce, *The Acts of the Apostles* (Grand Rapids: Eerdmans, 3rd edn, 1990 [2nd edn, 1952]) 360; C. Hemer, "First Person Narrative in Acts 27–28," *TynBul* 36 (1985) 81–82; S.M. Praeder, "The Problem of First Person Narration in Acts," *NovT* 29 (1987) 196.

[13] E. Plümacher, "Wirklichkeitserfahrung und Geschichtsschreibung bei Lukas: Erwägungen zu den Wir-Stücken der Apostelgeschichte," *ZNW* 68 (1977) 13–14; cf. H.J. Cadbury, "'We' and 'I' Passages in Luke-Acts," *NTS* 3 (1957) 128.

group as well, to establish it as an entity in its own right. A second example of distinguishing Paul from the others is found in 20:7 and 11. In the first, Paul is differentiated from the group gathered to break bread, and he becomes the speaker. Then, in v. 11, Paul leaves the first-person plural group to make their way without him to Assos, where they later pick him up (v. 14) and the group is reunited once more. It is difficult to determine which group the narrator is more interested in, since he does not give details concerning what either does during this time.

In Acts 21:11–14, Agabus's prophecy, a second instance of divine guidance is depicted, again with the same kind of understated acceptance of the divine will. Agabus is the one who is described in histrionic terms,[14] with his graphic, symbolic depiction of Paul's fate in Jerusalem.[15] Here too a division is made between Paul and the others of the group referred to by "we," made plausible in light of Agabus's prophecy and the members of the group joining with him in trying to convince Paul not to go to Jerusalem. But Paul's response is surprisingly well measured. As Polhill recognizes, acknowledging Paul's grief over separation from those in Ephesus, "Paul's conflict was not over whether or not to go."[16] He expresses his willingness, if occasion warrants, to die in Jerusalem. Perhaps an episode of this kind in a "we" passage can be contrasted, so far as narrative technique is concerned, with the episode in Philippi, in which Paul and Silas exorcise the slave girl, and then are arrested and put in prison (16:18–40). The events that unfold are all quite spectacular, including the presence of the unruly mob, Paul and Silas being beaten and thrown into prison, and then a violent earthquake shaking the foundations of the prison.[17] This kind of confrontation is handled with a significantly different emphasis in tone and a contrasting Pauline response in the "we" passages. Acts 21:15 resumes the inclusive use of "we" that continues until arrival in Jerusalem. Then the section closes in v. 18 with a distinction between Paul and "us," with "us" seen as accompanying Paul to see James (on this meeting, see

---

[14] Contrast the depiction in Acts 11:27–28 of a prophet named Agabus. Although there are parallels between the two (e.g. they both come down from Jerusalem, and they both engage in visual demonstrations), their differing depictions, as well as the independence of their accounts, are significant. See Johnson, *Acts*, 370, who notes that the author introduces Agabus in 21:10 "with no indication that the reader should remember him."

[15] See G. Schille, *Die Apostelgeschichte des Lukas* (THNT 5; Berlin: Evangelische Verlags-Anstalt, 1983) 408–409, esp. 409; J. Roloff, *Die Apostelgeschichte* (NTD 5; Berlin: Evangelische Verlags-Anstalt, 1981) 311.

[16] Polhill, *Acts*, 436 n. 115.

[17] On this episode, and its implications, see R. Seaford, "Thunder, Lightning and Earthquake in the Bacchae and the Acts of the Apostles," in A.B. Lloyd (ed.), *What is a God? Studies in the Nature of Greek Divinity* (London: Duckworth, 1997) 139–151.

Chapter Eight below). It is arguable that this distinction between Paul and the others is not completely necessary at this point in light of their common adventures, except that this is the style of the narrator of the "we" passages, and appears to be used to emphasize the independent existence and supporting role of these fellow travelers. Although throughout Acts there are various ways in which those participating in events are depicted, including differentiating a single figure from a group, the means found in the "we" passages, of depicting the major figure and others as two relatively equal and distinct groups, is not common. A more typical narrative technique is for the author to speak in terms of various individuals as part of a group event (e.g. Acts 2; 4:1–22), or in terms of a single individual or a couple of individuals only (e.g. 8:26–40), but rarely in terms of a single individual and a group of fellow travelers or companions on the same narrative level.

A third instance of divine guidance is relayed in Paul's comments to the sailors in Acts 27:21–26. In the midst of a horrific, life-threatening storm, and consistent with his understated previous warning in 27:10,[18] Paul calmly stands up among the men and rebukes them for not following his advice. He then relates a vision he had the previous night. In it, an angel of God (Paul parenthetically adds that this is the God whose he is and whom he serves, which in light of the circumstances is perhaps an unnecessary form of authentication of his message, but one delivered with a noticeable amount of calmness and understatement) told him not to be afraid, because he must stand trial before Caesar, and is to preserve the lives of his sailing companions.[19] Thus, they should pluck up their courage, because Paul is confident that events will transpire this way, even though the ship will run aground. It must be kept in mind that this rather matter-of-fact address is given in the midst of what is depicted as a raging storm, in which the sun and stars reportedly have not appeared for many days, so that "we" had finally given up hope of being saved. Paul is clearly distinguished from those who are on the verge of despair, especially since he has had the advantage of the revelation of the night before. Furthermore, the divine guidance, it is to be noted, is by means of an

---

[18] See Johnson, *Acts*, 447, who describes Paul's words in Acts 27:10 as "simple common sense and prudence." However, it is not uncommon for ancient heroes to deliver speeches in the midst of storms (e.g. Homer, *Od.* 5.299–312; Vergil, *Aen.* 1.92–101; Lucian, *Civil War* 5.653–671; Silius, *Punica* 17.260–667). See S.M. Praeder, "Acts 27:1–28:16: Sea Voyages in Ancient Literature and the Theology of Luke–Acts," *CBQ* 46 (1984) 696.

[19] See G. Lüdemann, *Early Christianity according to the Traditions in Acts: A Commentary* (trans. J. Bowden; Minneapolis: Fortress Press, 1987) 257.

angel, not by means of a direct revelation of God, something of which Paul is a recipient elsewhere (as I have noted above).

There have been various explanations of why Paul is depicted as he is in Acts. One is that these episodes reflect Lukan redaction that has resulted in interpolated scenes that are out of character with their contexts. Thus, in Acts 27:21–26, Paul delivers words that reflect Lukan style and literary concerns.[20] It seems that a more detailed consideration of context is necessary before such a conclusion can be posited. As it stands, it is simply an impressionistic conclusion that fails to consider larger features of the narrative. In one of the more recent discussions, Lentz says that this is part of Luke's consistent attempt to portray Paul as the man of virtue. More than simply a Jew or Greek or Roman, he is the classical *archetype* of Jew, Greek and Roman, the man who displays the cardinal virtues of bravery, wisdom, self-control and piety.[21] Unfortunately, Lentz does not rightly differentiate this episode from others he uses for comparison. He overlooks that this is a short speech utilizing understatement, rather than a lengthier more rhetorically-crafted effort, as, for example, is found in the non-"we" passage at 24:10–21, in Paul's speech before Felix (see Chapter Seven for analysis of this speech).[22]

b. Hellenism and Judaism in the "We" Passages

The orientation of the author of the "we" passages is very much that of the Hellenist, minimizing (though not disparaging) any distinctive importance of the Jews as being any other than simply part of the Greco-Roman world.[23] Although the relationship between Israel and the Gentiles as depicted in Luke–Acts has been widely discussed in scholarship,[24] this is not the apparent

---

[20] Roloff, *Die Apostelgeschichte*, 362; cf. Schille, *Die Apostelgeschichte*, 465. E. Haenchen (*The Acts of the Apostles: A Commentary* [trans. B. Noble *et al.*; Philadelphia: Westminster Press, 1971 (1965)] 709) describes the scene as unrealistic; H. Conzelmann (*Die Apostelgeschichte* [HNT 7; Tübingen: Mohr–Siebeck, 1963] 143) concurs. The redactional character of Acts is discussed in Chapter Two above.

[21] J.C. Lentz, Jr, *Luke's Portrait of Paul* (SNTSMS 77; Cambridge: Cambridge University Press, 1993) 94–95.

[22] M.L. Soards, *The Speeches in Acts: Their Content, Context, and Concerns* (Louisville: Westminster/John Knox, 1994) 118–119. By contrast, Soards's attempt to construct a single speech out of Paul's various comments in Acts 27 during the sea voyage is unconvincing.

[23] The classic treatment of this topic remains M. Hengel, *Judaism and Hellenism* (trans. J. Bowden; Philadelphia: Fortress Press, 1974). Perhaps a better title for this volume, and one that reflects the orientation of the author of the "we" passages, would be "Judaism within Hellenism."

[24] See M.A. Powell, *What are They Saying about Acts?* (New York: Paulist, 1991) 67–72, for a survey of opinions. Contrasting positions are represented by J.T. Sanders, *The Jews*

concern of the author of the "we" passages. Rather than outlining or differentiating any relationship between these groups, he simply shows little concern for the Jews as a specific group distinct from any other. The author includes virtually only non-Jewish cities within his discussion, even when he depicts Paul as being in Palestine. In the "we" passages, the first major city of visitation is Philippi in Macedonia, distinguished by being described as a Roman colony (the only time κολωνία is used in the Greek New Testament; Acts 16:12)[25] and having a place of prayer (16:13, 16). The place of prayer (προσευχή) is probably Jewish terminology for a Diaspora place of gathering, rather than a formal synagogue.[26] This passage is the only one to use such language in Acts. In 16:13, the group thinks that there is such a place of prayer in the city, although the women they encounter by the river are not necessarily part of it;[27] and, in 16:16, they are on their way to the place of prayer but never arrive. In this "we" passage, the successful meeting that the author records is with Lydia, who was a worshipper of God or a god-fearer (16:14). She may have been a Jew, but it is more likely that she was a Gentile.[28] The author of

---

in Luke–Acts (London: SCM Press, 1987), who sees high levels of anti-Semitism in Luke–Acts, and J. Jervell, The Theology of the Acts of the Apostles (New Testament Theology; Cambridge: Cambridge University Press, 1996), who sees the Jews depicted positively.

[25] On Philippi, see P. Pilhofer, Philippi. I. Die erste christliche Gemeinde Europas (WUNT 87; Tübingen: Mohr–Siebeck, 1995) esp. 205; and for more summative treatment, D.W.J. Gill, "Macedonia," in D.W.J. Gill and C. Gempf (eds.), The Book of Acts in its First Century Setting. II. The Book of Acts in its Graeco-Roman Setting (Grand Rapids: Eerdmans, 1994) 411–413; W.W. Gasque, "Philippi," in R.K. Harrison (ed.), Major Cities of the Biblical World (Nashville: Nelson, 1985) 198–207.

[26] See J. Gutman, "Synagogue Origins: Theories and Facts," in J. Gutman (ed.), Ancient Synagogues: The State of Research (BJS 22; Chico, CA: Scholars Press, 1981) 1–6; Pilhofer, Philippi, 165–174; and especially I. Levinskaya, The Book of Acts in its First Century Setting. V. The Book of Acts in its Diaspora Setting (Grand Rapids: Eerdmans, 1996) 207–225.

[27] As Johnson notes (Acts, 292), the use of νομίζω ("think") in Luke–Acts in every other instance introduces a false supposition (Acts 7:25; 8:20; 14:19; 16:27; 17:29; 21:29).

[28] On the issue of the god-fearers, with discussion of each of the pertinent passages in Acts, see M. Wilcox, "The 'God-Fearers' in Acts – A Reconsideration," JSNT 13 (1981) 102–122, esp. 110–111; C. Gempf, "Appendix 2: The God-Fearers," in C. Hemer, The Book of Acts in the Setting of Hellenistic History (ed. C. Gempf; WUNT 49; Tübingen: Mohr–Siebeck, 1989; repr. Winona Lake, IN: Eisenbrauns, 1990) 444–447; P.W. van der Horst, "Jews and Christians in Aphrodisias in the Light of their Relations in Other Cities of Asia Minor," in his Essays on the Jewish World of Early Christianity (NTOA 14; Freiburg: Universitätsverlag; Göttingen: Vandenhoeck & Ruprecht, 1990) 166–181; idem, "A New Altar of a Godfearer?" repr. from JJS 43 (1992) 32–37, in his Hellenism – Judaism – Christianity: Essays on their Interaction (Leuven: Peeters, 2nd edn, 1994) 65–72; L.H. Feldman, Jew and Gentile in the Ancient World: Attitudes and Interactions from Alexander to Justinian (Princeton: Princeton University Press, 1993) esp. 342–382; J.M. Lieu, "Do God-

the "we" passage apparently does not record the confrontation over the slave girl that leads to Paul's imprisonment, even though the account as we have it has all of the participants appropriate for such a passage (see 16:19, where "we" could have been used), leaving open the possibility of another authorial figure than those included in the "we" group. In the third passage (21:1–18), Paul and his companions travel the eastern Mediterranean but the account has them spending most of their time at Caesarea, a center of Hellenistic and Roman culture in Palestine,[29] only arriving at Jerusalem at the very end of the account (21:17). Even though Jerusalem is the purported goal of the journey, at least in the "we" passages as we have them, Jerusalem does not figure significantly, mention being reserved until the very end of the section.[30] It is again worth noting what happens in Caesarea. Agabus delivers his prophecy of impending doom in Jerusalem. In the only instance in the "we" passages where the Holy Spirit is said to have revealed a message (although we do not hear the Holy Spirit, except in a report of his message, a typical stylistic feature of the "we" narrator), Paul accepts the message, but not as a binding prophetic utterance. He states that he is ready to die in Jerusalem, if need be. The tenor is one of inevitable doom at the hands of the Jerusalem authorities (see Chapter Eight). Even the protests of Paul's companions are muted. The text says, "When he would not be dissuaded, we gave up and said, 'The Lord's will be done'" (21:14). Then they all prepared to go to Jerusalem. This is the last time that Jerusalem is part of the preserved "we" narrative; the action commences in 27:1, with sailing probably from Caesarea. Caesarea is not specifically mentioned, but it is logical to think in light of both the "we" passage and the rest of the Acts narrative, including the sailing course, that this is where the voyage began.

Fearers Make Good Christians?" in S.E. Porter, P. Joyce, and D.E. Orton (eds.), *Crossing the Boundaries: Essays in Biblical Interpretation in Honour of Michael D. Goulder* (BIC 8; Leiden: Brill, 1994) 329–346; M.C. de Boer, "God-Fearers in Luke–Acts," in Tuckett (ed.), *Luke's Literary Achievement*, 50–71; M. Hengel and A.M. Schwemer, *Paul between Damascus and Antioch: The Unknown Years* (trans. J. Bowden; Louisville: Westminster/John Knox, 1997) 61–68 with notes on 357–362; and especially Levinskaya, *Acts in its Diaspora Setting*, 51–126; and B. Wander, *Gottesfürchtige und Sympathisanten* (WUNT 104; Tübingen: Mohr–Siebeck, 1998) who includes many primary sources. On the story of Lydia's conversion, see D.L. Matson, *Household Conversion Narratives in Acts: Pattern and Interpretation* (JSNTSup 123; Sheffield: Sheffield Academic Press, 1996) 136–154.

[29] See A.B. Spencer, "Caesarea Maritima," in Harrison (ed.), *Major Cities of the Biblical World*, 63–71, for a brief summary, with reference to bibliography.

[30] Cf. Lüdemann, *Early Christianity*, 233, who sees Acts 21:1–16 as part of a source.

What did the narrator of the "we" passages know about Paul's fortunes in Jerusalem during this intervening period? We do not know. The author simply does not say, and Luke does not supplement the account with any other information. Jews as a distinctive group do not figure into the rest of the "we" narrative (they are part of the rest of Acts, however), but various Hellenistic features and people do appear. The centurion Julius is introduced (Acts 27:1 and following), Alexandria is mentioned in its only two appearances in the New Testament (27:6; 28:11; cf. 18:24, for reference to the city of Apollos), and the twin gods Castor and Pollux are depicted as being on an Alexandrian ship (28:11).[31] The author of the "we" passages cannot be characterized as in any overt way disparaging Jews. He simply says very little specifically about them, being instead concerned with the more general panoply of Hellenistic peoples and features, of which the Jews were a part.

c. Paul, the Man of Competence but not the Orator

The author of the "we" passages does not emphasize Paul the orator. Paul's speaking in the "we" passages is quite minimal, for the most part being confined to a few casual and underplayed remarks, nine verses in all (i.e. Acts 20:10; 21:13; 27:10, 21–26 [the last the longest section of Paul's words in the "we" passages]). By definition, according to my analysis, none of the lengthy speeches that occur in the contextual vicinity of the "we" passages belongs to the "we" narrative itself. Furthermore, in none of these speeches is the "we" convention used directly in any way to introduce the speech. In other words, there is always a noticeable break between a "we" passage, which is narrative in type, and a lengthy speech.

A secondary reason to think that these passages do not include any of the major speeches is the simple observation that the tone of the established "we" passages is much more muted and understated than in most of the speeches in Acts. This understated tone in the "we" passages, in contrast to the speeches, can be observed from the two speeches that are in closest proximity to the "we" passages. For example, after the second passage (Acts 20:5–15), Paul travels past Ephesus to Miletus, where he addresses the Ephesian elders (20:18–36).[32] The speech to the elders is full of hyperbole untypical of the author of the "we" passages, including reference to how Paul lived "the whole time," that is, "from the first day" he entered Asia, reference to his great humility, and

---

[31] On Castor and Pollux, see H.J. Rose, *Religion in Greece and Rome* (New York: Harper & Brothers, 1959) 239; W. Burkert, *Greek Religion* (Cambridge, MA: Harvard University Press, 1985) 212–213.

[32] Soards, *Speeches in Acts*, 104–108.

reference to the severe tests by the Jews. He considers his life nothing. He knows that none of them will ever see him again. Instead, savage wolves will come among them, although he has never stopped warning each of them night and day.[33] At his departure, there is much weeping, embracing and kissing. This hyperbolic tone is very different from the simple and straightforward comments Paul is said to have made with regard to Agabus's plea. The same kind of emotional farewell is not recorded, even though he is with similarly close friends.

The second speech in close proximity follows the last "we" passage, and is the one that Paul addresses to the Jews in Rome (Acts 28:17–20). This speech is also very different in tone from Paul's comments in the "we" passages, again being full of hyperbole.[34] For example, Paul begins by saying that he has done nothing against the Jewish people or against the laws (ἔθη)[35] of his ancestors. Although it may be that Paul is not to be seen as an outright breaker of Jewish law, it is also quite clear that Paul in Acts, as well as in his letters, cannot pass himself off as completely innocent when Jewish laws and traditions are involved, especially in his personal behavior and in relation to Gentiles. Upon his arrival in Jerusalem, James and the others tell Paul that there are Jews who are saying that Paul is teaching Jews who live among Gentiles to turn away from Moses by not performing circumcision or living according to Jewish laws (21:21).[36] Even if Paul never goes so far as to advocate Jews breaking the law, his own behavior could well have been interpreted by some as advocating such a position. In Acts, for example, Paul apparently travels on the Sabbath (16:13), and even stays with a Gentile woman (16:15). The book of Acts is replete with Jews reacting quite strongly to Paul and his message.

If Paul is not depicted in the "we" narrative as a great orator, how is he seen? In contrast to Lentz's undifferentiated picture of Paul, another characterization emerges from the "we" passages. Besides being one of several characters seen in their missionary travels, Paul is seen as the utilitarian man, one who acts and speaks as necessary and who is fully involved in the missionary endeavor, but without being unjustifiably the center of undue

---

[33] See R.C. Tannehill, *The Narrative Unity of Luke–Acts: A Literary Interpretation*. II. *The Acts of the Apostles* (FFNT; Minneapolis: Fortress Press, 1990) 254.

[34] Cf. Tannehill, *Acts*, 344.

[35] ἔθος is probably used synonymously with νόμος in Acts. ἔθος appears in Acts 6:14; 15:1; 16:21; 22:21; 25:16; 26:3; 28:17. On the usage of these terms, see Schneider, *Die Apostelgeschichte*, 2.309.

[36] See Lentz, *Luke's Portrait of Paul*, 139; contra B.S. Childs, *Biblical Theology of the Old and New Testaments: Theological Reflection on the Christian Bible* (Philadelphia: Fortress Press, 1992) 292–293. See Chapter Eight for discussion of this episode.

attention. It is Paul who apparently preaches at Philippi and to whom Lydia responds, even though his talk is never specifically mentioned (Acts 16:14); it is Paul who preaches all night at Troas, sufficiently long to put at least one person to sleep (who subsequently falls from the third story; 20:7, 9); it is Paul who travels by foot from Troas to Assos, when the others take the ship (20:13); it is Paul who is gathering a pile of wood when he is bitten by a snake (28:2–3); and it is Paul who offers a simple word of thanks on his arrival in Rome (28:15). Paul is recognizably the center of attention, but he is also depicted as a first among equals in the "we" passages.

d. Paul as Miracle Worker?

Haenchen posited that Luke portrayed Paul as a great miracle worker. However, of the six examples that he cites in support of his claim (Acts 13:6–12; 14:8–10; 14:19–20; 19:12; 28:3–6; 20:7–12),[37] only two occur in "we" passages (Haenchen does not distinguish the "we" passages in his analysis). At most, one might argue that only Luke (not the author of the "we" passages) depicts Paul as a miracle worker, but even this is a dubious conclusion to reach when all of the miracle passages themselves are examined more closely (see Chapter Nine, where such an analysis is made). Harnack has proposed a much more useful and variegated taxonomy of miracles and works of the Spirit in Acts. According to his analysis, the involvement of the supernatural is much stronger in Acts 1–15 than it is in the "we" sections. In the "we" sections, he cites miracles as occurring in 16:16–18, with Paul curing the woman possessed by a demon (which does not actually fall within the first "we" passage – see Chapter Two); 20:9–10, with Paul raising Eutychus; 28:13–16, where Paul is not harmed when a snake bites him; and 28:7, where Paul heals Publius.[38]

---

[37] Haenchen, *Acts*, 113. See also Schneider, *Die Apostelgeschichte*, 1.94, who characterizes this as one of the three characteristics of the "we" passages.

[38] See A. Harnack, *The Acts of the Apostles* (trans. J.R. Wilkinson; London: Williams & Norgate, 1909) 133–161, esp. 134–140, for a convenient chart. Note that Harnack places Acts 18:9 in a "we" passage. Cf. W.L. Knox, *The Acts of the Apostles* (Cambridge: Cambridge University Press, 1948) 91, for questioning of Harnack's analysis. Harnack had a far less moderated view in his earlier *Luke the Physician: The Author of the Third Gospel and the Acts of the Apostles* (trans. J.R. Wilkinson; London: Williams & Norgate, 2nd edn, 1909 [1907]) esp. 33–34, where he states that the author of the "we" passages is as fond of miracles as the author of the Gospel and the rest of Acts. Recent discussion of the issues in terms of source criticism (Petrine and Pauline comparisons) is by F. Neirynck, "The Miracle Stories in the Acts of the Apostles: An Introduction," in J. Kremer (ed.), *Les Actes des Apôtres: Traditions, rédaction, théologie* (BETL 48; Gembloux: Duculot; Leuven: Leuven University Press, 1979) 190–193, and in terms of ancient historiography by E. Plümacher, "TEPATEIA. Fiktion und Wunder in der hellenistisch-römischen Geschichtsschreibung und in der Apostelgeschichte," *ZNW* 89 (1998) 66–90.

An analysis of the miracle passages in Acts in terms of the "we" sections leads to a number of useful observations. In general terms, the author of the "we" passages recognizes the role of divine guidance and of the supernatural, but he does not depict Paul as a *flashy* miracle worker. Paul's mission is begun in response to a simple (or at least simply depicted) vision (Acts 16:10), and continues to be guided by understated divine influence (e.g. 21:14; 27:23–24). In three places, there is the potential for much to be made by the author of the "we" passages of what may be supernatural events, but in each case the author downplays the miraculous. In the second "we" passage (20:5–15), Paul and his companions travel to Troas, and then to Miletus in Asia Minor. The one extended account in this section is of the "raising up" of Eutychus. The passage does not unequivocally indicate that Eutychus was dead. Conzelmann asserts that ὡς ("as") is not used in Acts 20:9; the verse says ἤρθη νεκρός ("he was raised dead"), indicating that Eutychus was actually dead. However, vv. 10–12 compromises the idea that Paul thought that Eutychus was dead, with Paul's statement and the response.[39] Paul says that the boy's spirit or life is in him. It may be that Paul had already revivified him, or, perhaps, that closer examination showed that he was not in fact dead. The response by others is also quite restrained, v. 12 making use of litotes, a form of understatement: "they were comforted not moderately (οὐ μετρίως)."[40] Although many take this as a revivification story, and Luke may well have included it because of its appearance as such, it may well be nothing more than a resuscitation as it is presented in the "we" source.[41]

In the fifth "we" passage (Acts 28:1–16), the journey from Malta to Rome is recorded. Paul's encounter with the viper is included here (28:3). Again, the rhetorical possibilities of the miracle are not exploited to their fullest extent, but

---

[39] Conzelmann, *Die Apostelgeschichte*, 116, who claims that the uncertainty is introduced by redactional insertions in vv. 11–12.

[40] Schneider, *Die Apostelgeschichte*, 287 n. 361; R. Pesch, *Die Apostelgeschichte* (2 vols.; EKK 5.1, 2; Solothurn: Benziger; Neukirchen-Vluyn: Neukirchener, 1995 [2nd edn], 1986) 2.193 n. 31; Haenchen, *Acts*, 586; Talbert, *Acts*, 182–183, all of whom recognize the restraint. Johnson seems to miss the point (*Acts*, 358): "And the story itself is a strange blend of incidental detail and inconclusiveness. Luke's dramatic sense seems to have abandoned him completely." Of course, if the author (at least originally) responsible was the author of the "we" source, we would expect some differences, as I have tried to argue. Even so, there are literary features that Johnson has clearly missed.

[41] M. Dibelius, *Studies in the Acts of the Apostles* (ed. H. Greeven; trans. M. Ling; London: SCM Press, 1956) 117; cf. Haenchen, *Acts*, 586; Schneider, *Die Apostelgeschichte*, 2.283, but who take it as a depiction of a raising of the dead. It is interesting to note that neither Dibelius, Haenchen nor Schneider puts the Eutychus story in the "we" narrative, claiming that it was inserted into the narrative; cf. Tannehill, *Acts*, 248–249. See also Conzelmann, *Die Apostelgeschichte*, 116–117, who cites P.Oxy. III 475 as similar.

kept understated and matter-of-factly opposed to superstition.[42] Whereas the crowd responds by thinking that the bite is a sign of God's judgment against him, perhaps reflecting Gentile belief in divine retribution,[43] Paul simply shakes the snake off, and is said to show no signs of ill effect. Also in the fifth "we" passage is the episode with Publius's father (vv. 7–10), a man who is suffering from fever and dysentery. Paul simply prays and places his hands on him, the only time where both praying and laying on of hands are used together in a healing in Acts,[44] and he is healed. This is the most enthusiastic healing or miracle account in the "we" passages, but the results are hardly impressive, being conveyed in summary fashion.[45] Others who were sick on the island are said to have come to Paul and were healed, but there are no other explicit accounts of healings. It is, admittedly, said that Paul and his companions were honored in many ways, but this may translate into something as mundane as providing supplies for their journey to Rome, since the word for "honor" (τιμή) has financial implications (cf. Rom 13:7). This episode is in stark contrast to another Pauline healing story in 19:11–12, where it is said that God did extraordinary miracles and various items of cloth became the vehicles for healing.[46] In contrast to many other portions of Acts, including passages intercalated with the "we" source, the author of the "we" source provides a credible portrait of Paul the apostle, without exaggeration or embellishment. Not only is Paul not depicted as a miracle worker, but clear opportunities to depict him as such are passed by.

3. Luke's Use of the "We" Source and his Depiction of Paul

As is evident from what has been already stated, in several ways the "we" source has its own tone and narrative style. Consequently, it does not apparently depict Paul and his companions in the same light as does the rest of

---

[42] See Schille, *Die Apostelgeschichte*, 471; cf. Polhill, *Acts*, 531–532; and Talbert, *Acts*, 221–222, who cites examples from other literature of viper victims.

[43] Conzelmann, *Die Apostelgeschichte*, 147; cf. G.B. Miles and G. Trompf, "Luke and Antiphon: The Theology of Acts 27–28 in the Light of Pagan Beliefs about Divine Retribution, Pollution and Shipwreck," *HTR* 69 (1976) 259–267; D. Ladouceur, "Hellenistic Preconceptions of Shipwreck and Pollution as a Context for Acts 27–28," *HTR* 73 (1980) 435–449.

[44] Polhill, *Acts*, 534. Tannehill (*Acts*, 341–342) tries to draw parallels between this episode and Luke 4:38–40.

[45] Pesch, *Die Apostelgeschichte*, 2.299; contra Conzelmann, *Die Apostelgeschichte*, 147, who draws attention to the miraculous over the medical in this episode.

[46] See Polhill, *Acts*, 401.

Luke's writing. In light of this apparent orientation of the "we" narrative, the question must be raised of why it is that Luke has used the "we" source, and what Luke's theological and other reasons for doing so may have been, especially in his depiction of Paul.

On the basis of the analysis given here, and in conjunction with the previous chapter in this volume regarding the contents of the "we" passages, it is clear that the "we" source, at least as it is conveyed in Acts at this point and on the basis of its current style, is not the source of most of the major themes or ideas in Luke's theology.[47] For example, there is little in this "we" material to suggest Luke's great interest in the Spirit, especially when Paul disregards Agabus's warning and acts contrary to the Spirit's advice and leading (Acts 21:4, 11, the only uses of Spirit in the "we" passages – both instances not spoken by Paul); there is none of the language of "necessity" or "fulfillment" used in relation to God; there is not an emphasis upon Jesus as Savior (Jesus is only mentioned once, in 21:13); there is nothing eschatological about the account, however eschatology might be conceived in Acts; there is nothing apologetic about the material of the "we" passages, trying to show that Christians were not a threat to the Roman government; there is nothing of an overt defense of Paul and his teachings; there is nothing directed towards refuting heresy or promoting overt evangelism; there is no emphasis upon preaching or speech-making, so much so that we have very little idea what Paul believed, even regarding Jesus Christ, from what he says in the "we" passages; and there is no serious attention given to ecclesiology, with attendant issues such as baptism, wealth and possessions, and the like.[48] In other words, there is not that much in the "we" passages that does commend it so far as the usual categories in the discussion of Lukan theology are concerned.

There are perhaps two themes, one theological and the other historical, however, that Luke is developing in Acts that the "we" narrative responds to and helps him to develop. They are quite important, and form macrostructural principles[49] of organization for the book, thus perhaps warranting Luke's turning to the "we" source. The first is with regard to the progress of the gospel. For Luke, consistent with much of the rest of the New Testament, the

---

[47] One of the best accounts of Luke's theological and historical interests is still I.H. Marshall's *Luke: Historian and Theologian* (Grand Rapids: Zondervan, 1970) esp. chaps. 7–9. See also Powell, *What are They Saying about Acts?*, esp. chaps. 3–4.

[48] Of course not all commentators on Acts would agree that these are major themes. See, for example, Haenchen, *Acts*, 91–96.

[49] The term "macrostructure" comes from discourse analysis. See T.A. van Dijk, *Text and Context: Explorations in the Semantics and Pragmatics of Discourse* (London: Longman, 1977) 130–163.

progress of the gospel is seen in terms of its witness beginning with the Jews, hence Jerusalem, and progressing outwards to the rest of Judea, Samaria and the ends of the earth (Acts 1:8). Acts effectively traces this movement, beginning with the apostles observing Jesus' departure and then receiving the Holy Spirit, and ending with Paul being imprisoned in Rome. The "we" narrative does not exactly mirror this course of development, as was observed above. The "we" narrative pays little attention to things Jewish, including only brief mention of Jerusalem. Nevertheless, the "we" source does chart the progress of the gospel from its very beginnings as a message to those outside of Asia Minor to its ultimate destination in Rome. It traces this in a circuitous route, but one that nevertheless arrives in Rome.

More than this, and this is the second reason for Luke's apparent use of the "we" source, is that the "we" narrative does provide a very straightforward account of Paul's movement from Asia Minor to Europe, back to Palestine, and then on to Rome. The author of Acts not only speaks of Paul, but it is clear that Paul is one of his heroes. Although there are a few other interesting characters in Acts, such as Stephen and James, the major figures are Peter and Paul. It is interesting to note that for virtually everything that Peter does, Paul is seen by the author as doing the same – but better (healings, speeches, imprisonments, escapes, etc.).[50] The author of the "we" passages has written a narrative of Paul and his traveling companions, with very little, if any, significant interest in anyone else. This apparently appealed to Luke, since he has taken the account over and intercalated it into his larger narrative, or possibly used it as his own framework for telling the story of Paul. Apparently, the author of the "we" passages did not know or record much (or any?) of the intervening material that Luke has included in the account, such as most of Paul's second and third missionary journeys (from Acts 16:17–20:4). What he does know is that Paul traveled from Philippi to Miletus to Palestine. Likewise, he does not apparently know of the circumstances of Paul's arrest, lengthy captivity in Caesarea, several trials and then appeal to Caesar (from 21:19–26:32). The author does know that Paul was a prisoner (27:1), and perhaps he knew something of how Paul got into this predicament, but it is sheer speculation what he may have known or said in the rest of his source, since we do not have that. Luke apparently thought that his other materials suited his purposes better.

In some ways like Luke, in that he does not seem to (at least overtly) know or have access to Paul's writings (or possibly much of his theology) (see Chapter Five), the author of the "we" passages does not emphasize Paul the

---

[50] Bruce, *Acts*, 26–27.

writer, speaker or theologian, but Paul the practical man,[51] one willing simply to place himself in God's hands. Furthermore, what the source does know is that Paul did get to Rome, and that at every point along the way Paul was confident of his divine destiny.[52] For example, Agabus's prophecy states that Paul would be turned over to the Gentiles by the Jews (Acts 21:11). Not only is this part of the "we" source's minimization of the distinctiveness of the Jews, but it contains some reference to the Gentiles (to be read as the Romans) as part of God's plan for Paul. In 27:24, Paul is recorded as stating with quiet confidence that, despite the severe storm, he is to stand trial before Caesar. It is the author of the "we" passage who records the simple words, "And so we came to Rome" (28:14). The source ends with Paul living by himself with a guard in Rome. Throughout the account there is a consistently understated confidence that what is happening to Paul is in fact part of God's divinely ordained plan for Paul, and that this plan involves his being taken to Rome. This narrative movement can only be fully appreciated when the "we" passages are considered on their own. This is not as clearly seen when the intervening material is read. What Luke has done with the source, by intercalating other accounts of events, including some that are written from a different standpoint and reflect a different tone, is to lengthen the account considerably and even to dilute the force of this powerfully direct and unswerving "we" narrative.

4. Conclusion

Whereas in Chapter Two I differentiated and defined the "we" passages in Acts, in this chapter I have tried to discuss the orientation of the author and why his material apparently appealed to Luke. The material is sufficiently distinct in several respects, including its use of the first-person plural narrative convention, its approach to describing Paul and his companions, the kinds of events described, and its general tone, to raise anew the question of source criticism of Acts, this time in terms of the author's redactional interests. It

---

[51] See W. Neil, *The Acts of the Apostles* (NCB; London: Marshall, Morgan, Scott, 1973) 28–29.

[52] For a fuller development of the concept of Paul and divine destiny, in the context of this as a central theme in Luke–Acts, see J.T. Squires, *The Plan of God in Luke–Acts* (SNTSMS 76; Cambridge: Cambridge University Press, 1993) esp. 70–76; *idem*, "The Plan of God," in I.H. Marshall and D. Peterson (eds.), *Witness to the Gospel: The Theology of Acts* (Grand Rapids: Eerdmans, 1998) 19–39. Cf. Dibelius, *Studies in the Acts of the Apostles*, 197, who says that it is "inconceivable that Luke should have included insignificant and unimportant stations in his account of the journey if he had not had a description of the route at his disposal."

seems that the "we" source presented a picture of Paul that was very appealing to the author – though in many ways significantly different in perspective from his own – and it may well have provided the structural framework for him to construct his larger narrative regarding the progress of Paul and the gospel to Rome.

Chapter Four

Paul and the Holy Spirit in Acts

1. Introduction

Although a significant and growing number of exegetical works discuss the book of Acts, and a number discuss the role and function of the Holy Spirit, when the two are considered together, a number of shortcomings in the scholarly literature become evident.[1] The secondary literature that one finds can be classified into roughly five categories according to the nature of its discussion. The first category treats Acts, but does not give any emphasis to the role of the Spirit in the book. These studies are few, but some of their authors are worth noting, since they include arguably some of the most important recent interpreters of Acts.[2] The second are systematic-theological treatments, in which the Holy Spirit is discussed as a theological category.[3]

---

[1] For recent surveys of representative work on the Holy Spirit in Acts, see M. Turner, *Power from on High: The Spirit in Israel's Restoration and Witness in Luke–Acts* (JPTSup 9; Sheffield: Sheffield Academic Press, 1996) 20–79; cf. R.P. Menzies, *The Development of Early Christian Pneumatology with Special Reference to Luke–Acts* (JSNTSup 54; Sheffield: JSOT Press, 1991) 18–47; J.B. Green and M.C. McKeever, *Luke–Acts and New Testament Historiography* (IBR Bibliographies 8; Grand Rapids: Baker, 1994) 52–56; and M.A. Powell, *What are They Saying about Acts?* (New York: Paulist, 1991) 50–56. By far the most thorough study of the Holy Spirit in relation to Paul, but confined to his letters, is G.D. Fee, *God's Empowering Presence: The Holy Spirit in the Letters of Paul* (Peabody, MA: Hendrickson, 1994).

[2] See, for example, H. Conzelmann, *Die Apostelgeschichte* (HNT 7; Tübingen: Mohr–Siebeck, 1963) 9: "dazu kommt der Geist als ständiger Besitz der Kirche. Es ist bezeichnend, dass die Kontinuität der Kirchengeschichte nicht eine solche von Institutionen ist." This is perhaps surprising in light of the emphasis upon the Holy Spirit in Conzelmann's *The Theology of St Luke* (trans. G. Buswell; London: Faber & Faber, 1961 [1957]) 173–184. See also M. Dibelius, "Paul in the Acts of the Apostles," in *Studies in the Acts of the Apostles* (ed. H. Greeven; trans. M. Ling; London: SCM Press, 1956) 207–214; R. Maddox, *The Purpose of Luke–Acts* (Edinburgh: T. &. T. Clark, 1982) 66–90; and J.C. Lentz, Jr, *Luke's Portrait of Paul* (SNTSMS 77; Cambridge: Cambridge University Press, 1993), who avoids the Spirit at almost every turn.

[3] See, for example, C.F.D. Moule, *The Holy Spirit* (London: Mowbrays, 1978), who devotes one chapter to the Holy Spirit in the New Testament (pp. 22–42), and discusses it by topic.

This work often only mentions Acts in passing, or in terms of such an event as Pentecost (Acts 2). The third are those works that have a clear apologetic agenda in discussing the Holy Spirit and Acts, often in terms of justifying a particular way in which the Spirit operates in the life of the believer or the Church.[4] A fourth, and more productive, approach discusses the Holy Spirit in Acts, but only tangentially mentions Paul, if at all.[5] The fifth approach mentions and discusses Paul, but in relation to some larger topic with regard to Acts.[6] Several studies merit mention here, including Goulder's *Type and History in Acts*, in which he uses references to the Spirit on two planes. The first is in terms of finding the pattern for the entire book of Acts, and the

---

[4] See G.R. Beasley-Murray, *Baptism in the New Testament* (Grand Rapids: Eerdmans, 1973 [1962]) 93–125; C.S. Keener, *The Spirit in the Gospels and Acts: Divine Purity and Power* (Peabody, MA: Hendrickson, 1997) 190–213; and J.D.G. Dunn, *Baptism in the Holy Spirit: A Re-Examination of the New Testament Teaching on the Gift of the Spirit in Relation to Pentecostalism Today* (London: SCM Press, 1970) 38–102, who surveys opinion, and who has been responded to by many, including H. Ervin, *Conversion-Initiation and the Baptism in the Holy Spirit* (Peabody, MA: Hendrickson, 1984); Menzies, *Development of Early Christian Pneumatology*, esp. 245–277; and M. Turner, *The Holy Spirit and Spiritual Gifts Then and Now* (Exeter: Paternoster, 1996) esp. 36–57; *idem*, "The 'Spirit of Prophecy' as the Power of Israel's Restoration and Witness," in I.H. Marshall and D. Peterson (eds.), *Witness to the Gospel: The Theology of Acts* (Grand Rapids: Eerdmans, 1998) 327–348.

[5] A typical – but far from exhaustive – list would include F.J. Foakes Jackson and K. Lake, "The Development of Thought on the Spirit, the Church, and Baptism," in F.J. Foakes Jackson and K. Lake (eds.), *The Beginnings of Christianity. Part I. The Acts of the Apostles. I. Prolegomena I: The Jewish, Gentile and Christian Backgrounds* (London: Macmillan, 1920) 321–327; G.W.H. Lampe, "The Holy Spirit in the Writings of St Luke," in D.E. Nineham (ed.), *Studies in the Gospels: Essays in Memory of R.H. Lightfoot* (Oxford: Blackwell, 1957) 159–200; J.D.G. Dunn, *Jesus and the Spirit: A Study of the Religious and Charismatic Experience of Jesus and the First Christians as Reflected in the New Testament* (London: SCM Press, 1975); I.H. Marshall, *Luke: Historian and Theologian* (Grand Rapids: Zondervan, 1970) 197–202; *idem, The Acts of the Apostles* (NTG; Sheffield: JSOT Press, 1992) 66–69 (abbreviated *Acts Guide*); J.A. Fitzmyer, *Luke the Theologian: Aspects of his Teaching* (London: Chapman, 1989); W.H. Shepherd, Jr, *The Narrative Function of the Holy Spirit as a Character in Luke–Acts* (SBLDS 147; Atlanta: Scholars Press, 1994); Turner, *Power from on High, passim*.

[6] A typical – but again, far from exhaustive – list would include A. Harnack, *The Acts of the Apostles* (trans. J.R. Wilkinson; London: Williams & Norgate, 1909) 133–161; K. Lake, "The Holy Spirit," in F.J. Foakes Jackson and K. Lake (eds.), *The Beginnings of Christianity. Part I. The Acts of the Apostles. V. Additional Notes to the Commentary* (London: Macmillan, 1933) 96–111; W.L. Knox, *The Acts of the Apostles* (Cambridge: Cambridge University Press, 1948) 69–99; J.H.E. Hull, *The Holy Spirit in the Acts of the Apostles* (London: Lutterworth, 1967); H.C. Kee, *Good News to the Ends of the Earth: The Theology of Acts* (London: SCM Press; Philadelphia: Trinity Press International, 1990) 28–41; E. Franklin, *Luke: Interpreter of Paul, Critic of Matthew* (JSNTSup 92; Sheffield: JSOT Press, 1994).

second is in terms of the fourfold structure of the Pauline section of the book (see below, for further discussion of Goulder's analysis).[7]

What is significant in virtually all of these treatments of the Holy Spirit in Acts – many of which are quite insightful and have stood the test of time as "classic treatments" – is that few, if any, are specifically and directly devoted to the relationship between the Holy Spirit and Paul in Acts. There are treatments of individual episodes, such as the incident at Ephesus (Acts 19), but, as we shall see below, this is an incident in which, although the Holy Spirit plays a significant role, it plays this role almost apart from the role that Paul plays.

Whereas in the two previous chapters I have defined and then discussed the theology and perspective of the "we" passages in relation to the portrait of Paul, and in subsequent chapters I analyze various dimensions of Paul's speeches in Acts, in this chapter I wish to examine the relationship between the Holy Spirit and Paul in Acts. I do this not only because I wish to fill what I perceive to be a lacuna in the scholarly literature, but because, once the passages where Paul and the Holy Spirit are discussed in Acts are singled out for treatment, they reveal themselves to be of greater significance than has been heretofore realized. This can perhaps be accounted for by the relatively fewer references to the Spirit in the second or Pauline portion of Acts than in the first half.[8] Under closer scrutiny, however, I think that their significance is inversely proportional to their frequency.

2. Exegesis of Pauline Holy Spirit Passages in Acts

There are eight scenes in Acts where the Holy Spirit figures in the ministry of Paul. The first is when he meets Ananias (Acts 9:17); the second, his commissioning with Barnabas and initial missionary events (13:2, 4, 9); the third, the Jerusalem Council (15:8, 28); the fourth, Paul's thwarted missionary endeavors in Asia, which resulted in his visit to Macedonia (16:6, 7); the fifth, his initial visit to Ephesus (19:2, 6); the sixth, his farewell to the Ephesian elders (20:22, 23, 28); the seventh, the last warnings given to him before proceeding to Jerusalem (21:4, 11); and the eighth, the final encapsulation of Paul's mission to the Gentiles, found in Isa 6:9–10 (28:25). Each of these

---

[7] M.D. Goulder, *Type and History in Acts* (London: SPCK, 1964) 76–78, 105–106. Arguably the best book on the Holy Spirit in the New Testament (but with wider implications) is still H.B. Swete, *The Holy Spirit in the New Testament: A Study of Primitive Christian Teaching* (London: Macmillan, 2nd edn, 1910).

[8] See Lake, "Holy Spirit," 109; but cf. Lampe, "Holy Spirit," 159, who thinks that the theme of Luke's two volumes is "the operation of the Spirit of God."

passages merits brief exegetical comments. These are not meant to be full and complete studies of these passages, but are intended to draw out the interesting dynamics at play between Paul and the Holy Spirit as revealed in Acts.

a. Paul's Meeting with Ananias (Acts 9:17)

The almost incidental mentioning of the Holy Spirit in Acts 9:17 occurs in the meeting of Paul and Ananias in Damascus. When Ananias lays hands on Paul, he tells him that the Lord Jesus, who had appeared to him, had commanded Paul to come to him so that he could regain his sight and be filled with the Holy Spirit.

Several features related to this account are to be noted. The first is that this mention of the Holy Spirit is from the mouth of Ananias, not Paul. When Paul relates his conversion story later in Acts 22 and 26, he does not mention the Holy Spirit.[9] This might seem surprising in light of Luke's pattern of using repetition to emphasize an event to his readers, such as the repetition of the conversion account itself.[10] Nevertheless, in the first positive account of Paul in Acts (the previous account in 7:58 is at the stoning of Stephen, a negative depiction),[11] the Holy Spirit is linked in some way with his conversion. The second feature to notice is that the mention of the Holy Spirit in this account is one not taken up for extended discussion by many commentators,[12] apart from pondering its significance in the debate over determining the position of Acts on when the Holy Spirit is given – at the time of conversion (so-called conversion-initiation, a subject of widespread debate), or at some subsequent time.[13] It is quite astonishing to see how much is made of this particular

---

[9] On the three accounts, see C.W. Hedrick, "Paul's Conversion/Call: A Comparative Analysis of the Three Reports in Acts," *JBL* 100 (1981) 415–432; D. Marguerat, "Saul's Conversion (Acts 9, 22, 26) and the Multiplication of Narrative in Acts," in C.M. Tuckett (ed.), *Luke's Literary Achievement: Collected Essays* (JSNTSup 116; Sheffield: JSOT Press, 1995) 127–155.

[10] See E. Haenchen, *The Acts of the Apostles: A Commentary* (trans. B. Noble *et al.*; Philadelphia: Westminster Press, 1971 [1965]) 328; and G. Mussies, "Variations in the Book of Acts," *FN* 4 (1991) 165–182; 8 (1995) 23–62.

[11] G. Schneider (*Die Apostelgeschichte* [2 vols.; HTKNT 5.1, 2; Freiburg: Herder, 1980, 1982] 2.31) notes that there is probably a contrast between Acts 9:1 and Paul "breathing (ἐμπνέων) threats," and being filled with the Spirit in 9:17.

[12] For example, Conzelmann, *Die Apostelgeschichte*, 59. Noteworthy for their discussion is M.-E. Boismard and A. Lamouille, *Les actes des deux apôtres* (3 vols.; ÉB N.S. 12–14; Paris: Gabalda, 1990) 2.120–24, 182–88; 3.127–134.

[13] For an overview of the positions on the Holy Spirit and conversion, see Turner, *Holy Spirit*, 44–45; cf. Shepherd, *Narrative Function*, 192–193, who is apparently not concerned with the precise details of the account or their sequential ordering.

passage in determining the relationship between reception of the Holy Spirit and conversion.

What becomes clear – at least to me – is that much of the exegesis concerning this passage is apparently motivated by a given interpreter's prior conclusions. This, in turn, is affected by the desire to see the incidents in Acts as in some way normative for contemporary Christian experience. Two examples must suffice here. For example, Dunn devotes a chapter to this episode in his *Baptism in the Holy Spirit*, contending that the apparently clear position that Paul was converted and then three days later received the Holy Spirit must be seriously questioned. Rejecting this view on the basis of questioning the meanings of the words of address by Ananias (Dunn disputes that words such as "lord" and "brother" indicate accomplished incorporation in the Christian community), he argues for a three-day crisis experience of conversion. To do this, Dunn must appeal to Acts 22 to argue that Ananias did not see Paul's conversion as complete (v. 16 on forgiveness of sins) and that his commissioning actually came from Ananias, and to Paul's persistent blindness, which he contends represents a symbolic spiritual blindness only relieved at the end of his conversion experience.[14]

A second, and contrary, example is that of Menzies. He wishes to argue that Paul's being filled with the Holy Spirit is not a principal element in Paul's conversion, but is an endowment that is linked with Paul fulfilling his missionary calling. Relying on the position that the three Pauline conversion accounts must supplement each other, Menzies also draws on all three, thus arguing that the Ananias episode is not the culmination of Paul's conversion but linked with his commissioning as a missionary, in which Menzies finds many Old Testament parallels.[15] A number of other commentators have taken this episode as Paul's prophetic appointment as missionary to the Gentiles.[16]

The wish to read normative Christian practice from this single episode appears to have tainted attempts at dispassionate exegesis. Even though recent thought might well argue that Luke uses a common source for all three conversion stories,[17] the fact of the matter here is that mention of the reception of the Holy Spirit only occurs in this one passage. Furthermore, although reception of the Spirit is linked in a parallel grammatical fashion with Paul's

---

[14] Dunn, *Baptism in the Holy Spirit*, 73–78; supported by Turner, *Power from on High*, 375–378, esp. 375.

[15] Menzies, *Development of Early Christian Pneumatology*, 260–263.

[16] See, for example, F.F. Bruce, *Commentary on the Book of the Acts* (NICNT; Grand Rapids: Eerdmans, 1954) 200–201.

[17] See G. Lüdemann, *Early Christianity according to the Traditions in Acts: A Commentary* (trans. J. Bowden; Minneapolis: Fortress Press, 1987) 109–110.

receiving his sight, any further linkage is less easy to prove.[18] This is especially so in light of the lack of other references to the Spirit in Pauline conversion accounts. As a result, too much of specific value in this controversy cannot be made of Ananias's few words. As Johnson states, "The actual bestowal [of the Holy Spirit] is not described."[19] The narrative immediately proceeds to relate the healing of Paul's eyes, thus prompting Polhill to state: "Paul's receipt of the Spirit is not narrated. It did not seem to have come with Ananias's laying his hands on Paul. Recovery of his sight followed that. Perhaps it accompanied his baptism, since the two generally are closely connected in Acts,"[20] but as Polhill recognizes, this is not explicitly stated.[21] As Swete fittingly summarizes the passage, "In the case of Saul...it is not clear whether the gift of the Spirit preceded, accompanied, or followed baptism; nor is it necessary to distinguish the stages of an illumination which was practically a single act."[22] When this perspective is combined with Barrett's observation that "It is to be noted that at this point no visible or audible phenomena mark the giving of the Spirit,"[23] one is left with the reluctant conclusion – for both sides in the debate – that this passage provides very little detail regarding *how* and *when* the Spirit worked in Paul at or after his conversion, except to note that it did, and that its working is explicitly noted in the first account of his conversion in Acts.[24]

---

[18] See C.K. Barrett, *A Critical and Exegetical Commentary on the Acts of the Apostles* (2 vols.; ICC; Edinburgh: T. & T. Clark, 1994–) 1.457–458; Turner, *Power from on High*, 377; cf. Lüdemann, *Early Christianity*, 112, who sees a tension between Acts 9:17 and 18.

[19] L.T. Johnson, *The Acts of the Apostles* (SP 5; Collegeville, MN: Liturgical, 1992) 165; cf. B. Witherington, III, *The Acts of the Apostles: A Socio-Rhetorical Commentary* (Grand Rapids: Eerdmans, 1998) 319.

[20] J.B. Polhill, *Acts* (NAC 26; Nashville: Broadman, 1992) 238. Cf. also R.J. Knowling, "The Acts of the Apostles," in W.R. Nicholl (ed.), *The Expositor's Greek New Testament* (5 vols.; repr. Grand Rapids: Eerdmans, 1980) 2.237; Hull, *Holy Spirit*, 102–104; I.H. Marshall, *The Acts of the Apostles* (TNTC; Grand Rapids: Eerdmans, 1980) 172.

[21] Contra R.B. Rackham, *The Acts of the Apostles: An Exposition* (London: Methuen, 8th edn, 1919) 135, who creates a scenario on the basis of Acts and Paul's letters for the filling of the Spirit to follow baptism. See also K. Lake and H.J. Cadbury, *The Beginnings of Christianity. Part I. The Acts of the Apostles. IV. English Translation and Commentary* (ed. F.J. Foakes Jackson and K. Lake; London: Macmillan, 1933) 104; Lake, "Holy Spirit," 109; Haenchen, *Acts*, 438.

[22] Swete, *Holy Spirit*, 96.

[23] Barrett, *Acts*, 1.457.

[24] Paul's statement in Gal 1:12 that he did not receive his gospel message from any human is not contradicted here by the involvement of Ananias. See Lüdemann, *Early Christianity*, 115.

b. Paul's Commissioning with Barnabas and Initial Missionary Events (Acts 13:2, 4, 9)

Two points of dispute are still occasionally raised regarding the commissioning of Paul and Barnabas, and their initial missionary events in Cyprus. The first is the nature of their "ordination," and the second is whether the change of reference from Saul to Paul indicates a change of sources.[25] Regarding possible ordination, and, with it, whether it was the entire church or only a group of prophets and teachers involved in this event,[26] there has been much fruitless dispute over the fact that Paul and Barnabas are selected by the church at Antioch, Paul's statement in Gal 1:12 that he did not preach a gospel from men, and the laying on of hands in Acts 13:3. The dispute over ordination is in large part a much later controversy,[27] and Paul's having hands laid on him and preaching a gospel from God as opposed to men, especially with regard to the purpose of the letter to the Galatians, are not necessarily contradictory at all.[28] Most recent scholars are not concerned with differentiating sources in this passage.[29]

Even if various sources do lie behind the account, however, Luke effectively unites the sections together by his threefold reference to the Holy Spirit in Acts 13:2, 4, and 9,[30] one of the two largest concentrations of references to the Holy Spirit in a Pauline passage in Acts (see Acts 20:22, 23, 28, analyzed below). In his discussion of the fourfold structure of the Pauline section of Acts, in terms of the nine major themes of the book, Goulder cites Acts 13:2 as the first of four episodes involving the Spirit, thus indicating its importance in the overall frame of the book.[31] There is also a logical and

---

[25] On the first, see Rackham, *Acts,* 191–193; and on the second, Boismard and Lamouille, *Les actes,* 3.179–183.

[26] See Haenchen, *Acts,* 395–396; Marshall, *Acts,* 215; contra Barrett, *Acts,* 1.604, who endorses the prophets and teachers; see also J. Roloff, *Die Apostelgeschichte* (NTD 5; Berlin: Evangelische Verlags-Anstalt, 1981) 193. Swete (*Holy Spirit,* 104) argues that even if the church was involved, "it was felt that they had received their mission not from the Church, but directly from its Divine Guide; they were *sent out by the Holy Spirit.*"

[27] See Conzelmann, *Die Apostelgeschichte,* 73; D. Daube, *The New Testament and Rabbinic Judaism* (London: Athlone, 1956) 229–246; contra G. Schille, *Die Apostelgeschichte des Lukas* (THNT 5; Berlin: Evangelische Verlags-Anstalt, 1983) 283.

[28] See R. Wallace and W. Williams, *The Acts of the Apostles* (London: Duckworth, 1993) esp. 51, but also 9–11, on the relation of Paul's letters to Acts. See also W. Trollope, *The Acts of the Apostles* (rev. G.F. Browne; Cambridge: Hall & Son, 1877) 83.

[29] An exception is Lüdemann, *Early Christianity,* 146–151; contra Conzelmann, *Die Apostelgeschichte,* 74; Boismard and Lamouille, *Les actes,* 2.230–242.

[30] Cf. Shepherd, *Narrative Function,* 209, who prefers to speak of the Holy Spirit as "a direct actor" in the drama, speaking to those assembled.

[31] See Goulder, *Type and History,* 77–78 and 105.

literary progression to the references to the Spirit within this section. As Johnson states, "Luke emphasizes the divine character of the apostles' commission. The Holy Spirit had set them aside (13:2),...he now repeats [in 13:4] that they are 'sent out' by the Holy Spirit."[32] Reference to the Holy Spirit is picked up in 13:9 as well.[33]

The three individual passages require brief comment. In the first instance (Acts 13:2), the text says that the Holy Spirit spoke: "Set aside for me Barnabas and Saul for the work to which I have called them." Three points are worth noting. Although it is probable that the Spirit spoke through one of the prophets or teachers noted in v. 1 above (although one cannot differentiate who is a prophet and who is a teacher from those listed), and this is the view that most commentators take,[34] this is not certain in light of the Spirit's speaking elsewhere in Acts (8:29; 10:19).[35] Nevertheless, whether the Spirit spoke directly or through an intermediary, as Headlam states, "the missionary enterprise of the Church was the work of the Spirit."[36] Paul and Barnabas are described with commissioning language reminiscent of that used of Jesus ("being sent out by the Spirit"; cf. Luke 4:1, 14).[37] Secondly, although the "work" of Barnabas and Paul is not specified here, it has already been noted in Acts 9:15–16, where both Gentiles and Jews are mentioned, and confirmed by Paul's two-pronged approach to spreading the gospel in Acts, which involves both Gentiles and Jews. Thirdly, the language of "separation" used here in Acts 13:2 (ἀφορίσατε) involves the same verb used by Paul in Rom 1:1.[38]

---

[32] Johnson, *Acts*, 221, cf. 226, although he endorses the church sending Paul and Barnabas in Acts 13:3.

[33] T.E. Page, *The Acts of the Apostles* (London: Macmillan, 1886) 161.

[34] These include Swete, *Holy Spirit*, 103; F.F. Bruce, *The Acts of the Apostles* (Grand Rapids: Eerdmans, 3rd edn, 1990 [2nd edn, 1952]) 294; *idem*, *Commentary*, 261; Polhill, *Acts*, 290; Lüdemann, *Early Christianity*, 147; Schneider, *Die Apostelgeschichte*, 2.114; Witherington, *Acts*, 393.

[35] See Johnson, *Acts*, 226; Shepherd, *Narrative Function*, 210; cf. Barrett, *Acts*, 1.605; Turner, *Power from on High*, 41 (on the use of the language of speaking by the Spirit in Acts), 150, on the speaking of the Spirit.

[36] A.C. Headlam, *Christian Theology: The Doctrine of God* (Oxford: Clarendon Press, 1934) 401. Franklin (*Luke*, 251) sees mention of the Spirit here (and in Acts 15:28) as evidence of his "understanding of the present as the time of the eschatological activity of the exalted Lord." Although this may be Luke's understanding throughout Acts, it is not a theme apparently developed in the Pauline passages in Acts.

[37] Shepherd, *Narrative Function*, 210; Turner, *Power from on High*, 402.

[38] ἀφωρισμένος εἰς εὐαγγέλιον θεοῦ ("separated to [the] gospel of God"); cf. Gal 1:15: ὁ ἀφορίσας με ἐκ κοιλίας μητρός μου ("the one separating me from [the] womb of my mother"). See Schneider, *Die Apostelgeschichte*, 2.15 n. 36.

The second mention of the Holy Spirit, Acts 13:4, anaphorically picks up the reference in 13:2. The reference in 13:4 reiterates the idea that Barnabas and Paul are sent by the Holy Spirit, but places this reference in a subordinate participial phrase,[39] so that the thrust of the narrative can move forward.

In the third reference, Acts 13:9, Paul is defined using a participial phrase as one "filled with the Holy Spirit" (πλησθεὶς πνεύματος ἁγίου). This serves two functions.[40] First, the phrasing corresponds with language used throughout Acts to designate one who functions in light of divine calling or as a prophet (cf. 5:1–11; 8:2–24).[41] Secondly, the qualification at this point establishes the authority for Paul's confrontation with Elymas the magician, in light of his divine commissioning.[42] Johnson, in light of what he calls Luke's "penchant for parallelism," is not surprised to find reference to the Holy Spirit followed by a confrontation with demonic powers (see Luke 4:1–13; Acts 4:23–5:11).[43] However, Paul's imposition of blindness on Elymas – with blindness perhaps symbolically indicating spiritual blindness, reflecting Paul's own previous condition[44] – is the only occasion in Acts of Paul performing a miracle with direct reference to the Holy Spirit.[45]

c. Jerusalem Council (Acts 15:8, 28)

Much scholarly discussion revolves around the question of whether there in fact was a Jerusalem Council anything like the one recorded in Acts 15, and how this corresponds with Paul's visit to Jerusalem mentioned in Galatians 2.[46] These questions can be put aside here, however, since my immediate

---

[39] Schneider, *Die Apostelgeschichte*, 2.119 esp. n. 13. Note the Western textual variant in, for example, the Sahidic Coptic tradition, which has "by the saints," an accommodation to Acts 13:2 (see Barrett, *Acts*, 1.610).

[40] Contra Barrett, *Acts*, 1.616, who gives the impression that the phrase merely "emphasises that this was a notable occasion."

[41] Johnson, *Acts*, 223–224; Shepherd, *Narrative Function*, 211.

[42] See M. Turner, "The Spirit of Prophecy and the Power of Authoritative Preaching in Luke–Acts: A Question of Origins," *NTS* 38 (1992) 69; Schneider (*Die Apostelgeschichte*, 2.122) notes the contrast between Paul and Elymas.

[43] Johnson, *Acts*, 226; Shepherd, *Narrative Function*, 211; cf. Marshall, *Acts*, 217.

[44] See Bruce, *Commentary*, 265.

[45] Instances where the Holy Spirit is the subject or object of the action, such as receiving the Holy Spirit or the Holy Spirit speaking or foretelling events (see Acts 19, 20), are excluded. See Harnack, *Acts of the Apostles*, 134–140.

[46] On these closely related issues, see K. Lake, "The Apostolic Council of Jerusalem," in Foakes Jackson and Lake (eds.), *Additional Notes to the Commentary*, 195–212; Dibelius, "The Apostolic Council," in *Studies in the Acts of the Apostles*, 93–101; Haenchen, *Acts*, 455–472; M. Simon, "The Apostolic Decree and its Setting in the Ancient Church," *BJRL* 52 (1970) 437–460; M. Hengel, "The So-Called 'Apostolic Council' and its Consequences," in his *Acts and the History of Earliest Christianity* (trans. J. Bowden; London: SCM Press,

concern is not to harmonize the Pauline letters with Acts or to argue for or against the historicity of Acts. In point of fact, these references to the Holy Spirit are debatable for inclusion in this discussion, since they do not explicitly or directly concern Paul. Nevertheless, they occur in a context where Paul is present, and thus merit at least brief mention.

The first reference is made by Peter in his comments before the council. Scholars are agreed that he is referring to his own experience with evangelizing Gentiles, in particular the episode with Cornelius (Acts 10).[47] This passage would clearly need to be discussed in more detail in an exposition of the Holy Spirit in all of Acts, and especially in relation to Peter, but nothing further needs to be noted here with regard to Paul.

The second reference is made by James, when he is composing the letter to be sent with Paul, Barnabas, Judas Barsabas and Silas. In establishing practices for the Gentile Christians of Syria to ensure fellowship with Jewish believers, James says that "it seemed good to the Holy Spirit and to us" – expressed as almost a partnership between the leaders of the church and the Holy Spirit[48] – to establish four practices. The mention of the Holy Spirit here is significant for several reasons. First, the grammatical form of the statement, rather than asserting that human judgment is the same as divine, is a Greek (and possibly Semitic) way of indicating a decree.[49] Thus, what is to follow is meant to have binding force. Secondly, the decree has this force on the basis of the work of the Holy Spirit. This seems to be a recognition on the part of the church that the Spirit was involved in this last decision, in the same way that it had been involved in previous events in the development of the Church (cf. Acts 5:3, 9; 13:2), including the incorporation of the Gentiles (15:8, 12).[50] Thirdly, as Johnson points out, "The invocation of the Holy Spirit as a partner to the decision has an odd sound to contemporary ears, but it nicely captures

---

1979) 111–126; C.J. Hemer, *The Book of Acts in the Setting of Hellenistic History* (ed. C. Gempf; WUNT 49; Tübingen: Mohr–Siebeck, 1989; repr. Winona Lake, IN: Eisenbrauns, 1990) 247–251 and *passim*; F.J. Matera, *Galatians* (SP 9; Collegeville, MN: Liturgical, 1992) 24–26; J. Taylor, *Les actes des deux apôtres. V. Commentaire historique (Act. 9,1–18,22)* (ÉB N.S. 23; Paris: Gabalda, 1994) 198–225; and Witherington, *Acts*, 86–97, 440–49.

[47] See Bruce, *Commentary*, 306; Marshall, *Acts*, 249; Polhill, *Acts*, 326; Roloff, *Die Apostelgeschichte*, 230; Schille, *Die Apostelgeschichte*, 320; cf. Swete, *Holy Spirit*, 109; Turner, *Power from on High*, 378–380.

[48] Roloff, *Die Apostelgeschichte*, 234; contra Shepherd, *Narrative Function*, 218, who speaks in terms of the Spirit and the Church acting jointly. This seems to distort the concept of character.

[49] See Haenchen, *Acts*, 453, citing Josephus, *Ant.* 16.163 (from BAGD, 202); Schille, *Die Apostelgeschichte*, 324; Knowling, "Acts," 2.328; Witherington, *Acts*, 469.

[50] See Page, *Acts*, 180; Bruce, *Acts*, 338; Polhill, *Acts*, 335.

the dynamics of the process as portrayed by Luke," including the role played by the Spirit and humans in Acts 13:1-3 (see above).[51] Fourthly, there is no specification regarding how it is that James or others had it communicated to them or knew that it was good to the Holy Spirit to act in the way specified.

d. Paul's Thwarted Missionary Endeavors in Asia, and his Subsequent Visit to Macedonia (Acts 16:6, 7)

In Acts 16:6 and 7, Paul and his new companion, Timothy, along with others, are said to have passed through Phrygia and Galatia,[52] and then were forbidden by the Holy Spirit to speak the word in Asia.[53] When they came to Mysia, they tried to enter Bithynia, but the Spirit of Jesus did not permit them. They thus passed through Mysia and went to Troas, where, in a vision, a man of Macedonia called Paul to Macedonia. This marks a new episode in the missionary endeavor of Acts. Hence it is not surprising that Goulder cites 16:6 as the second significant episode in the Pauline section involving the Spirit.[54] Dibelius thinks this section is part of an itinerary that Luke used, but that he

---

[51] Johnson, *Acts*, 277. Contra Trollope, *Acts*, 101, who wants to see reference to the Cornelius episode in Acts 15:28 as well.

[52] The question of whether Phrygia and Galatia constitute one Roman province or refer to two separate regions following ethnic lines does not enter into the question here. I think that the first view is correct on the basis of Roman provincial organization, the language (with $\mathfrak{P}^{74}$, ℵ, A, B, D; see B.M. Metzger, *A Textual Commentary on the Greek New Testament* [London: UBS, 2nd edn, 1994] 441), and the Pauline itinerary in Acts. See Williams and Wallace, *Acts*, 23–24, 73–75; following the earlier study of W.M. Ramsay, *St Paul the Traveller and the Roman Citizen* (London: Hodder & Stoughton, 1895) 102–103, 194 ff. (also argued in his *A Historical Commentary on St Paul's Epistle to the Galatians* [London: Hodder & Stoughton, 1899] 1–234); supported by Hemer, *Book of Acts*, 280–299; and now argued at length in C. Breytenbach, *Paulus und Barnabas in der Provinz Galatien: Studien zu Apostelgeschichte 13f.; 16,6; 18,23 und den Adressaten des Galaterbriefes* (AGJU; Leiden: Brill, 1996). For discussion, see L.M. McDonald and S.E. Porter, *Early Christianity and its Sacred Literature* (Peabody, MA: Hendrickson, forthcoming 1999) chap. 10.

[53] The aorist participle following the main verb is to be taken here as referring to subsequent action, not preceding action or the reason for their passing through Phrygia and Galatia. See S.E. Porter, *Verbal Aspect in the Greek of the New Testament, with Reference to Tense and Mood* (SBG 1; New York: Lang, 1989) 385–387, where Acts 16:6, 7 are discussed on p. 386; Ramsay, *St Paul the Traveller*, 211–212 and xxi; *idem, The Church in the Roman Empire before A.D. 70* (London: Hodder & Stoughton, 4th edn, 1895) 89; Rackham, *Acts*, 275 n. 2; Lake and Cadbury, *English Translation*, 186, who, while recognizing the "timeless" character of the aorist participle, impose the past sense nevertheless; contra Page, *Acts*, 182; Bruce, *Acts*, 310 (2nd edn, 1952, but deleted on 354 of 3rd edn, 1990); *idem, Commentary*, 325 n. 11 and 326; Johnson, *Acts*, 285.

[54] Goulder, *Type and History*, 105.

must not have followed its account.[55] These few verses pose a number of interesting questions regarding the Holy Spirit and Paul in Acts, and merit extended discussion.

First, there are two different phrases used to refer to the Holy Spirit. Acts 16: 6 has the phrase "the Holy Spirit" (τοῦ ἁγίου πνεύματος), used elsewhere in Acts, as well as the New Testament, while v. 7 has the phrase "the Spirit of Jesus" (τὸ πνεῦμα Ἰησοῦ), a phrase unattested elsewhere in the New Testament.[56] The Byzantine textual tradition omits "Jesus," and some other traditions add "Lord" or "Holy," but "Spirit of Jesus" is almost assuredly the correct reading.[57] The question here is not ultimately whether S/spirit of Jesus should have the S capitalized or not, but rather the difference between the two sets of terms. In light of the context, where similar functions are performed by the two Spirits, and the presence and work of Jesus in the book of Acts (7:56; 9:5), it seems most likely that they are referring to the same divine Spirit. As Schneider says, both are used in light of God's instruction in vv. 9–10.[58] The alteration could be accounted for on several grounds: because of their following different sources,[59] because of simple stylistic variation, because the author is preparing the reader for the more intensely personal appearance in the vision of the man from Macedonia, which is meant to be seen as in some way Spirit-inspired as well, because the way that the Spirit communicated with Paul was different in each instance, with the second perhaps in a form that was reminiscent of the exalted Christ,[60] because there is a shift of emphasis, with the phrase "Spirit of Jesus" emphasizing the risen Jesus' directive presence,[61] or because there is a close association in Luke's mind between the Spirit and

---

[55] See Dibelius, *Studies in the Acts of the Apostles*, 12–13, 128–129, 169–170, 177; contra Schille, *Die Apostelgeschichte*, 334.

[56] Cf. "the S/spirit of Jesus Christ" (τοῦ πνεύματος Ἰησοῦ Χριστοῦ) in Phil 1:19, "S/spirit of Christ" (πνεῦμα Χριστοῦ) in Rom 8:9 and 1 Pet 1:11, and "the S/spirit of his son" (τὸ πνεῦμα τοῦ υἱοῦ αὐτοῦ) in Gal 4:6. See H. Stählin, "τὸ πνεῦμα Ἰησοῦ (Apostelgeschichte 16:7)," in B. Lindars and S.S. Smalley (eds.), *Christ and Spirit in the New Testament* (Festschrift C.F.D. Moule; Cambridge: Cambridge University Press, 1973) 229–252.

[57] See *UBSGNT*⁴ for the manuscript evidence. Cf. Metzger, *Textual Commentary*, 390–391.

[58] Schneider, *Die Apostelgeschichte*, 2.205. Shepherd (*Narrative Function*, 222 n. 214) tries to draw a literary conclusion from the use of the "we" convention, while claiming that the phenomenon has not been fully understood.

[59] Boismard and Lamouille, *Les actes*, 2.287–288.

[60] See Bruce, *Commentary*, 327, who notes 1 Cor 15:45, where Paul states that the last Adam became a lifegiving spirit; Polhill, *Acts*, 345.

[61] Turner, *Power from on High*, 304, 305, 430.

the person of Jesus.[62] It is simply impossible to answer this question with any certainty.[63]

Secondly, there is the means by which the Spirit spoke. The account in Acts simply does not say how. Several commentators have speculated that it may have been by inward monition, circumstances regarded as providential, some form of vision, or a prophetic utterance by one of the group.[64] Dibelius finds the various instances of divine guidance in this section of Acts quite strange, especially for a writer of history, since "We are told neither how the intervention of the Holy Spirit manifested itself nor whether Paul evangelised on the way...; we are told no names of stations or of persons." Dibelius speculates that perhaps the intervention of the Holy Spirit occurred in Paul's illness, recorded in Gal 4:3–14.[65] Haenchen, responding to Dibelius's despair over making sense of Paul's itinerary and the relation to divine guidance, especially in light of the image of Paul gained from his letters, argues that the account does not necessarily mean that Paul had left reason behind. Citing the work of Lake, who found three necessary conditions for Paul's preaching (a large Greek-speaking population, a prosperous Greek-speaking synagogue, and sufficient anti-Jewish sentiment to defuse hostility when he converted people away from the synagogue),[66] Haenchen states, "With all his obedience to the will of God he yet did not neglect at each point to consider the situation exactly, and although he tenaciously stuck to his major goals, he nevertheless reacted to new turns of events. We may therefore assume that at the beginning of his new missionary effort he had given consideration to the possible mission fields."[67] This is commensurate with two further points.

---

[62] Shepherd, *Narrative Function*, 223, but who is hard-pressed to develop this point, since this is the only use of this phrase in Acts. It is also pointless to try to define here more specifically the nature and character of this Spirit, especially as it relates to the various members of the godhead. See Lampe, "Holy Spirit," 160, who notes that "Although the activity of the divine spirit is the essential theme of his writings, St. Luke has little to say concerning the nature of that spirit (apart from its vitally important relationship to the person and work of Jesus) that is not already found in the Old Testament." See also Franklin, *Luke*, 76.

[63] See Dunn, *Jesus and the Spirit*, 180, who, after listing various options, states that "The picture given by Acts is so confused on this point anyway (multiplicity of heavenly voices) that we can neither integrate 16.7 into the whole or [sic] use the whole to clarify 16.7 with any certainty."

[64] Bruce, *Acts*, 311 (2nd edn, 1952); Knowling, "Acts," 2.341; cf. Marshall, *Acts*, 263.

[65] Dibelius, "The Acts of the Apostles in the Setting of the History of Early Christian Literature," in *Studies in the Acts of the Apostles*, 200.

[66] K. Lake, "Paul's Route in Asia Minor," in Foakes Jackson and Lake (eds.), *Additional Notes to the Commentary*, 237.

[67] Haenchen, *Acts*, 486.

Thirdly, one must consider the way in which the Spirit is mentioned as having led. As Swete points out, "It is remarkable that in both cases the guidance [of the Holy Spirit] was negative only, keeping the missionaries from a false move but not pointing out whither they should go. The actual step forward was determined by circumstances or, as in the latter instance, by a dream."[68]

Fourthly, the relation of the Spirit to human intention must be examined. Lake's hypothesis regarding Paul's missionary strategy may overextend what the evidence presents, but there is still merit in recognizing that divine guidance left latitude for human initiative. Again, citing Swete, "It was no part of the Spirit's work to supersede the reason or the judgement; but rather to leave them free to work upon the facts. In this method of procedure by *the Spirit of Jesus* we have the counterpart of the method of Jesus Himself, whose teaching usually indicated the direction in which His disciples should go without dictating a definite line of conduct."[69]

e. Paul's First Visit to Ephesus (Acts 19:2, 6)[70]

There is no doubt that Ephesus was one of the most important cities in the Pauline missionary strategy as recorded in Acts. As mentioned above, Goulder sees it functioning in several important ways. Regarding the fourfold Pauline structure of the book, and the nine significant themes, it is at Ephesus that the third major episode involving the Spirit occurs, and it is the most important of these episodes. As Goulder states, "The descent upon the dozen Gentiles at Ephesus is the descent of the Pauline section, and it is delayed till the Ephesian mission because Ephesus was the capital of Paul's mission to the Gentiles, where he spent two years – and also, no doubt, because no equally striking incident occurred earlier."[71]

In light of this structural importance, both in terms of the overall structure of Acts and the structure of the Pauline portion, it is not surprising that the coming of the Spirit at Ephesus has been subjected to intense scrutiny. As a result, the incident at Ephesus on Paul's first visit there has been another passage of widespread dispute regarding the reception of the Spirit. A number of scholars would probably question his analysis, but Hull aptly states the situation with regard to the passage:

---

[68] Swete, *Holy Spirit*, 106.

[69] Swete, *Holy Spirit*, 106.

[70] Acts 19:21 should probably not be included as a reference to the Holy Spirit, but as a reference to Paul's spirit. See Polhill, *Acts*, 406.

[71] Goulder, *Type and History*, 105.

The short paragraph which tells of the Ephesian disciples is the most puzzling and one of the most disappointing in Acts, raising tantalizing question after question but failing to supply sufficient information for satisfactory answers to be given to them. What prompted Paul's question to the disciples, "Did you receive the Holy Spirit when you became believers?" What is the meaning of their reply, "We have not even heard that there is a Holy Spirit"? Whose disciples were they?... How is the term, "John's baptism," which they had received, to be understood? Why were they rebaptized? Still more importantly for our purpose: Why did Paul lay his hands on them?[72]

There are at least six explanations of the difficulties of this passage worth recounting briefly. The first, recently argued by O'Neill,[73] is that the supposed tension between the two questions of Acts 19:2 and 3 reveals two different sources. The first question, O'Neill believes, implies baptism into the Holy Spirit, while the second raises the question of into whom they were baptized, a set of incompatible presuppositions being at play. O'Neill's sensitivity to the text, as well as his desire to integrate textual criticism into exegesis, is commendable; nevertheless, he seems to find insurmountable problems that others do not. These are based upon a set of assumptions that he brings to the text (such as that believing implies baptism into Jesus). Consequently, the sequence of questions in Acts 19:2, 3 has not raised the kinds of questions for others that O'Neill appears to have discovered.

The second position, recently advocated by Strelan, argues that the solution is to re-examine the question of Acts 19:2 as "when you became believers (in Jesus) did you receive a holy spirit which the [Holy] Spirit gives?"[74] By this interpretation of the anarthrous "holy spirit" ($\pi\nu\epsilon\hat{\upsilon}\mu\alpha$ $\mathring{\alpha}\gamma\iota\upsilon\nu$), invoking the support of Turner, Strelan appears to have eliminated the major problem of believers not having received the Holy Spirit – they did, only they did not receive such a gift from the Spirit. This exegesis is unconvincing for several reasons. One is Strelan's inadequate linguistic basis for such an interpretative adjustment. The support he cites from Turner in fact claims that the use of anarthrous "holy spirit" in Luke is "an unknown power. God's Spirit as opposed to that of men or demons,"[75] hardly the "gift" necessary for Strelan's

---

[72] Hull, *Holy Spirit*, 109–110. On John the Baptist, see R.L. Webb, *John the Baptizer and Prophet: A Socio-Historical Study* (JSNTSup 62; Sheffield: JSOT Press, 1991) esp. 69; and J.E. Taylor, *The Immerser: John the Baptist within Second Temple Judaism* (Studying the Historical Jesus; Grand Rapids: Eerdmans, 1997) esp. 97–98, 143–144.

[73] J.C. O'Neill, "The Connection between Baptism and the Gift of the Spirit in Acts," *JSNT* 63 (1996) 96–102.

[74] R. Strelan, *Paul, Artemis, and the Jews in Ephesus* (BZNW 80; Berlin: de Gruyter, 1996) 230–245, quotation 239.

[75] N. Turner, *Syntax*, vol. 3 of *A Grammar of New Testament Greek*, by J.H. Moulton (Edinburgh: T. & T. Clark, 1963) 175, cited in Strelan, *Paul*, 240. However, Turner qualifies

view. Another problem is consistency. When Strelan examines Acts 8:14–17, he takes the anarthrous phrase in v. 15 to refer to "the Holy Spirit,"[76] perhaps indicating that his view cannot be consistently maintained. A third problem for Strelan is the fact that this solution does not actually resolve the difficulty – how is it that in receiving the Holy Spirit his gift was not also received?

The third position, advocated by Käsemann,[77] argues that those in Ephesus were disciples of John the Baptist. The early Church, Käsemann contends, in its incipient days knew various independent missionaries, including Apollos (see Acts 18:24–28) and followers of John the Baptist (as well as Philip; see Acts 8). Unable to tolerate followers of John the Baptist being seen as legitimate missionary groups (with the implication that John was seen as the Messiah in certain circles), Luke attempts – though not entirely successfully, according to Käsemann – to subordinate the Ephesian followers of John the Baptist into the one legitimate Church. Therefore, Paul's question is an ad hoc construction and unexpected.[78] Käsemann raises legitimate questions regarding the Lukan narrative, including how subsequent exegetes have interpreted important terminology in the passage (e.g. such words as "disciple," "baptism," etc.), but his own explanation is flawed by the failure of his own historical method. Käsemann begins with an unfounded set of presuppositions regarding the fragmentary composition of the early Church, the messianic nature of John the Baptist and his ministry, especially as promoted by his followers, and Luke's highly tendentious historical method to arrive at an intriguing but ultimately indefensible conclusion – especially Luke's purported "early catholicism." Käsemann's reliance upon the last category is so significant that, in light of fundamental criticism of this construct, much of his argument is left indefensible.[79]

---

his description by calling it a Lukan tendency, with other factors also to be taken into account.

[76] Strelan, *Paul*, 243.

[77] E. Käsemann, "The Disciples of John the Baptist at Ephesus," in his *Essays on New Testament Themes* (trans. W.J. Montague; London: SCM Press, 1964) 136–148. He is followed by, among others, Conzelmann, *Die Apostelgeschichte*, 110–111; Haenchen, *Acts*, 554–557; Schneider, *Die Apostelgeschichte*, 2.264; Fitzmyer, *Luke the Theologian*, 132–133; Johnson, *Acts*, 331–345.

[78] Conzelmann, *Die Apostelgeschichte*, 110; Schille, *Die Apostelgeschichte*, 377.

[79] See C.K. Barrett, "Apollos and the Twelve Disciples of Ephesus," in W.C. Weinrich (ed.), *The New Testament Age: Essays in Honor of Bo Reicke* (2 vols.; Macon, GA: Mercer University Press, 1984) esp. 1.35–36; cf. also I.H. Marshall, "'Early Catholicism' in the New Testament," in R.N. Longenecker and M.C. Tenney (eds.), *New Dimensions in New Testament Study* (Grand Rapids: Zondervan, 1974) 217–231.

The fourth explanation, advocated by Marshall, following Haacker,[80] argues that the Lukan account in Acts is written from the standpoint of Paul as he first perceived the situation. The Ephesians Paul encounters are not to be considered true disciples or believers – they only appeared to be so before Paul had fully investigated. Once he had done so, he discovered that the Ephesian twelve had not received the Spirit when they were baptized.[81] According to Marshall, since there are no believers who have not received the Spirit,[82] these men must not have been Christians, and they needed to be baptized and to receive the Spirit. Thus what appears to be re-baptism was because the first baptism was not Christian baptism.[83] Marshall attempts to confront the difficulties of this passage, but two fundamental weaknesses in his approach mitigate the results. The first is his assumption that Luke has told the story from the standpoint of Paul. It is not clear that Luke uses this technique elsewhere in Acts, especially with regard to Paul.[84] Most would argue that he offers his own position, whether that position is more than a bit removed from the inner circle of Paul and his followers (as most scholars would advocate) or, as I would contend, is close to Paul's but still his own. Marshall's second assumption, that the New Testament does not know of one being a Christian without possessing the Spirit, begs the question of whether this passage does not in fact reflect just such a situation. The same is true of the argument regarding re-baptism.

The fifth position, advocated by Dunn,[85] is that those at Ephesus are clearly not disciples or believers, and that the language of the account indicates this. First, he argues that "disciples" for the twelve at Ephesus is used without the

---

[80] See Marshall, *Acts*, 305–308; following K. Haacker, "Einige Fälle von 'Erlebter Rede' im Neuen Testament," *NovT* 12 (1970) 70–77.

[81] Marshall (*Acts*, 306) (rightly) interprets the aorist participle in the construction εἰ πνεῦμα ἅγιον ἐλάβετε πιστεύσαντες; ("did you receive the Holy Spirit when you believed?") as indicating coincident rather than antecedent action. However, he cites Eph 1:13 as a parallel, where the aorist participle precedes the main verb, not a parallel construction at all (neither is Acts 11:17). See Porter, *Verbal Aspect*, 380–385.

[82] See also Bruce, *Commentary*, 386.

[83] See Bruce, *Commentary*, 386, who says that "this is the only account of re-baptism that we find in the NT."

[84] See Menzies, *Development of Early Christian Pneumatology*, 273 esp. n. 3.

[85] Dunn, *Baptism in the Holy Spirit*, 83–89. He is followed by, among others, Beasley-Murray, *Baptism*, 110–112; Turner, *Power from on High*, 390–394; cf. also Roloff, *Die Apostelgeschichte*, 282; Shepherd, *Narrative Function*, 227–229, who takes ζέων τῷ πνεύματι in Acts 18:25 as "burning enthusiasm" rather than "fervent in the Holy Spirit" (p. 228). Turner (*Holy Spirit*, 45), contra Shepherd, distinguishes between Apollos and the twelve disciples, believing the former to be a "spirit-inspired preacher of Jesus," while the twelve were only "in the process of conversion."

article (τινας μαθητάς),[86] whereas elsewhere in Acts the plural is used as virtually a technical term for believers, always with the article when used absolutely. When the sense is otherwise, Luke carefully modifies the usage. Thus, Dunn contends, Luke here is using the phrase "certain disciples" as a way of distinguishing them from true disciples, even though they may have been disciples of another sort (e.g. followers of John, etc.).[87] Secondly, Dunn rejects the idea that Paul's question, "Did you receive the Holy Spirit when you believed?" (εἰ πνεῦμα ἅγιον ἐλάβετε πιστεύσαντες;),[88] implies that they were believers, since the Paul of the epistles, like the Paul of Acts, finds it inconceivable that a Christian did not have the Spirit. Instead, Paul's question goes to the heart of his suspicion regarding their status. Thirdly, Dunn contends that baptism and the laying on of hands are one event, culminating in their reception of the Spirit and becoming Christians. Although Dunn attempts to make useful exegetical distinctions, each of his points can be contended. The distinction he makes regarding the word "disciples" (see on this further, below) is not as definitive as he asserts, his interpretation of Paul's question seems to overlook unstated assumptions in the question, with Dunn arguing similarly to Marshall regarding the question reflecting Paul's perspective on the Ephesians (see above), and he begs the question whether this is a passage that may indicate that receiving the Spirit and becoming a Christian are possibly separate events.

The sixth position, argued recently by Menzies,[89] is that Paul does consider the Ephesians to be believers, but that they have still not received the Holy Spirit, thus indicating two separate events. Menzies arrives at this position by means of his own historical reconstruction of Acts 19, having rejected the

---

[86] Dunn actually uses the words "definite article." This is a common mis-statement, since Greek does not know two articles (definite or indefinite), but only the single article. It does not function in the same way as the English definite article. See S.E. Porter, *Idioms of the Greek New Testament* (BLG 2; Sheffield: JSOT Press, 2nd edn, 1994) 103–105.

[87] See also Polhill, *Acts*, 399. Cf. A. Ehrhardt, *The Acts of the Apostles: Ten Lectures* (Manchester: Manchester University Press, 1969) 101–102, who argues that they were Alexandrian Christians as opposed to Jerusalem Christians.

[88] Dunn (*Baptism in the Holy Spirit*, 86–87) rightly rejects the aorist participle as antecedent, but on faulty grounds. He does not note the role that syntax plays in such a formulation, and not all of the examples he cites are germane. Bruce (*Commentary*, 385; *idem*, *Acts*, 406) argues similarly, but he cites in support J.H. Moulton, *Prolegomena*, vol. 1 of *A Grammar of New Testament Greek* (Edinburgh: T. & T. Clark, 3rd edn, 1908) 131 n. 1. Hull (*Holy Spirit*, 110) places too much stress on the aorist participle indicating "the moment when faith began," following an outdated *Aktionsart* approach to the aorist tense-form. On these issues, see Porter, *Verbal Aspect*, 17–65, 75–97.

[89] Menzies, *Development of Early Christian Pneumatology*, 268–277. Qualified support for this understanding is found in Hull, *Holy Spirit*, 112–116.

positions of Käsemann and others. He believes that there were groups of former disciples of John the Baptist who came to believe in Jesus, although they had not received baptism into the name of Jesus or instruction regarding the Spirit. Menzies also responds to other proposals. In response to Dunn, he attempts to directly rebut Dunn's three points. Although he misses Dunn's point regarding the use of the plural "disciples," Menzies is correct that there is similar phrasing in the singular (τις μαθητής) in Acts 9:10 and 16:1 to indicate that the usage in Acts 19:2 is not quite the unique usage that Dunn contends it is.[90] Menzies also rightly calls Dunn on his begging of the question whether Acts 19 is an instance where belief and receiving the Spirit are separated in the New Testament.[91] Lastly, Menzies indirectly suggests that Paul's question of whether the Ephesians received the Spirit when they believed implies that they did believe.[92] However, Menzies's position is also precarious at several points. His own reconstruction is no better grounded than those he rejects, since he simply posits a level of plausibility. Rather than putting forward positive arguments, he is better at refuting the arguments of others, as if these become positive arguments for his position.

Once more it is evident that one's theological position can easily intrude into exegesis, especially under the strain of a need to determine normativity for current Christian practice on the basis of the Acts account. Even if Menzies is correct – and he appears to have the better arguments regarding the situation in Acts 19 – it is highly dubious to extrapolate normative principles and practices from a passage that is so fraught with problems and fundamental disagreements on all sides. With regard to the Holy Spirit and Paul, however, there are three further observations to make, all in terms of unique features of this passage.

First, this passage is the only one in the Pauline sections of Acts where the coming of the Holy Spirit is directly associated with the laying on of hands (Acts 9:6); nevertheless, the text does not say that the Holy Spirit came as a direct result of this action.[93] More to the point, this is the only occasion in the Pauline material in Acts when Paul himself lays hands on anyone, even if it is probably fair to assume that the practice was common in the early Church.[94]

---

[90] See also Bruce, *Acts*, 406.

[91] Turner (*Power from on High*, 391–392) believes that the question implies that one could be a Christian without the Spirit.

[92] See also Lake, "The Twelve and the Apostles," 57.

[93] Cf. Lake, "Holy Spirit," 110, who says that this passage "is markedly different from the earlier part of Acts in that it connects the Spirit with a correct baptism." Nevertheless, the text does not establish what that connection is. See also Johnson, *Acts*, 338; Lüdemann, *Early Christianity*, 210.

[94] Swete, *Holy Spirit*, 107–108.

Secondly, this is the only time in Acts when the laying on of hands directly follows baptism.[95] Thirdly, this is the only instance in the Pauline material in Acts where the phenomena often associated with the coming of the Spirit (see Acts 2) – such as speaking in tongues and prophecying – occur. The prophecying is more easily recognized as being typically Pauline, even though this is the only clear case of it being done in conjunction with the Spirit in a Pauline portion of Acts. In his analysis of the passage, Johnson notes that one of the most striking things about Acts 19 is that this is the first time in Acts in which all of the noted phenomena have been applied to Paul, including his prophecying and involvement in bestowing the Spirit.[96] But Johnson appears to have overinterpreted. The passage does not in fact specifically say that Paul prophecied and spoke in tongues, although it leaves it open that he was part of the group that did (the text does not specify which of the disciples manifested which gifts, only that the group did).[97] In light of the contrast between "him" and "the Ephesian disciples," and his laying hands on them, it is perhaps better to note that, whereas the twelve manifested signs of the Spirit, one cannot say for sure that Paul did.[98]

f. Paul's Farewell to the Ephesian Elders (Acts 20:22, 23, 28)[99]

All references to the Holy Spirit in this section come from the mouth of Paul in his speech to the Ephesian Elders. Although the second and third references (Acts 20:23, 28) are clearly to the Holy Spirit, the first (in v. 22) may not be. Only the word "spirit" is used. It is arguable that the reference to "Holy Spirit" in v. 23 is designed to provide a contrast between the two spirits, even though Paul's spirit is clearly seen to be heavily influenced by the divine spirit.[100] Nevertheless, most commentators take the sense as referring directly to the Holy Spirit, especially because of the similar phrasing in 19:21 (but see above) and the use of the word "being bound" (δεδεμένος), initiating for the rest of the book an important theme of divine guidance with regard to Paul.[101] Verse 28 also raises questions about the way in which the Spirit worked. Most commentators are not nearly as concerned with the actual mechanism, in which

---

[95] Polhill, *Acts*, 400.

[96] Johnson, *Acts*, 343.

[97] See Turner, *Power from on High*, 395.

[98] In fact, I am skeptical that this passage provides any evidence that he did.

[99] For more detailed treatment of this speech, see Chapter Six below.

[100] See Page, *Acts*, 215; cf. Shepherd, *Narrative Function*, 233.

[101] See Bruce, *Acts*, 432; Schneider, *Die Apostelgeschichte*, 2.295; Conzelmann, *Die Apostelgeschichte*, 117; Johnson, *Acts*, 361; M.L. Soards, *The Speeches in Acts: Their Content, Context, and Concerns* (Louisville: Westminster/John Knox, 1994) 184–186; Shepherd, *Narrative Function*, 233–234.

the Holy Spirit is seen to be responsible for appointing the leaders, as they are with the nature of the "overseers" who are appointed.[102] Commentators are divided over whether the passage depicts a direct and unmediated work by the Holy Spirit or whether the Holy Spirit worked through some process of indicating its will.[103] Despite speculation, it is simply impossible to specify the means of communication, especially in a passage full of metaphorical language (e.g. talk of flocks and wolves). Several recent commentators have noted that Paul's speech to the elders has a number of unique features, including its being addressed to Christians.[104] For some, these unique features point to the use by Luke of a unique genre of the biographical encomium, in the form of a farewell address,[105] while for others the features point to the most pastorally oriented of the Pauline speeches and perhaps the best suited to comparison with the Paul of the letters.[106] The speech falls between two "we" passages in Acts (20:5–15 and 21:1–18), which raises further questions regarding how it is to be interpreted.[107] Even though the speech does not seem to originate in the "we" source, its placement raises questions regarding its relation to a first-hand witness.

Some of this speech's supposedly unique features can be overdrawn; nevertheless, when focus is restricted to Paul and the Holy Spirit in Acts, there remain several features worth noting. The first is that this is one of the two largest numbers of references to the Holy Spirit in any given section of the Pauline material in Acts (the other is Acts 19:2, 4, 9, discussed above). Soards states that mention of the Holy Spirit is a regular feature of speeches in Acts (he

---

[102] The question relates to the nature of their "ordination," and what this implies regarding ecclesiastical institutionalization (early catholicism). See above for discussion of the issues involved. One of the best treatments in a recent commentary is Polhill, *Acts*, 426–427; cf. Shepherd, *Narrative Function*, 234.

[103] On the two sides of the equation, see, for example, Menzies, *Development of Early Christian Pneumatology*, 224, 227; and Bruce, *Commentary*, 416; Conzelmann, *Die Apostelgeschichte*, 117. Swete (*Holy Spirit*, 108) is ambivalent.

[104] See D.F. Watson, "Paul's Speech to the Ephesian Elders (Acts 20.17–28): Epideictic Rhetoric of Farewell," in D.F. Watson (ed.), *Persuasive Artistry: Studies in New Testament Rhetoric in Honor of George A. Kennedy* (JSNTSup 50; Sheffield: JSOT Press, 1991) esp. 184–190.

[105] Dibelius, *Studies in the Acts of the Apostles*, 155–158; followed by Watson, "Paul's Speech to the Ephesian Elders," 190.

[106] C.J. Hemer, "The Speeches of Acts I. The Ephesian Elders at Miletus," *TynBul* 40 (1989) 76–82; F.F. Bruce, "Is the Paul of Acts the Real Paul?" *BJRL* 58 (1976) 304.

[107] See Chapter Two above; cf. Harnack, *Acts of the Apostles*, 129; contra M.-E. Rosenblatt, *Paul the Accused: His Portrait in the Acts of the Apostles* (Collegeville, MN: Liturgical, 1995) 65–66.

cites 1:16b–17),[108] but in the Pauline material, this simply is not the case. In fact, only relatively infrequently does Paul speak of the Holy Spirit in any one of his speeches in Acts. This passage is consistent in not specifying the means by which the Spirit has revealed its knowledge. The mention of the Holy Spirit in this passage, however, correlates well with the subject matter of the speech itself – the future direction of Paul's ministries and his closing words regarding the future of the Ephesian church convey what has been revealed by the Holy Spirit. This leads to the second point of significance. As Soards has pointed out, all three of the references to the Holy Spirit occur in sections where Paul is speaking of the future, rather than of the past or present: "Paul's comment concerning his uncertainty regarding the forthcoming visit to Jerusalem because of the certainty of the testimony of the Spirit pairs dramatically contrasting ideas, which together point to the superior role of the divine in divine-human relations." This applies both to Paul and to the elders: "the statement that the Holy Spirit gave the elders their charges recognizes divine initiative and authority in selection of church leadership…"[109]

Critical scholarship has viewed the theological significance of the words of Paul in at least two different ways. For those who tend to ascribe greater historical credibility to Acts, these words may well represent (even if in paraphrase or summary) the words Paul himself delivered on the occasion to the purported audience.[110] After all, this is the only speech of Paul in Acts delivered to Christians that Luke records, and it is not surprising that it has a number of Pauline features to it, including mention of the shedding of blood.[111] For those who doubt the historicity of Acts, there is the tendency to interpret this speech as a Lukan composition designed to offer a portrait of Paul the apostle, as his missionary campaign comes to an end (hence the prophecies that are offered regarding his future).[112] The speech does emphasize redemption in a way that is not typical of Lukan theology but is consistent with Pauline,[113]

---

[108] Soards, *Speeches in Acts*, 107.

[109] Soards, *Speeches in Acts*, 107.

[110] See, for example, P. Gardner, "The Speeches of St Paul in Acts," in H.B. Swete (ed.), *Cambridge Biblical Essays* (London: Macmillan, 1909) 401–404; Harnack, *Acts of the Apostles*, 129; Bruce, *Commentary*, 412–413.

[111] The phrasing is difficult at this point. The phrase probably refers to "the blood of his own," with "own" (ἴδιος) used as a term of endearment referring to Christ, rather than to God. See Moulton, *Prolegomena*, 90; Bruce, *Acts*, 434.

[112] See Dibelius, *Studies in the Acts of the Apostles*, 157–158; Haenchen, *Acts*, 596–597.

[113] See C.F.D. Moule, "The Christology of Acts," in L.E. Keck and J.L. Martyn (eds.), *Studies in Luke–Acts* (Philadelphia: Fortress Press, 1966) 171; contra Conzelmann,

whatever one wishes to make of that. Nevertheless, the Spirit is acknowledged as having played some role in ecclesiastical guidance, but without an emphasis upon the mode or extra-ordinary results of such influence.

g. Last Warnings to Paul before Going to Jerusalem (Acts 21:4, 11)

Paul does not mention the Holy Spirit in this passage, but the Spirit is mentioned twice, first by the narrator and then by Agabus. In Goulder's fourfold Pauline section of Acts, this marks the fourth and final episode involving the Holy Spirit, and indicates to Goulder that "the Holy Ghost is brooding over the waters..."[114] The first reference summarizes the fact that, during Paul's seven day stay in Tyre with disciples, they told Paul "through the Spirit" that he should not go to Jerusalem.[115] The means of revelation through the Spirit is not mentioned. More important in this verse than the form of mediation is the apparent contradiction between Paul's will (as stated, for example, in another passage with regard to the Holy Spirit, Acts 20:22) and the direction of the Spirit given to those in Tyre. As Shepherd says, this passage "raises the question of what it means for Spirit-filled, prophetic figures to disagree and be in conflict."[116] There have been several attempts to explain the apparent conflict of opinions. Haenchen argues that v. 4b is clearly secondary and inserted later.[117] Without textual support, this is sheer speculation to avoid the difficulty. Polhill argues that the Spirit would not be giving Paul contradictory messages, and so Paul's determination to go to Jerusalem must win out.[118] But this does not seem to be a satisfactory resolution of the theological problem that he has introduced, merely an avoidance of it. Witherington argues that New Testament prophecy, like Old Testament prophecy, is conditional in nature, and one is to weigh the words of the true prophets.[119] But this appears to be special pleading for a set of criteria that make the actual weighing of prophecy nearly impossible. As Dunn says, "The fact that Paul ignored what seem to have been regarded as clear directions of the Spirit through prophecy (21.4; cf. 21.10–4) is recorded without comment; no attempt is made to give guidance on what should be done when two inspired

---

Theology of St Luke, 201, but whose argument is without support; now endorsed by Franklin, *Luke*, 77–78.

[114] Goulder, *Type and History*, 106.

[115] See Porter, *Idioms of the Greek New Testament*, 148–151; but cf. Witherington, *Acts*, 630, who appears to become grammatically confused in an attempt to avoid the difficulty.

[116] Shepherd, *Narrative Function*, 237.

[117] Haenchen, *Acts*, 602–603; cf. also Boismard and Lamouille, *Les actes*, 2.322–323.

[118] Polhill, *Acts*, 433.

[119] Witherington, *Acts*, 630–631.

utterances, *both* from the Spirit (20.22; 21.4), not merely differ but contradict each other!"[120] Several argue that the Christians at Tyre had had revealed to them that Paul would suffer, and took upon themselves to warn Paul not to go to Jerusalem.[121] A possible solution, this certainly does not correlate with what the text says. Wallace and Williams argue that the warning is a suitable way to prepare the reader for the later, climactic events in Jerusalem and Rome.[122] Shepherd suggests that Luke appeals to his common prophetic pattern, in which appeal to Jesus and the prophets silences Paul's critics.[123] Although it is difficult to resolve the difficulty, the solution of Lake and Cadbury – mostly ignored by subsequent scholarship – seems the most likely. They question whether Paul doubted the inspiration of the prophets of Tyre.[124] The text does not say that he does, but he effectively does ignore them. In light of Paul's determination to go to Jerusalem, as well as Rome, despite what happens to himself, we as readers are apparently meant, if not to doubt, at least to disregard what those in Tyre said.

The second reference to the Holy Spirit is placed in the mouth of Agabus. During Paul's several days' stay in Caesarea on the way to Jerusalem, Agabus comes down from Judea, grabs Paul's belt and ties himself up, and then says that the Holy Spirit says that Paul will be bound by the Jews in Jerusalem.[125] Commentators also frequently raise questions regarding Agabus's prophecy, including the fact that it was not the Jews but the Romans who took Paul into custody.[126] This appears to be an unnecessary splitting of hairs, since the account in Acts 21 says that the Jews did, in fact, seize Paul, drag him out of the Temple, and were about to kill him, when the Roman cohort appeared, into whose hands Paul fell (Acts 21:30–33). Agabus appears to be speaking in

---

[120] Dunn, *Jesus and the Spirit*, 175–176. Cf. Schneider, *Die Apostelgeschichte*, 2.303.

[121] Trollope, *Acts*, 136; Page, *Acts*, 220; Knowling, "Acts," 2.443; Bruce, *Acts*, 439–440; *idem, Commentary*, 421; Marshall, *Acts*, 339, recognizing the problems with his solution.

[122] Wallace and Williams, *Acts*, 112; cf. Conzelmann, *Die Apostelgeschichte*, 120–121.

[123] Shepherd, *Narrative Function*, 238.

[124] Lake and Cadbury, *English Translation*, 266. Haenchen (*Acts*, 603) says that this explanation "has rightly met with no approval." It appears that it has been ignored, at least in part, because of the desire on both sides of the spectrum to maintain the "rightness" of each respective side.

[125] See Schille, *Die Apostelgeschichte*, 408, on the symbolic nature of Agabus's actions.

[126] See, for example, Bruce, *Acts*, 442; *idem, Commentary*, 425; Johnson, *Acts*, 372; cf. Turner, *Power from on High*, 325–326; R.G. Tannehill, *The Narrative Unity of Luke–Acts: A Literary Interpretation*. II. *The Acts of the Apostles* (FFNT; Minneapolis: Fortress Press, 1990) 265.

language reminiscent of legal decrees of the time, as well as in the language of the Septuagint when prophets delivered the divine message.[127]

There are several observations to be made about this set of passages. First, despite opinions to the contrary regarding Acts 21:4, these are the only references to the Holy Spirit clearly within one of the "we" passages of Acts (21:1–18) (see Chapter Two above). Although the previous reference appears in Paul's mouth in an extended speech between two "we" passages, in this case the references to the Holy Spirit are clearly within a "we" passage itself. This confirms that the Holy Spirit, as well as the phenomena often associated with it, are not emphasized in the "we" passages of Acts.[128] Secondly, in further confirmation of this, it is noteworthy that Paul is not the one depicted as referring to the Holy Spirit in either instance. As Soards says, "In comparison with the other speeches, Agabus's pronouncement is remarkable in that it not only mentions the Holy Spirit but portrays the Spirit as speaking through Agabus... Thus, the speech is one of those referring to the Holy Spirit..., and it shows clearly the theme of divine authority, especially in relation to divine awareness or control of the future."[129] The first is a summary statement by the narrator reflecting what was said by others, and the second is a quotation from Agabus. Thirdly, although the audience, including the "we" who are present, is greatly concerned by the forecasted events, Paul speaks against heeding the first warning and delaying or altering his trip to Jerusalem, affirming that the will of the Lord will be done as Agabus has stated (21:14).

h. Encapsulation of Paul's Mission to the Gentiles (Acts 28:25)

The final reference to the Holy Spirit and Paul in Acts occurs at the very close of the book, in a passage often passed over lightly by those commenting upon the Holy Spirit in Acts. After Paul had arrived in Rome, a number of Jews came to him and desired to hear directly from him about this new sect to which he belonged. Paul is cited as closing his discussions with them, with much disagreement among them, by stating that the Holy Spirit had rightly spoken through Isaiah the prophet, and then citing Isa 6:9–10 (essentially LXX),

---

[127] See Johnson, *Acts*, 370, who cites examples from Josephus, *Ant.* 11.26; Amos 3:11; 5:16; Nah 1:2; Hag 1:6; Zech 1:16; Isa 3:16; Jer 2:31; Ezek 4:13; cf. also Roloff, *Die Apostelgeschichte*, 310, who says that "Das spricht der Heilige Geist" stands for the Old Testament formula "So spricht Jahwe."

[128] Shepherd (*Narrative Function*, 238), citing Johnson (*Acts*, 370–372) and Haenchen (*Acts*, 605), contends that the emotional level of the passage is heightened by the vivacious "we" language. However, this is predicated upon his literary view of the "we" passages (pp. 221–222).

[129] Soards, *Speeches in Acts*, 109; contra Schneider, *Die Apostelgeschichte*, 2.304.

which emphatically[130] speaks of people not understanding what they hear because they have grown dull in their senses. This is one of the earliest and most widely used Old Testament testimonies to Christ found in the New Testament.[131] Paul interprets this as indicating that the lack of understanding of the Jews has justified taking the message of salvation to the Gentiles. This speech is emblematic of how the author of Luke–Acts has wanted to characterize Paul. He is a Jew who brought his prophetic message to his own people, only to find it rejected, as Scripture foretold, thus warranting his becoming the apostle to the Gentiles.[132] With that concluding statement, the book draws to a quick conclusion.

Two observations merit mention here. The first is that, although the number of statements about the Holy Spirit and Paul in Acts is relatively small, the statements are significant enough that it does not come as a surprise when Paul is quoted as introducing his final words by invoking the Holy Spirit's speaking through Isaiah. Secondly, Paul is cited as attributing the ultimate source of Isaiah's message to the Holy Spirit, with the further implication that his application of it to the contemporary situation of the Jews was something with the warrant of the Holy Spirit.[133] Although in other instances in Acts the Holy Spirit is said to have spoken through the Old Testament (cf. 1:16; 4:25),[134]

---

[130] Both the Greek and the Hebrew use cognate structures. On this type of syntax, see M.S. Krause, "The Finite Verb with Cognate Participle in the New Testament," in S.E. Porter and D.A. Carson (eds.), *Biblical Greek Language and Linguistics: Open Questions in Current Research* (JSNTSup 80; Sheffield: JSOT Press, 1993) 197–200; a feature not elucidated in the otherwise thorough study of G.J. Steyn, *Septuagint Quotations in the Context of the Petrine and Pauline Speeches of the Acta Apostolorum* (Kampen: Kok Pharos, 1995) 213–229, esp. 219–226.

[131] See C.A. Evans, *To See and Not Perceive: Isaiah 6.9–10 in Early Jewish and Christian Interpretation* (JSOTSup 64; Sheffield: JSOT Press, 1989).

[132] On the relationship of the Holy Spirit to Paul's prophetic function, see Shepherd, *Narrative Function, passim*, and 242–243. Whether the Jews are seen to be completely abandoned in Luke–Acts is highly debated. For opposing sides, see Maddox, *Purpose of Luke–Acts*, 42–46; J.T. Sanders, *The Jews in Luke–Acts* (Philadelphia: Fortress Press, 1987), who contend that Luke depicts the turning away from the Jews to be final, and E. Franklin, *Christ the Lord: A Study in the Purpose and Theology of Luke–Acts* (London: SPCK, 1975) 77–115 (cf. *idem, Luke*, 95–96); D.P. Moessner, "Paul in Acts: Preacher of Eschatological Repentance to Israel," *NTS* 34 (1988) 96–104; J. Jervell, *The Theology of the Acts of the Apostles* (New Testament Theology; Cambridge: Cambridge University Press, 1996) esp. 85–86, who argue that Paul's mission is first and foremost to Jews, and leaves open the possibility of repentance. The former position is probably closer to the Lukan perspective.

[133] On this quotation within a quotation, tying the past to the present, see F. Bovon, "'Schön hat der heilige Geist durch den Propheten Jesaja zu euren Vätern gesprochen' (Act 28 25)," *ZNW* 75 (1984) 226–232.

[134] Polhill, *Acts*, 543.

none of these instances involves Paul, except for this passage. Nevertheless, the effect here is to put Paul in a prophetic role similar to that of Isaiah.[135]

3. Implications of the Exegetical Study

In light of the exegesis of these passages, there are several observations worth making about the relationship between Paul and the Holy Spirit in Acts. Drawing these out should help to place the entire topic into several important literary and theological contexts.

The first is that, although there are a number of significant passages that bring Paul and the Holy Spirit together in the narrative, there does not appear to be a systematic way in which the two are presented together, nor does there seem to be a common theme that joins the two together (cf. the second observation below). For example, there is a mix of ways in which the Holy Spirit is mentioned, sometimes by Paul (e.g. Acts 19:2; 20:22, 23, 28; 28:25) but mostly by other characters or the narrator (e.g. Acts 9:17; 15:8, 28; 16:6, 7; 21:4, 11). Sometimes the message of the Holy Spirit points to the past (e.g. Acts 19:2) and other times to the present (e.g. Acts 20:22, 23, 28) or even the future (e.g. Acts 21:4, 11). Sometimes the Spirit is said to have spoken (Acts 13:2; 22:23; 28:25) and other times there is no statement of the means of mediation (e.g. Acts 13:4; 16:6, 7). In other words, the author of Acts does not seem to have a systematic means of presentation or to be making a systematic statement regarding the relationship between the Holy Spirit and Paul in Acts.[136] Therefore, to attempt to tease such a relationship out on the basis of several highly problematic passages, in particular the story of Paul's conversion in Acts 9 or the coming of the Holy Spirit to the Ephesians in Acts 19, is probably unjustified. These passages may well fit within a larger theology of Acts or Luke–Acts (although the interpretative problems mentioned above would need to be addressed), but the basis is not sufficient for clear statements regarding Paul.

The second observation, however, even if it may at first glance appear to contradict the first, is important to make as well. That is that, whereas it is arguable which incidents in Acts mark the most significant turning points in Paul's ministry, those above would certainly constitute many, if not most, of them. Thus, the Holy Spirit is seen either by the narrator or by the participants (and hence by the narrator as well) as playing a role in many of the crucial

---

[135] See Johnson, *Acts*, 476; Schneider, *Die Apostelgeschichte*, 2.418.

[136] See Marshall, *Luke*, 199.

events in the life and ministry of Paul, or (what Kee refers to as) functioning as an agent of guidance.[137] Of course, this is not to imply that the Holy Spirit was not thought to be working in Paul's ministry elsewhere, but it is noteworthy that his conversion (Acts 9), his commissioning (Acts 13), the Apostolic Council (Acts 15), his turning to Europe (Acts 16), his first and last contacts with Ephesus (Acts 19, 20), his proceeding to Jerusalem (Acts 20), and the closing summation regarding his mission (Acts 28), are all specifically marked as having been influenced by the Holy Spirit, wherever they may lead in relation to others' plans. In light of this evidence, Jervell is compelled to conclude that "Paul's work is determined by the Spirit."[138] Although it is difficult to see such a similar pattern in the first part of Acts due to the more diffuse nature of the material, there are more than passing similarities in this regard (cf. Acts 2). As Kee observes, what are indicated in Acts "are the ways in which the Spirit directs the itinerary of Paul, while at the same time making him aware of the personal difficulties which he must endure in the discharge of his ministry."[139] This consistent theme can be found in virtually all of the episodes above, where there is a sense of the Spirit's guidance, even if it leads to difficulty. Paul is depicted as selected by the Spirit for ministry (Acts 13), and his course of events can lead further than first expected (Acts 16), even into the hands of his enemies (Acts 21). For the Paul of Acts, this is all part of what it means to follow the Lord Jesus (Acts 21:13).

The third observation is that only a single instance that conjoins Paul and the Holy Spirit falls within a "we" section of Acts. This is consistent with what I have found earlier in describing the theology and perspective of the "we" passages (see Chapter Three), that is, that the author of this account creates an understated portrait of Paul, with little reference to performing extra-mundane phenomena.

The fourth observation, returning to what has been mentioned above, is that most of the statements about the work of the Holy Spirit are not uttered by Paul (see only Acts 20:22, 23, 28; 28:25; cf. 19:2, but in the form of a question), but are statements made by others, especially the author, Luke. Those uttered by Paul are mostly recapitulatory in nature, looking back on the course of his ministry, or even further. The sense is that the Holy Spirit is usually seen retrospectively to have been involved in Paul's ministry, whether the observation is being made by Luke or by Paul, as opposed to affirmations being made regarding the current or future governance of the Spirit (but see

---

137 Kee, *Good News*, 36.
138 Jervell, *Theology of Acts*, 92.
139 Kee, *Good News*, 38.

21:4). Th~ iemptation is to conclude that the inclusion of references to the Holy Spirit is as much a feature of Lukan narration as it is of Pauline affirmation, but the restrained way in which Paul is depicted in terms of the Holy Spirit indicates at the least a cautious editorial and authorial hand, perhaps consistent with what other sources, such as the 'we" source, revealed about Paul.

The fifth observation is that the means by which the Holy Spirit is said to work is unclear. There seem to be at least three ways in which the Holy Spirit's actions in Pauline passages of Acts are said to occur. The first simply states that the Holy spirit "spoke" (Acts 13:2). Although this may appear clear, as noted above, commentators are undecided whether this means by some form of direct divine speech or by some mediated prophetic speech of a prophet. A variation of this is that the Holy Spirit does other things, presumably accomplished by some form of spoken command, such as "send out" (Acts 13:4). The second is that it is said that people are given, filled by, or bound by the Spirit (Acts 13:9; 9:17; 15:8).[140] This language, too, is highly figurative (cf. Acts 15:28, where something is said to seem good to the Spirit), but it is not any clearer than the idea of the Spirit speaking, as has been observed in discussion of Acts 19. The third is that the Holy Spirit is simply invoked by the narrator as part of the flow of the narrative (Acts 16:6, 7). In this sense, the Holy Spirit takes on the function of a character, although the character is not fully developed,[141] and in the Pauline passages only makes spot appearances.

The sixth observation follows from the fifth, and that is that one of the common functions of the Spirit in Pauline passages in Acts is with regard to prophecy. However, it is difficult to specify the nature of this prophetic speech.[142] For example, in one instance, the prophecy of those at Tyre is disregarded by Paul (Acts 21:4). Whereas it appears to be a common function of the Spirit to be in some way involved in prophecy, in these passages, in only a few instances, is Paul seen to be the prophet – once when he curses Elymas (Acts 13:9), once when he is speaking to the Ephesian elders regarding his and their future ministries (Acts 20), and once when he speaks with the Jewish leaders in Acts 28. At other times, it is others who prophecy, such as

---

[140] See Marshall, *Acts* Guide, 67, on this kind of language.

[141] Contra Jervell, *Theology of Acts*, 44, who says "The Spirit is an impersonal, active force." He fails to account for the many places in Acts where the Spirit is depicted as "acting" in a personal way.

[142] See Turner, "Prophecy and Preaching," 74–75, although he does not single out Paul from the rest of the instances in Acts. See also E.E. Ellis, "The Role of the Christian Prophet in Acts," in W.W. Gasque and R.P. Martin (eds.), *Apostolic History and the Gospel: Biblical and Historical Essays Presented to F.F. Bruce on his 60th Birthday* (Exeter: Paternoster, 1970) 55–67, who notes that "the phenomenon of prophecy is ascribed to Christian disciples generally" (p. 55), including Paul in a few instances.

the leaders of the Antioch church (Acts 16) or Agabus (Acts 21:11). We may agree that one of the Spirit's functions is prophecy, but it is not something that apparently has a peculiar or particular relationship to Paul.

The seventh and final observation regards the relation between Paul and the Holy Spirit, and such things as miracles and other phenomena connected with the work of the Spirit. Of the (at most) seven miracles that Paul is said or seen to perform in Acts,[143] to only one is the Holy Spirit directly linked or even mentioned, and that is his commissioning (Acts 13:4–12).[144] Regarding other phenomena of the Spirit, only once is the Holy Spirit linked with phenomena sometimes equated with the Holy Spirit in modern discussion (and elsewhere in the New Testament, including Acts), but not even then directly linking them to Paul himself. In 19:6, when the Ephesians receive the Holy Spirit, they speak in tongues and prophecy, but Paul's commissioning is linked with fasting and prayer, and there is nothing said of how he was dissuaded from preaching in Asia. Any greater linkage of such phenomena with Paul must turn, not to Acts, but rather to his letters in order to attempt to substantiate the charismatic character of Paul and his ministry.

4. Conclusion

In all, the Holy Spirit is depicted in Acts as having functioned at significant junctures in Paul's ministry, though description of the Holy Spirit's work is treated in a way that notes the role of the Spirit, rather than emphasizing or describing more sensational phenomena. From the passages treated, it is difficult to answer questions regarding the sources of Acts and the role of the author of the book in creating the relation between the Holy Spirit and the Paul of Acts. Nevertheless, there is a certain consistency between the role of the Holy Spirit in relation to the Paul of Acts outside of the "we" passages (that is, the passages discussed above apart from Acts 21), and the character of Paul seen in the "we" passages. Whether that indicates a common editorial hand or a common conception of Paul is difficult to say. However, in light of the widespread mention of the Holy Spirit in the rest of Acts, including its active

---

[143] See Acts 13:4–12; 14:8–10; 16:16–18; 19:13–20; 20:7–12; 28:1–6, 7–8; although there is the (mistaken) impression given that Paul's ministry is characterized by the miraculous (cf. Acts 14:3; 15:12; 19:11–20; 21:19). See Harnack, *Acts of the Apostles*, 134–140; but cf. Knox, *Acts*, 91, for questioning of Harnack's analysis. This subject is discussed further in Chapter Nine below.

[144] Cf. Jervell, *Theology of Acts*, 92–93, who gives the impression that Paul as miracle worker, etc., is directly linked with the work of the Spirit.

engagement in a number of crucial episodes earlier in the book (e.g. Acts 2 at Pentecost, Acts 5 with Ananias and Sapphira, Acts 10 and the conversion of Cornelius), it is reasonable to think that the way that the Holy Spirit is depicted in relation to Paul is consistent with the way in which the author of Luke–Acts perceived Paul's relationship with the Spirit. That relationship appears to have been one in which the Spirit played a significant, yet muted role – present at most of the crucial events, but working with those involved, including Paul and others, in order to accomplish the divine purpose.

Chapter Five

Paul as Epistolographer *and* Rhetorician?
Implications for the Study of the Paul of Acts

1. Introduction

Our knowledge of Paul comes from two principal sources, his letters and the book of Acts, but these are not the same kinds of sources. One is a set of letters and the other a narrative, one being a primary and the other a secondary source, so far as Paul is concerned.[1] What we learn about Paul and his background from his letters is not nearly as great as we would like. In fact, much of what is tacitly assumed to be reliable knowledge of Paul is dependent upon the book of Acts. For example, a clear statement of Paul's conversion experience on the Damascus Road (Acts 9, 22, 26; but cf. Gal 1:11–24; 1 Cor 15:8), the itinerary of his several missionary journeys, the non-Jewish side of his background and experience, including his coming from Tarsus and his Roman citizenship – all of these are found primarily, if not exclusively, in Acts and not in the Pauline letters. Consequently, critical scholarship has often raised questions about whether these are accurate depictions of Paul. There are a number of other items related to Paul's life and experience that are only known from Acts, and these critical scholarship doubts even more seriously, such as his numerous public speeches, for example at Athens (Acts 17:22–31; see below, as well as Chapter Six, for discussion of different dimensions of this speech). This raises several important questions regarding the relationship between the Paul of Acts and the Paul of his letters, that is, between Paul the speechmaker and Paul the letterwriter. How do these relate to each other – are they compatible or exclusive? What can we make of the evidence that we get from each, especially in terms of analysis of Paul as a writer and speaker? In order to examine these questions adequately, general questions about the relationship between the Paul of Acts and of the letters must be asked, before discussing each of these corpora in more detail.

---

[1] The distinction between primary and secondary sources is not always an easy one to make. For example, both might be considered primary sources regarding some dimensions of the early Church, and both secondary sources regarding certain other dimensions.

2. The Relationship between the Paul of the Letters and the Paul of Acts

The traditional view of authorship of Acts is that the volume is the second of two composed by a traveling companion of Paul, Luke the physician.[2] Although this tradition is reasonably early (second century), it must be recognized that the Gospel of Luke and the book of Acts are formally anonymous, and so certainty regarding authorship cannot be established. Scholars have debated the evidence regarding how certain the traditional view is, giving various degrees of credibility to references in Paul's letters to Luke (Col 4:14; 2 Tim 4:11; Phlm 24). Further support for Lukan authorship is often found in the "we" passages of Acts (16:10–17; 20:5–15; 21:1–18; 27:1–29; 28:1–16) and the fact that Luke was among the faithful companions of Paul (Col 4:14; 2 Tim 4:11; Phlm 24). Critical scholarship of the last hundred years, however, has called this attribution into question. The thought that the author of Luke–Acts was a physician can no longer be definitively supported from the text itself, since the medical language appears to be typical of writers of Luke's level and style,[3] and the majority of references to Luke are found in the disputed Pauline letters.[4] Furthermore, there are a number of possibilities for explaining the use of the "we" passages, and the first-hand account is only one of them. The "we" passages have been viewed as a fictional device to tell of a sea voyage, they have been seen as an indication of the redactional activity of the author, they have been thought to indicate the incorporation of a source document, and they have been thought to indicate that the author is citing his own first-hand account (as discussed in Chapter Two above). Even if the "we" passages are thought to represent a first-hand account (the language does not necessarily mean an eyewitness), in light of the author's leaving this indicator in the text, the most that can probably be argued is that another, independent

---

[2] On authorship, see L.M. McDonald and S.E. Porter, *Early Christianity and its Sacred Literature* (Peabody, MA: Hendrickson, forthcoming 1999) chap. 8; cf. W.G. Kümmel, *Introduction to the New Testament* (trans. H.C. Kee; Nashville: Abingdon, 17th edn, 1975) 147–150; C.-J. Thornton, *Der Zeuge des Zeugen: Lukas als Historiker der Paulusreisen* (WUNT 56; Tübingen: Mohr–Siebeck, 1991) 8–81.

[3] On the use of medical language in Luke–Acts as reflecting simply a higher register of usage, see H.J. Cadbury, *The Style and Literary Method of Luke* (Cambridge, MA: Harvard University Press, 1920; repr. New York: Kraus, 1969) *passim*, arguing against W.K. Hobart, *The Medical Language of St Luke* (London: Longmans, Green, 1882) and A. Harnack, *Luke the Physician: The Author of the Third Gospel and the Acts of the Apostles* (trans. J.R. Wilkinson; London: Williams & Norgate, 2nd edn, 1909) esp. 175–198. For a recent treatment of language of healing, see L. Wells, *The Greek Language of Healing from Homer to New Testament Times* (BZNW 83; Berlin: de Gruyter, 1998) *passim*.

[4] On authorship of these letters, see McDonald and Porter, *Early Christianity and its Sacred Literature*, chap. 10.

source is being used (which is the conclusion of Chapter Two above). It does not resolve the issue of authorship, and certainly not the issue of the relationship between the Paul of Acts and the Paul of the letters, issues pursued in more detail in this volume in Chapter Nine in terms of the standard critical arguments against their correlation.[5]

Important still for the discussion are a number of questions that have been raised regarding the accuracy and reliability of Acts in relationship to what is known about Paul through his letters. A number of these factors seem to some scholars to be so at odds with the picture of Paul that is gained through his letters as to raise the question of whether the person who wrote Acts could possibly have been a first-hand witness or close acquaintance. In light of the concerns of this chapter, the following points are worth enumerating here briefly, before turning to the issues of rhetoric and epistolography.

1. Whereas Paul is only known as a letterwriter in the writings attributed to him in the New Testament, the author of Acts never depicts Paul as a letterwriter, but rather as a speechmaker or orator. Nowhere in Acts is Paul seen carrying on the kind of ministry that is depicted in his letters, that is, maintaining and guarding his relationships with his churches through his epistolary correspondence. Furthermore, the author of Acts, regardless of his knowledge of Paul's writing activities, does not overtly refer to or use the letters in his composition (although there may be allusions to them – see below on the Miletus speech).[6] Instead, in Acts, Paul carries out his missionary strategy through personal contacts and speaking in various ways.

---

[5] The standard treatments of these issues are P. Vielhauer, "On the 'Paulinism' of Acts," in L.E. Keck and J.L. Martyn (eds.), *Studies in Luke–Acts* (Philadelphia: Fortress Press, 1966) 33–50; and E. Haenchen, *The Acts of the Apostles: A Commentary* (trans. B. Noble *et al.*; Philadelphia: Westminster Press, 1971 [1965]) 112–116. For recent discussions of these issues, see L.T. Johnson, *The Writings of the New Testament: An Interpretation* (Minneapolis: Fortress Press, 1986) 231–238; B. Witherington, III, *The Acts of the Apostles: A Socio-Rhetorical Commentary* (Grand Rapids: Eerdmans, 1998) 430–438.

[6] For discussion of the intricacies of whether Paul knew and/or used Paul's letters, see W.O. Walker, "Acts and the Pauline Corpus Reconsidered," *JSNT* 24 (1985) 3–23 (repr. in S.E. Porter and C.A. Evans [eds.], *The Pauline Writings: A Sheffield Reader* [BibSem 34; Sheffield: Sheffield Academic Press, 1995] 55–74); and *idem*, "Acts and the Pauline Corpus Revisited: Peter's Speech at the Jerusalem Conference," in R.P. Thompson and T.E. Phillips (eds.), *Literary Studies in Luke–Acts: Essays in Honor of Joseph B. Tyson* (Macon, GA: Mercer University Press, 1998) 77–86; cf. also W. Schenk, "Luke as Reader of Paul: Observations on his Reception," in S. Draisma (ed.), *Intertextuality in Biblical Writings: Essays in Honour of Bas van Iersel* (Kampen: Kok, 1989) 127–133; R. Riesner, *Paul's Early Period: Chronology, Mission Strategy, Theology* (trans. D. Stott; Grand Rapids: Eerdmans, 1998) 318–326.

2. Whereas Paul apparently was not able to convince his audiences personally on several occasions, at least according to his own words in his letters (e.g. 2 Cor 10:10, although one must be careful in interpreting this passage),[7] in Acts, Paul is, for the most part, a highly convincing rhetorician (Acts 13:9–11, 16–41; 14:15–17; 17:22–31; 22:1–21; 24:10–21; 26:2–26). These speeches have been analyzed in some detail recently, and it is to this issue that I wish to return.[8]

3. One would not be able to gather from Acts alone that Paul jealously guarded his relationship as apostle with, for example, the Corinthian church, warranting the kind of epistolary exchange that we find in the letters themselves. Instead, he delivers speeches and then moves on, very much reminiscent of the itinerant evangelists ridiculed so severely in Lucian's *Peregrinus* and warned about in the *Didache* (11–13), as well as being similar to various other kinds of itinerant philosophers of the times, such as the Cynics.[9]

These kinds of contrasts can clearly be overdrawn (as I attempt to show in Chapter Nine), but they do illustrate that there are issues to be raised regarding the relationship between Paul the rhetorician and Paul the epistolographer, so much so that some would say that all we can know is Paul the epistolographer, since there is not an accurate depiction of Paul to be found in Acts. Is it possible to entertain his being both, or must we say that he is only one?

3. The Rhetoric of Paul and his Letters

That Paul was a letterwriter who apparently composed his letters following the conventions of ancient epistolary practice is beyond dispute, and will not be

---

[7] For the latest interpretation, see B.W. Winter, *Philo and Paul among the Sophists* (SNTSMS 96; Cambridge; Cambridge University Press, 1997) 203–230.

[8] For the most recent analyses of the speeches in Acts, see M.L. Soards, *The Speeches in Acts: Their Content, Context, and Concerns* (Louisville: Westminster/John Knox, 1994). Still valuable are H.J. Cadbury, "The Speeches in Acts," in F.J. Foakes Jackson and K. Lake (eds.), *The Beginnings of Christianity. Part I. The Acts of the Apostles. V. Additional Notes* (London: Macmillan, 1933) 402–427; and the older study of F. Bethge, *Die Paulinischen Reden der Apostelgeschichte: Historisch-grammatisch und biblisch-theologisch* (Göttingen: Vandenhoeck & Ruprecht, 1887). Many of the speeches are also analyzed in Chapters Six and Seven of this volume.

[9] See A.J. Malherbe, *The Cynic Epistles: A Study Edition* (SBLSBS 12; Missoula, MT: Scholars Press, 1977); *idem, Paul and the Popular Philosophers* (Minneapolis: Fortress Press, 1989) *passim*.

argued here.[10] Although the use of an amanuensis adds a heretofore unquantified (and probably unquantifiable) factor to authorial composition,[11] and although composition in the ancient world may well have been conceived of in terms other than those used today,[12] it cannot be seriously denied that Paul was the author of a number of letters in the New Testament. I would argue that these number thirteen, but, even if others argue for a smaller list, the point is that the authentic writings of Paul are all letters, regardless of their number.

A major issue in Pauline studies today is whether, in fact, Paul the letterwriter is also a rhetorician. Part of the problem with this dispute is what is meant by the terms rhetorician and rhetoric. A number of questions can be raised that will help to penetrate this issue.

Was Paul writing letters or was he in fact writing speeches, as did Demosthenes, Isocrates and Lysias?[13] That Paul was indeed writing speeches appears to be the position advocated by Kennedy.[14] Kennedy and his followers approach the letters of Paul essentially as speeches that must be interpreted along these lines, with the epistolary opening and closing treated as almost incidental features. This position is not confined to Kennedy, however, since those following the work of Betz strongly advocate the existence of a hybrid

---

[10] On Paul's letters, see W.G. Doty, *Letters in Primitive Christianity* (Philadelphia: Fortress Press, 1973); S.K. Stowers, *Letter Writing in Greco-Roman Antiquity* (LEC; Philadelphia: Westminster Press, 1986); J.L. White, "New Testament Epistolary Literature in the Framework of Ancient Epistolography," *ANRW* 2.25.2 (Berlin: de Gruyter, 1984) 1730–1756; *idem*, "Ancient Greek Letters," in D.E. Aune (ed.), *Greco-Roman Literature and the New Testament: Selected Forms and Genres* (SBLSBS 21; Atlanta: Scholars Press, 1988) 85–105; cf. *idem*, *Light from Ancient Letters* (FFNT; Philadelphia: Fortress Press, 1986); L. Alexander, "Hellenistic Letter-Forms and the Structure of Philippians," *JSNT* 37 (1989) 87–101 (repr. in Porter and Evans [eds.], *Pauline Writings*, 232–246); H. Probst, *Paulus und der Brief: Die Rhetorik des antiken Briefes als Form der paulinischen Korintherkorrespondenz (1 Kor 8–10)* (WUNT 2.45; Tübingen: Mohr–Siebeck, 1991) 29–105.

[11] See E.R. Richards, *The Secretary in the Letters of Paul* (WUNT 2.42; Tübingen: Mohr–Siebeck, 1991).

[12] See S.E. Porter, "Pauline Authorship and the Pastoral Epistles: Implications for Canon," *BBR* 5 (1995) 105–123.

[13] For discussion of the broader topic of ancient rhetoric and epistolography, see J.T. Reed, "The Epistle," in S.E. Porter (ed.), *Handbook of Classical Rhetoric in the Hellenistic Period 330 B.C.–A.D. 400* (Leiden: Brill, 1997) 171–193; and the classic study of E. Norden, *Die antike Kunstprosa* (2 vols.; 3rd edn, 1915; repr. Stuttgart: Teubner, 1995) 2.492–502.

[14] See G.A. Kennedy, *New Testament Interpretation through Rhetorical Criticism* (Chapel Hill: University of North Carolina Press, 1984) 86–87. See also K. Berger, "Hellenistische Gattungen im Neuen Testament," *ANRW* 2.25.2 (Berlin: de Gruyter, 1984) 1031–1432.

literary form that combines epistolary and rhetorical features.[15] As a result, rather than a single agreed-upon rhetorical outline for each Pauline letter, there are several types of analyses of Paul's letters that are to be found. For example, in some, the opening and closing are retained, but not seen to be integral to the rhetorical structure of the bulk of the letter. Kennedy's analysis of Galatians treats the salutation (1:1–5) as separate from the *proem/exordium* (1:6–10), with the epistolary closing labeled an epilogue (6:11–14).[16] In others, the opening and closing are jettisoned altogether. Thus Smit does not even treat the epistolary prescript (1:1–5) in his rhetorical analysis, seeing it as having a solely epistolary and hence non-rhetorical function. He labels the epistolary closing as *amplificatio* (6:11–18). He also excises from analysis 5:12–6:10, since (he contends) parenesis has no place within classical rhetoric.[17] Still others simply overlook the epistolary elements altogether. For example, Jewett analyzes 1 and 2 Thessalonians in entirely rhetorical terms. He begins with an *exordium* (1 Thess 1:1–5; 2 Thess 1:1–12) and closes with a *peroratio* (1 Thess 5:23–28; 2 Thess 3:16–18).[18]

Even though many rhetorical analysts of the Pauline letters have approached them as essentially speeches, or speeches in the disguise of letters, this approach is unsatisfactory, since it either minimizes or altogether neglects the clear epistolary features of the Pauline letters. Regardless of whether one argues for a three, four or five part Pauline epistolary structure, the failure to take into account the clear elements of the opening or the closing, whether this means bracketing them out of discussion or considering them to be appendages, starts off the entire discussion in the wrong direction; it demands that we analyze the clear in terms of the unclear, that is, the epistolary as secondary to the rhetorical. The epistolary features of the Pauline letters are the clear generic features that allow identification of the literary form, and, regardless of whatever else is done with the letters, these elements must be

---

[15] See H.D. Betz, *Galatians* (Hermeneia; Philadelphia: Fortress Press, 1979); *idem,* "The Literary Composition and Function of Paul's Letter to the Galatians," *NTS* 21 (1974–1975) 353–379; *idem, 2 Corinthians 8 and 9: A Commentary on Two Administrative Letters of the Apostle Paul* (Hermeneia; Philadelphia: Fortress Press, 1985); and M. Mitchell, *Paul and the Rhetoric of Reconciliation: An Exegetical Investigation of the Language and Composition of 1 Corinthians* (HUT 28; Tübingen: Mohr–Siebeck, 1991).

[16] Kennedy, *New Testament Interpretation,* 145. But see also Betz, *Galatians,* 14–25 and M. Bachmann, *Sünder oder Übertreter: Studien zur Argumentation in Gal 2,15ff.* (WUNT 59; Tübingen: Mohr–Siebeck, 1992) 156–160, who do similarly.

[17] J. Smit, "The Letter of Paul to the Galatians: A Deliberative Speech," *NTS* 35 (1989) 1–26.

[18] R. Jewett, *The Thessalonian Correspondence: Pauline Rhetoric and Millenarian Piety* (FFNT; Philadelphia: Fortress Press, 1986) 221, 225.

satisfactorily explained before moving to further explanation. The opening and closing clearly reflect the conventions of letter writing in the ancient world, abundantly attested in the documentary papyri. The rhetorical features are less clearly perceived, as can be seen in the simple fact that some rhetorical analysts include the epistolary opening, others exclude it, and still others re-label it. There is no consistency at this point, because the rhetorical features are not clear features in the same way that the epistolary opening and closing are. There is further lack of agreement when the other parts of the letter/speech are analyzed.[19]

Was Paul formally trained as a rhetorician, or were rhetorical categories in use in the ancient world no matter what the form of communication? Rhetorical analysts have argued both ways on this question. Some have wanted to maintain that Paul reflects formal training as a rhetorician. Although it is firmly established that Paul was born in Tarsus of Cilicia, a city known as a center of learning especially in the areas of philosophy and rhetoric (Strabo 14.5.3), and one with a fully-developed Greco-Roman educational system, it is doubtful that Paul proceeded very far in this educational system.[20] This is seen in two ways. The first is the lack of evidence from his letters of classical knowledge. At various times it has been argued that Paul reflects classical writers or uses classical or rhetorical language and terminology, but most remain firmly unconvinced.[21] His few quotations of classical writers can be attributed to common knowledge, and his use of such terms as ἀλληγορέω (Gal 4:24) is thought to be conventional and not technical.[22] The second line of evidence is

---

[19] Further examples and discussion are provided in S.E. Porter, "Paul of Tarsus and his Letters," in Porter (ed.), *Handbook of Classical Rhetoric*, 533–585.

[20] On Greco-Roman education, see H.I. Marrou, *A History of Education in Antiquity* (trans. G. Lamb; London: Sheed & Ward, 1956) esp. 229–329; D.L. Clark, *Rhetoric in Greco-Roman Education* (New York: Columbia University Press, 1957) esp. 59–66; and S.F. Bonner, *Education in Ancient Rome: From the Elder Cato to the Younger Pliny* (London: Methuen, 1977) *passim*.

[21] For recent discussion, see J. Fairweather, "The Epistle to the Galatians and Classical Rhetoric: Parts 1 & 2," *TynBul* 45.1 (1994) 23–30; D. Litfin, *St Paul's Theology of Proclamation: 1 Corinthians 1–4 and Greco-Roman Rhetoric* (SNTSMS 79; Cambridge: Cambridge University Press, 1994) 137–140. Cf. the still important finds of E.B. Howell, "St Paul and the Greek World," *Greece & Rome* 11 (1964) 7–29, although few biblical scholars would endorse his conclusions now (the same may not be true for classicists, however). See now also W.J. Porter, "λαλέω: A Word about Women, Music and Sensuality in the Early Church," in M.A. Hayes, W.J. Porter, and D. Tombs (eds.), *Religion and Sexuality* (RILP 4; Sheffield: Sheffield Academic Press, 1998) 101–124.

[22] For a list of such terms, as well as discussion, see C.J. Classen, "Philologische Bemerkungen zur Sprache des Apostels Paulus," *Wiener Studien* 107–108 (1994–1995) 321–335.

what he himself is recorded as saying in Acts 22:3. The statement there is grammatically ambiguous, but most interpreters believe that Paul is saying that, although he was born in Tarsus and may have lived there for a portion of his life, he was reared in Jerusalem.[23] Thus, he may have been able to receive primary education in Tarsus, but he does not seem to have been able to receive secondary or tertiary education, and therefore would not have been able to receive formal rhetorical training in Tarsus. Although there is significant influence of Hellenism on rabbinical methods of interpretation,[24] it is not sufficient to posit that this would constitute formal training in Greco-Roman rhetoric.

The supposition of a universal form of rhetoric does not go far toward answering the question either, since what is being discussed is not whether individuals have always had the ability to marshal persuasive arguments, but whether these arguments are clearly couched in the terminology and structure of ancient Greco-Roman rhetoric. The claim that Paul, even though he may not have received formal training in rhetoric, exemplifies a number of features of rhetoric simply because either he was intelligent and widely travelled enough to have availed himself of informal training in rhetoric, or there was sufficient rhetorical influence in the Greco-Roman world of the time to make it plausible that he inadvertently picked up the rudiments of rhetoric, overlooks the nature of rhetorical training and practice in the ancient world. Even though the times were litigious, we distort the social composition of the world to think that so many had clear access to the legal system; far fewer still were formally trained in rhetoric, especially when at most 20 to 30% of the *men* were probably even literate.[25] This training was intense and rigorous, as the ancient rhetorical handbooks attest – not the kind of thing that the vast majority had the luxury of time or sufficient money in which to engage.

---

[23] See M. Hengel with R. Deines, *The Pre-Christian Paul* (trans. J. Bowden; London: SCM Press, 1991) 18–39.

[24] See D. Daube, "Rabbinic Methods of Interpretation and Hellenistic Rhetoric," *HUCA* 22 (1949) 239–264.

[25] See W.A. Meeks, *The First Urban Christians: The Social World of the Apostle Paul* (New Haven: Yale University Press, 1983) *passim*, on the social composition of the early Church; and W.V. Harris, *Ancient Literacy* (Cambridge, MA: Harvard University Press, 1989) 116–146, on literacy in the Hellenistic period, with p. 141 for the statistics. For a sociologist's view of the development of the early Church, see R. Stark, *The Rise of Christianity: A Sociologist Reconsiders History* (Princeton, NJ: Princeton University Press, 1996).

Are ancient rhetorical and epistolary categories to be equated? Some have found it easy to do so,[26] but there are two major problems with such equations. The first is found in the analyses of arrangement of the Pauline letters themselves. Even by those who wish to "find" rhetorical categories appropriate to the Pauline letters, there is widespread divergence regarding what these categories are and the extent of their presence in a given letter. A survey of the rhetorical outlines of Paul's letters reveals virtually no two analyses the same, even by those who have worked together in the common task of doing such analyses. This failure to arrive at common results does not necessarily mitigate the task, but it does raise questions about the usefulness of the categories and the procedures being employed. This kind of confusion is certainly not to be found in discussion of the epistolary structure of the letters, where most if not virtually all commentators agree on the extent of the epistolary openings and closings, as well as the limits of the thanksgivings, bodies and parenesis, even if they do not always believe that they constitute discrete sections in epistolary structure. The second major problem is how the rhetorical categories are determined. When examining the rhetorical categories used in epistolary analysis, there is rarely a consistent utilization of categories from one of the handbooks or authors on rhetoric. Sometimes Roman and sometimes Greek categories are used, but in most instances treatments betray a mix of the two.[27] Since no clear set of categories appears to have been found, it is difficult to know how they can be in any way equated with the rather more straightforward categories of epistolary analysis. The only set of categories that seems to be consistently applied is that of Aristotle. Although it is plausible that Paul could have known and used the categories of Aristotelian rhetoric, there is little if any evidence that he did, and very few Aristotelian readings of Pauline letters have been advanced.[28] The relative simplicity of the categories has not resulted in the analyses proving to be the most penetrating or productive for interpretation.

If the terms of rhetorical and epistolary analysis are not to be equated, did the ancients recognize a cross-over between these two sets of categories and

---

[26] See, for example, F.W. Hughes, *Early Christian Rhetoric and 2 Thessalonians* (JSNTSup 30; Sheffield: JSOT Press, 1989) esp. 34–43, among many others.

[27] See H. Lausberg, *Handbuch der literarischen Rhetorik: Eine Grundlegung der Literaturwissenschaft* (Munich: Hueber, 1960) 148–149, for a synoptic chart of the categories of arrangement in the various authors and handbooks; and Porter, "Paul of Tarsus and his Letters," 539–561, for examples applied to the New Testament.

[28] Two Aristotelian rhetorical analyses of Pauline letters worth noting are R.G. Hall, "The Rhetorical Outline for Galatians: A Reconsideration," *JBL* 106 (1987) 277–287; T.H. Olbricht, "An Aristotelian Rhetorical Analysis of 1 Thessalonians," in D.L. Balch *et al.* (eds.), *Greeks, Romans, and Christians: Essays in Honor of A.J. Malherbe* (Minneapolis: Fortress Press, 1990) 224–236.

use rhetorical theory to discuss the composition and analysis of letters?[29] Such evidence is clearly lacking. This is seen in two major ways. The first is that epistolary theory only becomes a part of rhetorical theory much later than the composition of the New Testament. It is not until Julius Victor in the fourth century in an appendix to his *Art of Rhetoric* (§ 27) that there is a section devoted to letterwriting in a rhetorical handbook.[30] The second is that, where letters are mentioned in discussion of rhetoric, in virtually all instances a distinction between the two is made, apart from some consideration of elements of style. For example, Pseudo-Demetrius's *On Style*, perhaps written in the first century BC, has comments on letters in an excursus (223–235), but primarily to distinguish letterwriting from oratory, a distinction Seneca also makes (*Ep.* 75.1–2). There is certainly no theoretical basis assumed or established for analyzing letters according to the categories of rhetoric. The same can be said for the others who mention letters in their writings (e.g. Cicero). In none of the handbooks or other writers is the practice of epistolary composition evoked as a way of instruction in rhetorical composition. There is no evidence regarding the use of rhetorical categories to analyze letters until much later than the time of the composition of the New Testament. In the fourth and fifth centuries, such fathers of the Church as John Chrysostom and Augustine make rhetorical comments about the Pauline letters,[31] but this coincides with the (late) integration of epistolary theory with rhetorical theory, discussed above. The evidence clearly indicates that this was a later development in Christian hermeneutics, perhaps when the Church was concerned to establish itself as intellectually and literarily respectable in the ancient world, even though it was a religion based upon letters. Thus, the categories of rhetoric – apart, possibly, from recognition of elements of style – were not used for the analysis of letters, so far as the extant ancient evidence indicates. In fact, in the only sources that do remain – the epistolary theorists, most of whom are too late for serious inclusion in such a discussion, and a few

---

[29] The arguments used in the discussion that follows were first proposed in S.E. Porter, "The Theoretical Justification for Application of Rhetorical Categories to Pauline Epistolary Literature," in S.E. Porter and T.H. Olbricht (eds.), *Rhetoric and the New Testament: Essays from the 1992 Heidelberg Conference* (JSNTSup 90; Sheffield: JSOT Press, 1993) 100–122; and now developed in Porter, "Paul of Tarsus and his Letters," 562–584. Cf. also R.D. Anderson, Jr, *Ancient Rhetorical Theory and Paul* (Kampen: Kok Pharos, 1996) esp. 93–109, for similar conclusions.

[30] See A.J. Malherbe, *Ancient Epistolary Theorists* (SBLSBS 19; Atlanta: Scholars Press, 1988), for a collection of the epistolary theorists.

[31] See Fairweather, "Galatians and Classical Rhetoric," 2–22, and Kennedy, *New Testament Interpretation*, 11.

ancients who comment on letter-writing, such as Cicero – the letter is distinguished from the speech.

Is it, then, legitimate to use the categories of ancient rhetoric to study Paul's letters? It is evident that there are clear functional relations between some of the categories of ancient rhetoric and the categories of ancient letters.[32] This can be accounted for, however, by virtue of the need to communicate and the finite linguistic means by which this is possible. Therefore, no matter what form of discourse is concerned, there are bound to be a number of functional similarities of, for example, the opening gambit in most such discourses. Likewise, when such communication comes to an end, there is bound to be significant functional correspondence in light of the finite closing functions of these discourses. Similarly, the way that an argument unfolds is bound to have certain (although perhaps fewer) functional similarities. These functional similarities allow the interpreter to draw upon a much wider range of resources for analysis than simply those of the ancient rhetoricians. In fact, this is bound to have a certain liberating effect as categories of thought and analysis from a variety of disciplines are utilized. These could well include not only the New Rhetoric (as important as that is),[33] but also recent work in discourse analysis and other forms of what is sometimes called text-linguistics, as well as utilizing various other linguistic models that have a concern for the ways in which discourses are created and interpreted.[34] There is no necessary need to retain the categories of ancient rhetoric, and certainly not with reference to how they are defined and used in the ancient handbooks, or even utilized in the speeches themselves. We can recognize that the categories and conventions of ancient rhetoric were developed by practitioners of the time to aid them in their communicative tasks, in the same way that in our day and age we ought to develop and utilize useful sets of categories for our own analysis.[35] At best,

---

[32] See J.T. Reed, "Using Ancient Rhetorical Categories to Interpret Paul's Letters: A Question of Genre," in Porter and Olbricht (eds.), *Rhetoric and the New Testament,* 294–314; cf. C.J. Classen, "St. Paul's Epistles and Ancient Greek and Roman Rhetoric," in Porter and Olbricht (eds.), *Rhetoric of the New Testament,* 265–291.

[33] See, for example, the defining work of C. Perelman and L. Olbrechts-Tyteca, *The New Rhetoric: A Treatise on Argumentation* (trans. J. Wilkinson and P. Weaver; Notre Dame, IN: Notre Dame University Press, 1958).

[34] Cf. S.E. Porter, "Rhetorical Analysis and Discourse Analysis of the Pauline Corpus," in S.E. Porter and T.H. Olbricht (eds.), *The Rhetorical Analysis of Scripture: Essays from the 1995 London Conference* (JSNTSup 146; Sheffield: Sheffield Academic Press, 1997) 249–274.

[35] See, for example, D.L. Stamps, "Rhetorical Criticism of the New Testament: Ancient and Modern Evaluations of Argumentation," in S.E. Porter and D. Tombs (eds.), *Approaches to New Testament Study* (JSNTSup 120; Sheffield: JSOT Press, 1995) 151–157.

there is a sense in which rhetoric is universal, and as much with us today as it was in ancient times, but this does not necessarily mean that the categories of ancient rhetoric are the most useful for analysis of ancient discourse. In light of this, we must conclude that the Paul of the letters is Paul the epistolographer, not the rhetorician.

4. The Rhetoric of Paul and the Speeches in Acts

Having concluded that, on the basis of his letters, Paul is an epistolographer, and that the structure and organization of the letter-form must take priority in discussion of his letters, not rhetorical categories, I turn now to Acts, in order to see if there is a sense in which he is a rhetorician. The speeches of Paul in Acts are not the same as his letters, however. No matter how close a relationship we see between the Paul of the letters and the Paul of Acts (see Chapter Nine), the literary forms that they use are different. The Pauline letters are genuine letters; the speeches in Acts are not letters but are depicted as oral discourses delivered before varying audiences. It would appear, at least at a first glance, that the categories of ancient rhetoric would be ideally suited to analysis of Paul's speeches. Despite the *apparent* susceptibility of the speeches of Acts to rhetorical analysis, however, I believe that several words of caution are still necessary.

In dealing with the speeches in Acts, there are two major questions that must be addressed. The first is how speeches were recorded in the ancient world, including the book of Acts.[36] There have been two major positions regarding the speeches in Acts. The first holds that, since each speech suits the speaker, audience and circumstances of delivery, there is good reason to believe that the speeches were not invented by the author, but rather were condensed accounts

---

[36] For a fuller exposition of the issues involved, including an analysis of Thucydides 1.22.1, see S.E. Porter, "Thucydides 1.22.1 and Speeches in Acts: Is There a Thucydidean View?" *NovT* 32 (1990) 121–142 (repr. with modifications in S.E. Porter, *Studies in the Greek of the New Testament: Theory and Practice* [SBG 5; New York: Lang, 1996] 173–193), from which the following is summarized and occasionally quoted. For responses appreciating this article's concern for the difficulties of this passage, see C. Gempf, "Public Speaking and Published Accounts," 266, and P.E. Satterthwaite, "Acts against the Background of Classical Rhetoric," 355–356, both in B.W. Winter and A.D. Clarke (eds.), *The Book of Acts in its First Century Setting. I. Acts in its Ancient Literary Setting* (Grand Rapids: Eerdmans, 1993); J.B. Polhill, *Acts* (NAC 26; Nashville: Broadman, 1992) 45. See also W.J. McCoy, "In the Shadow of Thucydides," in B. Witherington, III (ed.), *History, Literature and Society in the Book of Acts* (Cambridge: Cambridge University Press, 1996) 3–23, esp. 15–16.

of speeches actually delivered and retained by the early Church.[37] The contrary position argues that the speeches are creations by the author of Acts, since such creation can be paralleled in other historical writing of the time, and purportedly reflect a later viewpoint than the chronological setting of the book.[38] Each of these positions establishes itself, in large part, by appeal to the well-known statement in Thucydides 1.22.1 regarding speeches. The first position usually assumes that there is such a thing as a "Thucydidean view" that endorses faithful retention and reproduction of the speeches, while the second maintains that Thucydides is speaking of reconstructing the intention of the speechmakers. But is there such a thing as a Thucydidean view of speeches?

An examination of Thucydides 1.22.1 reveals that there are at least seven problematic words or phrases in this passage. The Greek is given first, followed by the statement in Jowett's translation, with the contentious wording included for reference (note that, due to the nature of translation, the Greek wording does not necessarily appear in the same order):

καὶ ὅσα μὲν λόγῳ εἶπον ἕκαστοι ἢ μέλλοντες πολεμήσειν ἢ ἐν αὐτῷ ἤδη ὄντες, χαλεπὸν τὴν ἀκρίβειαν αὐτὴν τῶν λεχθέντων διαμνημονεῦσαι ἦν ἐμοί τε ὧν αὐτὸς

---

[37] See, for example, F.F. Bruce, *The Speeches in the Acts of the Apostles* (London: Tyndale, 1942) esp. 27; cf. also *idem*, "The Speeches in Acts – Thirty Years After," in R. Banks (ed.), *Reconciliation and Hope: New Testament Essays on Atonement and Eschatology* (Festschrift L.L. Morris; Grand Rapids: Eerdmans, 1974) 530–568; *idem*, "The Acts of the Apostles: Historical Record or Theological Reflection?" *ANRW* 2.25.2 (Berlin: de Gruyter, 1985) 2582–2588. See also W.W. Gasque, "The Speeches of Acts: Dibelius Reconsidered," in R.N. Longenecker and M.C. Tenney (eds.), *New Directions in New Testament Study* (Grand Rapids: Zondervan, 1974) 232–250; C.J. Hemer, *The Book of Acts in the Setting of Hellenistic History* (ed. C. Gempf; WUNT 49; Tübingen: Mohr–Siebeck, 1989; repr. Winona Lake, IN: Eisenbrauns, 1990) 63–100; Gempf, "Public Speaking and Published Accounts," 265–285; and B. Witherington, III, "Editor's Addendum," in Witherington (ed.), *History, Literature and Society*, esp. 24–26. Advocates of this position, even when they recognize the speeches as condensed summaries, tend to treat the words of the speeches as if they were the "words of Paul," and they become part of the corpus of "Pauline" material. Even Soards tends to analyze the speeches as if they were a body of hard data regarding Paul.

[38] See, for example, M. Dibelius, *Studies in the Acts of the Apostles* (ed. H. Greeven; trans. M. Ling; London: SCM Press, 1956) esp. 138–185; H.J. Cadbury *et al.*, "The Greek and Jewish Traditions of Writing History," in F.J. Foakes Jackson and K. Lake (eds.), *Beginnings of Christianity*. Part I. *The Acts of the Apostles*. II. *Prolegomena II: Criticism* (London: Macmillan, 1922) 7–29; B. Gärtner, *The Areopagus Speech and Natural Revelation* (trans. C.H. King; ASNU 21; Uppsala: Gleerup, 1955) esp. 7–36; E. Schweizer, "Concerning the Speeches in Acts," 208–216, and H. Conzelmann, "The Address of Paul on the Areopagus," 217–230, both in Keck and Martyn (eds.), *Studies in Luke–Acts*; Haenchen, *Acts*, 90–112; and G. Schneider, *Die Apostelgeschichte* (2 vols.; HTKNT 5.1, 2; Freiburg: Herder, 1980, 1982) 1.95–103, esp. 97.

ἤκουσα καὶ τοῖς ἄλλοθέν ποθεν ἐμοὶ ἀπαγγέλλουσιν· ὡς δ' ἂν ἐδόκουν ἐμοὶ ἕκαστοι
περὶ τῶν αἰεὶ παρόντων τὰ δέοντα μάλιστ' εἰπεῖν, ἐχομένῳ ὅτι ἐγγύτατα τῆς
ξυμπάσης γνώμης τῶν ἀληθῶς λεχθέντων, οὕτως εἴρηται (OCT).

As to the speeches which were made either before or during the war, it was hard (χαλεπόν)
for me, and for others who reported them to me, to recollect the exact words (τὴν ἀκρίβειαν
αὐτὴν τῶν λεχθέντων). I have therefore put into the mouth of each speaker the sentiments
proper to the occasion (τὰ δέοντα), expressed as I thought he would be likely (μάλιστα) to
express them (ὡς...ἂν...ἐμοὶ...εἰπεῖν), while at the same time I endeavoured, as nearly as I
could (ὅτι ἐγγύτατα), to give the general purport (τῆς ξυμπάσης γνώμης) of what was
actually said (τῶν ἀληθῶς λεχθέντων).[39]

The following items merit discussion. (1) The first is the meaning of the word
translated by Jowett as "hard" and by others often as "difficult" (χαλεπόν).
The question here is whether this should be rendered "difficult, but within the
realm of possibility," "difficult, and in fact not readily accomplishable, perhaps
under any circumstance," or the intermediary position, "difficult, even
impossible, unless some intervening action or circumstance occurs." It is not
altogether clear which is the best understanding. The last has probably the most
to commend it, with Thucydides saying that, whereas reconstructing the
speeches was virtually impossible, he was able to render a close
approximation, if he applied his particular method. (2) The second is the
meaning of the phrase rendered by Jowett and most interpreters as "the exact
words" (τὴν ἀκρίβειαν αὐτὴν τῶν λεχθέντων). The question is whether this
refers to the specific, individual utterances themselves, or to the accuracy of the
statements taken as a whole. The word "exact" itself is not an absolute but a
relative term, depending upon the nature of the action spoken about. (3) Third
is the phrase that should probably be glossed "as they [the speakers] seemed to
me as they would have spoken (if they could have been heard)"
(ὡς...ἂν...ἐμοὶ...εἰπεῖν), in which there is an apparent contrast with the
similar phrase in the next section, 1.22.2 (οὐδ' ὡς ἐμοὶ ἐδόκει). The adverb
"likely" or, better, "especially" (μάλιστα) can be taken with "the things that are
necessary," as in "what was roughly or precisely required," with "to speak" as
in "to speak roughly or precisely," or with the entire clause, as in "to speak the
things that are required, as certainly as possible." (4) The phrase rendered by
Jowett "proper to the occasion," or more precisely "the necessary things" (τὰ
δέοντα), raises the question of for whom or for what purpose they were
necessary. Is it that these things are necessary for Thucydides, the occasion,
his audience, or the individual speakers involved? A case can be, and has been,
made for each of them. (5) The fifth is the phrase "that is nearest" (ὅτι

[39] B. Jowett, *Thucydides* (2 vols.; Oxford: Clarendon Press, 2nd edn, 1900) 1.16.

ἐγγύτατα), meaning either "keeping as close as possible to the general sense of what Thucydides himself saw as necessary," or "keeping as close as possible to the general sense of what was said in light of what was necessary for whatever reason." (6) The sixth is the phrase given by Jowett as "general purport" and often rendered "general sense" (τῆς ξυμπάσης γνώμης). This interpretation is often objected to, however. Two suggestions are that it means "the gist of the message" or "the line taken by the speaker." (7) The seventh is the phrase "truly said" (τῶν ἀληθῶς λεχθέντων), interpreted to mean either "spoken truthfully" or "truly spoken."

In light of the varied interpretations suggested above, the degree of precision that one can attribute to this statement by Thucydides is open to serious question. Certainly more weight has been placed on it by both sides in the debate than the statement itself can hold. As a result of various interpretative configurations, Thucydides's statement can be construed as saying something from the fairly conservative "it has been difficult (but I have done it) to remember with accuracy the things which were stated, but the speeches are given as they were required on the basis of the events, possessing an accuracy of the specific words which were spoken truthfully," to the more skeptical "it has been impossible to remember with any accuracy the things which were stated, so the speeches are given as seemed required for my purposes, possessing an accuracy equivalent to a consensual view of the things said by those who would have really spoken." Thus, it is difficult to appeal to any sort of notion of a programmatic statement in Thucydides to justify a particular kind of recording of the speeches in Acts. Neither side in the discussion has clear support from Thucydides for its supposition regarding accuracy of recording.

With the theoretical issue inconclusive, the second issue in Acts, the actual speeches themselves, must be raised. Since there is not a clear systematic statement in Thucydides to which to appeal either way regarding the accuracy of the speeches, one must turn to the issue of the speeches themselves in order to proceed with discussion of whether, and to what degree, Paul was a rhetorician.

Before proceeding with discussion of any actual speeches, however, several preliminary observations must be made, which threaten the entire enterprise. First, if what was said above regarding the lack of formal knowledge of rhetoric by the Paul of the letters is true, then it is only logical to think that, if it is the same Paul found in Acts, he has the same lack of formal rhetorical training. (Of course, if the Paul of Acts has no actual relation with the Paul of the letters, rhetoric alone cannot establish such a link.) The issue is just as apt if all of the speeches are Luke's creations. There is widespread disagreement about how much rhetoric one would have known simply by being a member of

Greco-Roman society and somehow exposed to rhetorical handbooks, and how much would have normally come through the educational system.[40] I am doubtful that many, if any, in the New Testament actually had significant exposure to the kind of informal or formal training that a rhetorician would have had, the kind of training that would have exposed him to other rhetoricians and to the handbooks. Paul is a possible exception to this, although, as noted above, scholars are not agreed that Paul had much, if any, formal training. He may have simply had the kind of mind that allowed him to create a persuasive argument as the occasion warranted. Although this is a commendable feature, it may exclude his speeches of Acts, if they are genuinely his, from formal rhetorical analysis that relies upon conscious imitation of known and accepted models.

A second preliminary point is that there is a tendency, as discussed above, and seen perhaps most clearly in Kennedy, simply to impose in a heavy-handed way the categories of ancient rhetoric as found in the rhetorical handbooks.[41] These ancient rhetorical handbooks were written to aid in the creation and analysis of speeches, not in providing the kind of critique that modern interpreters are seeking. Further, these handbooks themselves show a decided evolution in thought (e.g. regarding stasis theory from Aristotle to Quintilian). There is no such thing as a static conception of the ancient speech, either in the handbooks or in actual practice.[42] Besides, the speeches of the ancient rhetoricians themselves – such as Demosthenes, Isocrates, and others – are far more diverse than the handbooks and most subsequent analysis allow for. For example, it is typical for modern scholars to debate whether a piece of rhetoric conforms to one of the three species, that is, epideictic, deliberative or forensic rhetoric. Often they arrive at differing answers to the question. What is often overlooked is that even the speeches that were delivered in particular contexts, such as a judicial context, often contain distinct elements of at least one other species of rhetoric.[43]

A third observation, and perhaps the single most limiting factor for analysis of the speeches of Acts, is that we do not know whether we have any single example of a complete speech, as advocates of both positions on the statement

---

[40] See Kennedy, *New Testament Interpretation*, 10.

[41] See Kennedy, *New Testament Interpretation, passim*; followed by, for example, R.N. Longenecker, *Galatians* (WBC 41; Dallas: Word, 1990) c–cxix, esp. cxii–cxiii; C.A. Wanamaker, *Commentary on 1 and 2 Thessalonians* (NIGTC; Grand Rapids: Eerdmans, 1990) esp. 46.

[42] Cf. Quintilian's own warnings regarding strict adherence to the manuals and the models they provide: 4.2.85; 5.13.59.

[43] See Porter, "Paul of Tarsus and his Letters," 541–561 *passim*.

in Thucydides usually recognize. This may well be true of even the one or two sentences occasionally treated as "speeches" that are recorded in Acts (e.g. 1:4b–5, 7–8, 11; 18:6; 21:11; 21:13, 28; 23:9), but is virtually certain to be true of the so-called "major speeches," none of which is more than a couple of minutes in reading length. It is very difficult to believe that these "major speeches" in Acts are all that was said on the occasion, especially given the dramatic effects that some of them seem to have had. This says nothing of what to do with those that are interrupted for one reason or another. One must appreciate the importance of these factors in any analysis of the speeches in Acts. Ancient rhetorical analysis is designed to examine the process by which an ancient rhetorician formulated his argument, whether it was designed to praise or blame (epideictic), persuade to future action (deliberative), persuade regarding a past action (forensic), or a combination of them.[44] In order to do this, various conventions were maintained regarding invention, or how an oration is planned and argued; arrangement, or how the various parts are fitted together; style, or how these various elements are expressed in words and larger units; and memory and delivery, in which how the speech itself was presented becomes part of the rhetorical exercise.[45] It is difficult to know how much the integrity of a given speech in Acts has been maintained, even if it were an actual oration that followed these conventions at all. If the speeches are not preserved in their entirety, even if one takes the view that the speeches in Acts reflect the content of what was actually said on the occasion (one of the several possible interpretations of Thucydides 1.22.1), and a possibility in light of apparent ancient practice of recording summaries of forensic speeches (see Diodorus Siculus 1.76),[46] one must wonder whether the categories of rhetoric can be systematically or comprehensively applied. If the speeches are analyzed as they appear in Acts, all that may result is rhetorical analysis of either a summary or the final form constructed by Luke, not the actual speech of Paul (or anyone else). Perhaps the interrupted speeches provide more fertile ground for such analysis, but, in these instances, one cannot find the structure of an

---

[44] On the "species" of rhetoric, for the most recent treatment, see G.A. Kennedy, "The Genres of Rhetoric," in Porter (ed.), *Handbook of Classical Rhetoric*, 43–50.

[45] On invention, see M. Heath, "Invention," 89–119; on arrangement, see W. Wuellner, "Arrangement," 51–87; on style, see G.O. Rowe, "Style," 121–157; and on delivery and memory, see T.H. Olbricht, "Delivery and Memory," 159–167, all in Porter (ed.), *Handbook of Classical Rhetoric*.

[46] See B.W. Winter, "Official Proceedings and the Forensic Speeches in Acts 24–26," in Winter and Clarke (eds.), *Acts in its Ancient Literary Setting*, 307. Winter admits that this process results in a summary made by a scribe, which makes the basis for his subsequent detailed analysis difficult to understand. See also Witherington, *Acts*, 518, who does the same.

entire speech. The interrupted speeches, however, have been debated with regard to whether the interruptions are genuine.[47] It appears to many that, if there was more to be said by Paul, there was not much more, leaving us again with very short speeches for analysis. Consequently, in the analysis that follows below and in Chapters Six and Seven, although there will be reference to some of the categories of ancient rhetoric, these categories are not used rigidly or dogmatically as heuristic tools for analysis of the argumentative structure of the Pauline speeches. They are invoked where there appears to be some clear pattern of usage that may be informative, not because it is thought that any complete ancient oration can necessarily be reconstructed from what is found in Acts. In other words, ancient rhetoric does not seem to provide a useful tool for understanding the relationship of the Paul of Acts and the Paul of the letters.

Analysis of two of the most important speeches by Paul in Acts confirms what has been said above.

a. Paul's Speech to the Ephesian Elders at Miletus (Acts 20:18–35)

The first speech to consider is Paul's speech to the Ephesian elders at Miletus (Acts 20:18–35). This speech must take priority in examining the speeches of Acts in relation to the letters of Paul, since, as Hemer has pointed out, following others, it is "the only one of the larger speeches addressed to a Christian audience, actually of leaders of a church previously founded by Paul, and so likely to be nearer to the pastoral function of Paul's writing in the epistles than any other. It therefore offers the best prospect of direct comparison between the Paul of Acts and the Paul of the letters."[48] Several scholars accept this relationship of the speech to the writings of Paul, but this is where the agreements apparently end. The disputes over the speech include at least the following.

The first dispute is over the type of speech that it is. Dibelius calls it an encomium biography. Hemer and Soards, among others, say that it is a speech of farewell, apparently a category based on its function, rather than a set of formal criteria. Watson agrees that it is a speech of farewell, which (he notes) is a type of epideictic speech, although he provides no rationale for introducing

---

[47] For example, some have argued that the interruptions come only after the content of the speech has been given, indicating that the interruption was used as a way of marking the conclusion of the speech. See below for discussion of instances.

[48] C. Hemer, "The Speeches of Acts I. The Ephesian Elders at Miletus," *TynBul* 40 (1989) 77. See also Cadbury, "Speeches in Acts," 412; Bethge, *Die Paulinischen Reden*, 117–167. Witherington (*Acts*, 610–611) provides a synoptic chart of Acts and Paul's letters, illustrating points of conceptual correlation.

the categories of classical rhetoric, apart from citing Menander Rhetor 2.15 (also noting, however, that the *topoi* he discusses are not found in this speech). Kennedy says it is a speech of farewell as well, but he states categorically that Paul's speech here does not conform to the rhetorical conventions of Menander Rhetor. Conzelmann notes that it has elements of popular rhetoric.[49] Thus, whereas we may well be able to agree that it is a farewell speech, it is difficult to equate it easily with any kind of rhetoric, including an epideictic speech.

The second dispute is concerning the structure of the speech. Opinions here also vary considerably. Dibelius posits four sections: Acts 20:18–21 retrospect and self-defense, vv. 22–27 anticipation of death, vv. 28–31 the apostle's statement, and vv. 32–34 the closing (blessing, conclusion). Soards proposes: Acts 20:18b–21 Paul's recalling of his Asian ministry, vv. 22–27 words about the future, vv. 28–31 advice for the elders, and vv. 32–35 concluding blessing and admonition. Whereas the first two analyses have much in common, Kennedy's, a third, is quite different. Kennedy posits that Acts 20:18–27 constitutes an extended *proem*, v. 28 a proposition, v. 29 a metaphor, v. 31 an example, and vv. 32–35 an epilogue (he does not treat v. 30). Different still is that of Lambrecht, who posits six sections within two larger sections: self-defense and announcement (Acts 20:18b–27), consisting of vv. 18b–21, previous conduct, vv. 22–25, announcement of departure and future suffering, and vv. 26–27, previous conduct (apology); and exhortations and farewell (18:28–35), consisting of vv. 28–31, warning: vigilance in face of imminent dangers, v. 32, farewell, and vv. 33–35, warning: help for the weak. Whereas the first four analyses at least stayed within the boundaries of the speech itself, a fifth, by Watson, does not. His includes five sections: Acts 20:17–18a historical preface, vv. 18b–24 *exordium*, vv. 25–31 *probatio*, vv. 32–35 *peroratio*, vv. 36–38 narrative summary.[50] Watson's analysis is instructive, since it is not merely an analysis of the Pauline speech, but also an analysis of

---

[49] See Dibelius, *Studies in the Acts of the Apostles*, 155; Hemer, "Speeches of Acts," 81; Soards, *Speeches in Acts*, 105; D.F. Watson, "Paul's Speech to the Ephesian Elders (Acts 20.17–38): Epideictic Rhetoric of Farewell," in D.F. Watson (ed.), *Persuasive Artistry: Studies in New Testament Rhetoric in Honor of George A. Kennedy* (JSNTSup 50; Sheffield: JSOT Press, 1991) 190–191; Kennedy, *New Testament Interpretation*, 132–133; H. Conzelmann, *Die Apostelgeschichte* (HNT 7; Tübingen: Mohr–Siebeck, 1963) 117. See also J. Dupont, *Le discours de Milet: Testament pastoral de Saint Paul (Actes 20, 18–36)* (LD 32; Paris: Cerf, 1962) esp. 11–21.

[50] Dibelius, *Studies in the Acts of the Apostles*, 157; Soards, *Speeches in Acts*, 105; Kennedy, *New Testament Interpretation*, 133; J. Lambrecht, "Paul's Farewell-Address at Miletus (Acts 20, 17–38)," in J. Kremer (ed.), *Les Actes des Apôtres: Traditions, rédaction, théologie* (BETL 48; Gembloux: Duculot; Leuven: Leuven University Press, 1979) 318; Watson, "Paul's Speech," 208.

Acts 20:17–38. There seems to be some ambiguity in Watson's analysis regarding what constitutes the speech and what constitutes the rhetorical unit, and what this may imply regarding the contribution of Paul and that of the author of Acts.

The third dispute is over the relationship of the speech to Pauline style in the letters. It is routinely denied that Luke knew or represents authentic Pauline material in Acts, including in the speeches, since the style of Acts is often said to be thoroughly consistent. However, there are a number of parallels between this speech and the Pauline letters worth considering.[51] The first are verbal parallels, including the following phrasing: "being a servant of the lord" (Acts 20:19; Rom 12:11), "with all humility" (Acts 20:19; Eph 4:2),[52] "Jews and Greeks" (Acts 20:21; and especially Romans), "complete the course" (Acts 20:24; 2 Tim 4:7), "complete service" (Acts 20:24; 2 Tim 4:5; Col 4:17), "the service which we received from our Lord Jesus" (Acts 20:24; Col 4:17), "grace of God" (Acts 20:24, 32; frequently in Paul), "the church of God" (Acts 20:28; frequently in Paul), "watch out for yourselves" (Acts 20:28; 1 Tim 4:16), "consider" (Acts 20:31; 1 Cor 16:13; Col 4:2; 1 Thess 5:6, 10), "build up" (Acts 20:32; Rom 15:20; 1 Cor 8:1, 10; 10:23; 14:4, 17; Gal 2:18; 1 Thess 5:11), "inheritance among the saints" (Acts 20:32; Col 1:12), "hands...working" (Acts 20:34–35; 1 Cor 4:12; Eph 4:28), and repeated language of earnestness (Acts 20:31; 1 Thess 2:7–8). The second set of parallels includes biographical details: for example, Paul's not wishing to be a burden to his churches (Acts 20:33–34; 1 Corinthians 9; 2 Cor 11:7–11; 1 Thess 2:9–12), and the length of his stay with the Ephesians. The third set of parallels covers theological similarities, including reference in Acts 20:28 to "the blood of his own." This redemptive language is untypical of Luke, both in the Gospel and in Acts.[53]

How to assess all of this material has been highly debated. Some have contended that all of these individual elements can be found in various ways and forms in the language and thinking of the larger Christian community.[54] The confluence of such factors prompts most scholars to claim that Luke's

---

[51] On the authorship of the various Pauline letters, see McDonald and Porter, *Early Christianity and its Sacred Literature*, chap. 10.

[52] See Conzelmann, *Die Apostelgeschichte*, 117.

[53] See Hemer, *Book of Acts*, 425–426; Cadbury, "Speeches in Acts," 412–413; R. Pesch, *Die Apostelgeschichte* (2 vols.; EKK 5.1, 2; Solothurn: Benziger; Neukirchen-Vluyn: Neukirchener, 1995 [2nd edn], 1986) 2.201–206; among others. Contra Lambrecht, "Paul's Farewell-Address," esp. 325–326, who emphasizes Lukanisms, disputing Pauline parallels (pp. 319–320).

[54] See Cadbury, "Speeches in Acts," 416–417.

inclusion of them was designed to render his work with an authentic Pauline stamp. This raises the question, however, of how Luke knew what was or was not an authentic Pauline stamp. There seem to be only two real options. The first is that he knew the Pauline letters, the only documents known to have been written by Paul and that have remained extant. If this is the case, then Luke, in fact, did know and use the Pauline letters, something denied by many if not most scholars. The second is that, if he did not know the letters, he must have known Paul, or someone very like him. In either case, it is difficult to show that this speech is a reflection of Paul as rhetorician. It is more likely that this speech shows Paul delivering a farewell testimony to close friends, reflecting a similar pastoral and theological approach to that found in his letters (which have already been shown not to be formally rhetorical according to ancient standards). The other alternative, of course, to which Watson's analysis seems to point, is that any rhetorical analysis is not of Paul's speech to the Ephesian elders, but rather of what Luke has done with it.

b. Paul's Speech on the Areopagus in Athens (Acts 17:22–31)

The second speech for analysis is Paul's speech on the Areopagus (Acts 17:22–31). This, the best known of Paul's speeches in Acts, has generated a large number of analyses and interpretations (see Chapter Six, below, for more detailed discussion, in a different context). As many scholars have noted, the body of this speech discusses three main, intertwined themes: God's self-sufficiency, humans created to need God, and worship of God excluding images (this topic of natural theology is discussed in Chapter Six).[55] Paul moves directly from the assertion of knowledge of this god to the God who made the world and everything in it, as a way of beginning to discuss these themes.[56] The transition is rough, whether that was because Paul himself was

---

[55] See, for example, Dibelius, *Studies in the Acts of the Apostles*, 27; D.L. Balch, "The Areopagus Speech: An Appeal to the Stoic Historian Posidonius against Later Stoics and the Epicureans," in Balch *et al.* (eds.), *Greeks, Romans, and Christians*, 54. But cf. Conzelmann, *Die Apostelgeschichte*, 98; Kennedy, *New Testament Interpretation*, 130–131; Soards, *Speeches in Acts*, 96. Specific similarities with Stoic thought have been noticed by J.T. Squires (*The Plan of God in Luke–Acts* [SNTSMS 76; Cambridge: Cambridge University Press, 1993] 72–73). These include parallel thinking regarding God as creator (Acts 17:24; Dio Chrysostom 12.29, 37), being lord of all (Acts 17:24; Dio Chrysostom 12.27, 34), giving life and breath (Acts 17:25; Dio Chrysostom 12.24, 30), as well as determining the nations (Acts 17:24; Dio Chrysostom 12.29) and nature (Acts 17:26; Dio Chrysostom 12.32).

[56] The theme of God as creator of the universe is common to Greek thought, including that of the larger Greek world (e.g. Plato, *Tim.* 28C, 76C; Epictetus 4.7.6; *Corpus Hermeticum* 4.1), as well as Hellenistic Judaism (e.g. Gen 1:1; 3:14; Isa 42:5; 2 Macc 7:23,

pushing to get to the point, or whether the editor has excised several important steps in the logical process. Paul characterizes the level of knowledge of the Athenians at this point as "unknowing" or, in some translations, as "ignorance." Their interest in the divine has led them to erect an altar in ignorance of the god to whom it is specifically addressed. Paul contends that that god is knowable and that he can clarify their god's identity for them. This is an intriguing logical maneuver on Paul's part. Paul clearly has in mind the introduction of his God. However, in the way that he states the case, it appears at first as if he sees this God as only one of a number of gods, and that he is simply filling in a blank that is still left in the pantheon. The way Paul goes on to define this God makes clear, however, that he is thinking of one particular God, whom the Athenians have a dim idea about, but whom they have been unable heretofore to define fully.[57]

Paul then explicates who this God is in terms of his relation to the natural world. This involves several different dimensions, the first mentioned being his creative role. Paul says that this is the God who made the world and all the things in it. The language, very similar to that of Acts 14:15[58] (see Chapter Six for discussion of this speech), but not organized in quite the same way, begins by stating, simply and directly, that this creator God is the one who made the universe and its inhabitants. Paul then clarifies and elucidates these two dimensions of the creative role. He defines this God using the translation of YHWH in the Septuagint – Lord of heaven and earth, in other words, of the entire known universe. Concerning the inhabitants of this world, it is God who has "inspirated" them. Restated, Paul says that it is God who gives to all living things their life and breath.[59] Paul does not say here whether he has in mind only the initial creation of the world or whether there is a sustaining function in mind, although it seems likely that the continuing life of respirant creation necessitates reference here to a creating and sustaining role of God. In other

---

28; Philo, *Op. Mund.* 2, and *passim*; Aristobulus fr. 5). See Conzelmann, *Die Apostelgeschichte*, 98.

[57] That Paul's strategy here is not inconsistent with pagan or even Jewish theology of the time is perhaps confirmed by Jewish inscriptional evidence. For example, there apparently were Jews who recognized a number of gods, besides their traditional one. P.Cair.Zen. I 59076 (= C.P.Jud. I 4; third century BC) gives thanks in line 2 to "the gods" (τοῖς θεοῖς) (republished in White, *Light from Ancient Letters*, 39–40, no. 16), and two inscriptions from El-Kamis (second or first century BC) are by Jews offering blessings to Pan (C.I.J. II 1537, 1538; repr. in W. Horbury and D. Noy, *Jewish Inscriptions of Graeco-Roman Egypt* [Cambridge: Cambridge University Press, 1992] 207–210, nos. 121, 122).

[58] See Conzelmann, *Die Apostelgeschichte*, 98.

[59] There may be a word-play on words for life and breath (ζωή and πνοή). See Conzelmann, *Die Apostelgeschichte*, 98.

words, there is a clear divine providential element to Paul's thought, perhaps one of the major points of connection with his audience.[60]

That the speech is probably a summary is made apparent by the quick transition back from creation of the world and being Lord of heaven and earth, to the dwelling place of this God. Paul states that this God does not dwell in hand-made temples and is not served by humans, as if he had some kind of human-like need.[61] Paul's specification of the realm of inhabitance of God serves two useful purposes. One is to define the character of this God by means of what he does, that is, to create; the other is to differentiate this God from what he has created by saying that he cannot be located in or equated with his creation, and certainly is not to be seen as in any way dependent upon his creation. God is in fact the creator of humanity, with the purpose of their seeking after him. The syntax, as Squires has pointed out, supports this providential action of God, since he is the subject of the speech, and, from Acts 17:24–27, the agent of the action.[62] The Stoics and Paul would perhaps understand this creator-God differently; nevertheless, Kennedy thinks that the argumentation in vv. 24–25 that God's not living in temples is proved by his not needing humans would have been mutually intelligible.[63] For example, Paul and the Stoics have at least parallel thinking regarding God as creator. This set of distinctions is important to ensure that natural theology does not become pantheism or panentheism, that is, so that it is the God from without who initiates and sustains creation, but also who remains apart from and not intertwined with (and hence dependent upon) his creation.[64] To the contrary, as Paul states in v. 28, the human's existence is intricately dependent upon God, for "in him we live and move and exist." In support of the notion that humanity exists only because of this God, Paul may cite two lines from pagan poets in v. 28. There is disagreement whether "in him we live and move and exist" is actually from the poet Epimenides (also cited by Paul in Titus 1:12).[65] More

---

[60] See Squires, *Plan of God in Luke–Acts*, 72; B.W. Winter, "In Public and in Private: Early Christian Interactions with Religious Pluralism," in A.D. Clarke and B.W. Winter (eds.), *One God, One Lord in a World of Religious Pluralism* (Cambridge: Tyndale House, 1991) 119–128.

[61] Epicurean thought apparently held similarly. See Winter, "In Public and in Private," 123–124.

[62] Squires, *Plan of God*, 73–74.

[63] Kennedy, *New Testament Interpretation*, 130.

[64] The independence of God is a common concept in Greek thought. See Euripides, *Herc. Fur.* 1345–1346; Seneca, *Ep.* 95.47; Corpus Hermeticum 6.1.

[65] See F.F. Bruce, *The Acts of the Apostles* (Grand Rapids: Eerdmans, 2nd edn, 1952) 384–385 (the text is reconstructed from a later Syriac text by Isho'dad and references in Clement of Alexandria, *Strom.* 1.14.59.1–2; Diogenes Laertius 1.111, 112); although most

certainly, there is citation in the second part of the verse of a line from the poet Aratus, *Phaenomena* 5: "for we also are his offspring" (cf. Cleanthes, *Hymn to Zeus* 4). Aristobulus, the Hellenistic Jewish philosopher, also cites this poem (fragment 4 in Eusebius, *Prep. Evang.* 13.12.3). As Johnson says, "Luke has Paul citing pagan *auctoritates* in virtually the same way that he cites Torah for his Jewish listeners."[66] The link between God and humanity through this concept of generation allows Paul to dismiss idolatry as foreign to the divine nature, and aptly places the creature in its creaturely relation to the creator. Paul then turns the argument around by stating that, if humans are the offspring of God, by logically thinking backward one can surmise that the divine nature or divinity (θεῖον) is not of material substance, or represented by such things as gold, silver, stone or any of the other images that human beings fashion. These are part of the created order, and represent items in the material world. They are of a different category than that which God created in the human being, who in some way is seen as the created offspring of God.

In light of what has been said regarding the divine and human natures, it is appropriate that, in Acts 17:26, Paul address the question of ethnic distinctions (again, as in 14:16, using the word ἔθνος). Paul says that, from "one," every nation of humanity was made or created. The main verb (ἐποίησεν) may be a helping verb, in the sense of "he *allowed* humanity to live...," but, more likely, it is an independent verb, meaning that "he *made* humanity, so that they would live...."[67] The "one" may be a single human, or it may be a single nation. If it is a single human, Paul does not say anything here about Adam (though most commentators interpret it this way);[68] likewise, it is impossible to know if Paul is perhaps alluding to one of the creation myths of the ancient Greeks.[69] It may be that he is alluding to the Stoic doctrine of the logos or permeating rational presence that was the one thing that was disseminated to all racial or ethnic groups, or to the Epicurean concept of unitary materiality. These allusions are a distinct possibility, in light of his audience, although nothing is made of them

---

do not agree: e.g. L.T. Johnson, *The Acts of the Apostles* (SP 5; Collegeville, MN: Liturgical, 1992) 316. Similar is the thought of Corpus Hermeticum 5.10: "but all things are in you, all things are from you, giving all things you take nothing." For a discussion of possible quotations of pagan writers in Acts, see H.J. Cadbury, *The Book of Acts in History* (London: A. & C. Black, 1955) 44–52.

[66] Johnson, *Acts*, 316. This of course does not mean that Paul believed that the pagan authors had the same status or authority as the Old Testament for him.

[67] Conzelmann, *Die Apostelgeschichte*, 99.

[68] E.g. G. Schille, *Die Apostelgeschichte des Lukas* (THNT 5; Berlin: Evangelische Verlags-Anstalt, 1983) 357.

[69] For a handy summary of such myths, see R. Graves, *The Greek Myths* (vol. 1; Harmondsworth: Penguin, rev. edn, 1960) 27–39.

by the author or speaker. Paul seems to be promoting the idea of the common origins and nature of humanity, even if human existence is spread much wider across the earth (or at least the earth known to him at the time). This process of procreation and dispersement, Paul says, is itself controlled by God. He says that God determined the appointed times and boundaries of habitation. This may refer to God's ordaining the historical epochs of various people groups and their boundaries, or the natural boundaries of their habitation.[70] The result is the same, and that is that this creator God is involved in the life of his creatures. This may also characterize the time period to which Paul refers in v. 30 as the times of ignorance, before God holds all humans accountable.

Paul states that there was an overall divine purpose in all of this activity – from creation to the places and times in which humans lived – and this was for humans to seek God. Paul recognizes that there is an instilled or natural human urge to have some relationship with the divine. He has already perceived this in the Athenians, as he has pointed out. Now he explicates this in terms of the God whom he has defined, recognizing and focusing more particularly upon the human need to find God. Paul qualifies this seeking in two ways, however. The first is that he uses the protasis of a fourth-class conditional statement to raise the question of whether humanity might possibly grope after and find God. The use of the fourth-class conditional in Acts 17:27 grammaticalizes the most condition-laden form of conditional supposition in Greek,[71] and leaves open the chances that any human being might have of reaching God on one's own. The second qualifier is that Paul says that God is not far from each one. These two qualifications might at first seem to be contradictory. On the one hand, Paul says that the seeking of God is something after which one must grope and, even then, might only *possibly* accomplish. On the other hand, Paul says that God is nearby (note the use of litotes)[72] and presumably reachable. I think that the only way to understand this juxtaposition is in terms of what has already been said regarding the relation of God to his creation (God has made this world and is intimately connected with it, but is not to be equated with it), and in anticipation of what Paul is going to say (but does not fully explicate) regarding God's setting the time and conditions of human repentance. The chance of a human finding God is, in other words, minimal. The burden of this rests with God as well, as is suitable since a human is, in one sense, merely a part of the divinely created order.

---

[70] Conzelmann, *Die Apostelgeschichte*, 99.

[71] See S.E. Porter, *Idioms of the Greek New Testament* (BLG 2; Sheffield: JSOT Press, 2nd edn, 1994) 263–264; Witherington, *Acts*, 528.

[72] On the nearness of God as a topic of Greek popular philosophy, see Dio Chrysostom 12.28; Josephus, *Ant.* 8.108; Seneca, *Ep.* 41 (Schille, *Die Apostelgeschichte*, 358).

Paul extrapolates from what he has so far presented – what he seems to see is a compelling formulation of natural theology (see Chapter Six for further discussion) – to an instance of special revelation. Paul says that God, having overlooked the previous times of ignorance, now declares that all should repent, because God intends to judge the world. This declaration seems consistent with Paul's understanding and use of natural theology in this speech, since all of the categories appear to be logical extensions or developments of what he has said to this point regarding God as creator and the place of his created order, including human beings. The worship of things made out of gold, silver or stone reveals ignorance, which God has been willing to overlook until the designated time of his divine judgment (cf. Rom 3:25–26). The concept of the judgment of the world, not found frequently in Acts, is found abundantly in Paul. It was also a familiar concept to the Stoics, who believed that the world would end in destruction (Diogenes Laertius 7.156).[73] This judgment, according to Paul, is going to be carried out by a man designated for such a purpose, and shown to be worthy of this task because of God having raised him from the dead. Kee notes that

The strategy of this address is remarkable. The choice of Stoic principles as a point of entry and the quotation of familiar Greek writers virtually guarantees attention and a sympathetic hearing – at least initially. The degree of overlap between the concepts in this popular philosophy and what the author regards as the basic Christian worldview is striking, and serves the reader as a demonstration of what can be done in approaching with the gospel those who have no familiarity with the teachings of the Jewish scriptures.[74]

The proof for Paul of the appointment of this man as the worthy judge of humanity is his having been raised from the dead (Acts 17:30–31). Paul does not appeal to natural theology but to the proof of the resurrection that God has appointed a man for such a judgmental purpose, a distinctly Christian element to the speech. For Paul, it appears to be a natural step to progress from natural revelation in the created order – the relation of the creator and the creature, racial and natural distinctions, and what all of this implies regarding the role and place of the human – to suggest that there is a further day of reckoning. The fact that he appeals to an act that is not a part of the natural order, however,

---

[73] See Balch, "Areopagus Speech," 58–67, on the Stoic view of judgment. On belief in cosmic conflagration, see P.W. van der Horst, "'The Elements Will Be Dissolved with Fire.' The Idea of Cosmic Conflagration in Hellenism, Ancient Judaism, and Early Christianity," in his *Hellenism–Judaism–Christianity: Essays on their Interaction* (Leuven: Peeters, 2nd edn, 1994) 271–292.

[74] H.C. Kee, *The Good News to the Ends of the Earth: The Theology of Acts* (London: SCM Press; Philadelphia: Trinity Press International, 1990) 65.

seems to have disrupted the flow of thought on the part of his audience, and his audience reacts to this. It is not that Paul's logic has been grossly inconsistent. It appears more that he has introduced something into the argument that his audience would not have fully accepted. The problem for Greek thinking was not the idea of spiritual existence or even continual existence after death. The point of contention would have been the apparent revivification to physical life of a dead body. This apparent conflict is what leads Paul's audience to interrupt him and not allow him to continue. Some scholars believe that this is not a genuine interruption, seeing the speech as complete.[75] This cannot be correct, however, since the balance of the speech is completely wrong, with the only distinctly Christian part, mention of the resurrection, coming at the very end of v. 31.

Concerning Acts, it is difficult to posit on the basis of what has been said above that we have sufficient evidence to provide an analysis of the rhetoric of Paul. We might well posit that we have sufficient confidence in the speeches of Acts to have a firm idea of what Paul said on the occasion, even in terms of his approach (*stasis*) to various topics (*topoi*),[76] but we do not have a sufficient quantity of those words to allow us to perform rhetorical analysis of the speeches as *speeches* of Paul. As conservative a commentator as Hemer says that "The crucial question of historicity here concerns only the essential content of the speeches. We need not be concerned with any supposition that they are verbatim reports; there is a clear argument against such an extreme position." As Hemer states further, Paul must have spoken at great length (see Acts 20:7; cf. 2:40; 9:22; 14:1, 3): "The brief summary paragraphs we possess do not purport to reproduce more than perhaps a *précis* of the distinctive highlights. They do not read as transcripts of oral delivery and the responses of the audience to them do not relate realistically to the bald words reported."[77] The same conclusion is reached by Cadbury: "the probability is against any extensive verbal agreement of the ultimate record with the original. Memory must have considerably condensed the actual utterance, and, indeed, the speeches that we have are all relatively brief and succinct and capable of explanation as summaries of longer addresses."[78] Thus, as clearly Pauline rhetoric, there is little firm ground for positing Paul the rhetorician even in the

---

[75] For example, Dibelius, *Studies in the Acts of the Apostles*, 57; followed by Haenchen, *Acts*, 526; Soards, *Speeches in Acts*, 100.

[76] See Porter, "Paul of Tarsus and his Letters," 570–576.

[77] Hemer, *Book of Acts*, 418.

[78] Cadbury, "Speeches in Acts," 406–407.

book of Acts, at least in any way that provides firm data for close analysis of his speeches.

5. Conclusion

Others would obviously conclude differently regarding the rhetoric of Paul, wishing to assert that Paul the rhetorician can be found in both his letters and his speeches in Acts. However, I am compelled to conclude that we cannot find Paul the ancient rhetorician in the letters, primarily because, in writing letters, Paul was a letterwriter. To be a letterwriter was to be doing something different than being a speechmaker in the Greco-Roman world. On the basis of the letters, we cannot examine Paul as a rhetorician in terms of the categories of construction of speeches in the ancient world. More to the point for this chapter, can we find Paul the rhetorician in Acts? The answer here must be yes and no. On the one hand, it is highly debatable whether we have direct access to the historical Paul as speechmaker, for two reasons. The first is that there is a highly debatable relationship in ancient historiography between the delivery of speeches and their record in later literary works. The second is that what are found in Acts are, for various reasons, not complete Pauline speeches but, at best, later summaries, or even prematurely curtailed speeches possibly designed to give the gist of the original speech. These cannot provide an adequate basis for rhetorical analysis of the speeches of the historical Paul. Nevertheless, if these strictures are taken into account, there are still grounds for examining the speeches in Acts, including those of Paul, in terms of how they are presented by the author of the book. In that case, although the speeches may have had their origins with the historical Paul and reflect the context of what was said by him, the rhetorical analysis is of the speeches in Acts as they were shaped and presented by its author.

Chapter Six

The Argumentative Dimension of Paul's Missionary Speeches in Acts

1. Introduction

In this chapter and the next one, I wish to return to the question of the speeches in Acts. In particular, I wish to analyze Paul's speeches in Acts, with a view to their argumentative dimension. In this chapter, after a brief discussion of the purposes of the speeches in Acts, I will analyze the major missionary speeches by Paul in Acts. In Chapter Seven, I will analyze the major apologetic, or defensive, speeches by Paul in Acts, before providing a brief assessment of the common traits that distinguish Pauline argumentation in them, and conclude with a comment on the relationship between Paul's speeches and his letters. To anticipate my conclusions, I believe that it can be shown that the Paul of Acts has a fundamental structure to his argumentation, but that he is also depicted as adapting his argumentation to his particular context, especially whether the speech is missionary or apologetic in orientation. Although this technique of speech-giving cannot be equated with Paul's epistolary style, and, in fact, clearly represents the language of the author of Acts, there are sufficient similarities to suggest that the same mind may well stand behind the speeches in Acts and the Pauline epistles.

2. Speeches in Acts: Their Purpose or Purposes

That Acts is a book full of speeches no one can deny. Soards has recently suggested that there are 36 speeches in Acts.[1] His is probably the most

---

[1] M.L. Soards, *The Speeches in Acts: Their Content, Context, and Concerns* (Louisville: Westminster/John Knox, 1994). A smaller number of speeches is treated in more detail in F. Bethge, *Die Paulinischen Reden der Apostelgeschichte: Historisch-grammatisch und biblisch-theologisch* (Göttingen: Vandenhoeck & Ruprecht, 1887), one of few sources devoted to study of Paul's speeches in Acts. Cf. W.L. Liefeld, *Interpreting the Book of Acts* (Grand Rapids: Baker, 1995) 61–77, esp. 73–77.

comprehensive analysis of the speeches, or at least the most inclusive list. Not only does he include the lengthy speeches of Paul and Peter, but he includes, for example, 1:4b–5, 7–8, 11, the words of the risen Jesus; 18:6, Paul's speech to the Corinthian Jews; 21:11, Agabus's speech in Caesarea; 21:13, Paul's speech to the disciples in Caesarea; 21:28, the speech of the Jews from Asia; 23:9, the Pharisees' and scribes' speech in the council; among others. Although there is merit to be found in listing and analyzing all of the spoken utterances in Acts, it may be misleading to consider these incidental comments as speeches, either narrowly or broadly defined. Some appear to be exclamations, others simply conversation, and still others at best a *précis* of what must have been much longer comments. A more realistic estimate, and so most scholars, is that there are around 24 or 25 actual speeches in Acts. Even with this reduced number, as Horsley has estimated, there is a greater frequency of speeches in Acts than there is in other writings of the Greek and Roman worlds (Tacitus's *Annals* 2 times, Herodotus 2 times, Josephus's *Jewish War* 4 times, Thucydides 8 times, Polybius 16 times).[2]

This raises a very important question – why are the speeches used, especially with such frequency? Soards states that there are at least three possible explanations for the use of the speeches: stylistic, historiographic or theological.[3] For example, some have argued that the author uses the speeches to increase the vividness of the narrative.[4] Some have argued that they were a convention of ancient historiography, whether they were actually uttered by the purported speakers or not.[5] Lastly, many, especially recent interpreters, have seen the speeches as a device used by the author to develop his theological ideas.[6] What is clear to me from these explanations is that none of them is adequate to describe what the speeches as a whole are doing, to say nothing of what any individual speech is doing. So far as the speeches as a whole are concerned, it seems that one may well need to combine two or more of the three explanations above, plus possibly developing and adding others. These explanations are not mutually incompatible. Although the majority of criticism in this century has striven hard to show that Acts is a

---

[2] G.H.R. Horsley, "Speeches and Dialogue in Acts," *NTS* 32 (1986) 609–614.

[3] Soards, *Speeches in Acts*, 9–10. See M.A. Powell, *What are They Saying about Acts?* (New York: Paulist, 1991) esp. chaps. 3, 5 and 6.

[4] Horsley, "Speeches and Dialogues," 613.

[5] W.W. Gasque, "The Book of Acts and History," in R.A. Guelich (ed.), *Unity and Diversity in New Testament Theology* (Festschrift G.E. Ladd; Grand Rapids: Eerdmans, 1978) 58–63, among others.

[6] M. Dibelius, *Studies in the Acts of the Apostles* (ed. H. Greeven; trans. M. Ling; London: SCM Press, 1956) 138–185; E. Haenchen, *The Acts of the Apostles: A Commentary* (trans. B. Noble *et al.*; Philadelphia: Westminster Press, 1971 [1965]) *passim*.

theological book, theology is not necessarily incompatible with history (or even "historical narrative," if one wishes to be cautious). Dibelius himself, for example, recognized that speeches were an important part of ancient historiography, even though he believed that those in Acts were not actually uttered by those purported to do so.[7] Recent work in Acts, if it has not proven that Acts is a reliable historical source, has at least shown the plausibility that many accounts in Acts have a basis in the early activities of the Christian church.[8] To be either theologically or historically well-informed does not mean that one cannot be literarily astute. This disjunction does not take into account the perhaps even more important fact that a speech in a given context within the book may require a different analysis altogether regarding its purpose than another, regardless of what one might think regarding the historicity of any of the speeches, or of any of the events one may purport to describe. For example, one might think that Peter's speech before Matthias's selection as a disciple (Acts 1:16–22, 24–25) serves the primarily historiographic purpose of explaining the succession of the apostles, while contending that Peter's speech at Pentecost (2:14–36, 38–40) is primarily theological, explaining belief in the presence of the Holy Spirit. Thus, a far more context-sensitive discussion of the speeches in Acts is needed, one that recognizes that different speeches may serve different purposes, or even that a given speech may serve multiple purposes.

Recent attempts to utilize ancient rhetoric seem *prima facie* to display such an approach.[9] As Soards has recently shown, the speeches readily evidence many of the features of ancient rhetoric. This is understandable for several reasons, including the nature of speech-giving in the Greco-Roman world, and the nature of their delivery before audiences of varying degrees of sympathy. Nevertheless, application of the categories of ancient rhetoric to even the speeches in Acts is not as straightforward as it might appear to be, as I have shown in Chapter Five. However, when it is realized that ancient rhetoric, as well as modern rhetoric, has the primary purpose of persuasion, it

---

[7] See Dibelius, *Studies in the Acts of the Apostles*, 175.

[8] See C. Hemer, *The Book of Acts in the Setting of Hellenistic History* (ed. C. Gempf; WUNT 49; Tübingen: Mohr–Siebeck, 1989; repr. Winona Lake, IN: Eisenbrauns, 1990) *passim*.

[9] See, for example, G.A. Kennedy, *New Testament Interpretation through Rhetorical Criticism* (Chapel Hill: University of North Carolina Press, 1984) 114–140; B.W. Winter, "Official Proceedings and the Forensic Speeches in Acts 24–26," 315–331, and P.E. Satterthwaite, "Acts against the Background of Classical Rhetoric," 337–379, both in B.W. Winter and A.D. Clarke (eds.), *The Book of Acts in its First Century Setting. I. Acts in its Ancient Literary Setting* (Grand Rapids: Eerdmans, 1993); and Soards, *Speeches in Acts*, *passim*.

becomes apparent that the speeches of Acts might well be analyzed as examples of early Christian rhetoric before various audiences, both Jewish and Gentile, Christian and non-Christian. In light of the comments in Chapter Five above, however, the best way to proceed may well be not to start with a thesis regarding the speeches as a whole, but to work in reverse, beginning with the speeches themselves and seeing if there are any common patterns, rhetorical or otherwise, that unite them together. So far as Paul's speeches in Acts are concerned, there are a number of common features that merit investigation.

3. Paul's Missionary Speeches in Acts: An Analysis

Rather than trying to determine the species of each of the speeches by Paul in Acts, I intend to look at them in terms of two basic form-critical categories: missionary and defensive or apologetic speeches.[10] This chapter discusses the missionary speeches. Even though the categories are form-critical, they are also based upon the function and content of the speeches. In looking at each of them, I will be concerned with the argumentative dimension, that is, the elements of the speeches that go towards Paul creating his particular argument, whether it be in terms of evangelization or apologetic. I will begin with these categories, but the analysis itself will suggest the need for further refinement of such categorization.

Before I examine these speeches, however, it is worth noting that there are other speeches of Paul that could be analyzed, but that are not treated here. One worth noting is his farewell speech in Acts 20:18–35 before the Ephesian elders (discussed in Chapter Five).[11] However, for the purposes of this chapter, I am concentrating upon the speeches that have explicit *argumentative* aims, especially here those that are described as concerned with Paul's missionary endeavor (and his defense of his ministry in the chapter that follows). The speech to the Ephesian elders does not resemble these speeches in many ways. For example, there is no formal introduction, but simply an abrupt beginning, since Paul would supposedly have been

---

[10] See, for example, G. Schneider, *Die Apostelgeschichte* (2 vols.; HTKNT 51.1, 2; Freiburg: Herder, 1980, 1982) 1.95–103, with a useful chart on p. 96.

[11] On this speech, among others, see C.J. Hemer, "The Speeches of Acts I. The Ephesian Elders at Miletus," *TynBul* 40 (1989) 77–85; D.F. Watson, "Paul's Speech to the Ephesian Elders (Acts 20.17–38): Epideictic Rhetoric of Farewell," in D.F. Watson (ed.), *Persuasive Artistry: Studies in New Testament Rhetoric in Honor of George A. Kennedy* (JSNTSup 50; Sheffield: JSOT Press, 1991) 184–208.

already well-known to his Christian audience, the only explicit one he addresses in Acts. The speech consists of only a partial recounting of his personal history. After noting important points of their contact with each other (Acts 20:18–21), he turns to the future, describing what he sees as the future course of events for him (vv. 22–26). He then offers them a word of exhortation in light of the fact that he will no longer be able to be with them (vv. 28–32). He concludes regarding his personal standard of morality (vv. 33–35). With the speech finished, his auditors begin to respond to what he has said by kneeling, praying, weeping and grieving. One should not make too much of the differences of this speech from the others, using it alone to form the basis for arguing that the speeches in Acts, although they may agree in language, are not clearly the same in structure and content. However, this does appear to be the case in at least this instance.

A second factor to consider is the similarity in language and style between the speeches, and between the speeches and the rest of Acts.[12] This has been interpreted in various ways, but the overall consistency is conceded by virtually all when discussing the reliability of Acts and the place of the speeches with regard to the rest of the book. One might reasonably have expected (or at least hoped for) wider divergences of language from speech to speech depending upon the orators, if they are actually by the different people concerned. However, this kind of hoped-for divergence is not to be found in any other significant ancient historian who includes speeches, such as Thucydides. One must ask, nevertheless, whether this similarity of style and language precludes the speeches originating with their purported authors. It is commonly acknowledged that the author of Luke–Acts used sources, as he admits in Luke 1:1–4, and as is quantified in traditional explanations of the Synoptic source theories (whether one argues for Markan or Matthean priority!). As noted in Chapter One, even Harnack, who argues for consistent style in Acts admits that, in the Gospel, where it is clear that Luke is dependent upon Mark, introductory καί ("and") is the only evident proof of Luke's dependence, the narrative otherwise having been re-written in Luke's own style (one notes that the "we" passages provide some exception to these

---

[12] On the uniformity of the language of Acts, see A. Harnack, *Luke the Physician: The Author of the Third Gospel and the Acts of the Apostles* (trans. J.R. Wilkinson; London: Williams & Norgate, 2nd edn, 1909) 26–120; H.J. Cadbury, *The Style and Literary Method of Luke* (Cambridge, MA: Harvard University Press, 1920; repr. New York: Klaus, 1969) 1–39. On the similarity in structure of the speeches, now followed by many commentators on the speeches in Acts, see E. Schweizer, "Concerning the Speeches in Acts," in L.E. Keck and J.L. Martyn (eds.), *Studies in Luke–Acts* (Philadelphia: Fortress Press, 1966) 208–216.

statements; see Chapter One).[13] This pattern is consistent with other historians of the ancient world. Common practice was to reshape one's sources, so that the original source was closely conformed to the author's own style.[14] Nevertheless, if distinctions are to be made regarding the authenticity of the speeches of Paul in Acts, that is, whether they were spoken by the historical Paul or written by Luke (to state the opposition boldly), one would need firmer evidence than merely stylistic differences between the speech material and the surrounding narrative in Acts to insist upon authenticity.[15]

According to Schneider,[16] Paul delivers three missionary speeches: (1) Paul's speech at Pisidian Antioch (Acts 13:16–41), (2) the speech of Barnabas and Paul at Lystra (14:15–17), and (3) Paul's speech at the Areopagus (17:22–31). A number of scholars have discussed these missionary speeches, noting that they tend to occur in the first half or so of Acts, with Pauline defensive speeches being found in the second half. The missionary speeches have a number of common characteristics worth noting, in an attempt to get a picture of Paul's argumentative strategy.

a. Paul's Speech at Pisidian Antioch (Acts 13:16–41)

Next to Paul's speech in Athens, this is probably the most widely discussed Pauline speech in Acts, the two major topics of discussion being the use of the Old Testament quotations and its relationship to other speeches, in particular Peter's and Stephen's.[17] This is Paul's first speech in the book of

---

[13] Harnack, *Luke the Physician*, 93.

[14] See M. Hengel, *Between Jesus and Paul* (trans. J. Bowden: London: SCM Press, 1983) 4, 135 n. 17, citing Livy, Dionysius of Halicarnassus, Philo and especially Josephus when he uses the Septuagint, 1 Ezra, *Letter of Aristeas*, and 1 Maccabees.

[15] I have purposely avoided the topic of how Paul's speeches in Acts are to be seen in relation to the speeches of others in Acts, such as Peter.

[16] Schneider, *Die Apostelgeschichte*, 1.96.

[17] See, for example, M.L. Strauss, *The Davidic Messiah in Luke–Acts: The Promise and its Fulfillment in Lukan Christology* (JSNTSup 110; Sheffield: Sheffield Academic Press, 1995) 148–197, for a recent survey of opinion; D.L. Bock, *Proclamation from Prophecy and Pattern: Lucan Old Testament Christology* (JSNTSup 12; Sheffield: JSOT Press, 1987) 240–257; G.J. Steyn, *Septuagint Quotations in the Context of the Petrine and Pauline Speeches of the Acta Apostolorum* (Kampen: Kok Pharos, 1995) 159–202. See also Kennedy, *New Testament Interpretation*, 124–125; Soards, *Speeches in Acts*, 79–88. G. Lüdemann (*Early Christianity according to the Traditions in Acts: A Commentary* [trans. J. Bowden; Minneapolis: Fortress Press, 1987] 153) compares the speech with Jesus' initial speech in Luke 4:16–30.

Acts, and it is addressed to a Jewish-oriented audience, though not one exclusively Jewish in composition.[18]

The circumstance is that Paul and his companions have gone to the synagogue of Pisidian Antioch, and, after the reading of the law and the prophets, and an invitation from the synagogue officials, Paul stands up and addresses the congregation. It cannot be determined whether (if authentic) this is a speech extemporaneously delivered on the occasion or planned in advance, but there is every reason to believe that it may well be the kind of speech that one could have expected from a person who was planning to address a crowd such as this. Several scholars have given rhetorical outlines of the speech,[19] but, although it is represented as a complete speech, it is probably not valid to present such analyses, as if they are all that Paul would have said on the occasion. At best, they would be outlines of the summary that Luke presents, to my mind a questionable focus of rhetorical analysis (see discussion in Chapter Five). Paul begins by standing and making a gesture to his audience (Acts 13:16). Much is made by various commentators of these actions as particular to an orator, but they may well have been common motions for speakers, even those in a synagogue.[20] What is worth noting in Acts, however, is that Peter makes a similar gesture in Acts 12:17, when speaking to a small prayer meeting, and Paul also begins his speech in Acts 26:2–23 before Agrippa with a gesture.

There are four significant parts to this speech: (1) Paul's direct address of his audience, (2) the use of a historical narrative to speak of the actions of God, (3) emphasis upon the promise or good news of salvation, and (4) support for the argument by quotation from the Old Testament.[21]

---

[18] See J. Roloff, *Die Apostelgeschichte* (NTD 5; Berlin: Evangelische Verlags-Anstalt, 1981) 202. Cf. G.W. Hansen, "The Preaching and Defence of Paul," in I.H. Marshall and D. Peterson (eds.), *Witness to the Gospel: The Theology of Acts* (Grand Rapids: Eerdmans, 1998) 297–317, who divides mission speeches to Jews from those to Gentiles, with the result that he has one, the speech in Antioch, in the first category.

[19] See Soards, *Speeches in Acts*, 79–80; cf. R.C. Tannehill, *The Narrative Unity of Luke-Acts: A Literary Interpretation*. II. *The Acts of the Apostles* (FFNT; Minneapolis: Fortress Press, 1990) 165–166, 167 n. 1.

[20] See Haenchen, *Acts*, 408, who notes that Philo describes the synagogue service in terms similar to that of Luke (*Spec. Leg.* 2.61.102). Philo's evidence is worth noting, since the context here is a Diaspora synagogue, not a Palestinian one (cf. Luke 4:20). He is followed by G. Schille, *Die Apostelgeschichte des Lukas* (THNT 5; Berlin: Evangelische Verlags-Anstalt, 1983) 293.

[21] This outline is very similar to that of Kennedy: *proem* (Acts 13:16a), narration (vv. 17–25), proposition (v. 26), and proof (vv. 27–37) (*New Testament Interpretation*, 125). It is also similar to the kind of primitive preaching that Dodd saw in the early part of Acts. See C.H. Dodd, *The Apostolic Preaching and its Developments* (London: Hodder & Stoughton, 1944)

Paul begins by addressing his audience as "Israelite men and those who fear God" (ἄνδρες Ἰσραηλῖται καὶ οἱ φοβούμενοι τὸν θεόν) (Acts 13:16), with a word of admonition for listening ("hear," ἀκούσατε). The phrase "Israelite men" is used here for the fourth of five times in an address in Acts (cf. 2:22; 3:12; 5:35; 21:28, the last not by an apostle), and here is the only time it is linked with the "god-fearers" (on whom, see Chapter Three). These words of address are clearly limited to a Jewish audience, or at least one sympathetic to Judaism, and it is appropriate that they are used in the first part of Acts by the apostles. The last instance is by the crowd, when they think that they have discovered Paul taking a Gentile into the Temple. There is perhaps greater significance than first realized in the linking of "Israelite men" with "god-fearers," an address that includes the Jewish members of his audience, as well as that class of Gentiles who were attracted to and associated with the Jews because of their legal and personal morality, without being willing to be circumcised (cf. v. 43 also, where there is a distinction made between Jews and "god-fearers," though the verb σέβομαι is used here).[22] In Paul's first major speech, he is seen to be creating a bridge in his person, and in his audience, between the Jewish origins and original Jewish audience of the gospel and the subsequent presentation of the gospel to Gentiles by the Apostle to the Gentiles. Similar words of address are repeated in vv. 26 and 38.[23] In v. 26, Paul re-addresses the audience as "men brothers" (ἄνδρες ἀδελφοί), defining them more particularly as "sons of the line of Abraham," and "god-fearers." The phrase "men brothers" is used frequently

---

29–30; cf. M. Dibelius, *From Tradition to Gospel* (trans. B.L. Woolf; London: Nicholson and Weidenfeld, 1934) 16–17. But see F.F. Bruce, "The Speeches in Acts – Thirty Years After," in R. Banks (ed.), *Reconciliation and Hope: New Testament Essays on Atonement and Eschatology Presented to L.L. Morris on his 60th Birthday* (Exeter: Paternoster, 1974) 58, who notes that this schema is not followed in missionary speeches to pagans; and Roloff, *Die Apostelgeschichte*, 202, who outlines the speech as following the pattern: Acts 13:16–25, 26–31, 32–37, 38–41, according to themes and ideas, especially christological ones.

[22] Schneider (*Die Apostelgeschichte*, 2.131) raises the question of whether the "god-fearers" of Acts 13:16 are the same as the "god-fearing proselytes" of v. 43. The phrasing is different, but there seems to be conceptual overlap. See M. Wilcox, "The 'God-Fearers' in Acts – A Reconsideration," *JSNT* 13 (1981) 102–122; C.K. Barrett, *A Critical and Exegetical Commentary on the Acts of the Apostles* (2 vols.; ICC; Edinburgh: T. & T. Clark, 1994–) 1.629–631.

[23] Cf. D. Ellul, "Antioche de Pisidie: Une predication... trois credos? (Actes 13,13–43)," *FN* 5 (1992) 3–14, esp. 6; J.B. Polhill, *Acts* (NAC 26; Nashville: Broadman, 1992) 300; C.H. Talbert, *Reading Acts* (New York: Crossroad, 1997) 129, who use the words of address as a means of conceptually structuring the speech; and F.S. Spencer, *Acts* (Readings; Sheffield: Sheffield Academic Press, 1997) 146, who sees a development in the inclusiveness of the language conveyed by the words of address.

in Acts,[24] as one might expect with such an unspecific phrase (the synagogue officials use it in 13:15 to call upon anyone with a word of exhortation, and Paul uses it again in this speech in 13:38), but the address to those of the line of Abraham is unique to Acts.[25]

Secondly, Paul uses a historical narrative based upon God's actions towards Israel[26] as the major vehicle for making his missionary speech (Acts 13:17–31; cf. 7:2–50, where Stephen also gives a historical summary).[27] As Squires notes, in the historical survey, the syntax itself emphasizes God's role with Israel, with nine of ten indicative verbs indicating God's care for Israel.[28] Because the god-fearers would have congregated at the synagogue, Paul is on good ground for utilization of a historical narrative that appeals directly to Jewish history. The influence of the LXX is pervasive (besides quotation in v. 22),[29] as would have been appropriate for both Jews and god-fearers. He begins by stating that the God of Israel chose these people and made them great in Egypt, and moves forward from that time, recounting the wilderness wandering, conquest, judges, and kings.[30] Throughout, God is seen to have kept his promises to those who fear him. As Soards says, Paul makes a "theologically saturated survey of history, which ended in a christological claim."[31] It was from the kingly line of David that the savior, Jesus, was brought forward by God, proclaimed by John the Baptist, but executed by unaccepting Jews in Jerusalem and raised by God from the dead (he mentions the resurrection several times: vv. 30, 37).[32] Although Soards divides the historical survey into the portion concerned with Israel and that

---

[24] Acts 1:16; 2:29, 37; 7:2; 13:15, 26, 38; 15:7, 13; 22:1; 23:1, 6; 28:17.

[25] Soards (*Speeches in Acts*, 84), perhaps in an effort to emphasize Lukan influence on the speeches in Acts, notes that mention of Abraham is for the seventh and final time in the speeches here, but he fails to note the difference in usage.

[26] Note the phrasing regarding Israel in Acts 13:17–18, 23–24, 26, 31. See Schneider, *Die Apostelgeschichte*, 2.133; Hansen, "Preaching and Defence," 300–301.

[27] Although there are similarities in the speeches in Acts 7 and 13, there are also a number of differences, as shown in J.T. Squires, *The Plan of God in Luke–Acts* (SNTSMS 76; Cambridge: Cambridge University Press, 1993) 70–77; cf. H.-W. Neudorfer, "The Speech of Stephen," in Marshall and Peterson (eds.), *Witness to the Gospel*, 275–294.

[28] Squires, *Plan of God*, 70.

[29] See Haenchen, *Acts*, 408. Examples of clear LXX influence include use of wording such as "the God of Israel."

[30] The major events are found in Genesis, Exodus 6, Deuteronomy 1 and 7, Joshua 14–17, 1 Samuel 7–10, 15–16 and 2 Samuel 7 and 22, according to Soards, *Speeches in Acts*, 82; cf. Schille, *Die Apostelgeschichte*, 293–294.

[31] Soards, *Speeches in Acts*, 83.

[32] Cf. Steyn, *Septuagint Quotations*, 165, who notes the jump from David to Jesus, indicating that a typological equation is probably being made. The resurrection is a common motif in Acts. The same verb, ἐγείρω, is used also in Acts 3:15; 4:10; 5:30; 10:40.

concerned with Jesus, he admits that "in the interpretation of the significance of these events one sees that God is still the overarching, controlling figure whose own divine purposes were accomplished through Jesus."[33]

Thirdly, the historical narrative forms the basis for Paul's proclamation of the good news (Acts 13:32), introduced with the explicitly grammaticalized subject "we" (καὶ ἡμεῖς).[34] Paul only uses the word for "proclaiming good news" (εὐαγγελίζομαι) once in this speech (cf. 14:15), but it is clear that he uses this as a way of drawing his historical narrative to bear upon what he wishes to say about Jesus. He then develops his description of who Jesus is, speaking of him as fulfilment[35] of the promise.

Fourthly, Paul cites a number of scriptural quotations in support of what he has said regarding who Jesus is.[36] These form a kind of proof for his various assertions regarding Jesus. For example, as proof that Jesus is the one raised by God, he cites Ps 2:7 (Acts 13:33);[37] that Jesus is raised from the dead and no longer will decay, he cites Isa 55:3 and Ps 16:10 (vv. 34, 35); and that there is danger in scoffing at what he has said, he cites Hab 1:5 (v. 41).[38] Each of these citations, which essentially follow the LXX in each instance (with some variations), is introduced by some form of specific labeling, such

---

[33] Soards, *Speeches in Acts*, 84; see also Schneider, *Die Apostelgeschichte*, 2.131; U. Wilckens, *Die Missionsreden der Apostelgeschichte: Form- und traditionsgeschichtliche Untersuchungen* (WMANT 5; Neukirchen-Vluyn: Neukirchener, 3rd edn, 1974) 144–150.

[34] Tannehill, *Acts*, 169. Cf. Barrett, *Acts*, 1.644, who takes the use of the pronoun as contrastive.

[35] Soards (*Speeches in Acts*, 86) makes far too much of the fact that ἐκπληρόω occurs only in Acts 13:33, when πληρόω occurs throughout the book.

[36] H.C. Kee (*Good News to the Ends of the Earth: The Theology of Acts* [London: SCM Press; Philadelphia: Trinity Press International, 1990] 14) calls the argument from Scripture here "an amazing synthesis of what might seem to be disparate texts." See also D.P. Moessner, "The 'Script' of the Scriptures in Acts: Suffering as God's 'Plan' (βουλή) for the World for the 'Release of Sins,'" in B. Witherington, III (ed.), *History, Literature and Society in the Book of Acts* (Cambridge: Cambridge University Press, 1996) 233–241, who emphasizes the unifying thread being the will or plan of God.

[37] It is debated whether the use of ἀνίστημι refers to the entire course of Jesus' life or specifically the resurrection. Even if the use of ἀνίστημι in Acts 13:33 refers to raising up Jesus for this purpose, v. 34 uses the same verb in conjunction with ἐκ νεκρῶν, indicating that the resurrection is still in view in the passage. Cf. Schille, *Die Apostelgeschichte*, 296; Bock, *Proclamation*, 244; Hansen, "Preaching and Defense," 302–303.

[38] For thorough, recent discussion, see Steyn, *Septuagint Quotations*, 169–185 on the first two, and 185–194 on the third, where there are a number of interesting variants; and C.A. Evans, "Prophecy and Polemic: Jesus in Luke's Scriptural Apologetic," in C.A. Evans and J.A. Sanders, *Luke and Scripture: The Function of Sacred Tradition in Luke–Acts* (Minneapolis: Fortress Press, 1993) 202–205. See also E. Schweizer, "The Concept of the Davidic 'Son of God' in Acts and its Old Testament Background," in Keck and Martyn (eds.), *Studies in Luke–Acts*, 186–193.

as a statement that it is a Psalm or comes from the prophets or "is stated" (using the perfect tense, a form often used in the New Testament to introduce quotations).[39] The quotations emphasize that the covenant of David is fulfilled in Jesus,[40] already suggested in vv. 32–33.

Paul's speech ends abruptly but is greeted with a warm response, with people begging that they might speak of these things on the next Sabbath.[41] Soards wishes to include Acts 13:46–47 in this speech of Paul,[42] but most scholars do not. There are reasonable grounds for excluding them from the speech, since the following words are said to have been given on the next Sabbath, when the city assembled again to hear God's word. Even though the Jews were jealous of the success that Paul had in his first speech, and consequently tried to contradict him, the author says that the Gentiles rejoiced.

b. The Speech of Barnabas and Paul at Lystra (Acts 14:15–17)

Paul and Barnabas came to Lystra, and Paul performed a miracle of healing a man who had been lame from birth. When the crowd saw this, they began to proclaim that the gods had become like men and had come down to them. They called Barnabas Zeus and Paul Hermes, possibly influenced by the myth of a man named Philemon and his wife, Baucis, Phrygians who gave hospitality to Zeus and Hermes, when they tested the piety of humanity, disguised. Philemon and Baucis, told by the gods to climb a mountain, were saved from being drowned by an ensuing flood.[43] This place in Asia Minor

---

[39] See S.E. Porter, *Verbal Aspect in the Greek of the New Testament, with Reference to Tense and Mood* (SBG 1; New York: Lang, 1989) 269 and n. 16.

[40] Steyn, *Septuagint Quotations*, 179–180; contra P. Bolt, "Mission and Witness," in Marshall and Peterson (eds.), *Witness to the Gospel*, 205.

[41] Contra Barrett, *Acts*, 1.653, who believes that the response in Acts 13:42 ff. is Luke's creation.

[42] Soards, *Speeches in Acts*, 80, 87–88.

[43] See Ovid, *Met.* 8.611–725, summarized in B.W. Winter, "In Public and in Private: Early Christian Interactions with Religious Pluralism," in A.D. Clarke and B.W. Winter (eds.), *One God, One Lord in a World of Religious Pluralism* (Cambridge: Tyndale House, 1991) 116; cf. also C. Breytenbach, "Zeus und der lebendige Gott: Anmerkungen zu Apostelgeschichte 14.11–17," *NTS* 39 (1993) 404–407; L.H. Martin, "Gods or Ambassadors of God? Barnabas and Paul in Lystra," *NTS* 41 (1995) 152–156; G.W. Hansen, "Galatia," in D.W.J. Gill and C. Gempf (eds.), *The Book of Acts in its First Century Setting. II. The Book of Acts in its Graeco-Roman Setting* (Grand Rapids: Eerdmans, 1994) 392–395. On Zeus and Hermes within the Greek pantheon, see M.P. Nilsson, *Geschichte der griechischen Religion. I. Bis zur griechischen Welthenschaft* (Munich: Beck, 1941) 364–400 and 471–480; W.K.C. Guthrie, *The Greeks and their Gods* (Boston: Beacon, 1950) 87–94; W. Burkert, *Greek Religion* (Cambridge, MA: Harvard University Press, 1985) 156–159.

apparently still followed the Greek pantheon, as also witnessed by their having a priest of Zeus, probably with a temple outside of the city. The fact that the inhabitants are described as speaking in the Lycaonian dialect may also indicate that they conservatively followed and preserved certain linguistic and other traditions.[44] The Lystrans wished to worship Barnabas and Paul, who tried to persuade them otherwise. This missionary speech is said to be given by both Paul and Barnabas. In light of the fact that the brief speech is a reaction to the people of Lystra wishing to worship Barnabas and Paul as Zeus and Hermes, and since Hermes is the messenger god, it is not unreasonable to attribute the speech to Paul, if assignment must be made.[45] This is strengthened by the fact that nowhere in Acts do we have another speech of Barnabas recorded.

This speech of Paul and Barnabas is addressed to a Gentile audience. It is important to keep in mind, however, that this is not the same kind of speech as the first in Pisidian Antioch, where Paul is speaking on a formal occasion in a synagogue. In fact, the speech may be better analyzed as not a speech at all, if it were not for several factors.[46] The first is that what is said is surprisingly consonant with other speeches by Paul in Acts, as will become evident. The second is that, although the circumstances that warrant the speech are unusual, to say the least, this was not the first time that Paul and Barnabas had been in Gentile cities on their missionary journey. During this journey, they had already encountered a variety of unusual circumstances (cf. Acts 14:5–6), giving credence to the idea that, in this kind of a situation, reasoned words might have been expected, even if the circumstances were unreasonable.[47] If the words are not those of Paul, but those of the author only, it is still significant to note that he has put into Paul's mouth words that are consistent with Paul's other missionary speeches.

---

[44] On this dialect as one of the Greek dialects of Asia Minor, see C. Brixhe, *Essai sur le grec anatolien au début de notre ère* (Travaux et mémoires: Études anciennes 1; Nancy: Presses universitaires, 1987) *passim*; cf. C. Consani, "La koiné et les dialectes grecs dans la documentation linguistique et la réflexion métalinguistique des premiers siècles de notre ère," in C. Brixhe (ed.), *La koiné grecque antique: Une langue introuvable? I* (Travaux et mémoires: Études anciennes 10; Nancy: Presses universitaires, 1993) esp. 32–33.

[45] Secondary literature on this speech is surprisingly sparse, probably because the speech is so short and is not given in the rhetorical circumstances that one might expect. Paul is quoted as using the plural, clearly with reference to himself and Barnabas. See R. Pesch, *Die Apostelgeschichte* (2 vols.; EKK 5.1, 2; Solothurn: Benziger; Neukirchen-Vluyn: Neukirchener, 1995 [2nd edn], 1986) 2.58.

[46] See Schille, *Die Apostelgeschichte*, 306, who clearly views it as a Lukan creation for the context.

[47] In this regard it is surprising that Kennedy does not treat this speech in his analysis.

There are four major features of this speech worth noting: (1) words of
direct address to the audience, (2) an appeal to the commonalty of human
nature, (3) mention of the gospel, and (4) the use of a form of natural
theology based upon nature having been created by God.[48] In light of the
shortness of the speech, each of these features is much shorter than in the first
missionary speech.

First, in the haste of the situation, Paul does not develop or modify his
reference to his audience as simply "men" (ἄνδρες) (Acts 14:15). Although
the word "men" is used elsewhere in Acts as a word of address, it is only used
by Paul here and in 27:10, 21, 25, under pressure of shipwreck. So far as Paul
is concerned, it appears that he uses it because of the haste required in the
situation. It is also true that this is a more appropriate form of address for his
Gentile audience, a group with which, at least by race and religion, he does
not have the same kinds of bonds as he does with the Jews.

Secondly, after his direct address of his audience, Paul's first major point
is introduced by means of a question – "why are you doing these things?"
(Acts 14:15; phrasing similar to Luke 16:2 and Demosthenes 55.5). He
answers his rhetorical question by emphatically stating that we all (καὶ ἡμεῖς)
are humans of the same nature. His address of them as "men" suitably
indicates that Paul sees them all – Paul, Barnabas and the Lystrans – as
having the same human nature. The element of creation will be noted further
below, but here appeal to a common human nature points to a common
conception of humanity, with common origins, common destiny, and
common functions. This commonalty is to be seen in distinction to those who
would appeal to one race or group of people as manifesting a particular kind
of character, perhaps because of a special or different origin or destiny, thus
placing them above or superior to another group. Even though his audience
consists of Gentiles, the line of division here is not between Jews and
Gentiles but between humans and those thought to be gods. This would
perhaps have been a significant admission on Paul's part because of his being
Jewish, and his belief (admittedly known from the letters) that the Jewish
people occupied (or, at least, had occupied at one time and would occupy
again) a special purpose in the plan of God (Romans 9–11). In any case, Paul
attempts to erase any such distinctions, and places all of humanity on
common ground.

Thirdly, Paul invokes the preaching of the gospel as the purpose of their
visit (Acts 14:15). His command to turn away from foolish things, apparently

---

[48] See the outline of Soards, *Speeches in Acts*, 88, which resembles more a contemporary
sermon outline.

meaning idolatry, and to turn to the living God is found in a variety of Hellenistic Jewish apologetic literature, and reflects LXX language.[49] The vain things are not actually specifically defined here, but seem to be referring to all of the practices involved in the worship of the Greek pantheon, no doubt involving the kinds of superstitions and gullibility that would lead them to proclaim Paul and Barnabas to be gods on the basis of a single event, their quickness in getting the priest of Zeus into the affair, and their corporate willingness to bring animals to offer sacrifice, all with a huge crowd of thoroughly convinced people. For Paul, these practices can only be described as vain things. The sentiment to worship may be right, but the object is clearly wrong. In his juxtaposition of the vain rituals and assertion regarding the living God, Paul makes the transition from looking at natural phenomena as an indication of the non-existence of other divine beings to looking at the common nature of humanity, including its desire to worship, as pointing to the existence of a real and living God.

Would this particularly Jewish and Christian view of God have been understandable to a Gentile audience,[50] if Paul had actually delivered these words or ones resembling them? The monotheistic language may well be addressed directly at a belief in Zeus as the creator God, reflecting beliefs held in southern Asia minor at the time, and reflected in the way Paul and Barnabas were met by the Lystrans.[51] This approach would have served as a useful means of directly addressing the Lystrans in an attempt to steer their belief toward God. As Rackham states, Paul "uses the method of accommodation. He starts with a doctrine they would readily accept – creation by God; he appeals to that evidence which would be most obvious to country folk – the witness of nature; and he makes use of their present state of feeling – the gladness and joy of a festival."[52] Furthermore, Paul is recorded as using very similar language regarding the "living God" in 1 Thess 1:9, to a church probably of mixed Jewish and Gentile composition.[53] As a way of defining who this living God is, in Acts Paul cites an Old Testament passage from the LXX, Exod 20:11 (but cf. Gen 1:1 and Ps 145:6 LXX, which have

---

[49] See L.T. Johnson, *The Acts of the Apostles* (SP 5; Collegeville, MN: Liturgical, 1992) 249, for references.

[50] See K. Lake and H.J. Cadbury, *The Beginnings of Christianity*. Part I. *The Acts of the Apostles*. IV. *English Translation and Commentary* (ed. F.J. Foakes Jackson and K. Lake; London: Macmillan, 1933) 166.

[51] See Breytenbach, "Zeus und der lebendige Gott," 396–413.

[52] R.B. Rackham, *The Acts of the Apostles: An Exposition* (London: Methuen, 8th edn, 1919) 233.

[53] On the common features of 1 Thess 1:9–10 and Acts 14:15–17, as well as Acts 17:22–31, see Wilckens, *Die Missionsreden der Apostelgeschichte*, 81–91.

similar echoes), although it is not introduced by any words of citation. The passage is simply incorporated into the wording that Paul uses, and therefore does not constitute an appeal to Old Testament authority as much as a means of explicating this God in opposition to other gods, whether that be "a living god" as opposed to "the non-existent gods of the heavens,"[54] or "the living god" as opposed to those who are not gods.[55]

Fourthly, instead of the invocation of scriptural citations in defense of his position, in this speech Paul appeals to a form of natural theology (see below for a comparison of this speech, the Areopagus speech of Acts 17:22–31, and Rom 1:18–32 on natural theology).[56] In fact, the Old Testament citation noted above forms a part of this appeal to natural theology, because Paul designates who God is in terms of his creative role. In that sense, natural theology is ultimately made clear and explained by means of direct divine revelation, such as early Christians saw in Scripture. The definition of God in terms of the language of Scripture might well indicate that, for the Paul of Acts at least, natural theology has its basis in the God of Scripture. For those who do not recognize such a verbal similarity, the point is still much the same, however. In this instance, the common human nature is explicitly justified in terms of one creating God. The living character of this God is defined in terms of a creative function, one that is all inclusive. This includes the expanse of the known universe, with heaven and earth providing the extremities of this physical creative act. It includes more than simply the realm of habitation, however, since Paul specifies that it is not only these realms, but all of the things in them that God has created, as well. He is the one who made the heaven and the earth and all in it; he is the one who permitted humanity to go its own way; yet he did not leave himself without witness (ἀμάρτυρον is a New Testament *hapax legomenon*), an instance of poignant litotes.[57]

Paul here provides a brief recapitulation of the course of human history. This has included a permissive will of God, which has allowed for various human groups to be able to live their lives as they willed. There are a number of features here that figure into Paul's explication of natural theology. One is

---

[54] T.E. Page, *Acts of the Apostles* (London: Macmillan, 1886) 172.

[55] Haenchen, *Acts*, 428. The concept of the living God is one known to both Greek and Jewish thought. See discussion of Acts 17:22–31 below.

[56] By way of a rough definition, natural theology may be described as drawing upon elements of the natural world, in its various forms, as a means of revealing something about the nature, character, actions, purposes or intentions of God. On this passage, see Polhill, *Acts*, 316–317.

[57] Schneider, *Die Apostelgeschichte*, 2.161.

the multifarious character of humankind. ἔθνη, the word used here, refers to various nationalistic or racial groups, each permitted in the past to develop on its own. When Paul says that God permitted them to go their own way (Acts 14:16), it is not clear whether he is saying that the ethnic groups were allowed to find their own places of habitation, or that they were allowed to define the terms in which they lived.

During this time, in which nations were permitted to develop on their own, Paul says, God was not without a specific witness. Here Paul directly appeals to a form of natural theology, that is, he refers to the natural phenomena in terms of the cycles and patterns of the natural world. Paul says that there were rains from heaven and fruitful seasons, and the result was that people, because they were able to live by having food, were full and glad (a series of participial phrases conveys this in Acts 14:17). Of course, he does not mean that every person was happy during this time, but that basic provisions for life were made possible through nature, because God had set up this system in nature. For this, Paul says that it is appropriate to characterize God as doing good.

In sum, there are three clear elements to Paul's explication of God from nature (each with parallels in Paul's speech in Acts 17 – see below in this chapter): reference to God's role in the destiny of nations, their ignorance, and God's not being without witness through nature.[58] With the speech complete,[59] the narrative states that Paul was only just successful in convincing the crowd not to offer sacrifices to them.

c. Paul's Speech on the Areopagus in Athens (Acts 17:22–31)

This is certainly the best known of Paul's speeches in Acts, and one that has generated a number of analyses and interpretations (see Chapter Five for an analysis in terms of its rhetorical dimensions).[60] Schneider categorizes the

---

[58] See Soards, *Speeches in Acts*, 89–90; Schille, *Die Apostelgeschichte*, 307.

[59] Contra Polhill, *Acts*, 317, who believes that Paul and Barnabas were cut short, because the theology is incomplete, such as leaving out reference to Christ. A theological agenda seems to be influencing Polhill's exegesis at this point.

[60] A sample of the most important secondary literature (excluding commentaries) includes Dibelius, *Studies in the Acts of the Apostles*, 26–83; E. Norden, *Agnostos Theos: Untersuchungen zur Formengeschichte Religiöser Rede* (Stuttgart: Teubner, 1913; repr. Darmstadt: Wissenschaftliche Buchgesellschaft, 1956) 1–124; B. Gärtner, *The Areopagus Speech and Natural Revelation* (trans. C.H. King; ASNU 21; Uppsala: Gleerup, 1955); P. Schubert, "The Place of the Areopagus Speech in the Composition of Acts," in J.C. Rylaarsdam (ed.), *Transitions in Biblical Scholarship* (Chicago: University of Chicago Press, 1968) 235–261; H. Conzelmann, "The Address of Paul on the Areopagus," in Keck and Martyn (eds.), *Studies in Luke–Acts*, 217–230; N.B. Stonehouse, *Paul before the Areopagus*

Areopagus speech as a missionary speech before Gentiles,[61] but not all scholars agree that this is what is occurring in this incident, and "its literary significance has not been equally appreciated."[62] Several interpreters have noticed that Paul begins his discussions in Athens by reasoning in the synagogue with the Jews and god-fearers, and in the market place with whoever happened to be there. This would have included the Stoics and Epicureans. As a result of his discussions with the philosophers, on one occasion he is taken to the Areopagus, in response to the question that they desire to know about his new teaching, which sounds strange to their ears. It is in this setting (not that of the synagogue) that Paul makes his speech.[63] But what exactly is the context? On the one hand, there is a distinct missionary feel about the situation, in that the philosophers are responding to the discussions that Paul has previously had in the market place. The narrative in Acts states that Paul first spent some time noticing their various religious monuments, which provoked him to discussion. This would not have required that Paul be taken to the Areopagus to be examined, however. On the other hand, therefore, some have claimed that Paul is actually undergoing a form of trial, or at least a preliminary hearing, before the leading people of the city, to determine if he is perhaps disseminating some form of subversive doctrine. In this case, the question that is asked of Paul may be more of an informal charge.[64] One cannot help but notice that it is a charge that in some ways resembles that brought against Socrates in the same city almost 450 years before.[65] It is difficult to know the full extent of the context, since so little information is given. Dionysius, one of the converts on the occasion of Paul's speech, is called an Areopagite, perhaps conveying that he had a position of responsibility in the proceedings. In most other trial scenes, however, Luke

---

and Other New Testament Studies (London: Tyndale, 1957) 1–40; C.J. Hemer, "The Speeches of Acts: II. The Areopagus Address," *TynBul* 40.2 (1989) 239–259; D.L. Balch, "The Areopagus Speech: An Appeal to the Stoic Historian Posidonius against Later Stoics and the Epicureans," 52–79, and J.H. Neyrey, "Acts 17, Epicureans, and Theodicy: A Study in Stereotypes," 118–134, both in D.L. Balch, E. Ferguson and W.A. Meeks (eds.), *Greeks, Romans, and Christians: Essays in Honor of Abraham J. Malherbe* (Minneapolis: Fortress Press, 1990).

[61] Schneider, *Die Apostelgeschichte*, 1.96.

[62] Squires, *Plan of God*, 71. See Schille, *Die Apostelgeschichte*, 360–361, for a survey of opinion on the origin of this speech.

[63] As Schille (*Die Apostelgeschichte*, 354) reminds us.

[64] See, for example, Kennedy, *New Testament Interpretation*, 129–130; T.D. Barnes, "An Apostle on Trial," *JTS* 20 (1969) 407–419; contra B.W. Winter, "On Introducing Gods to Athens: An Alternative Reading of Acts 17:18–20," *TynBul* 47.1 (1996) esp. 79–80, 90.

[65] See Haenchen, *Acts*, 518; cf. K.O. Sandnes, "Paul and Socrates: The Aim of Paul's Areopagus Speech," *JSNT* 50 (1993) 20–24; and Hansen, "Preaching and Defense," 310.

leaves no ambiguity regarding the nature of the enquiry.[66] If this is a form of legal hearing, Paul's speech takes on a different cast. It is no longer simply a call to repentance, but it becomes a form of defense of himself and his message. Noteworthy in this regard is the importance of the resurrection in his speech, as discussed below and in terms of the speeches of defense in the next section.

There are three features of this speech of significance for this discussion: (1) Paul's words of direct address of his audience, (2) an appeal to a form of natural theology in which the known God is defined, and (3) mention of the resurrection.

First, standing in their midst (a posture used elsewhere by Paul and by others in Acts), Paul addresses his audience as "Athenian men" (ἄνδρες 'Αθηναῖοι) (Acts 17:22). This is consonant with his speeches elsewhere, in which he often specifies his audience. Nevertheless, Kennedy has drawn attention to the fact that this may well have been an improper word of address in light of the circumstances. Instead of "Athenian men," Paul perhaps should have addressed them as "gentlemen."[67] It is unclear what bearing this has on the account in terms of its authorship, since the author of Acts may have recorded what he knew to be true just as much as he may have conformed the word of address to many of Paul's other speeches. Nevertheless, Paul does address his audience with a specific title, perhaps warranted on the basis of his having discussed with them previously and established a certain degree of familiarity.

Secondly, Paul appeals to his audience's "religiousness" (not "superstition") as a way of invoking a form of natural theology (Acts 17:22–29). The word that is used, δεισιδαιμονεστέρους, can be translated in a number of different ways.[68] In light of Paul's desire at this point to capture the interest and solicit the favor of his audience, it is unlikely that Paul is using the word pejoratively here, as one would use the word "superstitious"

---

[66] See Haenchen, *Acts*, 518–519. Debate over whether this speech is Greco-Roman in orientation (e.g. Dibelius, *Studies in the Acts of the Apostles*, 26–77 *passim*) or a Hellenistic Jewish apologetic (e.g. Gärtner, *Areopagus Speech*, 248–252) is to a large extent unnecessary due to the nature of the Hellenistic world of which Judaism was a part. See M. Hengel, *Judaism and Hellenism* (trans. J. Bowden; Philadelphia: Fortress Press, 1974) *passim*; *idem*, *The 'Hellenization' of Judaea in the First Century after Christ* (trans. J. Bowden; London: SCM Press, 1989), who describes the nature of this world; and D. Mendels, "Pagan or Jewish? The Presentation of Paul's Mission in the Book of Acts," in his *Identity, Religion and Historiography: Studies in Hellenistic History* (JSPSup 24; Sheffield: Sheffield Academic Press, 1998) 394–419.

[67] Kennedy, *New Testament Interpretation*, 130.

[68] See BAGD, s.v. δεισιδαίμων; and Theophrastus, *Character* 16: Δεισιδαιμονίας.

to describe people who have a simple-minded or gullible view of the supernatural. This introduction is a form of *captatio benevolentiae*,[69] designed to curry their favor and find a common ground for discussion, even if, as some have suggested, it may have alienated some of the Epicurean elements of his audience.[70] Instead, he is probably wishing to say, even if partly tongue-in-cheek in light of what he goes on to say, that he recognizes that they have a preoccupation with things related to the gods (a well-known trait of the Athenians; see Sophocles, *Oed. Col.* 260; Josephus, *Apion* 2.130). He supports this by noting that, in his travels around the city, he had noted their numerous objects of worship, which undoubtedly would have included both the large number of spectacular altars and temples erected to various deities, many of them located on the Acropolis of Athens, and numerous private and personal shrines, monuments and altars. He notes as an example an altar dedicated "to an unknown god" (ἀγνώστῳ θεῷ),[71] and bluntly states that he can proclaim that unknown god to them. Despite not having found an altar with this very inscription on it (the singular use of the noun, in a dative phrase), the fact that a number of ancient authors speak of altars to unknown gods in and around Athens shows that the speech, if not completely historically accurate, is at least placed in the right religious and grammatical context to provide clear and compelling parallels.[72] Paul's comments indicate

---

[69] The *captatio benevolentiae* was the part of a speech designed, at the outset, to capture the goodwill of the audience, and thus find a point of contact from which to proceed. See B.W. Winter, "The Importance of the *Captatio Beneuolentiae* in the Speeches of Tertullus and Paul in Acts 24:1–21," *JTS* 42 (1991) 507–515.

[70] Conzelmann, *Die Apostelgeschichte*, 97; Johnson, *Acts*, 314; cf. D. Zweck, "The Exordium of the Areopagus Speech, Acts 17.22–23," *NTS* 35 (1989) 94–103; contra B. Witherington, III, *The Acts of the Apostles: A Socio-Rhetorical Commentary* (Grand Rapids: Eerdmans, 1998) 520.

[71] See Schille, *Die Apostelgeschichte*, 356.

[72] See Pausanias 1.4.1; 5.14.8; Philostratus, *Apol. Tyana* 6.3.5; cf. Diogenes Laertius 1.110. For recent inscriptions, see P.W. van der Horst, "The Altar of the 'Unknown God' in Athens (Acts 17:23) and the Cult of 'Unknown Gods' in the Graeco-Roman World," repr. from *ANRW* 2.18.2 (Berlin: de Gruyter, 1989) 1426–1456 in his *Hellenism – Judaism – Christianity: Essays on their Interaction* (Leuven: Peeters, 2nd edn, 1994) 187–220, who makes a very plausible case for the accuracy of Luke's language, as well as suggesting that the reference may be to the God of the Jews (contra Haenchen, *Acts*, 521 n. 2; Schille, *Die Apostelgeschichte*, 356, who takes the reference as merely literary). Winter ("Introducing Gods," 84) notes that singular and plural are often interchangeable in Greek discussion of god/s. See also Winter, "In Public and in Private," 118–119, for examples, such as Cleanthes's *Hymn to Zeus* 1–7 and Diogenes Laertius 7.119. On the appropriateness of Paul's words, especially to a Stoic audience, but less so to an Epicurean one, see Balch, "Areopagus Speech," esp. 54–79; Neyrey, "Acts 17, Epicureans, and Theodicy," 122–129. The points of similarity include providence in nature and history, and opposition to images of deity. The

that he takes this as confirmation of the religious nature of the Athenians. In other words, what Paul says is that he recognizes in the Athenians a common interest in the divine. It is not limited to that which they consciously know and recognize, but they are also interested in the realm of the divine that they have not been able to discover yet. They have ensured that they have done what is appropriate to that unknown realm by erecting an altar to such a god.[73]

Many commentators in the past have drawn attention to what are often labeled as superficial similarities between Rom 1:18–32 and the speeches in especially Acts 17:22–31 and 14:15–17.[74] The general tenor of much recent discussion, especially in light of the kinds of distinctions drawn between the Paul of Acts and the Paul of the letters (see Chapter Nine), is to find little or no connection between the Acts material and that in Romans. In other words, fine distinctions are often drawn that purport to show that, for example, if there is natural theology to be found in Romans, it is sufficiently different to point away from a relationship between the material in Acts and Romans.[75] Before any conclusions are drawn, however, an examination of the evidence must be undertaken. Despite what is sometimes asserted, there are, in fact, a number of features of natural theology to be found in Rom 1:18–32,[76] discussed here in terms of their relationship with the material in Acts 17:22–31, along with Acts 14:15–17.

In structuring his argument, Paul in Romans does not present the individual elements of that argument in the same order as seems to be found

---

concept of a living God is known in Stoic thought (see Plutarch, *Mor.* 1034B; cf. Seneca, *Div. Inst.* 6.25). The classic survey of the evidence remains Norden, *Agnostos Theos*, 31–124.

[73] The theme of knowing/unknowing (ignorance) is important throughout the speech. See Witherington, *Acts*, 524.

[74] See Witherington, *Acts*, 425–426, 511, for a recent advocate.

[75] See, for example, E. Käsemann, *Commentary on Romans* (trans. G.W. Bromiley; Grand Rapids: Eerdmans, 1980) 39–41, who finds natural theology in tension with Paul's theology; Roloff, *Die Apostelgeschichte*, 267–268, who cites three major areas of difference between the Paul of the letters and of Acts: the possibility of knowing God through nature, whether humans understand the wrath of God and their blameworthiness, and the roles of justification and reconciliation, versus resurrection.

[76] Among those who see Paul developing some form of natural theology in this passage, see, for example, O. Kuss, *Die Briefe an die Römer, Korinther und Galater* (Das Neue Testament 6; Regensburg: Pustet, 1940) 28; M. Black, *Romans* (NCB; Grand Rapids: Eerdmans, 1973) 49; J.D.G. Dunn, *Romans* (2 vols.; WBC 38A, B; Waco, TX: Word, 1988) 1.56–57; J.A. Fitzmyer, *Romans* (AB 33; New York: Doubleday, 1993) 273; D.J. Moo, *The Epistle to the Romans* (NICNT; Grand Rapids: Eerdmans, 1996) 97. For noting of verbal parallels between Acts 17:22–31 and the Pauline letters, see F. Blass, *Acta apostolorum sive Lucae ad Theophilum liber alter* (Göttingen: Vandenhoeck & Ruprecht, 1895) 191–194.

in Acts 14:15–17 or 17:22–31. In Rom 1:19, he states that knowledge about God is plain and evident within human beings (Jews and Gentiles alike, although with an emphasis on Gentiles),[77] for the simple reason that God has made it evident to them.[78] Thus, Paul begins in Romans with his conclusion, which he proceeds to clarify in the following verses. What Paul means exactly by knowledge of God being "plain" and what it means for this knowledge to be "in them" is not stated here,[79] and not fully clarified in what follows, especially in light of Paul's negative attitude regarding human redemption. All Paul says regarding knowledge of God being plain is that God made it plain. Does "in them" mean located physically, mentally, psychologically, or what? Does it mean in each individual, or in the corporate sense (hence the possible rendering "among them")? Paul tends to use the plural in this passage, so it is possible that he has a corporate sense of knowledge, in which each individual would not necessarily have the same knowledge. This would be consistent with the discussion of racial and ethnic distinctions made in Acts 14 and 17.

In Rom 1:18, as a means of providing the context for his statements about what can be known of God through nature, Paul states that the wrath of God is being revealed against all ungodliness and unrighteousness of humanity. Whereas, in Acts 17, Paul does not introduce the idea of judgment until he is well into his speech (and just before he is interrupted, as explained above), here he introduces God's judgment right at the beginning. Nevertheless, the concept is more than passingly similar, that is, that God holds humanity responsible for the knowledge that has been given to it, such that God, according to Paul, seems to be well within his rights as God (his role as creator in Romans 1 is discussed below) to punish humans for failing to uphold these standards of righteousness. Here, in Rom 1:18, Paul explicates, in a way that he does not in Acts 17, what the relationship is between human unrighteousness and divine judgment. At the outset, it is said that humans suppress the truth in or by (ἐν) unrighteousness. There is a sense that their unrighteousness is, in some way, involved with restraining or holding down their access to knowledge of God. Then, in Rom 1:21–23, Paul, by means of several sets of useful parallels (note the use of the verbs with the prefixed

---

[77] F.J. Leenhardt, *L'épître de Saint Paul aux Romains* (CNT 6; Geneva: Labor et Fides, 3rd edn, 1995) 35; L.L. Morris, *The Epistle to the Romans* (Grand Rapids: Eerdmans, 1988) 74. See Moo, *Romans*, 96–97, on recent discussion of the audience addressed in these verses.

[78] See Fitzmyer, *Romans*, 273; contra Moo, *Romans*, 99, who seems to contradict his position on natural theology by his assertion that the capacity to access God through natural human capacities is excluded.

[79] On complexities with the rest of the syntax, see Moo, *Romans*, 104.

preposition παρά), explains the cause of human sinfulness, painting a bleak picture of it. This sinfulness seems to function on two levels. There is a marked contrast between humanity's knowledge of God (see below) and their failure to honor or give thanks. One senses that failure in these regards is the direct cause of futile human speculation and a darkened, ignorant, or foolish heart. Further, there is the substitution of divine glory for various manufactured images – as in Acts 17, Paul invokes images of the kinds of figures made for human worship, here not discussing the materials out of which they are made, but the shapes that they take (humans, birds, animals and reptiles). The point regarding human sinfulness is essentially the same.

In Rom 1:20, Paul speaks in terms of God as creator, using language familiar to Stoic thought.[80] He does not offer the same amount of detail as is presented in Acts 14 or 17, but he marks the creation of the world as the starting point for God's characteristics to be present in nature. He also speaks of the world in which this knowledge is manifested as a "made" or created world. Paul draws a similar distinction between the creator and the creature, through an exposition of the means by which knowledge of the former is made known in the latter, and by a play on the concept of "seeing" the "unseen." Paul specifies three characteristics that distinguish the knowledge of God in the created order, and these include invisible attributes, eternal power, and divine nature. He says (oxymoronically) that they have been "clearly seen or perceived" (καθορᾶται).[81] These things are seen, not through physical means, such as sight, however, but are understood through what has been made. In other words, humans have a responsibility for deducing from the surrounding phenomena. This phrasing is intriguing, but is understandable if seen in relation to the need to differentiate the creator from the created order. The characteristics of God perceived in nature are not to be equated with nature, and they are not part of nature such that they can be perceived without an intelligible act of understanding.

Some say that, whereas in Acts 17 the words of Paul have an optimistic slant, allowing for human groping after and finding God, here in Romans 1 there is only despair, caused by God giving humans over to their impure desires. These desires are inclusive, encompassing physical degradation and a depraved mind, something Paul develops here in detail over a number of

---

[80] See Dunn, *Romans*, 1.57, who cites, for example, Pseudo-Aristotle, *De Mundo* 399b.14 ff.; Plutarch, *Mor.* 398A, 665A.

[81] See M.-J. Lagrange, *Saint Paul épître aux Romains* (ÉB; Paris: Gabalda, 1950) 23; contra Käsemann, *Romans*, 40.

verses, including the use of a vice list (Rom 1:29–31).[82] The situation in Acts 17 is not nearly so optimistic as some have thought, however, since the protasis of a fourth-class conditional structure is used, with the optative, the most condition-laden Greek mood form, being used in v. 27.[83] In fact, in some ways the situation in Acts 17 is more frustrating, because God is said to be very near to those who are groping after him, though with little reasonable chance of their finding him. The situation is equally desperate in Romans 1.[84]

This analysis, I think, shows that – despite differences in order and emphasis – there is much in common among the accounts in Acts 14:15–17, Acts 17:22–31 and Rom 1:18–32 with regard to natural theology.[85] The common elements are the recognition of the creator God and his creation, that the creation includes humans but is not to be equated with it, that humans have various ways of trying to reach God through human-made means, that these humans are accountable to God and are to be judged on this knowledge that they have of him, that humans have neglected the knowledge that they have of God, that human attempts to reach God are not hopeful, and that God has until this point not judged them as he is now prepared to do. Not each of these is emphasized or developed in the same way in each passage (especially Acts 14:15–17, which is significantly shorter), but the common pattern is clear.

The third feature of Paul's speech in Acts 17 is his mention of the resurrection. In Paul's argument in Acts, proof for Paul of the appointment of this man as the worthy judge of humanity is his having been raised from the dead (Acts 17:30–31). At the mention of the resurrection, Paul's audience reacts strongly. Some are entirely dismissive, others say that they will hear

---

[82] See L.T. Johnson, *Reading Romans* (New York: Crossroad, 1997) 35, who cites Philo, *Sacr.* 2, who has a vice list of 140 elements. On virtue and vice lists, see D.L. Balch, *Let Wives Be Submissive: The Domestic Code in I Peter* (SBLMS 26; Atlanta: Scholars Press, 1981) 21–80; J.D. Charles, *Virtue amidst Vice: The Catalog of Virtues in 2 Peter 1* (JSNTSup 150; Sheffield: Sheffield Academic Press, 1997) 99–127.

[83] See S.E. Porter, *Idioms of the Greek New Testament* (BLG 2; Sheffield: JSOT Press, 2nd edn, 1994) 263–264.

[84] Often overlooked in any treatment of possible natural theology in Romans 1 is that there may be further appeal to general revelation by Paul in other places in Romans 1–3. In fact, the evidence is that the use of natural theology is fundamental to laying the foundation for what Paul wishes to say in Romans. For example, in Rom 2:14–15 (see Moo, *Romans*, 148–153), Paul says that the moral nature is a point of contact between God and humanity, such that God reveals himself to humanity through conscience. As a result, all humans, Jews and Gentiles, are incapable of salvation on their own merits but stand condemned before God (e.g. Rom 3:9); in Rom 3:25 (Stonehouse, *Paul before the Areopagus*, 21), Paul speaks of the passing over of sins because of God's patience.

[85] See also F.F. Bruce, *Romans* (TNTC; Grand Rapids: Eerdmans, 2nd edn, 1985) 78.

Paul on this topic at another time, possibly indicating a more polite dismissal or even the need for time to contemplate fully what it is that they have just heard, and still others seem to believe what Paul has said. Although Paul appears to have created an argument that makes sense of his mention of the resurrection, his audience reacts negatively to this. As noted in Chapter Five, it is not that Paul's logic has been inconsistent. It appears more that he has introduced something into the argument that his audience would not have fully accepted. The problem for Greek thinking was not the idea of spiritual existence or even continual existence after death. The point of contention would have been the apparent revivification to physical life of a dead body. Both the Epicureans and Stoics were materialists.[86] The Epicureans believed that the world as we know it was made up of very small particles, an early form of atomic theory. At death, one simply returned to the condition of one's particular state. The Stoics believed that the material substance of the universe was the principle of rationality, the logos, etc., and that the goal of life was to align oneself with this divine principle of rationality. Both were agreed that death was an escape from physical existence. Therefore, the idea of continued existence was not a problem, since both believed that material did in fact persist. The problem was that one would return to a human physical state. This was a condition of which one ought to be glad to be relieved.[87] This conflict is what apparently leads Paul's audience to interrupt him and not allow him to continue. This interruption is not typical of the two other missionary speeches of Paul, as noted above, and will be discussed further in Chapter Seven on Apologetic Speeches.

---

[86] On Stoic and Epicurean thought, besides Gärtner, Balch and Neyrey, see T.R. Glover, *The Conflict of Religions in the Early Roman Empire* (London: Methuen, 1909) 33–74; W. Tarn and G.T. Griffith, *Hellenistic Civilisation* (London: Edward Arnold, 3rd edn, 1952) 325–360; W.T. Jones, *The Classical Mind* (New York: Harcourt Brace Jovanovich, 2nd edn, 1970) 317–333; A.A. Long (ed.), *Problems in Stoicism* (London: Athlone, 1971); F.H. Sandbach, *The Stoics* (London: Chatto & Windus, 1975) esp. 149–178; A.A. Long, *Hellenistic Philosophy: Stoics, Epicureans, Sceptics* (London: Duckworth, 2nd edn, 1986) 14–74, 107–209; E. Ferguson, *Backgrounds of Early Christianity* (Grand Rapids: Eerdmans, 1987) 281–301; and Winter, "In Public and in Private," 118–122.

[87] F.F. Bruce (*The Acts of the Apostles* [Grand Rapids: Eerdmans, 3rd edn, 1990 (2nd edn, 1952)] 387) cites Aeschylus, *Eum.* 647–648 against the idea of Greeks believing in a bodily resurrection. But cf. Euripides, *Alcestis*, where Heracles brings Alcestis back from the dead. This topic is discussed in S.E. Porter, "Resurrection, the Greeks, and the New Testament," in S.E. Porter, M.A. Hayes, and D. Tombs (eds.), *Resurrection* (JSNTSup; RILP 5; Sheffield: Sheffield Academic Press, forthcoming 1999); cf. B.W.R. Pearson, "Resurrection and the Judgment of the Titans: ἡ γῆ τῶν ἀσεβῶν in LXX Isaiah 26.29," in Porter, Hayes, and Tombs (eds.), *Resurrection*, on the pattern of entry into and exit from the underworld in early Greek mythology, and its possible influence on later Jewish thinking.

4. Conclusion

Conclusions regarding Paul's speeches in Acts are preliminary at this point, until discussion of his apologetic speeches is completed in Chapter Seven. The three missionary speeches, however, have a number of common elements to their structure. Some of these elements are to be found elsewhere in the book of Acts, but a number of them, including terms of address and the structure and shape of the argument, seem more particular to these Pauline speeches. These features suggest either that the author of Acts has fashioned these speeches in some ways to create a Pauline persona, or that the author has drawn upon some information, possibly historical information, regarding Paul and included this material at appropriate points.[88] Analysis of Rom 1:18–32 in relation to Acts 14:15–17 and Acts 17:22–31 suggests greater theological commonalties between the two bodies of material than is often admitted.

---

[88] See Lüdemann, *Early Christianity*, *passim*, for discussion of the relationship between tradition and redaction in this material, as well as the rest of Acts.

Chapter Seven

The Argumentative Dimension of Paul's Apologetic Speeches in Acts

1. Introduction

According to Schneider, Paul offers four apologetic or defensive speeches: (1) Paul's speech to the Jerusalem Jews (Acts 22:1–21), (2) Paul's speech before Felix (24:10–21), (3) Paul's speech before Agrippa and others (26:2–23), and (4) possibly Paul's speech to the Roman Jewish leaders (28:17–20), although Schneider is less than certain about this last one (and his uncertainty is warranted).[1] There are a number of common argumentative features in these speeches requiring comment in an attempt to get a picture of Paul's apologetic strategy. As Jervell has stated, the apologetic speeches in Acts have received what he calls "second-rate treatment" compared to the speeches in Acts 1–17.[2] As the discussion in this chapter makes clear, these speeches deserve more considered examination than they have previously received. Once these features have been discussed in these four speeches, the conclusions of this and the previous chapter are drawn together in a discussion of the emerging figures of the Paul of Acts and the Paul of the letters.

---

[1] G. Schneider, *Die Apostelgeschichte* (2 vols.; HTKNT 5.1, 2; Freiburg: Herder, 1980, 1982) 1.95–103, with chart on p. 96. I choose to call these apologetic or defensive speeches to avoid a number of the problems associated with the inappropriate imposition of the categories of classical rhetoric on them (see Chapter Five above). This avoids the unnecessary debate over whether Paul's apologetic speeches are actually forensic or not, as debated in F. Veltman, "The Defense Speeches of Paul in Acts," in C.H. Talbert (ed.), *Perspectives on Luke–Acts* (Danville, VA: Association of Baptist Professors of Religion, 1978) 243–256 and J. Neyrey, "The Forensic Defense Speech in Acts 22–26: Form and Function," in C.H. Talbert (ed.), *Luke–Acts: New Perspectives from the Society of Biblical Literature Seminar* (New York: Crossroad, 1984) 210–214.

[2] J. Jervell, *The Theology of the Acts of the Apostles* (New Testament Theology; Cambridge: Cambridge University Press, 1996) 85–86 n. 159.

2. Paul's Apologetic or Defensive Speeches in Acts: An Analysis

a. Paul's Speech to the Jerusalem Jews (Acts 22:1–21)

In Acts 22:1–21, after Paul has been taken into custody in the Temple precinct, the Jews having accused him of taking a Gentile into the Temple, he asks for permission from the Roman centurion to address the primarily Jewish audience. He is given permission to do so.

There are four features of this speech meriting analysis: (1) Paul's word of direct address, (2) mention of the fact that he is making a defense, (3) recounting of his personal history, and (4) emphasis upon Jesus. Paul is then interrupted and no longer able to continue.

The first feature is Paul's word of address. After standing and motioning to the people (Acts 21:40), as he has done elsewhere (13:16; 17:22; 26:1), Paul addresses his audience as "men brothers and fathers" (ἄνδρες ἀδελφοὶ καὶ πατέρες), and requests that they hear him. This interesting combination of terms of address is only otherwise found in Stephen's speech in Acts 7:2, also followed by a request for hearing. Some commentators wish to emphasize the difference in audience,[3] but it is perhaps noteworthy that, even though the two groups are not exactly the same, both Stephen and Paul use these words to address hostile Jewish crowds in Jerusalem near the Temple area. The words show attention to the hierarchy and ethnic relations among those present. Paul is perhaps also anticipating reference in Acts 22:3–21 to his own personal background (and mention of Stephen in v. 20?), and using the terminology here to place himself in the appropriate place with regard to his peers and his superiors, to ensure the greatest receptivity to what he is about to say.

Secondly, Paul mentions that he is offering an apology or defense (ἀπολογία) (Acts 22:1). Schneider has used mention of the fact that the speech is a defense as the primary means of categorizing it as a defensive speech on form-critical grounds.[4] The labeling is a helpful means of distinguishing this speech from others, and it is possible that the word, "apology," indicates the theme for the concluding portion of Acts,[5] or that Paul is following a particular convention of offering a defensive speech

---

[3] For example, E. Haenchen, *The Acts of the Apostles: A Commentary* (trans. B. Noble *et al.*; Philadelphia: Westminster Press, 1971 [1965]) 624.

[4] Schneider, *Die Apostelgeschichte*, 2.319–320. Cf. J. Roloff, *Die Apostelgeschichte* (NTD 5; Berlin: Evangelische Verlags-Anstalt, 1981) 321, who refers to it as a "Rede als persönliche Apologie."

[5] Haenchen, *Acts*, 624.

(judicial speech?),[6] but Paul does not actually say what it is that he is defending.[7] Is it his recent behavior, or is it his entire career? One might expect his speech to be a direct refutation of what it is that he has just been accused of doing, if he was intending to get to this point in his speech, but he never does.

Thirdly, in his attempt to offer a defense of his actions, either recent or extended, Paul engages in a recounting of his personal history (Acts 22:3–21). This personal narrative is the basis of his entire speech, up to the point when he is interrupted. He states that he is a Jew,[8] was born in Tarsus, was brought up in either Tarsus or Jerusalem (the syntax is ambiguous),[9] and was educated under Gamaliel. He was zealous, persecuting Christians (referred to here as "the Way"), thereby identifying himself with the actions of his

---

[6] L.T. Johnson, *The Acts of the Apostles* (SP 5; Collegeville, MN: Liturgical, 1992) 387; M.L. Soards, *The Speeches in Acts: Their Content, Context, and Concerns* (Louisville: Westminster/John Knox, 1994) 112. The word ἀπολογία appears here and in Acts 25:16; the verb form in 24:10; 25:8; 26:1–2, 24.

[7] See G. Schille, *Die Apostelgeschichte des Lukas* (THNT 5; Berlin: Evangelische Verlags-Anstalt, 1983) 421, who finds in it a general defense before Jews, similar to that of Acts 7:2 before the Sanhedrin; R. Pesch (*Die Apostelgeschichte* [2 vols.; EKK 5.1, 2; Solothurn: Benziger; Neukirchen-Vluyn: Neukirchener, 1995 (2nd edn), 1986] 2.233) goes further and thinks that this is based on the Stephen speech, and shows distinct similarities with those in Acts 8 and 9; and R.C. Tannehill (*The Narrative Unity of Luke–Acts: A Literary Interpretation. II. The Acts of the Apostles* [FFNT; Minneapolis: Fortress Press, 1990] 276–277) thinks that it is a failed attempt to respond in general to the charge that Paul teaches "against the people."

[8] See Roloff, *Die Apostelgeschichte*, 322, who emphasizes "I am a Jew" as a motto in the speech; he also (p. 320) says that the speech itself becomes background material for Luke to present the conversion of Paul. M.-E. Rosenblatt (*Paul the Accused: His Portrait in the Acts of the Apostles* [Collegeville, MN: Liturgical, 1995] 72) contends that, after this speech, Luke represents Paul as a secular, rather than a religious, person, emphasizing his Roman connections.

[9] There is a variety of odd argumentation in the commentators attempting to prove that Paul was brought up in Jerusalem, apparently designed to keep Paul from having contact with any pagan religion in Tarsus. Paul's life was filled with such contact, however. See R.E. Witt, *Isis in the Ancient World* (Baltimore: Johns Hopkins University Press, 1997) 255–268. To note also is that, in Acts 21:39, Paul emphasizes his connections to Tarsus. We are, of course, studying the Greek text, but Acts 22:2 states that Paul spoke in the Hebrew dialect (probably Aramaic). Bi- or tri-lingualism would have been fairly common for many in the Greco-Roman world, including Jews of both the Diaspora and Palestine (if such a distinction can even be made in this instance). See S.E. Porter, "Jesus and the Use of Greek in Galilee," in B. Chilton and C.A. Evans (eds.), *Studying the Historical Jesus: Evaluations of the State of Current Research* (NTTS 19; Leiden: Brill, 1994) 123–154. For recent discussion of Paul's tripartite reference to his upbringing, see G. Lüdemann, *Paul, Apostle to the Gentiles: Studies in Chronology* (trans. F.S. Jones; Philadelphia: Fortress Press, 1984) 39 n. 72.

audience.[10] In particular, he was on his way to Damascus to do just such a thing, when he was confronted by Jesus the Nazarene. As a blind man, he was led to Damascus, where a man named Ananias informed him of his new purpose in life: God had appointed him to be a witness for God. Having returned to Jerusalem, he was praying in the Temple, when he fell into a trance and was informed that he was not yet welcome in Jerusalem. This is the only time such a revelatory episode is mentioned in the New Testament for Paul (not at Acts 9, where it would appear to belong), and Johnson is probably right that it implicitly offers a rebuttal of the charge against him while proving his piety.[11] Instead of being welcome in Jerusalem, he was sent to the Gentiles. It is at this point that the crowd interrupts and calls for his death. Johnson states that Luke "has had Paul make all the points required," so that the interruption is not genuine.[12] But how can this be determined, since the speech is so different from the others that Paul has made? Paul's message was apparently again rejected in Jerusalem.

Fourthly, although God is mentioned once, in Acts 22:14, as the "God of our fathers" (ὁ θεὸς τῶν πατέρων ἡμῶν) (cf. 3:13; 5:30; 7:52), Paul does not dwell on God but on Jesus the Nazarene. In the recounting of his personal history, it is the Lord who confronts Paul on the Damascus Road (Acts 22:8), and who tells him what to do (v. 10). It is the "Righteous One" (τὸν δίκαιον) (v. 14; cf. 3:14; 7:52) whom, Ananias says, Paul will see. It is the Lord whom Paul sees and hears from during his trance in the Temple (Acts 22:18, 19). It is surprising that these references to appearances of Jesus are not what arouse the ire of the crowd, however. It is the mention of the Lord telling Paul to go to the Gentiles.

b. Paul's Speech before Felix (Acts 24:10–21)

In this speech before the Roman procurator Felix, a Gentile,[13] Paul responds to the accusations made against him by Tertullus, the orator representing the Jewish authorities in Jerusalem.[14]

---

[10] See Tannehill, *Acts*, 279. The language is similar to that of 1 Cor 15:9, Gal 1:13 and Phil 3:6.

[11] Johnson, *Acts*, 390.

[12] Johnson, *Acts*, 391; contra Tannehill, *Acts*, 283–284.

[13] Cf. J.C. Lentz, Jr, *Luke's Portrait of Paul* (SNTSMS 77; Cambridge: Cambridge University Press, 1993) 95–97, who contrasts Paul and Felix, but who misses the gist of the narrative and speech.

[14] On this episode, see B. Rapske, *The Book of Acts in its First Century Setting. III. The Book of Acts and Paul in Roman Custody* (Grand Rapids: Eerdmans, 1994) esp. 158–163; A.N. Sherwin-White, *Roman Society and Roman Law in the New Testament* (Oxford: Clarendon Press, 1961) 48–57; and H.W. Tajra, *The Trial of St Paul: A Juridical Exegesis of*

In Paul's speech there are five elements of importance: (1) direct address of the procurator Felix, (2) specification that he is making a defense, (3) a recounting of Paul's personal history, (4) emphasis upon the role God has played in events, and (5) mention of the resurrection.[15]

The first item to note is Paul's word of direct address to his audience. Whereas in other speeches Paul uses some kind of a word of direct address, such as "brothers" or "men," in this speech, perhaps because he is addressing a single person, he simply uses the word "you" in the singular (Acts 24:10, 11). If a word of direct address of Felix by name or title was made on the occasion, Luke does not know of it or has deleted it.

Secondly, Paul engages in a more formalized *captatio benevolentiae*, one shorter than and not pitched as loftily as that of Tertullus.[16] He states directly to Felix that he is pleased that he has the occasion to make his defense before him, using here the verb form ἀπολογέομαι (Acts 24:10).[17] Felix, according to Paul's words of introduction, had been the arbitrator of affairs in that region for a number of years (ἐκ πολλῶν ἐτῶν). This temporal phrase may well be conventional,[18] but Felix had apparently already been procurator for five years at this time, as well as serving three or four years under Cumanus before that.[19] The question must be asked why Paul should be pleased to

---

the Second Half of the Acts of the Apostles (WUNT 2.35; Tübingen: Mohr–Siebeck, 1989) 118–124.

[15] Cf. the outline of G.A. Kennedy, *New Testament Interpretation through Rhetorical Criticism* (Chapel Hill: University of North Carolina Press, 1984) 136: *proem* (Acts 24:10), narration (v. 11), proposition (v. 12), proof (vv. 13–21). Cf. also J.B. Polhill, *Acts* (NAC 26; Nashville: Broadman, 1992) 481–484; C.H. Talbert, *Reading Acts* (New York: Crossroad, 1997) 206, who divide the speech differently. F.S. Spencer (*Acts* [Readings; Sheffield: Sheffield Academic Press, 1997] 219) speaks of an alternation between narrative and declarative statements, but the alternation is not as pronounced as Spencer implies.

[16] Schille, *Die Apostelgeschichte*, 432; Tajra, *Trial of St Paul*, 125.

[17] According to Haenchen (*Acts*, 654), the verb is the "real catchword" of the last chapters of Acts. Cf. Tajra, *Trial of St Paul*, 125–126, who probably over-theologizes the implications of the word, claiming that its use points to a divine inspiritual element that underlies all the apologetic speeches in Acts; and P.F. Esler, *Community and Gospel in Luke–Acts* (SNTSMS 57; Cambridge: Cambridge University Press, 1987) 217, who notes the socio-political implications of Paul's use of the word.

[18] Cf. P.Lond. VI 1912.22 with ἐκ πολλῶν χρόνων. See K. Lake and H.J. Cadbury, *The Beginnings of Christianity. Part I. The Acts of the Apostles. IV. English Translation and Commentary* (ed. F.J. Foakes Jackson and K. Lake; London: Macmillan, 1933) 300; followed by H. Conzelmann, *Die Apostelgeschichte* (HNT 7; Tübingen: Mohr–Siebeck, 1963) 132, quoting H.I. Bell, *Jews and Christians in Egypt* (London: British Museum, 1924).

[19] F.F. Bruce, *The Acts of the Apostles* (Grand Rapids: Eerdmans, 3rd edn, 1990 [2nd edn, 1952]) 478; contra G. Lüdemann, *Early Christianity according to the Traditions in Acts: A Commentary* (trans. J. Bowden; Minneapolis: Fortress Press, 1987) 248.

appear before him, however. Is this simply a rhetorical means of currying favor with Felix, is it an appeal to his experience with the Jews in his region, is it his being perceived as a good, neutral judge,[20] or is it a recognition that Felix was married to Drusilla, the daughter of Herod Agrippa I? It is unclear. In this instance, it is much more readily apparent what circumstances warrant a defense on Paul's part, since he has just been accused by Tertullus of being a pest (λοιμός) because he had stirred up dissension among the Jews all over the world and was a ringleader of the sect of the Nazarenes, even going so far as trying to desecrate the Temple. The charges are clear, and, in terms of Roman law, especially with regard to the stirring up of people to the point of riot, are quite serious charges indeed. That Felix would have been particularly sensitive to such activities is confirmed in the way he quelled several rebellions during his administration.[21]

Thirdly, Paul again engages in a recounting of his personal history, although in an abbreviated form that dwells mostly upon very recent events (Acts 24:11–21).[22] He states that twelve days ago he came up to Jerusalem to worship. He then states what he did not do in Jerusalem – such as disputing or causing a riot, as he had been charged, the very thing that would have aroused the attention of a Roman procurator. In a surprising rhetorical move,[23] Paul does confess (v. 14) that it was because of his devotion to Christianity, described here again as "the Way," though called by some a "sect,"[24] that Paul came to Jerusalem with a charitable gift for the Christians there (v. 17; the only mention of the gift in Acts).[25] It was in conjunction with this gift that he went to the Temple, where he was accused. As Spencer emphasizes, however, when presented here, the charges against Paul appear even weaker than those brought against others, such as Peter and John, in Acts.[26]

---

[20] Schille, *Die Apostelgeschichte*, 432.

[21] See B.W. Winter, "The Importance of the *Captatio Beneuolentiae* in the Speeches of Tertullus and Paul in Acts 24:1–21," *JTS* 42 (1991) 505–531, esp. 516–519.

[22] See Roloff, *Die Apostelgeschichte*, 337, who recapitulates the "twelve days" in Jerusalem.

[23] See Johnson, *Acts*, 412.

[24] Conzelmann (*Die Apostelgeschichte*, 133) notes that "way" corrects "sect," and clarification of what Christianity was is fundamental in understanding Christianity as the fulfilment of Judaism; cf. Schneider, *Die Apostelgeschichte*, 2.347; Tajra, *Trial of St Paul*, 126–127. Important discussion of the term "way" is to be found in S.V. McCasland, "The Way," *JBL* 77 (1958) 222–230; cf. J.A. Fitzmyer, "Jewish Christianity in Acts in Light of the Qumran Scrolls," in L.E. Keck and J.L. Martyn (eds.), *Studies in Luke–Acts* (Philadelphia: Fortress Press, 1966) esp. 140–141.

[25] See Schille, *Die Apostelgeschichte*, 434; Johnson, *Acts*, 413–414, on dispute whether this is in fact Paul's gift mentioned in the letters.

[26] Spencer, *Acts*, 220.

Fourthly, it is perhaps surprising, but Jesus does not enter into Paul's defense. It is God who is mentioned in conjunction with the purpose of his activities. Paul says that he has served or worshipped the "ancestral God" (Acts 24:14; the wording is semantically similar to that used elsewhere for "God of the fathers," but the phrasing is unique to this verse), has followed the law and the prophets (v. 14), and has had a hope in God and a good conscience before him (v. 15). Paul makes clear that he – at least, in his mind – never left Judaism.[27]

Fifthly, with regard to what has been done, Paul says that certain Jews from Asia were the ones who formed the crowd that brought accusations against him (Acts 24:19).[28] When he entered the Temple there was no crowd or uproar, so if this group has a charge against him, they should appear before Felix too. The only statement that he shouted out, he says, was that he was on trial for the resurrection (ἀνάστασις) of the dead (v. 21). Paul does not mention that it is the resurrection of Jesus, but simply the resurrection of the dead, using his typical phrase for this in Acts and the letters (see discussion in Chapter Nine). A dispute about the resurrection was not a chargeable crime under Roman or Jewish law.[29]

This explanation is apparently enough to prompt Felix to interrupt the proceedings. The reason is not clear, except that the text says that he had a more exact knowledge about the Way and that he needed to consult with Lysias, the chiliarch who took Paul into custody (Acts 24:22). Either he appreciated the force of Paul's argument that he was not being charged by the proper witnesses,[30] or he knew that what was being disputed was not a matter of Roman criminal law, but an internecine religious factionalism.[31] In any case, this interruption is different than that of other defensive speeches of Paul. This is not a hostile or reactive interruption, but one apparently based on substantive issues.[32] The account goes on to say that Felix was married to a Jew (Drusilla), who later heard Paul talk about faith in Christ Jesus (v. 24); however, discussing such things as righteousness, self-control and the judgment caused Felix to become frightened.

---

[27] See Tajra, *Trial of St Paul*, 127.

[28] Roloff, *Die Apostelgeschichte*, 338.

[29] See Johnson, *Acts*, 414.

[30] See Sherwin-White, *Roman Society and Roman Law*, 52–53.

[31] Cf. Rapske, *The Book of Acts and Paul in Roman Custody*, 164–167.

[32] Contra Polhill, *Acts*, 485, who labels Felix as indecisive.

c. Paul's Speech before Agrippa and Others (Acts 26:2–23)

Schneider sees this speech as without doubt the highpoint of the apologetic speeches of Paul.[33] There are legitimate reasons for his view on this. When Felix was replaced by Festus, Felix, as a favor to the Jews, and perhaps influenced by the apparent fact that his wife was a Jew, left Paul in prison. It was during his imprisonment under Festus that Paul had occasion to speak to Herod Agrippa II, the Romanized king, and others.[34] Festus is recorded as being a bit perplexed by the imprisonment of Paul, since he cannot seem to find anything guilt-worthy about him, despite the accusations of the Jews.

In speaking to Agrippa and his sister Bernice, in Acts 26, Paul, after making a gesture (Acts 13:16; 21:40), (1) directly addresses Agrippa, (2) specifies that he is making a defense, (3) engages in a personal history, (4) recounts the role of God in these events, and (5) mentions the resurrection.[35] It is at this point that Festus accuses Paul of being out of his mind. The arrangement of the material and the topics discussed in this speech are surprisingly similar to those in Paul's speech before Felix, as well as his speech before the Jews outside the Temple in Jerusalem. Soards, along with others, includes Paul's subsequent response in Acts 26:25–29 (except v. 28) with his speech here, but these appear to be more spontaneous remarks.[36] Nevertheless, they serve a useful purpose – their evangelistic and hence apologetic nature, in which Paul implores his hearers, including Agrippa, to become like him, is clearly evident. They may well recount the kinds of words that Paul may have planned for the endings of his speeches, but that we do not hear because, in many cases (noted above and in Chapter Six), his words are cut off before he has had an opportunity to conclude fully. In any case, they cannot be included as part of the speech itself.

The first element to notice – after Paul's gesture, noted above, and the narrator's statement that Paul is making a defense (on the verb form, see b above) – is that Paul directly addresses King Agrippa (βασιλεῦ 'Αγρίππα).

---

[33] Schneider, *Die Apostelgeschichte*, 2.364; cf. Tajra, *Trial of St Paul*, 163, who notes that it is the longest; and B. Witherington, III, *The Acts of the Apostles: A Socio-Rhetorical Commentary* (Grand Rapids: Eerdmans, 1998) 735.

[34] Cf. Lentz, *Luke's Portrait of Paul*, 83–91, who contrasts the characters at the expense of the narrative and the content of the speech.

[35] This speech, Bruce contends (*Acts*, 496), may be the closest to his defense of his life, for which Bruce provides a detailed outline. See also Kennedy, *New Testament Interpretation*, 137. The problems that literalistic rhetorical analysis of a summarized speech can cause are well illustrated in Witherington, *Acts*, 737–738 and n. 456.

[36] See Soards, *Speeches in Acts*, 122–126; but cf. Kennedy, *New Testament Interpretation*, 137–138.

Paul states that he considers himself to be in a fortunate state (ἥγημαι ἐμαυτὸν μακάριον) that he is able to make his defense before him (Acts 26:2),[37] an instance of what Roloff calls "eine kunstvolle gebaute *captatio benevolentiae*."[38] Paul considers himself fortunate because, he says, Agrippa is an expert in the laws and questions of the Jews.[39] Although there is the chance that Agrippa may have undertaken special study of Jewish law due to his own background, there is no substantial evidence that this was the case, especially in light of his strong Roman connections (actually Bernice had more involvement in Jewish practice, taking a Nazirite vow; cf. Josephus, *War* 2.310–314). This may well have been simply Paul's way of drawing Agrippa into the nature of the dispute at hand. That he is attempting to draw Agrippa into the discussion is perhaps further established by his several other instances of direct address in the speech, including vv. 7, 13, and 19, all with the vocative.

Secondly, Paul recognizes that he is making a defense before Agrippa (Acts 26:3; cf. his reference to his "standing, being on trial" in v. 6). His statement that he is making a defense is especially appropriate at the beginning of his speech before Felix, but it is also probably appropriate before Agrippa in light of the circumstances, in which he defends himself, even if this is not a formal trial. The situation is probably that Festus has not given up his responsibility to make a decision in this matter, although he is apparently relying upon Agrippa to give him some kind of advice on what should be done with this perpetual prisoner, against whom there are no substantive charges. Paul apparently realizes this situation, as indicated not only by his address of Agrippa and his explicitly calling his speech a defense,[40] but also his re-casting his approach in the course of his speaking so that he refers to his speech as "bearing witness" (μαρτυρόμενος) in v. 22.[41]

---

[37] On the use of the perfect here, see J.H. Moulton, *Prolegomena*, vol. 1 of *A Grammar of New Testament Greek* (Edinburgh: T. & T. Clark, 3rd edn, 1908) 148.

[38] Roloff, *Die Apostelgeschichte*, 351, as does Pesch, *Die Apostelgeschichte*, 2.276; cf. also Schille, *Die Apostelgeschichte*, 447, who compares it to the one in Acts 24:3; Tajra, *Trial of St Paul*, 164; and Witherington, *Acts*, 739.

[39] See Schille, *Die Apostelgeschichte*, 447, who notes that the Pauline speech here is unusual, but he still calls it "lukanische[n] Paulus-Reden." See F. Blass and A. Debrunner, *A Greek Grammar of the New Testament and Other Early Christian Literature* (trans. R.W. Funk; Chicago: University of Chicago Press, 1961) § 262(1). Schille (p. 447) calls the phrasing in Acts 26:3 (γνώστην ὄντα σε) a solecism (see also Blass and Debrunner, *Greek Grammar*, §§ 136[2], 137[3]). But it may be an accusative absolute. See S.E. Porter, *Idioms of the Greek New Testament* (BLG 2; Sheffield: JSOT Press, 2nd edn, 1994) 91–92; Blass and Debrunner, *Greek Grammar*, § 200(3).

[40] Witherington, *Acts*, 735–736.

[41] Tannehill, *Acts*, 316.

Paul appears to have taken the initiative in light of the legal situation (note that he has already appealed to Caesar), and turned the context to his favor.

Thirdly, in offering his defense, and in conjunction with his flattery of Agrippa that he is expert in matters Jewish, Paul again engages in a personal history, or what Rosenblatt calls "autobiography"[42] (Acts 26:4–21; cf. 22:3–21). Paul begins with a few comments about how Jews knew of his manner of living[43] as a youth, moving quickly to his time in Jerusalem and then to Pharisaism. It is as a Pharisee, and engaged in hostile activities against Jesus of Nazareth, including attempting to force Christians to blaspheme, that he had his confrontation on the Damascus Road.[44] Perhaps in light of his audience, in this conversion account, Paul goes into the most detail regarding the steps that he had taken to suppress the Church, a sign of his Pharisaical Jewishness, and mentions that the voice that spoke to him spoke in Aramaic (v. 14).[45]

Fourthly, in comparison to the other defensive speeches, Paul does not dwell on God's activity as much. He does not address God as the God of our fathers, speaking instead of the promise made by God "to our fathers" (Acts 26:6). It is for this hope, Paul claims, that he is accused (v. 7). Paul does not specify what this hope is. It is unclear whether this is because the speech has been abbreviated by an editor, or whether Paul, as depicted here, simply assumes that his audience would have known what this hope was. In any case, the connecting material is not present, even though Paul proceeds to ask the question of why it is considered incredible if God raises someone from

---

[42] Rosenblatt, *Paul the Accused*, 83; cf. Tannehill, *Acts*, 317.

[43] It is interesting to note that the earliest forms of βιόω are from Jewish sources: Ben Sira pref. and a Phrygian inscription of AD 60–80 (Bruce, *Acts*, 497), perfectly compatible with Paul delivering the speech. Less so is his use of ἴσασι, a classical form of οἶδα, which he does not use in his letters.

[44] D.B. Gowler (*Host, Guest, Enemy, and Friend: Portraits of the Pharisees in Luke and Acts* [ESEC 2; New York: Lang, 1991] 294 and n. 231), following R. O'Toole (*Acts 26: The Christological Climax of Paul's Defense* [Rome: Biblical Institute Press, 1978] 28), claims that the aorist, ἔζησα, in Acts 26:5 "should not be seen as a singular past event." I am in great sympathy with O'Toole's and Gowler's attempts to rid the aorist of the traditional past and punctiliar sense (a fault of, among others, J. Darr, *On Character Building: The Reader and the Rhetoric of Characterization in Luke–Acts* [Louisville: Westminster/John Knox, 1992] 125; Witherington, *Acts*, 740, both of whom equate tense and time). In context, however, this aorist is not to be seen as present-referring (O'Toole) or gnomic, culminative or dramatic (Gowler), but past-referring on the basis of the historical narrative context and the use of the contrastive καὶ νῦν ("and now") in v. 6. See S.E. Porter, *Verbal Aspect in the Greek of the New Testament, with Reference to Tense and Mood* (SBG 1; New York: Lang, 1989) chap. 4 and 265.

[45] On further literary features of Paul's description of his conversion, especially in Acts 16:16–18, see Schille, *Die Apostelgeschichte*, 450–451.

the dead (v. 8). Therefore, it appears that the hope is the resurrection of Jesus, a clearly Pauline idea in Acts (cf. 23:6; 24:15; see Chapter Nine for further discussion). As Spencer insightfully indicates, there is a development in Paul's thought in this speech regarding Jesus. The risen Jesus first appears to Paul as a light from heaven (v. 13), then commissions Paul (vv. 16–17), and, finally, proclaims a message to both Jews and Gentiles (v. 23).[46]

Fifthly, mention of the resurrection in Acts 26:23 prompts Festus's response, even though this is not Paul's first reference to it. In v. 8, as mentioned above, Paul asks why it is incredible if God raises someone from the dead, but this elicits no response from his audience. It is only in v. 23, when he brings the prophets and Moses to bear on his situation, that Festus reacts. Moses and the prophets are said to have foretold two things: the capability of the Messiah's suffering,[47] and his being the first resurrected (ἀναστάσις) from the dead. The prophets and Moses are mentioned, but there is no explicit quotation from the Old Testament given. This pattern occurs also in Peter's words to Cornelius (Acts 10:43) and later on in this episode with Agrippa and Festus (see also 26:27), both contexts where Gentiles rather than Jews are involved.[48] Paul declares that it was within the prophetic message that the Christ was to suffer, and that he was to be resurrected from the dead in order to proclaim light to Jews and Gentiles. Festus says that Paul's learning has driven him mad or insane. Kennedy is correct that Acts 26:23 and 22:21 both mention the Gentiles, just before the ensuing interruption,[49] but here it is probably not simply the mention of Gentiles that prompts Festus's outburst, especially since "the people" and the Gentiles are mentioned. It appears more likely than Paul's insanity that Paul's conjunction of the Messiah suffering and the resulting resurrection from the dead, including both Jews and Gentiles – ideas that struck home – proved too disturbing for Festus.[50]

---

[46] Spencer, *Acts*, 228. Cf. Talbert, *Reading Acts*, 211–212, who tries to use the resurrection motif to outline the speech; and D.P. Moessner, "The 'Script' of the Scriptures in Acts: Suffering as God's 'Plan' (βουλή) for the World for the 'Release of Sins,'" in B. Witherington, III (ed.), *History, Literature and Society in the Book of Acts* (Cambridge: Cambridge University Press, 1996) 242–248.

[47] On the use of these two εἰ phrases, see Johnson, *Acts*, 438.

[48] Soards (*Speeches in Acts*, 125) wishes to include this episode with Acts 3:18, 22, 24, where no explicit quotation is given, but the context in Acts 3 is much different.

[49] Kennedy, *New Testament Interpretation*, 137.

[50] See Witherington, *Acts*, 748–749.

d. Paul's Speech to the Roman Jewish Leaders (Acts 28:17–20)

Soards, along with others, defines the entire pericope of the speech as Acts 28:17–28,[51] but it is better to confine the speech to vv. 17–20, since the words that Paul is recorded as speaking were delivered on two separate occasions separated by days. Nevertheless, when the group reconvenes, it is simply stated by the narrator that Paul was explaining to them the kingdom of God and trying to persuade them concerning Jesus from the law and the prophets. His final words are quoted, and this passage consists almost entirely of an extended quotation of Isa 6:9–10.[52] In other contexts where Paul is interrupted, he has had occasion to refer to the prophets and to speak of Jesus, but he is not recorded as devoting time to speaking of the kingdom of God. The fact that the kingdom is the further topic of discussion indicates that this may well have been the further content of his speeches on other occasions, had he been allowed to continue. Of the other mentions of the kingdom associated with Paul, on two occasions he is quoted as speaking of the kingdom (Acts 14:22; 20:25), and on two occasions speaking of the kingdom is said to constitute the content of his preaching (19:8; 28:31). These occasions are virtually all associated with Jewish audiences or believers. Perhaps Paul would have moved on to proclaiming the kingdom in those speeches where he was interrupted. At the least, this calls into further question the view that these interruptions are manufactured, on the grounds that Paul has supposedly said all that he wishes to say. There obviously is more that he said – or at least Luke thinks he said.[53]

In this speech to the Roman Jews, Paul organizes his comments according to three primary characteristics: (1) a word of direct address, (2) the use of his personal history, and (3) very brief mention of the hope of Israel. Those listening say that they have never heard of Paul, but that they know of the sect of which he is a member (note again that Paul's term is "the Way," while the Jews, probably quite properly, refer to Christians as a sect; cf. Acts 24:5, 14).[54] In the words recorded, Paul has not mentioned any particular sect. This seems to indicate that Paul's recorded comments are only a part of the information conveyed, whether the Roman Jews had information regarding

---

[51] Soards, *Speeches in Acts*, 130–133.

[52] See G.J. Steyn, *Septuagint Quotations in the Context of the Petrine and Pauline Speeches of the Acta Apostolorum* (Kampen: Kok Pharos, 1995) 213–229, on the entire larger unit, including the use of the Old Testament quotation.

[53] See Roloff, *Die Apostelgeschichte*, 372, on this speech as a "summarische Bemerkung."

[54] See Johnson, *Acts*, 470.

Christians already, whether there were other things said that are not recorded or whether the speech itself is only a summary of longer comments.[55]

The first element of Paul's speech is his word of direct address, "men brothers" (ἄνδρες ἀδελφοί) (Acts 28:17), words of address used always in Acts by Jews to Jews (1:16; 2:29, 37; 7:2; 13:15, 26, 38; 15:7, 13; 22:1; 23:1, 6; 28:17; except 13:16, where god-fearers are included, though Jews are not excluded). Here he addresses, not the Jews of a synagogue, perhaps since Paul cannot search out such an audience, but the leaders of the Jewish community in Rome.[56]

Secondly, Paul immediately launches into his personal history (Acts 28:17–19), insisting that he had done nothing against "our people" or the laws of "our fathers." Nevertheless, he was taken into Roman custody, and would have been released had it not been for the insistence of Jews from Jerusalem, forcing him to appeal to Caesar, even though he has no charge to make against his nation.[57]

Thirdly, Paul claims that the only reason that he is in chains is on account of (ἔνεκεν) the hope of Israel (Acts 28:20).[58] Paul does not define what this hope means, but, in the context of his Jewish audience, it must have meant either hope in the coming Messiah or hope in the resurrection, realized in Jesus, or both.[59] Those hearing him invite Paul back to hear from him again.

3. The Argumentative Dimension of the Speeches of Paul in Acts

In analyzing the speeches of Paul in Acts in this chapter and the one previous, several elements of his argumentative strategy emerge. The findings of the two chapters are synthesized here.

First, Paul has two major kinds of speeches that he delivers, the missionary speech and the apologetic or defensive speech, although it is impossible to make a firm distinction between the two. One of the relatively firm distinguishing features of the apologetic or defensive speeches is their use of

---

[55] R.B. Rackham (*The Acts of the Apostles: An Exposition* [London: Methuen, 8th edn, 1919] 501) thinks it surprising that the Roman Jews should know so little about Paul and why he is in Rome; cf. Tajra, *Trial of St Paul*, 188. Bruce (*Acts*, 477 [2nd edn, 1952]), in light of Roman law's punishment of unsuccessful prosecutors, thinks it very understandable.

[56] Schneider, *Die Apostelgeschichte*, 2.414.

[57] Witherington (*Acts*, 798) takes this as a veiled threat of a countersuit, but this reveals too great an effort to equate items of each speech with forensic rhetoric.

[58] See Blass and Debrunner, *Greek Grammar*, §§ 35(3), 216(1), on the grammar here.

[59] See Bruce, *Acts*, 539; Johnson, *Acts*, 469; Schille, *Die Apostelgeschichte*, 478.

the word "defense" at the outset to forecast what the purpose is. The missionary speeches have no such indication, but they tend to be found where Paul is addressing larger groups in Gentile cities, rather than appearing before government officials.

Secondly, Paul always begins his speeches with some form of address, and this varies according to the kind of speech. When he is addressing Jews, he calls them either "brothers" or "Israelite men." When he is addressing Gentiles, he calls them simply "men" or by their place names. Individuals are also directly addressed, although not always by name.

Thirdly, in all of his speeches, apart from the one to the Jews in Jerusalem (Acts 22:1–21), Paul makes explicit statements about God and the role that he has played. In the speech in Jerusalem, Paul only briefly mentions God, instead dwelling on God's designated righteous one, Jesus.

Fourthly, in all of his speeches, as a means of establishing common ground with his audience, and as a means of developing his argument, Paul relies upon some form of external argumentative support for his claims. In his missionary speeches, this usually consists of an appeal to some form of natural theology. In his apologetic speeches, this usually consists of a retelling of his personal history.

Fifthly, as a means of reinforcing his argument in his missionary speeches, Paul often makes an appeal to common authority. When he is speaking to Jews this seems to be an explicit and marked appeal to the Old Testament. When he is speaking to Gentiles, in the Areopagus speech Paul cites the Greek poet Aratus, a parallel use of an established authority, and in his speech at Lystra he alludes to the Old Testament but does not label his citation as such – he just weaves it into his argument. As a means of reinforcing his argument in his apologetic speeches, Paul apparently relies simply on divine endorsement as the basis of his personal history.

Sixthly, in his missionary speeches, apart from the Areopagus speech, Paul is able to complete the speech, but in his apologetic speeches, on every occasion Paul is interrupted. This interruption often comes when he has mentioned the resurrection (e.g. in his speeches before Felix, Agrippa, and possibly the Roman Jews, as well as the Areopagus speech).

Thus, in sum, Paul begins with an explicit address of his audience, determined apparently according to the composition of his audience. With those with whom he is more familiar, namely Jews, he has more specific words of address that illustrate his common bond with them. When he is offering an explicit defense of who he is and what his mission entails, he virtually always labels his speech as a "defense." When he is in a missionary context, Paul tends to rely upon a natural-theology argument, whereas in his apologetic speeches Paul relies upon his personal history to demonstrate the validity and lack of threat of his mission. The rationale for these two different approaches seems to be the common intent of finding a point of contact before proceeding. When he is addressing a Jewish audience, Paul makes a direct appeal to authority by invoking the Old Testament, something he does not apparently feel as free to do in his speeches to Gentiles. Instead, he on one occasion integrates a quotation from the Old Testament and on another cites at least one pagan poet. In virtually every speech that Paul makes, the emphasis is upon God. He elucidates God's actions in various ways – sometimes seeing him as the creator and sustainer of the universe, and other times as the one who has acted specifically in Jesus of Nazareth – but God is the common figure who is never far from Paul's mind. It is perhaps surprising to note that Jesus does not loom nearly so large, apart from in his speech before the people of Jerusalem (Acts 22:1–21). Rather than dealing with the life of Jesus, when Paul does mention Jesus, he moves virtually directly to the resurrection, often causing his audience to react strongly. This is even true of the speeches at Pisidian Antioch (13:16–41) and Lystra (14:15–17), where, even though we may not have all of Paul's words, he is at least recorded as having completed these speeches.

In light of these common features, it is perhaps worth noting that the Areopagus speech fits least comfortably within the definition offered above. On the one hand, it is categorized by Schneider as a missionary speech. It is presented before a group of people who have expressed interest in Paul's teaching, and it is not prefaced by the explicit label of "defense." It relies upon an argument from natural theology, using the poet Aratus as a means of invoked authority. On the other hand, it has two qualities of the apologetic or defensive speech. These are the mention of the resurrection, and the resultant interruption of the speech. Whereas Paul is able to complete his missionary speeches before those at Pisidian Antioch and Lystra, in Athens he is not able to do so. Perhaps the reception of Paul's speech is a form of confirmation of the theory that the speech at the Areopagus, although in some ways appearing to be simply a discussion among philosophers regarding some new form of teaching, is much closer to being a kind of legal hearing.

4. Comparison of the Paul of Acts and the Paul of the Letters

The Paul of the letters and the Paul of Acts, it is often said, are two very different individuals (see Chapter Nine for discussion of these assertions). Is it possible, on the basis of what has been presented above regarding the major

Pauline speeches in Acts, to say anything about the relationship between the Paul of these two sets of writings? It is certainly not possible to make definitive statements, but it would appear that, if anything in Acts were instructive for deciding the possible relationships between the letters and Acts, it would be the speeches. The speeches would have highest claim to capturing the explicit teaching of Paul, such as is found in his letters.

One of the major difficulties, however, is determining what counts for evidence. As has been noted above, there are a number of common features to the speeches of Paul in Acts, but there are also a number of differing features, depending upon the audience and the nature of the speech. Thus, there is a difference between a speech addressed to Gentiles and a speech addressed to Jews, or a speech delivered as a missionary appeal and one offered as a defense, or a speech offered before a crowd and one offered before an individual or two. On the one hand, this kind of variation is what one might expect from any kind of reasonably competent speaker – a recognition that different approaches are needed for different occasions, while maintaining a certain commonalty of approach. On the other hand, one of the major theories regarding how ancient historians wrote speeches that they placed in their narratives (as discussed in Chapter Five) was that they wrote what would have been appropriate and plausible for a given occasion. The common features could be accounted for on the basis that the same writer – the author of Acts, or Paul? – was responsible for all of the speeches, and the differences on the basis of the occasion for which the speech was being composed. Further complicating this scenario is the fact that the speeches – whether they originated with the historical Paul or not – are, in any event, mediated through the authorship of Luke. For those who dismiss any connection between Paul and Luke, there is little ground for arguing for an accurate reflection of Paul. However, even for those who argue that Luke may have known and possibly been the traveling companion of Paul, there are various views of how faithful he was in reflecting Paul and his theology. For example, it has been argued that Luke captures much of what Paul said, but completely misses the significance of his vital doctrine of the cross.[60] This situation makes it very difficult to know how to proceed in analysis of the speeches of Paul in Acts. Perhaps the following comments may be of use.

As many have recognized, the Paul of Acts has concern for both Jews and Gentiles in the book of Acts, and this is reflected in the speeches that we have examined, as well. Three of the seven speeches we have analyzed are

---

[60] See R. Maddox, *The Purpose of Luke–Acts* (Edinburgh: T. & T. Clark, 1985) 68, for this opinion.

addressed to distinctly Jewish audiences of some sort (Acts 13:16–41; 22:1–21; 28:17–20), three are addressed to distinctly Gentile audiences (14:15–17; 17:22–31; 22:1–21), and one to a mixed audience of Agrippa, the Romanized king, and others (26:2–23). This reflects the similar kinds of proportions as are probably reflected in such a place as Rome. Scholars are clearly in disagreement regarding the proportions of Gentiles and Jews in the church or churches at Rome, but it is agreed by most that there was some kind of mixed congregation or congregations. Thus, it is not surprising that Paul has comments in Romans that appear more specifically addressed to the Jewish members of the audience (e.g. Rom 2:17; 3:1; 4:1–25), and comments more specifically addressed to the Gentile members (chs. 9–11, esp. 11:13; 14:1–15:17).[61]

For the Paul of both Acts and the letters, the foundational belief is that it is God who is at work in the world, including raising up Jesus of Nazareth from the dead. Although it could be asserted that this is what distinguishes most, if not all, New Testament writers, the way this fundamental assumption is used in Paul is different than it is in other early Christian writers. Many scholars have noticed that the Paul of the letters is not apparently overtly concerned with the earthly life of Jesus, making little reference to any of the events surrounding his birth and ministry.[62] The Paul of the letters is instead concerned with the death and resurrection of Jesus. The same can be said of the Paul of Acts, at least in his speeches. Specific vocabulary cannot be used to distinguish references in Acts as either distinctly Pauline or Lukan, since, for example, both ἐγείρω and ἀνίστημι are used in the speeches,[63] but the resurrection is clearly the emphasis of Paul when he speaks.

Paul also utilizes a natural-theology argument in several of his speeches, in particular those before Gentile audiences at Lystra and Athens. It is especially in the book of Romans that Paul uses a natural-theology argument, as well. Many scholars are unconvinced, however, that these natural-theology arguments reveal the same mind. Maddox offers four arguments to establish the differences between Luke's and Paul's use of natural theology in Acts

---

[61] See, for example, J.D.G. Dunn, *Romans* (2 vols.; WBC 38A, B; Waco, TX: Word, 1988) xliv–liv; cf. L.M. McDonald and S.E. Porter, *Early Christianity and its Sacred Literature* (Peabody, MA: Hendrickson, forthcoming 1999) chap. 10.

[62] See, for example, D.E.H. Whiteley, *The Theology of St Paul* (Oxford: Blackwell, 2nd edn, 1974) 99. This conclusion needs to be tempered, however. See S.E. Porter, "Images of Christ in Paul," in S.E. Porter, M.A. Hayes, and D. Tombs (eds.), *Images of Christ: Ancient and Modern* (RILP 2; Sheffield: Sheffield Academic Press, 1997) 97–100.

[63] ἐγείρω is used approximately 12 times, and ἀνίστημι approximately 44 times.

17:22–34 and Romans, especially 1:18–32.[64] First, Maddox says, there is "a difference in mood, in that [Acts] looks hopefully on the possibility that human beings will, with the moral encouragement given by the warning of coming judgment (v. 30 f.), at last find God, who has all the time been accessible to them (v. 27–29), whereas in Rom. 1:18 ff. Paul looks on human society as in a desperate state, because of willful ignorance of God (v. 19–21, cf. 3:22b–23)."[65] But perhaps these lines of contrast are overdrawn. In Acts 17:22–31, Paul does indeed hold out the hope that humans will perhaps be able to grope after him and find him, but one cannot help but note (as I have above) that he here twice uses the optative verb form in a fourth-class conditional structure (v. 27), conveying the idea that, though they are groping, there is little if any certainty of their actually grabbing hold of him.[66] This is confirmed by the fact that the next clause states that they are groping even though God is not far from each one, a picture of perpetual frustration. The image is of humans struggling to make contact with the divine, but not being successful, despite the proximity of the creator-God. This is not too far removed from the image of humans failing to find God in Rom 1:18–32. Nevertheless, although Romans 2 is subject to much disagreement, according to at least one reading it appears that Paul does indeed hold out the possibility that, in some sense (even if only hypothetical), humans can find their way to God, on the basis of the witness that he has provided in the universe (e.g. Rom 2:7, 10, 14–15).[67] There may be other extenuating circumstances, but there is in Romans at least the hope of finding God. Acts 14:15–16, Paul's speech at Lystra, seems to capture some of this middle ground, holding out the hope for humans of finding a witness to him, even though they have gone their own way.

Secondly, Maddox argues that "in Acts 17:30 human sin seems to be treated rather lightly, being identified with the ignorance shown in worshipping cult-objects of human manufacture (v. 29, cf. v. 16, 22b–23), but in Rom. 1:23 f., 25 f., 28 idolatry is interpreted as a deep-seated perversion of

---

[64] These are essentially the same arguments used by P. Vielhauer, "On the 'Paulinism' of Acts," in Keck and Martyn (eds.), *Studies in Luke–Acts*, 34–37, following M. Dibelius, *Studies in the Acts of the Apostles* (ed. H. Greeven; trans. M. Ling; London: SCM Press, 1956) 26–77 *passim*.

[65] Maddox, *Purpose of Luke–Acts*, 83.

[66] See Porter, *Idioms of the Greek New Testament*, 263–264; cf. *idem*, *Verbal Aspect*, 173–177.

[67] For recent discussion of these difficult verses, but with different conclusions, see F. Thielman, *Paul and the Law: A Contextual Approach* (Leicester: InterVarsity Press, 1994) 169–174; and T.R. Schreiner, *The Law and its Fulfillment: A Pauline Theology of Law* (Grand Rapids: Baker, 1994) 193–196.

the honour due to God, which leads to moral depravity."[68] Two comments must be made in response. The first is that Maddox has perhaps overdrawn the contrast for the sake of his argument. Though he cites Rom 1:23, he neglects Paul's argument that the failure to honor God results in the substitution of images of corruptible humans, birds, four-footed creatures and reptiles. It is from this substitution that perversion results. He also fails to consider Rom 3:25–26, where Paul says that God had passed over former sins in his forbearance. The second comment is that the different audiences must be taken into account. Romans is addressed to a group of Christians, so Paul speaks firmly to them of the dangers of human neglect of God. In Acts, Paul's speech at the Areopagus is addressed to the unconverted. He begins with a *captatio benevolentiae* in order to capture their attention and win their favor, rather than alienate them from the beginning. As Bruce says in comparing these two passages, "I find it difficult not to imagine [Paul] as saying something very much along the lines of the summary in Acts 17:22–31. Here he is talking to pagans, not writing to Christians; he will not cut off his hearers' ears as the first step towards gaining their attention."[69]

Thirdly, Maddox states that "Acts 17:28b–29a regards kinship with God as an innate characteristic of humanity, whereas in Romans human beings are by nature children of Adam (5:12) and divine sonship is the gift of election realized through faith in Christ (8:14)."[70] Again, Maddox has drawn the lines of distinction too exclusively. In Acts 17:28–29, Paul refers to the pagan poet(s) as a form of support for his argument. This is not quite the same as saying that he regards them or what they say as theologically definitive. The rest of the speech in Acts draws very clear lines of division between God and humanity, as does the speech in Acts 14:15–17. Furthermore, Rom 5:12 does not present humans as by nature children of Adam, only that sin spread throughout humanity because of one man. As Maddox rightly points out, there is significant adoption language in Paul, to my mind very much reflecting adoption language of the Greco-Roman world.[71]

---

[68] Maddox, *Purpose of Luke–Acts*, 83.

[69] F.F. Bruce, "The Speeches in Acts – Thirty Years After," in R. Banks (ed.), *Reconciliation and Hope: New Testament Essays on Atonement and Eschatology Presented to L.L. Morris on his 60th Birthday* (Exeter: Paternoster, 1974) 64.

[70] Maddox, *Purpose of Luke–Acts*, 83.

[71] On adoption in Paul, see J.M. Scott, *Adoption as Sons of God: An Exegetical Investigation into the Background of ΥΙΟΘΕΣΙΑ in the Pauline Corpus* (WUNT 2.48; Tübingen: Mohr–Siebeck, 1992), but whose evidence moves in a completely different direction, to my mind. The concept of adoption seems to me to be one that grows out of the larger Greco-Roman world, not solely the Old Testament, at least as Paul uses it.

Fourthly, Maddox states that "the motives for repentance suggested in Acts 17:24–31 are gratitude for the providence of creation and fear of the coming judgment, whereas in Romans they are not only the coming judgment (2:12) but also the seriousness of the present human plight (1:18–32) and the power of God's salvation in the cross of Christ (1:16 f.; 3:21–26)."[72] Maddox, in essence, is conceding a great area of overlap between what Paul purportedly says in Acts and Romans, with the judgment being a serious and important motivation for human repentance. What Maddox fails to note, however, is Acts 17:30, which speaks of God's having overlooked the times of ignorance and his present (νῦν) announcement to repent, because the day of judgment has been fixed and the man to do it has been appointed. The account in Acts does not have the sense of distance regarding judgment that Maddox's position requires.

Although the evidence is far from conclusive, there are legitimate grounds for seeing the Paul of Acts as sharing a similar voice to that of the Paul of the letters, at least at those points where direct comparison can be made. In other words, from a conceptual standpoint, there is little of substance in the speeches that stands in the way of this conclusion. What Gärtner says of the Areopagus Speech in Acts 17 can, I think, be said of the other speeches as well:

A summary of the results of the present study shows that no item in the discourse clashes with what is otherwise known of Paul's theology. There are also certain reasons for presuming that the speech is not sheer invention by Luke but builds on a solid tradition proceeding from Paul's sojourn in Athens: namely, the character of the narrative framework, and certain details in the speech, notably its take-off from the altar "To an unknown God."[73]

5. Conclusion

In Chapters Six and Seven, I have tried to show the argumentative strategy of the Paul of Acts by analyzing his major speeches in the book. What comes to the fore is that there is an apparent underlying theoretical foundation from which Paul constructs his argument. It is not altogether clear that the Paul of Acts is the Paul of the letters, but there is no conclusive argument in this area to show that he was not. Even if there is no such argument, however, it is nevertheless clear that the author of Acts has not retained all of the words of

---

[72] Maddox, *Purpose of Luke–Acts*, 83–84.

[73] B. Gärtner, *The Areopagus Speech and Natural Revelation* (trans. C.H. King; ASNU 21; Uppsala: Gleerup, 1955) 249–250.

Paul in Acts. But he has retained a sufficient quantity of his wording so that we can gain at least an impression of how Paul approached his several different argumentative situations, whether he was addressing a missionary context or offering an apologetic speech, whether he was addressing Jews or Gentiles, or a combination of them, or whether he was addressing a crowd or individuals. The Paul of Acts builds his case around the person of God, who is at work in the world, bears witness to himself, and has raised Jesus from the dead, but Paul is also seen in his speeches in Acts to be a man of incredible complexity and argumentative skill. When the character of Paul as seen in Acts is compared with the Paul of history (so far as he can be known), and compared with the kind of person he must have been to have written and accomplished what he did, perhaps the lines of demarcation fade even further. As Blaiklock, the classical historian, has aptly and passionately said, Paul "was the first citizen of Europe, if the true European is one who carries in his culture, character and outlook, the threefold heritage of the ancient world. The rabbi of Jerusalem, the Greek of Tarsus, the citizen of Rome; trilingual, participant in three civilizations, interpreter of East to West; Paul, the apostle of Christ, emerges from the record more real than any other personality known to us from his generation."[74]

---

[74] E.M. Blaiklock, "The Acts of the Apostles as a Document of First Century History," in W.W. Gasque and R.P. Martin (eds.), *Apostolic History and the Gospel: Biblical and Historical Essays Presented to F.F. Bruce on his 60th Birthday* (Exeter: Paternoster, 1970) 54.

Chapter Eight

Acts 21:17–26 and Paul, the Man for All Seasons, or the Man Betrayed by his Friends?

1. Introduction

One of the significant concepts for understanding Luke–Acts is the theme of salvation; in the second of the two volumes, Acts, this theme is transmitted by means of the apostolic message. As van Unnik stated several years ago, "There is a solid bridge between the saving activity of Jesus and people being at a distance Jerusalem with the incarnate Lord. The solidity of this bridge consists in the confirmation of the salvation by the apostles, sanctioned by God..."[1] From Mary's first description of God as savior (Luke 1:47),[2] to focusing upon the saving activity of Jesus, this theme can be seen developing: "Here the great salvation Israel and the world had longed for took its beginning." In Acts, according to van Unnik, "this 'Good News' was proclaimed by telling who Jesus was... This salvation is proclaimed in the world."[3]

The Gospel of Luke ends climactically in Jerusalem with the ascension of Jesus; Acts begins with this same event and propels the action to new heights. To change metaphors, there is a "concentric ring" structure to the book that reflects the movement of the gospel. The Church has a humble beginning in Jerusalem (Acts 1:1–2:47), proclaiming the message of salvation. When God's Holy Spirit descends, however, those gathered in Jerusalem from the Diaspora hear the message proclaimed and believe (2:47). With Peter serving as the initial center of attention as he preaches in the synagogue and heals (6:7), the Church continues to expand (6:1–12:25) to other areas and peoples

---

[1] W.C. van Unnik, "Luke–Acts, a Storm Center in Contemporary Scholarship," in L.E. Keck and J.L. Martin (eds.), *Studies in Luke–Acts* (Philadelphia: Fortress Press, 1966) 48. For other views, see van Unnik, "Luke–Acts," 23–26.

[2] See I.H. Marshall, *Luke: Historian and Theologian* (Grand Rapids: Zondervan, 1970) 92, 97, 103–104.

[3] Van Unnik, "Luke–Acts," 49. On this and other themes in Acts, see W.L. Liefeld, *Interpreting the Book of Acts* (Grand Rapids: Baker, 1995) 79–98.

Cornelius (10:1–11:18), and the city of Antioch (11:19–30). A transition occurs in 9:19b–11:30, from the heavily Jewish focus of the Church to the beginning and development of the Gentile mission. In chs. 7 and 8, we read about Stephen, with Paul comprising a subtle background figure (7:58; 8:1) until God calls him (9:1–19a). He then looms large on the field, as a prize in the spread of the gospel's salvific message (9:31), but also as its greatest instigator. Peter then fades from the picture (12:1–15; his last appearance is in ch. 15).

The author of Acts then depicts the three missionary journeys of Paul (or Barnabas and Paul, at the very beginning). In his poem the *Prelude*, William Wordsworth describes his life in a series of ever-expanding circles: he ventures away from home – to Cambridge, continental Europe, etc. – only to return each time.[4] So with Paul. Each one of his missionary trips takes him further from Antioch, but he always returns to Antioch, the center of his missionary endeavor.[5] This inevitably leads to a tension with the church at Jerusalem, seen both in his letters (e.g. Galatians 2; 2 Cor 11:5) and also in Acts. His return after completing his first missionary journey warrants the occasion for the so-called Jerusalem Council (Acts 15:1–25; note that there are at least two other previous visits to Jerusalem before embarking on his missionary journeys, in 9:25 ff.; 11:30; 12:25). Based upon the literary structure of the book of Acts and the way the episode is constructed, it seems likely that Paul was present at this Council.[6] On the second trip, Paul "went up and greeted the church," which most take as a trip to Jerusalem, although nothing more is said.[7] On the third missionary journey, according to the book of Romans, Paul talks about his plans to visit Rome (cf. Rom 1:11 ff.), but, according to Acts, he also realizes before he leaves Miletus that trouble awaits him in Jerusalem (Acts 20:18–35 [see Chapter Five above]; at

---

[4] See W. Wordsworth, *The Prelude*, in C. Baker (ed.), *William Wordsworth's The Prelude with a Selection from the Shorter Poems and the Sonnets and the 1800 Preface to Lyrical Ballads* (New York: Rinehart, 1948) 130–365.

[5] Contra I.H. Marshall, *The Acts of the Apostles* (TNTC; Grand Rapids: Eerdmans, 1980) 302, who sees Jerusalem as the center.

[6] See R.N. Longenecker, "The Acts of the Apostles," in F.E. Gaebelein (ed.), *The Expositor's Bible Commentary* (vol. 9; Grand Rapids: Zondervan, 1981) 448; F.F. Bruce, *Commentary on the Book of Acts* (NICNT; Grand Rapids: Eerdmans, 1954) 298–302; Marshall, *Acts*, 242–247; contra D.R. Catchpole, "Paul, James and the Apostolic Decree," *NTS* 23 (1977) 430–432; M. Dibelius, *Studies in the Acts of the Apostles* (ed. H. Greeven; trans. M. Ling; London: SCM Press, 1956) 100; S.G. Wilson, *The Gentiles and the Gentile Mission in Luke–Acts* (SNTSMS 23; Cambridge: Cambridge University Press, 1973) 191.

[7] H. Conzelmann, *Die Apostelgeschichte* (HNT 7; Tübingen: Mohr–Siebeck, 2nd edn, 1972) 117.

Caesarea, Agabus prophecies of Paul's impending imprisonment, Acts 21:11 [see Chapter Six above]). But Paul continues to make his way to Jerusalem.[8]

2. Acts 21 and Paul's Participation in the Temple Ritual

Though clearly foreshadowed, the events of Acts 21 comprise another significant turning point in Paul's ministry, and begin the last group of events in Luke–Acts.[9] Just as a centrifugal force throws an object away from the center, the incidents of Acts 21 hurtle Paul (figuratively, since the length of time is spread over several years) away from Jerusalem and toward Rome. The sense of distance is seen both geographically and also ideologically. The events that precipitated these significant events warrant further exegetical attention.

In Acts 21:17, when Paul and his companions arrived in Jerusalem, possibly in time for Pentecost (although this is uncertain),[10] they were first received gladly by the brethren.[11] The next day they reported to James and the elders[12] the many things God had done among the Gentiles.[13] At this time,

---

[8] F.F. Bruce, *Paul, Apostle of the Heart Set Free* (Grand Rapids: Eerdmans, 1977) 344.

[9] P. Schubert, "The Final Cycle of Speeches in the Book of Acts," *JBL* 87 (1968) 4–10; H.S. Songer, "Paul's Mission to Jerusalem: Acts 20–28," *RevExp* 71 (1974) 499–510.

[10] See K. Lake and H.J. Cadbury, *The Beginnings of Christianity*. Part I. *The Acts of the Apostles*. IV. *English Translation and Commentary* (ed. F.J. Foakes Jackson and K. Lake; London: Macmillan, 1933) 270; T.E. Page, *The Acts of the Apostles* (London: Macmillan, 1886) 221; and R.B. Rackham, *The Acts of the Apostles* (London: Methuen, 8th edn, 1919) 413.

[11] Contra J. Kürzinger, *The Acts of the Apostles* (2 vols.; New York: Herder & Herder, 1971) 2.111.

[12] Nothing is said of the other apostles being in Jerusalem. According to the portrait in Acts, those such as Peter and John were seen as undertaking missionary responsibilities elsewhere, while James remained in Jerusalem as the church's leader, along with a group of elders, possibly seventy. See Bruce, *Commentary*, 429; R.J. Knowling, "The Acts of the Apostles," in W.R. Nicholl (ed.), *Expositor's Greek Testament* (5 vols.; repr. Grand Rapids: Eerdmans, 1980) 2.449; Page, *Acts*, 221; C.S.C. Williams, *A Commentary on the Acts of the Apostles* (London: A. & C. Black, 1957) 240; Conzelmann, *Die Apostelgeschichte*, 131. From what is to be said below, it is clear that James was in charge of a legalistic faction. See M. Goulder, *A Tale of Two Missions* (London: SCM Press, 1993), for development of the Pauline/Jacobian opposition.

[13] The third "we" section of Acts concludes at Acts 21:18. Some scholars think that the "we" passages indicate that Luke the author is present throughout this episode, but that for purely literary reasons he uses the third person in 21:19 ff. because he focuses the narrative upon Paul. See Longenecker, "Acts," 518–519; Williams, *Acts*, 239–240. To the contrary, R.P.C. Hanson (*The Acts in the RSV* [Oxford: Clarendon Press, 1967] 210) discredits the

Paul probably presented the collection from the Gentile churches, especially those in Macedonia, though Luke (perhaps somewhat surprisingly) does not mention it (Rom 15:31; Acts 24:17).[14]

When James and the elders heard these things, Acts says, they glorified God, possibly for some time, although the verbal tense-form does not necessarily imply this.[15] This joyful scenario is purportedly attributed to the conversion of the Gentiles, as evidenced by their contribution to the church at Jerusalem. Some scholars think that the joy of the Jerusalem leaders also stemmed from the elders' relief on learning that the allegations of Acts 21:21 against Paul were false.[16] However, the narrative does not make it clear that the leaders were convinced that the accusations were false. It appears that not only were possibly more conservative members of the Jerusalem church still suspicious of Paul, but the leaders of the church may well have been as well,[17] thereby causing consternation for the entire church there,[18] especially as they were trying to find a way of cohabitation in Jerusalem with other Jews. At the least, as Rosenblatt states, "It is not clear what degree of support Paul has from the Church's leadership in Jerusalem."[19] As a result, "they"

---

entire speech of vv. 20–25 as "clearly only a convention used in order to advance the story." On the "we" passages, see Chapter Two in this volume.

[14] See Marshall, *Acts*, 342; Longenecker, "Acts," 2.519; Knowling, "Acts," 2.448; E. Haenchen, *The Acts of the Apostles: A Commentary* (trans. B. Noble *et al.*; Philadelphia: Westminster Press, 1971 [1965]) 612–614; G. Schille, *Die Apostelgeschichte des Lukas* (THNT 5; Berlin: Evangelische Verlags-Anstalt, 1983) 415; and B. Witherington, III, *The Acts of the Apostles: A Socio-Rhetorical Commentary* (Grand Rapids: Eerdmans, 1998) 646, on reasons for omission of this in the account. On the collection, cf. K.F. Nickle, *The Collection: A Study in Paul's Strategy* (SBT 48; London: SCM Press, 1966); D. Georgi, *Remembering the Poor: The History of Paul's Collection for Jerusalem* (Nashville: Abingdon, 1992).

[15] See F. Blass and A. Debrunner, *A Greek Grammar of the New Testament and Other Early Christian Literature* (trans. R.W. Funk; Chicago: University of Chicago Press, 1961) § 327; N. Turner, *Syntax*, vol. 3 of *A Grammar of the Greek New Testament*, by J.H. Moulton (Edinburgh: T. & T. Clark, 1963) 66; S.E. Porter, *Verbal Aspect in the Greek of the New Testament, with Reference to Tense and Mood* (SBG 1; New York: Lang, 1989) 198–208, 209–211, on the use of the imperfect tense-form.

[16] See F.F. Bruce, *The Acts of the Apostles* (Grand Rapids: Eerdmans, 3rd edn, 1990 [2nd edn, 1952]) 391 (2nd edn, 1952); W. Neil, *The Acts of the Apostles* (NCB; London: Marshall, Morgan, Scott, 1977) 218.

[17] Contra Marshall, *Acts*, 342.

[18] Bruce, *Commentary*, 430.

[19] M.-E. Rosenblatt, *Paul the Accused: His Portrait in the Acts of the Apostles* (Collegeville, MN: Liturgical, 1995) 68. See also p. 69: "Luke minimizes the evidence of conflict between Paul and the Church's elders, but ironically suggests that Paul's religious integrity is as much their own question as that of the community at large."

address Paul (v. 20),[20] "You see" (θεωρεῖς), implying that he may have been aware of some of the difficulty.[21] As a recognized brother in the faith (note use of the vocative of address),[22] he can be told that many thousands (probably hyperbole to introduce and emphasize the point; note use of πάντες in v. 20c)[23] of the Jews who have believed[24] are still zealous for the Mosaic law.[25] These "zealots" may have been those who were former members of or sympathizers with the Pharisaic party (cf. 15:5), and who were, in any case, enthusiastic for God's law as a gift to Israel (similar phrasing is found in 1 Macc 2:26–27, 50, 54, 58), but who were certainly not members of any group, formal or informal, that represented the political Zealot party – but it was probably not restricted to this group. The phrasing sounds much more like it represents a larger general group, such as possibly were involved in insurrection during the time purportedly represented by the narrative.[26]

---

[20] Regarding the use of "they," Lake and Cadbury (*English Translation*, 271) raise the question of whether this is ecclesiastical propriety rather than a physical possibility. According to the scenario being laid out above, it is probably indicative of the widespread sentiment of the church in Jerusalem, including both leaders and members. However, J. Roloff (*Die Apostelgeschichte* [NTD 5; Berlin: Evangelische Verlags-Anstalt, 1981] 314) believes that James speaks for the elders, and in an almost threatening tone.

[21] Knowling, "Acts," 2.448.

[22] See R. Pesch, *Die Apostelgeschichte* (2 vols.; EKK 5.1, 2; Solothurn: Benziger; Neukirchen-Vluyn: Neukirchener, 1992 [2nd edn], 1986) 2.219, who also notes the hyperbole involved in the language used toward Paul, especially regarding the numbers involved in accusing Paul.

[23] See Marshall, *Acts*, 344; Haenchen, *Acts*, 608–609. Others suggest that the reference to thousands is idiomatic for "many": Bruce, *Acts*, 445; Page, *Acts*, 221; or is a reference to all Judea: Neil, *Acts*, 218; Knowling, "Acts," 2.449. Cf. Roloff, *Die Apostelgeschichte*, 314; L.T. Johnson, *The Acts of the Apostles* (SP 5; Collegeville, MN: Liturgical, 1992) 374; and F.S. Spencer, *Acts* (Readings; Sheffield: Sheffield Academic Press, 1997) 199, who, citing such parallels as Acts 2:41, 47; 4:4; 5:14, seem to take the numbers literally.

[24] J. Munck (*The Acts of the Apostles* [rev. W.F. Albright and C.S. Mann; AB 31; Garden City, NY: Doubleday, 1967] 209) proposes non-Christian Jews, but this can only be if τῶν πεπιστευκότων is eliminated. See also B. Newman and E.A. Nida, *A Translator's Handbook on the Acts of the Apostles* (London: UBS, 1972) 409.

[25] The issue here does not appear to be the validity of the law for salvation. See G. Krodel, *Acts* (Philadelphia: Fortress Press, 1981) 69. On the general question of law in the New Testament, there has been much recent discussion. See Chapter Nine below for basic bibliography.

[26] See Page, *Acts*, 222; J.B. Polhill, *Acts* (NAC 26; Nashville: Broadman, 1992) 447. For more historical information on this time, with the steps taken by the Romans to suppress insurrection, see E. Schürer, *The History of the Jewish People in the Age of Jesus Christ* (ed. and rev. G. Vermes *et al.*; 3 vols.; Edinburgh: T. & T. Clark, 1973–1987) 1.426–445; M. Hengel, *The Zealots* (trans. D. Smith; Edinburgh: T. & T. Clark, 1989) esp. 149–183.

These people, characterized as zealots, apparently readily believed the rumors they were told about what Paul was teaching (Acts 21:21). κατηχέω, the word used to characterize Paul's teaching, often implies definite instruction,[27] possibly with a deliberate purpose from a position of authority,[28] and this clearly bothered them. Their accusation is, therefore, twofold: Paul is accused of teaching those Jews in the Diaspora (κατὰ τὰ ἔθνη)[29] to forsake (ἀποστασίαν; cf. 1 Macc 2:15; 2 Thess 2:3)[30] Moses and to do this by not circumcising their children and not walking (περιπατέω)[31] according to the customs laid down by the Jewish law. Circumcision, the most distinctive rite of the Mosaic law, was a sign of obedience, and quite clearly a boundary marker for what it meant to be an obedient Jew. To not perform this rite could easily call forth contempt from other Jews (cf. 1 Sam 17:26).[32]

On the basis of what is seen elsewhere in Acts with regard to Jews that he encounters (to say nothing of Paul's letters), this is clearly a mistaken characterization of Paul's teaching (regardless of what one thinks of his personal behavior), especially with regard to his thoughts on the law's place and relevance. Conzelmann states this even more strongly: "Der Leser der Act weiss, dass die Vorwürfe falsch sind."[33] However, one can understand the origin of the rumors, and even the responsiveness of the Jerusalem church's leaders to them, because Christian Jews of the Diaspora were probably taking seriously Paul's statements to Gentiles regarding "freedom from the Law" (see Gal 4:9; 5:6; Rom 2:25–30) and his denial of being a preacher of circumcision to the Gentiles (Gal 5:11), and even his own behavior that reflected such teaching.[34] But neither in Paul's letters nor especially in Acts

---

[27] Knowling, "Acts," 2.29.

[28] Page, *Acts*, 222; H.W. Beyer, "κατηχέω," *TDNT*, 3.638.

[29] Haenchen, *Acts*, 609. On the Jews of the Diaspora, see now the work of J.M.G. Barclay, *Jews in the Mediterranean Diaspora: From Alexander to Trajan (323 BCE–117 CE)* (Edinburgh: T. & T. Clark, 1996) *passim* but esp. 424–426.

[30] ἀποστασία is a strong word for rebellion or abandonment in a religious sense. See BAGD s.v.

[31] This is the only use of this verb in Luke–Acts. See BAGD s.v.

[32] See Page, *Acts*, 222.

[33] Conzelmann, *Die Apostelgeschichte*, 131; see also Knowling, "Acts," 2.449; G. Schneider, *Die Apostelgeschichte* (2 vols.; HTKNT 5.1, 2; Freiburg: Herder, 1980, 1982) 2.309; Pesch, *Die Apostelgeschichte*, 2.220; B. Rapske, "Opposition to the Plan of God and Persecution," in I.H. Marshall and D. Peterson (eds.), *Witness to the Gospel: The Theology of Acts* (Grand Rapids: Eerdmans, 1998) 244.

[34] See Marshall, *Acts*, 344; Schneider, *Die Apostelgeschichte*, 2.220; and F.F. Bruce, "Is the Paul of Acts the Real Paul?" *BJRL* 58 (1976) 295; Witherington, *Acts*, 648; contra Lake and Cadbury, *English Translation*, 271.

(see Acts 15) does Paul suggest that Jewish believers give up their ancestral practices, even if he does not endorse them for Gentiles (see Acts 16:3) or personally follow all precepts of the law in every detail.[35] The distinction between Paul's message for Jews and Gentiles was apparently missed, or even willfully overlooked, by a number of Jews, and even those in the Jerusalem church. One may even detect here a distinct hint of jealousy toward Paul on the part of the Jerusalem leaders entering into the repetition of the accusations.[36]

The rhetorical question, "What, therefore, is it [that is, what is to be done to correct the false opinion about Paul]?" (τί οὖν ἐστιν;),[37] not only expresses residual or suspicious doubt regarding Paul, even by the Jerusalem Christians,[38] but implies by its very rhetorical nature that Paul is in some way being positioned in such a way to compensate for the difficulties that he has purportedly caused. At the least, the Jerusalem church has already devised a plan and set it in motion.[39] Silence is not the answer, because, of course (πάντως),[40] "they" will have heard that Paul has arrived in Jerusalem. The "they" here probably refers to those who are characterized as being zealots for the law,[41] not Jews in general[42] but Jews – both Christian and not – who believed rather in the abiding validity of the law; hence, it probably also includes, by association, the Jerusalem leaders, who are apparently equally

---

[35] See Bruce, *Acts*, 446; Haenchen, *Acts*, 609.

[36] Several critics use reference in this episode to the apparent thriving of Jewish Christianity as an aid to dating the composition of Acts. They also note that this illustrates that Pauline Christianity was attempting a compromise with Jewish Christianity. See Lake and Cadbury, *English Translation*, 271; Haenchen, *Acts*, 609; cf. also W. Gasque, *A History of the Criticism of the Acts of the Apostles* (BGBE 17; Tübingen: Mohr–Siebeck; Grand Rapids: Eerdmans, 1975) 132–133; contra J.C. O'Neill, *The Theology of Acts in its Historical Setting* (London: SPCK, 1961) 17–18.

[37] Haenchen, *Acts*, 609; cf. Johnson, *Acts*, 375, who notes this type of rhetorical question in diatribal literature such as Epictetus (1.6.12; 1.7.7; 2.4.8).

[38] See G. Lüdemann, *Opposition to Paul in Jewish Christianity* (trans. M.E. Boring; Minneapolis: Fortress Press, 1989) 58; contra Conzelmann, *Die Apostelgeschichte*, 131.

[39] Polhill, *Acts*, 448.

[40] πάντως possibly has a weakened sense of assurance, although that is not readily evident in this context. See Lake and Cadbury, *English Translation*, 272.

[41] See Knowling, "Acts," 2.449; Marshall, *Acts*, 344. Schneider (*Die Apostelgeschichte*, 2.309) labels it a genitive of content.

[42] See Conzelmann, *Die Apostelgeschichte*, 131. Schille (*Die Apostelgeschichte*, 413) says that the charges were falsely repeated not by Christian Jews but by Jews in Asia Minor (see Acts 21:29). This interpretation appears to conflate this and the following episodes, and to attempt to avoid the implications of this scenario for the Christian Jews in Jerusalem.

suspicious.[43] The use of the third person is a way of grammatically distancing those making the claims from those reporting them, even if the two groups overlap.[44]

A practical suggestion is presented, which will both make clear to the Jewish Christians that accusations against Paul are false and protect the leaders of the Jerusalem church against recrimination for supporting Paul.[45] There is also a clear sense that this will put Paul in his proper place as subordinate to the Jerusalem leaders, something he had apparently resisted throughout his missionary career (e.g. Gal 2:5). It is not enough that Paul has probably brought a gift from other Christians to the Jews in Jerusalem – he also must do something.[46] The ease with which this solution is found, and the fortuitous timing involved, give the impression that this is a plan that may have in fact been some time in the making. It clearly is not "absurd" to think that Paul was in some way, if not directly lured into, at least not prevented from, stepping into a trap,[47] or to think that James "would never have consented to it."[48] It appears that four men, almost assuredly part of the Jerusalem church,[49] happened to be under a vow (Acts 21:23). εὐχή probably refers here to a temporary Nazirite vow, since the participants are Jews intending to shave their heads (v. 24).[50] They are in the process of fulfilling

---

[43] The Western text (D), plus ℵ A C, has δεῖ συνελθεῖν πλῆθος or the like (Bruce, *Acts*, 446), which could support either interpretation of "they," plus suggest others (see Haenchen, *Acts*, 609; contra G.A. Deissmann, *Bible Studies* [trans. A. Grieve; London: Hodder & Stoughton, 2nd edn, 1909] 232–233, who says πλῆθος means community or congregation). The reading is strongly based upon the manuscript evidence, but it appears to be a Western addition that gained wide circulation (B.M. Metzger, *A Textual Commentary on the Greek New Testament* [Stuttgart: Deutsche Bibelgesellschaft, 2nd edn, 1994 (1971)] 429).

[44] On the use of person, and what it entails, see S.E. Porter, *Idioms of the Greek New Testament* (BLG 2; Sheffield: JSOT Press, 2nd edn, 1994) 76–77.

[45] Longenecker, "Acts," 529.

[46] So Roloff, *Die Apostelgeschichte*, 314.

[47] See R. Bauckham, "James and the Jerusalem Church," in R. Bauckham (ed.), *The Book of Acts in its First Century Setting. IV. The Book of Acts in its Palestinian Setting* (Grand Rapids: Eerdmans, 1995) 478, who uses such language in rejecting the idea of A.J. Mattill, "The Purpose of Acts: Schneckenburger Reconsidered," in W.W. Gasque and R.P. Martin (eds.), *Apostolic History and the Gospel: Biblical and Historical Essays Presented to F.F. Bruce on his 60th Birthday* (Exeter: Paternoster, 1970) 115–116, Mattill's proposal, to my mind, being a very plausible and convincing explanation of what happened in Jerusalem.

[48] Witherington, *Acts*, 650, who is clearly overlooking the possibility of the Judaizers of Galatians having come from James (see Gal 2:12).

[49] Knowling, "Acts," 2.449.

[50] The phrase is a LXX formula. See also Acts 18:18, the only other occurrence in the New Testament of the noun form. See H. Greeven, "εὔχομαι," *TDNT*, 2.777; cf. H. Danby, *The Mishnah* (London: Oxford University Press, 1958) 280–293; H.L. Strack and P. Billerbeck, *Das Evangelium nach Markus, Lukas und Johannes und die Apostelgeschichte*

the vow (ἔχοντες – present participle) but it at present lies unfulfilled (it is still ἐφ' ἑαυτῶν).[51] This is possibly because the four were unable to pay for the appropriate sacrifices,[52] but more likely because this situation was set up to put Paul in his place, and for him to be seen to be in his place of subordination to the Jerusalem leaders by the church and the Jews of Jerusalem.

The proposal requires that Paul purify himself along with the four, and that he pay their expenses for the vow. To pay the expenses of those participating in a Nazirite vow was deemed an act of great Jewish piety (see Josephus, *Ant.* 19.294, regarding Herod Agrippa's similar actions).[53] It is unlikely that Paul used money he brought for the Jerusalem church, since this would have diluted the benefit to the church and detracted from the resources that Paul had brought, as well as compromising the plan of the leaders. Ramsay speculates that Paul probably had access to reasonably large sums of money, possibly from an inheritance,[54] but we simply do not know where his money came from in this instance, if it transpired as reported. What we do know is that, outside of Jerusalem, Paul appears to have had a significant number of supporters, some of them with sufficient money to have met this and similar expenses.

Paul is told to join in the purification rites with the four (Acts 21:24). The verb παραλαβών ("join") implies that Paul became the companion of the four in the ritual (σὺν αὐτοῖς), but, although ἁγνίζω ("purify") does have cultic associations, this does not necessarily mean Paul also took the Nazirite vow – the verb here is ambiguous.[55] Four major views of what happened in this event have been proposed. (1) With the four others, some say, Paul undertook the terminal sacrifice of a Nazirite vow previously begun at Cenchrea when he had his hair cut (Acts 18:18). All five require a period of purification and then a thirty-day period (in Paul's case never completed) to terminate the

---

(vol. 3; Munich: Beck, 1961) 755–761; and most commentators, especially Lake and Cadbury, *English Translation*, 272–273.

[51] Knowling, "Acts," 2.449.

[52] Longenecker, "Acts," 520.

[53] See Knowling, "Acts," 2.450; Page, *Acts*, 223.

[54] W.M. Ramsay, *St Paul the Traveller and the Roman Citizen* (London: Hodder & Stoughton, 1895) 310–311.

[55] See Schille, *Die Apostelgeschichte*, 414. In fact, according to G. Lüdemann, so is the entire episode (e.g. a Nazirite vow was thirty days, but only seven days are involved in the Acts account), indicating (to him) Lukan redaction to try to preserve a tradition of Paul being a faithful Jew to the end (*Early Christianity according to the Traditions in Acts: A Commentary* [trans. J. Bowden; Minneapolis: Fortress Press, 1987] 232); see also Polhill, *Acts*, 449.

vow.[56] (2) The four men had contracted some ceremonial defilement and had to undergo a seven-day purification rite in the Temple before consummating their Nazirite vows. According to this view, Paul joins the men for the purification rites (see Acts 24:18), although he himself may not have contracted defilement and is not actually participating in the Nazirite vow itself.[57] (3) The four Nazirites had already completed their period of devotion, but they could not afford their final expense for the sacrifice. Paul, wanting to enter fully into the ritual, offered to pay the sacrifice, but, since he had come from a foreign land, needed first to regain levitical purity before he could be present at the absolution ceremony for the four.[58] (4) Luke misunderstood the account of the incident, so that although Paul's vow appears to be Nazirite, insufficient time is allowed for it to have actually taken place.[59] As Haenchen admits in assessing the situation, the story in Acts need not be contradictory or confused (contra view 4 above),[60] but it appears to eliminate a Nazirite vow for Paul because of insufficient time (contra views 1 and 3).[61] It is not clear that traveling to Gentile lands defiled a Jew (contra view 3), and it is possible for various rites to be performed in the Temple by one not defiled.[62] Thus, it appears (with view 2) that Paul joins the four men in their ritual, though probably not participating in the Nazirite vow itself, not least because of insufficient time due to the pressure of the Jerusalem leaders for Paul to show his Jewish identity as quickly as possible.

Some scholars rightly question whether Paul would have participated in such a ceremony, even if there had been sufficient time.[63] This is a logical question to ask, especially in light of Paul's relationship to the Jerusalem church, and the preceding prophecies in Acts regarding his forthcoming fate in Jerusalem (see Acts 20:38; 21:11). On one level, Paul participates,

---

[56] See V. Stolle, *Der Zeuge als Angeklagter* (Stuttgart, 1973), 76–78, cited in Marshall, *Acts*, 345; Knowling, "Acts," 2.450; Page, *Acts*, 223; Longenecker, "Acts," 520; R. Wallace and W. Williams, *The Acts of the Apostles* (London: Duckworth, 1993) 113.

[57] Bruce, *Commentary*, 430–431; *idem, Acts*, 393 (2nd edn, 1952); Roloff, *Die Apostelgeschichte*, 315.

[58] Haenchen, *Acts*, 611–612; Schneider, *Die Apostelgeschichte*, 2.310.

[59] Conzelmann, *Apostelgeschichte*, 31; Hanson, *Acts*, 211; Haenchen (*Acts*, 611) hints at this.

[60] Haenchen, *Acts*, 611.

[61] See Danby, *Mishnah*, 281.

[62] Bruce, *Acts*, 393 (2nd edn, 1952); see Knowling, "Acts," 2.450.

[63] Contra A. Harnack, *The Date of the Acts and the Synoptic Gospels* (trans. J.R. Wilkinson; New York: Putnam, 1911) 76, who states, "This account...bears the stamp of perfect trustworthiness"; Roloff, *Die Apostelgeschichte*, 315.

however, so that (ἵνα)[64] the four Nazirites might be able to shave their heads (cf. Num 6:14),[65] which solves the immediate problem.[66] On another level, Paul participates so that all, Jewish Christians primarily and all Jews generally, might know that the accusations, whether real or manufactured by the Jerusalem leaders (see Acts 21:21 for the same use of the verb κατηχέω), are invalid, and that Paul himself obeys the law when dealing with Jewish Christians. The situation is very realistic, in so far as it accurately shows that Paul was convinced that he was no longer under the law, but he was also a Jew and able to share in his people's religious duties.[67] στοιχέω here assumes an ethical sense like περιπατέω (v. 21). Paul apparently was willing to keep the law both as a conciliatory gesture in light of the situation, and, in terms that reflect the letters, as a means of looking forward to the salvation of Israel (Romans 9–11), and as part of being all things to all men, including a Jew to Jews (1 Cor 9:20).[68]

James apparently anticipated a possible Pauline objection (περὶ δέ; Acts 21:25), and says that the fact that Paul participated in this way with the Jews did not affect his behavior toward believing Gentiles. James and the elders, speaking for the Jerusalem church, as well as themselves, now reaffirm the resolution sent to the Gentiles (Acts 15); the use of ἡμεῖς emphasizes that they had agreed to the Gentile conditions,[69] which they are obviously less concerned about than the standards Jews were expected still to fulfil. Many scholars have questioned the reason for the repetition of these four edicts here. For example, some say (as mentioned above) that Paul was not at the

---

[64] See Turner, *Syntax*, 100; Blass and Debrunner, *Greek Grammar*, § 369(3), regarding the future form. See also Porter, *Verbal Aspect*, 403–439.

[65] See Danby, *Mishnah*, 282.

[66] See Longenecker, "Acts," 571, who says that ξυράω is the equivalent of the Hebrew word for the entire Nazirite offering.

[67] Harnack, *Date of Acts*, 80–81; cf. Lüdemann, *Opposition to Paul*, 59, who also believes that this is from a continuous source, other than the "we" source.

[68] Lake and Cadbury, *English Translation*, 273; Roloff, *Die Apostelgeschichte*, 315; J. Jervell, "Paul in the Acts of the Apostles: Tradition, History, Theology," in J. Kremer, (ed.), *Les Actes des Apôtres: Traditions, rédaction, théologie* (BETL 48; Gembloux: Duculot; Leuven: Leuven University Press, 1979) 300–301. Jervell introduces unnecessary difficulties when he asserts that the Paul of Acts's view of the law as not giving salvation has no relation to the Pauline idea that the law cannot be fulfilled (*The Theology of the Acts of the Apostles* [New Testament Theology; Cambridge: Cambridge University Press, 1996] 89 and n. 168, following P. Vielhauer, "On the 'Paulinism of Acts," in L.E. Keck and J.L. Martyn [eds.], *Studies in Luke–Acts* [Philadelphia: Fortress Press, 1966] 33–34). Cf. G. Bornkamm, "The Missionary Stance of Paul in I Corinthians 9 and in Acts," in Keck and Martyn (eds.), *Studies in Luke–Acts*, 194–207.

[69] Knowling, "Acts," 2.450; Pesch, *Die Apostelgeschichte*, 2.221.

Jerusalem Council, so this would have been his first hearing of the matter, and thus provides a means of exonerating his supposed failure to follow the requirements;[70] others that Luke as redactor has failed to eliminate the words in his source, so that inclusion here is an unfortunate accident, perhaps best ignored;[71] some that the words are not for Paul but for the reader, although there is nothing in the structure of the text to make this indication;[72] others that there is a change from what was decided at the Apostolic Council, so that what was permitted is now seen as sinful,[73] a retrogressive and even reactionary step in Jewish and Gentile relations; and that James and the elders, though glad Paul does not teach abandonment of the Jewish law, want to reaffirm their support of Paul's mission to the Gentiles, although it is unclear why citing these legalistic requirements helps to do that.[74] However, there may be another, even more plausible, explanation. Since the decrees arose originally in the relations between Jewish and Gentile Christians, and arise again here in a similar context,[75] they should probably be seen as being

---

[70] Catchpole, "Paul," 431; cf. Spencer, *Acts*, 199.

[71] Conzelmann, *Die Apostelgeschichte*, 131–132.

[72] Haenchen, *Acts*, 610. One must ask the further question of whether there is anything in the text that is not for the reader, and what difference that really makes here.

[73] Schneider, *Die Apostelgeschichte*, 2.311.

[74] Bruce, *Acts*, 447–448; *idem*, *Commentary*, 431.

[75] The four requirements – to abstain from what was sacrificed to idols, from blood, from what is strangled, and from unchastity – conform to Acts 15:29 (different order in 15:20). It is quite clear that the "ritual" interpretation is to be accepted (see Haenchen, *Acts*, 499–500, 455–472; M. Simon, "The Apostolic Decree and its Setting in the Ancient Church," *BJRL* 52 [1969] 437–460; Catchpole, "Paul," 428–444; R.P. Martin, *New Testament Foundations*. II. *The Acts, the Letters, the Apocalypse* [Grand Rapids: Eerdmans, 1978] 112–115), and that the textual variants are designed to promote a solely "moral" or an "ethical" interpretation (Harnack, *Date of Acts*, 248–263; A.C. Clark, *The Acts of the Apostles: A Critical Edition with Introduction and Notes on Selected Passages* [Oxford: Clarendon Press, 1970] 360–361; P. Head, "Acts and the Problems of its Texts," in B.W. Winter and A.D. Clarke [eds.], *The Book of Acts in its First Century Setting*. I. *The Book of Acts in its Literary Setting* [Grand Rapids: Eerdmans, 1993] 438–442). A thorough, though not necessarily convincing, study of Acts 15:20, 29 and 21:25 is found in W.A. Strange, *The Problem of the Text of Acts* (SNTSMS 71; Cambridge: Cambridge University Press, 1992) 87–105.

εἰδωλόθυτον refers to meat offered to idols and then eaten either in a Temple feast or sold in a shop. The reference here is to the meat which came out of the Temple (F. Büchsel, "εἰδωλόθυτον," *TDNT*, 2.378–379). αἷμα means animal flesh from a strangled animal, forbidden by Jewish law because of the thought that the life or soul resided in the blood (Bruce, *Acts*, 342). πνικτόν refers to strangulation itself. This is the item omitted by the Western (D) text. πορνείαν refers variously to breaches of the Jewish marriage laws or, perhaps more accurately, illicit sexual intercourse (Marshall, *Acts*, 253). On further theological implications of the Western text, see E.J. Epp, *The Theological Tendency of Codex Bezae Cantabrigensis in Acts* (SNTSMS 3; Cambridge: Cambridge University Press, 1966) 107–112.

used now by the Jerusalem leaders to establish common ground in the Church, and a common ground that at the least shares institutionalized respect for Jewish practices.[76] This seems to be the overwhelming concern of the leaders of the Jerusalem church, and something that they wish to convey very strongly to Paul, represented both in word and in deed.

With the speech over (τότε), Paul accedes to the request to be involved in the ritual in the Temple (Acts 21:26). There is no indication in the narrative that he does so begrudgingly, but based on subsequent actions, the wisdom of his participation could well be questioned.[77] The motivation of the Jerusalem leaders is also brought into serious question, because they should have known the potentially unstable and explosive climate of religious belief in Jerusalem. They appear to be responding to such pressure in their compelling Paul to be involved in this act in the first place. The imperfect tense-form in v. 26, εἰσῄει, has been interpreted to designate a specific entrance by Paul to announce the fulfilment of the purification ritual (cf. v. 18),[78] Paul's repeated visits to the Temple to talk about the matter,[79] or separate trips Paul made with each of the four Nazirites.[80] The reference is probably to participation by Paul with the Nazirites in their week-long purification rites (see τῇ ἐχομένῃ ἡμέρᾳ with σὺν αὐτοῖς; cf. v. 27).[81] He also announces the day on which the purification rites will be completed (Num 6:5) and when (adverbial use of the participle διαγγέλλων)[82] the Nazirite offerings (Num 6:14–15)[83] will be offered up.[84]

---

[76] Cf. Simon, "Apostolic Decree," 459; R.N. Longenecker, *Paul: Apostle of Liberty* (New York: Harper & Row, 1964) 223.

[77] E.M. Blaiklock, *The Acts of the Apostles: An Historical Commentary* (TNTC; Grand Rapids: Eerdmans, 1959) 172; Bruce, *Commentary*, 432. Knowling ("Acts," 2.451) dismisses this view.

[78] See Bruce, *Acts*, 448; Blass and Debrunner, *Greek Grammar*, § 99(1).

[79] Lake and Cadbury, *English Translation*, 274.

[80] Longenecker, "Acts," 520.

[81] Knowling, "Acts," 2.451; cf. Pesch, *Die Apostelgeschichte*, 2.219.

[82] Lake and Cadbury, *English Translation*, 274. διαγγέλλω is used here with the sense of "give notice," in this case pertaining to a "cultic announcement." See BAGD s.v.; J. Schniewind, "διαγγέλλω," *TDNT*, 1.69; Schneider, *Die Apostelgeschichte*, 2.311.

[83] Danby, *Mishnah*, 288.

[84] See K. Weiss, "προσφέρω," *TDNT*, 9.66–67. Some take ἕως οὗ with εἰσῄει: "he entered in…[and stayed] until the offering." See Knowling, "Acts," 2.451.

3. Conclusion

Acts 21:17-26 presents numerous problems for the interpreter, including that of the relationship between the Paul of Acts and the Paul of the letters.[85] At the conclusion of three missionary journeys, according to the account in Acts, Paul comes to Jerusalem to report his success and, probably, to convey the collection to James and the elders.[86] Though the church leaders apparently rejoice, on closer examination it appears that they are in full agreement with a more strongly Pharisaical group in the Jerusalem church who wish to accuse Paul of encouraging Diaspora Jews to abandon the law of Moses. To clear himself of suspicion, Paul accepts James's transparently unspontaneous suggestion to demonstrate that, as a servant of Christ, he still remains a loyal Jew: Paul pays the expenses for four Nazirites and himself to participate in a purification ritual in the Temple. Thus Paul, maintaining his love for Israel and remembering that God is determined to bring Israel to salvation (Rom 11:11 ff.), clearly illustrates in the book of Acts what he articulates in his letters elsewhere: he made himself a "slave to all, that I might win more" (1 Cor 9:19). This means that "to the Jews I become as a Jew, in order to win Jews, to those under the law I become as one under the law" (1 Cor 9:20), without believing that he has compromised himself. This does admittedly result in an inconsistency in Paul's conduct, between in some contexts practicing the law and in others not. In this instance, the resulting events turn sour. What at first appears to be a sign of willing devotion (probably in concession to those elsewhere characterized as "the weak" [see Rom 14:1–15:13]) becomes an unforeseen catastrophe, with the Jerusalem church apparently standing passively by.[87] When the Jews grab him in the Temple and try to kill him, Paul makes one last rather surprising defense to his Jewish countrymen in the Hebrew/Aramaic language (Acts 22:1–21).[88] From this point on, Paul's life is in the hands of the Romans. One cannot help but notice that his missionary endeavors thrive more under these conditions than they do in the hands of the leaders of the Jerusalem church. According to Acts, we do not know what happens to Paul in Rome, but it is significant that the last

---

[85] Vielhauer ("Paulinism," 39–40) throws the passage out because of its problems.

[86] Note again that the collection, even though meant as a relief fund for the church in Jerusalem, is not mentioned in Acts 21. See Krodel, *Acts*, 69.

[87] See Lüdemann, *Opposition to Paul*, 61; J.D.G. Dunn, *Unity and Diversity in the New Testament* (Philadelphia: Westminster Press, 1977) 256–257. On relations between the Jews and the Romans in Palestine during this period, see Schürer, *History of the Jewish People*, 1.381–392 and 455–470.

[88] Schubert, "Final Cycle," 5.

speech by Paul, as noted in Chapter Seven above, is addressed to the Jews in Rome, telling of their rejection of the gospel and that "this salvation of God [God's salvation] has been sent to the Gentiles; they will listen" (28:28). These words serve as the formal renunciation of the events that took place in Acts 21. The Jews, apparently both Christian and non-Christian Jews, having rejected him, Paul preaches the kingdom of God and the teaching of Jesus Christ openly and unhindered in Rome to Gentiles (28:30–32).

Chapter Nine

The Paul of Acts and the Paul of the Letters: Some Common Conceptions and Misconceptions

1. Introduction

The portrait of the Apostle Paul gleaned from the book of Acts and from his letters is not the item of serious contention that it once was among scholars. To survey the past discussion very briefly, in the nineteenth century, due in large part to the work of F.C. Baur,[1] skepticism was introduced regarding the reliability of Acts as an early historical document, and, with it, there was a separation of its account from both an accurate depiction of the ancient world of the time and its portrait of Paul. Around the turn of the century, much of this resultant skepticism was countered by the ambitious and adventuresome discoveries of William Ramsay. In English-speaking scholarship, he has been followed in his work by such scholars as F.F. Bruce, Ward Gasque, I.H. Marshall, now Rainer Riesner, and, perhaps most significantly, Colin Hemer.[2]

---

[1] See F.C. Baur, "Die Christuspartei in der korinthischen Gemeinde, der Gegensatz des petrinischen und paulinischen Christentums in der alten Kirche, der Apostel Petrus in Rom," *Tübinger Zeitschrift für Theologie* 4 (1831) 61–206, repr. in F.C. Baur, *Historisch-kritische Untersuchungen zum Neuen Testament* (ed. E. Käsemann; Stuttgart: Frommann, 1963) 1–146; *Paulus, der Apostel Jesu Christi: Sein Leben und Wirken, seine Briefe und seine Lehre* (Stuttgart, 1845; 2nd edn, 1866–1867), trans. as *Paul: His Life and Works* (trans. A. Menzies; 2 vols.; London: Williams & Norgate, 1873, 1875); and *Das Christenthum und die christliche Kirche der drei ersten Jahrhunderte* (Tübingen, 1853; 2nd edn, 1860; 3rd edn, 1863), trans. as *The Church History of the First Three Centuries* (trans. A. Menzies; 2 vols.; London: Williams & Norgate, 1878, 1879). That Baur has not always been interpreted correctly on Acts, however, is made clear by C.K. Barrett, "How History Should Be Written," in B. Witherington, III (ed.), *History, Literature and Society in the Book of Acts* (Cambridge: Cambridge University Press, 1996) esp. 36–37. For a history of Baur and his followers, see H. Harris, *The Tübingen School: A Historical and Theological Investigation of the School of F.C. Baur* (Oxford: Oxford University Press, 1975; repr. Grand Rapids: Baker, 1990).

[2] Only a selection of their works can be given: W.M. Ramsay, *The Bearing of Recent Discovery on the Trustworthiness of the New Testament* (London: Hodder & Stoughton, 1915); F.F. Bruce, *The Acts of the Apostles* (Grand Rapids: Eerdmans, 3rd edn, 1990 [2nd edn, 1952]); W.W. Gasque, *A History of the Criticism of the Acts of the Apostles* (BGBE 17; Tübingen: Mohr–Siebeck; Grand Rapids: Eerdmans, 1975); I.H. Marshall, *The Acts of the*

This opinion seems to continue to be the trend among much classical scholarship. However, throughout the century much German biblical scholarship has simply ignored this predominantly English-language work, continuing to develop the disjunction between the Paul of Acts and the Paul of the letters.[3] This work perhaps reached its definitive statement in the work of the 1950s and 1960s of Ernst Haenchen and Paul Vielhauer, originally published in German.[4] This work has also had widespread influence in the English-speaking world, resulting in what appear to be several of the assured results of scholarship – that the book of Acts is anything but primarily a historical document, and that its depiction of Paul is at odds with that of the Pauline letters. Those who deny that the book of Acts is primarily a book of ancient historiography have proposed a variety of re-interpretations, including

---

Apostles (TNTC; Grand Rapids: Eerdmans, 1980); R. Riesner, *Paul's Early Period: Chronology, Mission Strategy, Theology* (trans. D. Stott; Grand Rapids: Eerdmans, 1998); and C. Hemer, *The Book of Acts in the Setting of Hellenistic History* (ed. C. Gempf; WUNT 49; Tübingen: Mohr–Siebeck, 1989; repr. Winona Lake, IN: Eisenbrauns, 1990).

[3] For a history of the scholarship on Acts, see Gasque, *History of the Criticism of Acts*, *passim*; W.G. Kümmel, *The New Testament: The History of the Investigation of its Problems* (trans. S.McL. Gilmour and H.C. Kee; Nashville: Abingdon, 1972) *passim*; cf. also E.E. Ellis, *The Gospel of Luke* (NCB; Grand Rapids: Eerdmans, rev. edn, 1974) 42–51; M.A. Powell, *What are They Saying about Acts?* (New York: Paulist, 1991); J.B. Green and M.C. McKeever, *Luke–Acts and New Testament Historiography* (IBR Bibliographies; Grand Rapids: Baker, 1994) *passim*.

[4] See E. Haenchen, *The Acts of the Apostles: A Commentary* (trans. B. Noble *et al.*; Philadelphia: Westminster Press, 1971 [1965]) 112–116; P. Vielhauer, "On the 'Paulinism' of Acts" (originally published as "Zum 'Paulinismus' der Apostelgeschichte," *EvTh* 10 [1950–1951] 1–15), in L.E. Keck and J.L. Martyn (eds.), *Studies in Luke–Acts* (Philadelphia: Fortress Press, 1966) 33–50. The Germans have been clear in following this position. See, for example, H. Conzelmann, *Die Apostelgeschichte* (HNT 7; Tübingen: Mohr–Siebeck, 1963); J. Roloff, *Die Apostelgeschichte* (NTD 5; Berlin: Evangelische Verlags-Anstalt, 1981) 2–5; G. Schille, *Die Apostelgeschichte des Lukas* (THNT 5; Berlin: Evangelische Verlags-Anstalt, 1983) 48–52; but cf. U. Wilckens, "Interpreting Luke–Acts in a Period of Existentialist Theology," in Keck and Martyn (eds.), *Studies in Luke–Acts*, 60–83. A response to Vielhauer that fails to engage with the substantive issues is Gasque, *History of the Criticism of Acts*, 283–291. More useful are J. Jervell, "Paul in the Acts of the Apostles: Tradition, History, Theology," in J. Kremer (ed.), *Les Actes des Apôtres: Traditions, rédaction, théologie* (BETL 48; Gembloux: Duculot; Leuven: Leuven University Press, 1979) 297–305; and L.T. Johnson, *The Writings of the New Testament: An Interpretation* (Minneapolis: Fortress Press, 1986) 231–238. Along similar lines was the position of G. Harbsmeier ("Unsere Predigt im Spiegel der Apostelgeschichte," *EvTh* [1950–1951] 352–368), responded to by O. Bauernfeind, "Zur Frage nach der Entscheidung zwischen Paulus und Lukas," *ZST* 23 (1954) 59–88; repr. in *idem, Kommentar und Studien zur Apostelgeschichte* (WUNT 22; ed. V. Metelman; Tübingen: Mohr–Siebeck, 1980) 353–382; cf. *idem*, "Die Geschichtsauffassung des Urchristentums," *ZST* 15 (1938) 347–378; repr. in *Kommentar und Studien*, 425–448; and *idem*, "Vom historischen zum lukanischen Paulus," *EvT* 13 (1953) 347–353.

that it is a heavily redacted document, possibly from some (now virtually unrecoverable) sources, that it is a kind of travelogue conforming to ancient conventions of sea voyages, or that it is of a kind with ancient romantic or novelistic literature (see Chapter Two for discussion of these theories in relation to the "we" passages).[5] If this is the consensus of modern scholarship, one might well ask why this chapter is included here at all. Elsewhere in this volume, I deal with some issues regarding the nature of the book of Acts as a literary document. Here, I wish to scrutinize the arguments put forward by Haenchen and Vielhauer, still considered to be the authoritative statements on this issue,[6] regarding the Paul of Acts and the Paul of the letters. These arguments have left an enduring legacy in New Testament scholarship, one that must constantly be re-considered because of the serious implications that derive from them regarding the use of the book of Acts to inform study of Paul's letters.

2. The Paul of Acts and of the Letters

There seem to be two main sets of arguments marshalled by Vielhauer and Haenchen against the Paul of the letters being the Paul of Acts. It is fair and right to admit from the outset that their work, representative of much of the discussion over the previous century, has many suggestive contributions to make. The arguments raised have helped all Acts and Pauline scholars to come to terms with what is found in both corpora of New Testament writings. The question, however, is whether their description and assessment of the evidence are the fairest, or even the most plausible ones.

Haenchen tends to concentrate upon the person and depiction of Paul in Acts, while Vielhauer concentrates upon the theology revealed about Paul in

---

[5] See B.W.R. Pearson and S.E. Porter, "The Genres of the New Testament," in S.E. Porter (ed.), *Handbook to Exegesis of the New Testament* (NTTS 25; Leiden: Brill, 1997) 142–148.

[6] See C.M. Tuckett, "The Gospels and Acts," in Porter (ed.), *Handbook to Exegesis of the New Testament*, 483, who discusses these issues on 483–484; cf. R. Wall, "Israel and the Gentile Mission in Acts and Paul: A Canonical Approach," in I.H. Marshall and D. Peterson (eds.), *Witness to the Gospel: The Theology of Acts* (Grand Rapids: Eerdmans, 1998) 440–441 and n. 4. To use the taxonomy of Mattill, Haenchen and Vielhauer represent the Two-Paul View of the School of Creative Edification. As he states, this view "is dominant overall, and has succeeded in putting the burden of proof on others. Interpreters not only cannot ignore the work of [this group], but usually must begin with its conclusions and proceed to build upon, modify, or reject them." See A.J. Mattill, Jr, "The Value of Acts as a Source for the Study of Paul," in C.H. Talbert (ed.), *Perspectives on Luke–Acts* (Danville, VA: Association of Baptist Professors of Religion, 1978) 76–98, quotation 83.

Acts. I will treat these two issues in that order. There are other issues that have indicated some points of difference between the Paul of Acts and of the letters, but these are raised elsewhere in this volume.[7]

a. The Person of Paul in Acts and in the Letters

There are five reasons suggested by Haenchen to reject the tradition that "Luke" the author of Acts was the companion of Paul. One need not intertwine the issue of authorship with the question of how faithful a chronicler of Paul the author was, however. It is sufficient to consider the arguments in order to establish the degree of authorial knowledge of information regarding Paul.

1. *Paul's Mission and the Law*. Haenchen recognizes that "For both 'Luke' and Paul, the overriding problem was that of the *mission to the Gentiles without the law*. But 'Luke' is *unaware* of Paul's *solution*."[8] Haenchen then offers what has come to be known as the standard, Lutheran appraisal of the problem of law:

Paul was able to justify the mission without the law on *internal* evidence: the law leads not to God, but into sin [Gal 3:19; see also Rom 4:13–16; 2 Cor 3:6; 1 Cor 15:56]. For it causes man to put his trust not in God, but in his own righteousness [Rom 10:3]. Even so, admittedly, it still has served the purposes of God, who has shut up all under unbelief [Gal 3:21–22]. But Christ is the end of the law for all who believe [Rom 10:4]. For when the sinner places his trust in Christ, the son of God, he thereby enters into the right relationship to God.[9]

I believe that Haenchen is very close to being exactly right in depicting Paul's view of the law. That is, of course, because I believe that the traditional view of Paul and the law is correct, contrary to much recent discussion led by Sanders, Dunn, and others, regarding the so-called New Perspective on Paul.[10] It is worth asking what this new perspective might indicate with

---

[7] For example, the issue of Pauline rhetoric is treated primarily in Chapter Five, as well as in Chapters Six and Seven.

[8] Haenchen, *Acts*, 112, emphasis his.

[9] Haenchen, *Acts*, 112–113.

[10] See, for example, E.P. Sanders, *Paul and Palestinian Judaism: A Comparison of Patterns of Religion* (Philadelphia: Fortress Press, 1977); *idem*, *Paul, the Law and the Jewish People* (Philadelphia: Fortress Press, 1983); J.D.G. Dunn, "The New Perspective on Paul," *BJRL* 65 (1983) 95–122; cf. J.D.G. Dunn (ed.), *Paul and the Mosaic Law* (WUNT 89; Tübingen: Mohr–Siebeck, 1996), for a recent set of studies; and the monograph by S. Westerholm, *Israel's Law and the Church's Faith: Paul and his Recent Interpreters* (Grand Rapids: Eerdmans, 1988), for a summary of opinions and critique. This position is assessed also in L.M. McDonald and S.E. Porter, *Early Christianity and its Sacred Literature* (Peabody, MA: Hendrickson, forthcoming 1999) chap. 9.

regard to dissolving this barrier between the Paul of the letters and the Paul of Acts. This is not the place to define the position of those involved in promoting the new perspective, except to note the following. The new perspective wishes to emphasize continuity over discontinuity regarding the issue of covenant, with Christianity and Judaism both predicated upon a relationship of grace with God. The law is not a matter of legalism, but something that guides in proper behavior within the covenant of grace, or perhaps was used by some to define themselves as Jews, rather than as a set of entrance requirements into one's relationship with God. If this new perspective is correct, then it would appear that the Jewish elements that typify the account in Acts, such as Paul's beginning much of his local preaching with a visit to the synagogue (see Chapters Six and Seven on Paul's speeches), his agreeing to participate in the ritual in Jerusalem (Acts 21:17–26; see Chapter Eight above), and his defenses focusing upon his continuity with Judaism, all point toward continuity between the Paul of Acts and of the letters. Thus, the new perspective on Paul would appear to render this criticism of Haenchen no longer valid.

However, I reject the new perspective on Paul as being a correct understanding of Paul's view of the covenant and of the role of the law, and think that Haenchen's formulation of the issue is much closer to what Paul thought. If this is the case, it would appear that Haenchen's perceived problem regarding the Paul of Acts and of the letters remains.

Haenchen makes two further comments worth noting. The first elucidates the statement cited above:

Of this view of the law [Paul's], with its simultaneous affirmation and negation, there is no trace in Acts. When in 15.10 Peter says of the law that "neither we nor our fathers could bear" this "yoke," something quite different is meant: here the Judaic law is regarded as through the eyes of a Gentile Christian, who would see in it a mass of commands and prohibitions such as no-one could unravel or master.[11]

This, however, does not seem to be inconsistent with what Haenchen has said above regarding Paul's depiction of the law. This attitude is also consistent with Paul's position as articulated in Acts 13:39, where he speaks of being freed from the law of Moses, and Acts 21:17–26, especially v. 21, as described in Chapter Eight above. Further in Galatians, Paul says that "while we were children, we were held in bondage under the elemental things of the world" (Gal 4:3). Whatever the precise interpretation of the "elemental

---

[11] Haenchen, *Acts*, 113. See also J. Jervell, *The Theology of the Acts of the Apostles* (New Testament Theology; Cambridge: Cambridge University Press, 1996) 89 and n. 168.

things,"[12] they seem related to the law, because Paul goes on to say that Christ was born "under the law, in order that he might redeem those who were under the law" (Gal 4:4–5). In ch. 5 he depicts a fairly hopeless picture, when he says that everyone who receives circumcision "is under obligation to keep the whole law" (Gal 5:3).

Haenchen's second comment is that "Luke has no doubt whatever of the legitimacy of the Gentile mission; on the contrary he takes it for granted. Yet he is incapable of justifying it, like Paul, 'from within.' He must therefore seize on a justification 'from without' – God willed the mission, and that was sufficient."[13] This comment warrants further elucidation. There seems to be some imprecision regarding what justification from "within" and "without" means. Above, Haenchen has cited the fact that Paul in his letters appears to recognize the positive and negative dimension of the law, a pattern found also in Acts. At times, Paul is depicted as one who sees virtue in the law, and at other times as one who does not (see Chapter Eight above). More to the point, however, is the framing of Haenchen's observation. Just because Paul may justify his mission as he does does not mean that Luke must justify the mission in the same way. Furthermore, it simply does not logically follow to say that, because Luke does not *justify* the mission in the same way Paul does, this means that Luke does not know of Paul's solution. There is not a necessary logical contradiction here. It may simply be a different perspective. Is it a difference in perspective that two different people on the same missionary venture could have? Since there is no formal logical contradiction, this possibility cannot on logical grounds be excluded without a more persuasive argument.

More can be said, however. Haenchen speaks of the idea of a "majestic divine will" being present in Acts, smacking of "that ineluctable destiny known to pagan belief."[14] He cites as an instance Luke's use of the proverb of the goads in relation to Paul's calling (Acts 26:14). This suggests two further problems with Haenchen's analysis, however. The first is that there are plenty of instances in Paul's letters that reflect a "majestic divine will" working with "ineluctable" force. One needs only to look at Romans 9–11, especially those verses that reinforce such a sense of divine destiny as the story of Jacob and Esau (9:9–13), quotations from the Old Testament regarding God's actions (e.g. 9:15–17), the analogy of the potter and clay (9:19–23), among many

---

[12] See A.J. Bandstra, *The Law and the Elements of the World: An Exegetical Study in Aspects of Paul's Teaching* (Kampen: Kok, 1964) 5–72.

[13] Haenchen, *Acts*, 113.

[14] Haenchen, *Acts*, 113.

others. This sense of vocation coming from "without" is very readily present in Paul's own writings. The second problem is that Haenchen himself admits as much. As he states, "Of course Paul himself speaks (in I Cor. 9.16) of a necessity which is laid upon him, but here it represents his being subjectively conquered by his recognition of the glory of God in the countenance of Christ..."[15] I am not sure that I recognize what Haenchen is stating in the second part of the sentence quoted, since the passage noted says nothing about any subjective conquering by a recognition of the glory of God. To the contrary, it sounds much more like something regarding which Paul has no choice (i.e. an ineluctable force), subjective or no subjective response.

2. *Paul the Miracle Worker*. Haenchen cites what he sees as a discrepancy between the Lukan Paul and the Paul of the letters, with regard to Luke portraying Paul as a great miracle worker. He cites the following instances: blinding Elymas (Acts 13:6–12), healing the cripple at Lystra (14:8–10), Paul's recovering after being stoned (14:19–20), his being unaffected by snake venom (28:3–6), and his bringing Eutychus back to life (20:7–12). As opposed to this evidence in Acts, Haenchen notes that "Now it is true that the real Paul did on one occasion lay claim to the 'signs of an Apostle' (II Cor. 12.12), but the exploits in question were so little out of the ordinary that his opponents flatly denied his ability to perform miracles."[16]

A number of responses may be made to Haenchen's analysis of Paul the miracle worker. The first is contained in Chapter Three, above, where a more nuanced treatment of Paul the miracle worker is presented in light of possible sources of the book of Acts. The conclusion that I reach there is that there is still much more to be said about Paul the miracle worker in Acts. The second response is that, simply on surface appearances, the number of miracles that Haenchen cites is not particularly large in terms of the significance of Paul in the book of Acts, and when compared with, for example, Jesus, who, by comparison, is a bona fide miracle worker. Of the five examples that Haenchen cites, three of them are bunched together in what might be considered one extended episode (Acts 13:6–12; 14:8–10, 19–20). We might also look more closely at the examples that Haenchen cites of Paul as miracle worker. Paul's recovery after being stoned is perhaps not best categorized as a miracle.[17] The text says that they stoned and dragged Paul out of the city,

---

[15] Haenchen, *Acts*, 113.

[16] Haenchen, *Acts*, 113; cf. A. Harnack, *The Acts of the Apostles* (trans. J.R. Wilkinson; London: Williams & Norgate, 1909) 133–161, esp. 134–140, with a chart that distinguishes various types of miracles, distinguishing them from other types of works of the Spirit.

[17] For the several questions raised by this episode, see L.T. Johnson, *The Acts of the Apostles* (SP 5; Collegeville, MN: Liturgical, 1992) 253.

supposing (νομίζοντες) him to be dead. It is at best questionable whether Paul was in need of a miracle, and that there is any substantive evidence in the text in that regard. But even if he were dead, this would be a different sort of miracle than, for example, striking Elymas with blindness. Did Paul raise himself up from being dead? If there is any miracle here, it is an act of God, not of Paul. A similar objection as to whether a miracle actually was involved can be raised regarding the incidents with Eutychus and with the snake venom (see Chapter Three above). This leaves at best two miracles in Acts performed by Paul, hardly warrant for labeling him a "miracle worker."

The evidence from the letters of Paul must also be considered, however. Haenchen is dismissive of this evidence, citing only one passage, which is, he claims, undermined by how Paul was actually treated. There are several other factors in this analysis. For one, the question must be raised of how much occasion there would be in the letters to speak of miracles. The accounts of the miracles related in Acts occur, not in expository or oratorical material, but in narrative accounts. The amount of narrative in the Pauline letters is very small, being confined to a few passages, such as Gal 1:11–2:14/21, and a few others.[18] When several of these passages, as well as others, are examined, however, what might be construed as miraculous events *are* to be found. Of course, this depends upon how one defines miracle.[19] One might confine the definition to healing miracles, as Haenchen does, but one might well wish to include other instances in which there is supernatural intervention in the course of human affairs. In that case, one would need to include Paul's conversion, not noted by Haenchen above in Acts, but found not only in Acts 9, 22 and 26 but also in Gal 1:16 and 1 Cor 15:8–10. In 1 Cor 12:4–11, Paul speaks of various gifts of the Spirit. These include the ability to perform miracles (v. 10; note that, in 1 Cor 12:28, Paul himself distinguishes between miracles and healings, contra Haenchen). Paul does not state here that he has that gift, but he does note that he has others of the gifts (1 Cor 14:18). Paul also relates the story of the man who was caught up into the third heaven (2 Cor 12:2–5). Perhaps this story offers some insight into Paul's view of the miraculous, when he states in v. 5 that he will not boast on his own behalf.[20]

3. *Paul as Orator.* In conjunction with his previous analysis, Haenchen also offers as a difference between the Paul of Acts and of the letters that the

---

[18] On a related topic, see G. Lyons, *Pauline Autobiography: Toward a New Understanding* (SBLDS 73; Atlanta: Scholars Press, 1985).

[19] On the problem of miracles, see C. Brown, *Miracles and the Critical Mind* (Grand Rapids: Eerdmans, 1984), who traces the history of debate.

[20] See C.K. Barrett, *The Second Epistle to the Corinthians* (HNTC; New York: Harper & Row, 1973) 311–312.

Lukan Paul is an "outstanding orator," who is able to offer improvised speeches to great effect before whatever audience presents itself, Jew, Gentile, governmental or philosophical. By contrast, Haenchen continues, "the real Paul, as he himself admits, was anything but a master of the improvised speech...as a speaker he was feeble, unimpressive (II Cor. 10.10)."[21] Haenchen concludes that it is not Luke's faulty memory at work here, but that the author of Acts writes generations later, imagining that Paul must have been a great orator.

There is no doubt that in many places the Paul of Acts is a great speaker, as Chapters Six and Seven have tried to show. As noted in Chapter Three as well, there are also a number of places, especially connected with the "we" passages, where it is *not* emphasized that Paul is an orator. Since Haenchen wrote, however, there has been much further work done on the rhetorical dimension of Paul's letters. Much of this work minimizes the epistolary features of his letters and claims to identify in a systematic way various classical rhetorical features, in terms of the type of rhetoric used, the arrangement of the parts of the letters, the forms of argumentation, and even some of the elements of style. By this estimation, Paul, through his letters, ends up an accomplished rhetorician of the ancient world.[22] If these assessments are correct, the conclusion that one might well reach is that the Paul of both Acts and his "letters" is really an orator or rhetorician in both instances, and thus Haenchen's argument does not hold.

I, however, wish to argue that Paul is clearly an epistolographer, and that the application of the categories of classical rhetoric to analysis of his letters is, in fact, a mistake (see Chapter Five, where this is argued in more detail). However, I do not wish to deny that the Paul of Acts is depicted as a successful speaker. Nevertheless, this is not to say that Haenchen's argument shows that the Paul of Acts and the Paul of the letters have little, or nothing, in common with each other at this point. Haenchen's argument is vulnerable at the very point where he sees the greatest contrast. In and of itself, there is nothing inherently contradictory in one person being both a speechmaker and a letterwriter. In fact, the ancient world knew of several who were examples of such, including Plato and especially Cicero. We also have both speeches and letters attributed to Demosthenes (Demosthenes is the example that Haenchen uses for comparison with the Paul of Acts as an excellent orator),

---

[21] Haenchen, *Acts*, 114.

[22] See S.E. Porter, "The Rhetoric of Paul and his Letters," in S.E. Porter (ed.), *Handbook of Classical Rhetoric in the Hellenistic Period 330 B.C.–A.D. 400* (Leiden: Brill, 1997) 433–485, for discussion; and Chapter Five above for an assessment of these arguments.

although it was recognized then and now that Demosthenes's letters are pseudepigraphal. The fact that letters were attributed to the orator Demosthenes simply shows that the ancients did not think that the two genres were such that a single person could not be adept at both.

Haenchen makes the further point that, in his letters, Paul admits to being a feeble and unimpressive orator (2 Cor 10:10).[23] This verse has the potential for being greatly misunderstood, however. There are those who take this and other Pauline denials of oratorical competence as, in fact, instances of his utilization of the categories of rhetoric, especially that of assuming a suitable level of humility with regard to his oratorical skill. This is especially appropriate in a book such as 2 Corinthians, where Paul wishes to be seen boasting, not in his own abilities, but in what he has seen accomplished among the believers in Corinth – they themselves are his commendation (2 Cor 3:2). Another important dimension of analysis of this verse is the fact that its larger context is rarely taken into consideration – Haenchen certainly neglects this factor. Several observations are worth making. The first is that Paul does not directly claim that this is what he believes about himself. The comments about his letters being weighty and his speech unimpressive are attributed to others who say such things. Does Paul agree with these comments? I doubt this. He continues in 2 Cor 10:11 by saying that a person who does hold to this view should be prepared for Paul to be very firm when present. Furthermore, whether one accepts this chapter as part of the third or the fourth Pauline letter to Corinth, Paul's experience of dealing with the Corinthians by letter (as well as by personal visitation, it is true) was not a resounding success due to strong and weighty epistles. All of these factors call into question whether one can accept a statement such as is found in 2 Cor 10:10 at face value. In other words, there is dubious warrant for making the claim that Paul disparaged his own oratorical ability, and little to no ground for excluding a person from being both a successful orator and an epistolographer. At the least, as a suitable explanation, one does not require the supposition that "Luke" wrote generations later to justify a work such as Acts in its depiction of Paul as a speaker.

4. *Paul the Apostle*. Haenchen also posits that the author of Acts, despite the splendor with which he depicts Paul, actually missed the major claim that Paul made regarding himself. According to Haenchen, when Paul was engaged in his missionary venture, according to the letters, he demanded that

---

[23] For recent discussion of this passage, and those related to it, see B.W. Winter, *Philo and Paul among the Sophists* (SNTSMS 96; Cambridge: Cambridge University Press, 1997) 203–230.

he should be recognized as an Apostle, with the same rights and claims as the other Apostles, such as Peter. This can be seen in the confrontation between Peter (or Cephas) and Paul in Gal 2:1–11 (see esp. v. 8), and is elucidated at some length in 1 Cor 15:5–8, when Paul says that the risen Christ appeared to him at the end of a chain of appearances.[24]

The case that Haenchen makes must die the death of numerous qualifications, however. First, Haenchen admits in a footnote that Paul and Barnabas are called Apostles in Acts 14:4 and 14. He says, however, that "It makes no difference that in 14.4 & 14 Paul and Barnabas, as envoys from Antioch, are called 'Apostles.'"[25] Since Haenchen's case is argued on the basis of who is called what in two corpora, I find it hard to believe that it makes "no difference" that two of the 28 instances of the use of the word ἀπόστολος in Acts are ascribed to Paul. There is also evidence that there are two different senses of the word Apostle being used in Acts and the Pauline letters. This becomes clear if one looks more closely at 1 Corinthians 15. In 1 Cor 15:5, Paul says that the risen Christ appeared to Cephas (or Peter) and then to the twelve disciples. In 1 Cor 15:7, he says that Christ appeared to James and then to all of the Apostles, before appearing to Paul. Thus, contrary to Haenchen, it appears that Paul has a larger concept of apostleship, into which he can fit, even if he does consider his authority to be equal to that of the twelve. In Acts, especially in ch. 15 at the Jerusalem Council, reference is made to "apostles and elders," with there being no clear way of determining whether James is considered one or the other. However, it seems that Acts 15 uses the word Apostle in the way that Paul uses the word "twelve" in 1 Corinthians 15, with Paul thinking of himself as an Apostle in a broader sense that Acts also employs (see 14:4, 14). There is apparently a high degree of similarity in usage of the word Apostle in Acts and the Pauline letters, but usage that also allows for differences (though clearly not contradictions) between authors.

5. *Jewish and Christian Relations in Acts and the Pauline Letters*. As a last point of difference in depiction of the person of Paul in Acts and in the letters, Haenchen claims that Acts depicts Jewish and Christian relations in a way that contradicts those of Paul's letters. According to Acts, Haenchen says, the major bone of contention was that Paul preached about the resurrection, a doctrine to which Acts itself depicts certain Jews holding (see Acts 23:6; 24:15, 21; cf. 26:6–7, 27; 28:20; Haenchen goes further and notes that the Pharisaic doctrine of the resurrection was not congruent with the Christian

---

[24] Haenchen, *Acts*, 114.
[25] Haenchen, *Acts*, 114 n. 5.

belief in it). According to the letters, it was Paul's teaching regarding the law, which had manifestations in his missionary strategy, that put Paul in conflict with the Jews.[26]

This argument used by Haenchen looks like an instance of the excluded middle (resurrection vs. law), besides neglecting other linguistic evidence to be found both in Acts and in the Pauline letters. An examination of the use of ἀνάστασις in Acts reveals that, of the twelve instances, six appear in phrases or contexts that make reference to the resurrection of Christ (Acts 1:22; 2:31; 4:2, 33; 17:18, 32). Four instances use the phrase "resurrection of the dead" (ἀνάστασις τῶν νεκρῶν; Acts 17:32; 23:6; 24:21; 26:23), a problematic phrase for Haenchen since it is not overtly Christian; and two instances simply mention the resurrection (Acts 23:8; 24:15). The linguistic picture is more complex than Haenchen has indicated, however, with fully half of the uses in Acts indicating not just the general resurrection but the specific one of Christ, with two of these instances in contexts where Paul is present (Acts 17:18, 32). A response might be that the *crucial* instances in Acts 23 and 24, where resurrection was a bone of contention, make use simply of the phrase "resurrection of the dead" or the word "resurrection." A consideration of the Pauline use of the word ἀνάστασις, however, shows that this usage may not be as problematic as Haenchen thought. Of the eight uses of the word (seven in the accepted seven letters), five of them use the same phrase "resurrection of the dead" (Rom 1:4; 1 Cor 15:2, 13, 21, 42), with the two others using a phrase equivalent to "his resurrection," referring to that of Jesus (Rom 6:5; Phil 3:10). In other words, the phrase that Haenchen cites as showing the difference between the Paul of Acts and of the letters is in fact the very phrase that the undisputed Paul uses most frequently. It is difficult to see how this evidence divides the two Pauls. Clearly resurrection was an issue in certain contexts for the Paul of the letters.

Regarding the issue of the law, similar comments may be made. There is no doubt that the issue of law was a crucial one in Paul's relationship with his churches, especially as revealed in such correspondence as the letters to the Galatians and Romans. But the issue of law also appears at crucial junctures in Acts, as well. For example, in Acts 13:38, Paul explicitly states that through Christ there is a forgiveness for sins that cannot be gained through the law, a message very similar to what Paul proclaims in his letters. Acts 15 is clearly concerned with establishing which elements of the law Gentile Christians will need to obey (cf. v. 5). A minimal set of requirements is laid down, which is then brought up once more in Acts 21 when Paul is "asked"

---

[26] Haenchen, *Acts*, 115.

by the leaders of the Jerusalem church to help four men fulfil their ritualistic (Nazirite?) vows as a way of appeasing the distrust of those who think that Paul has completely abandoned the practice of keeping the law, even by Jews (see Acts 21:20, 24). In Acts 18:13, 21:28, 22:3, 23:29 and 25:8, in each of these instances, Paul is either being accused of disobeying the law or of instructing others to disobey the law, or defending himself against such accusations. This evidence indicates that it is an unfair generalization to claim that Acts is concerned with resurrection and the letters of Paul with the law, when both are issues of concern in each corpus.

Haenchen concludes his discussion by stating that "The time has come to strike the balance" regarding the "representation of Paul in Acts."[27] He certainly is correct. However, on the basis of the evidence above, there is little warrant for concluding, as Haenchen does, that the author of Acts is "someone of a later generation trying in his own way to give an account of things that can no longer be viewed in their true perspective," and that the Paul depicted is not the "real Paul" but "a Paul seen through the eyes of a later age."[28] To the contrary, the evidence above suggests that there is a surprisingly large amount of continuity and similarity between the two bodies of material. A fresh analysis of this evidence seems, rather, to indicate that there must have been some close lines of connection between the authors of the book of Acts and of the Pauline letters. How one accounts for these similarities is another question. Differences between the two accounts seem easily to fall within the realm of the kinds of differences one would expect from two different authors writing in two different literary genres (narrative and epistle), even when writing about the same subject.

b. The Theology of Paul in Acts and in the Letters

There is further evidence to be discussed, however, and this includes purported theological differences between the two bodies of literature. Vielhauer, in what has come to be regarded as a classic article, marshals a number of arguments in an attempt to determine "whether and to what extent the author of Acts took over and passed on theological ideas of Paul, whether and to what extent he modified them... [and] whether or not he and Paul belong together theologically."[29] Vielhauer treats four areas, drawing primarily on the speeches in Acts, since he considers the speeches to be the

---

[27] Haenchen, *Acts*, 116.

[28] Haenchen, *Acts*, 116.

[29] Vielhauer, "Paulinism," 33.

locus of the Pauline theology in the book. These four areas are natural theology, law, Christology and eschatology. Elsewhere in this volume I have dealt with the speeches and the issue of natural theology (see Chapters Five, Six and Seven). The topic of law has been dealt with earlier in this chapter and in Chapter Eight of this volume on Acts 21. Here I wish to deal with Christology and eschatology.

1. *Christology*. Regarding Pauline Christology in Acts, compared to that of the letters, Vielhauer characterizes Paul's message in Acts as related to the "kingdom" or "kingdom of God" (Acts 19:8; 20:25; 28:23, 31), Jesus and the resurrection (17:18; 23:11; 25:19), the content of the gospel of grace (20:27, 24, 20), and the promise of the Scriptures regarding a resurrection of the dead. However, Vielhauer states that there are only two Pauline christological statements of any length in Acts, found in his speeches before Jews in Antioch (13:13–43) and before Agrippa (26:22–23). The message of Acts, according to Vielhauer, is that "Jesus is the Messiah who was promised in the Old Testament and expected by the Jews and…that his suffering and resurrection were according to the scripture."[30] The death and resurrection of Jesus are the fulfilment of the Scriptures (see Acts 26:34–37, citing Ps 16:10) and the impetus for the Christian mission (Acts 26:32); and Jesus, seen as a descendant of David, is the savior (see Acts 26:23, 33, citing Ps 2:7).

Vielhauer goes on to note that there are parallels to these two major christological statements in Paul's letters: Rom 1:3–4 regarding Jesus being descended from David and becoming the son of God in fulfilment of Scripture (v. 2), and 1 Cor 15:3–4 where the death, burial and resurrection of Jesus are said to be according to the Scriptures. Both of these passages, Vielhauer claims, however, are traditional, pre-Pauline formulations.[31] Vielhauer is correct in so far as Paul admits that he received the statements in 1 Cor 15:3–4 from other Christians. One may not necessarily wish to equate this with the statement being a pre-Pauline formulation, however, since 1 Corinthians 15 seems to reflect a heavy shaping influence of Paul on whatever material he may have been using. Further, Vielhauer is not on nearly as certain ground regarding Rom 1:3–4. There is serious debate among scholars whether this is indeed a traditional formulation.[32] Mention of the lineage of David is admittedly unique to Paul (apart from 2 Tim 2:8, if we assign the Pastorals to a later author), and there is notable syntactical and

---

[30] Vielhauer, "Paulinism," 43.

[31] Vielhauer, "Paulinism," 43–44.

[32] See D.J. Moo, *The Epistle to the Romans* (NICNT; Grand Rapids: Eerdmans, 1996) esp. 45–46 n. 31; J.A. Fitzmyer, *Romans* (AB 33; New York: Doubleday, 1993) 235–237.

conceptual parallelism. However, there has been an undervaluing of what Paul does know about the man Jesus,[33] and the much-used arguments about parallelism, which stem from Norden to Käsemann to the present, involve misconstruals both of the wider context of Greco-Roman literature and of Paul's writing ability.[34] A more important oversight on Vielhauer's part, however, is that he cites the formulation in Romans as being found in 1:3–4, but the reference to fulfilment of the Scriptures as occurring in v. 2. Thus, the major feature that Vielhauer sees as constituting the Pauline Christology of Acts, its basis in Scripture, is on Vielhauer's own admission contained within admittedly distinctively Pauline material in the letter, right here at the beginning of the book of Romans. Thus, Vielhauer's claim that the christological statements of Paul in Acts (13:16–37 and 26:22–23) are not specifically Pauline or Lukan does not seem to be sustainable. The major plank regarding fulfilment of Scripture seems to be Pauline.

Vielhauer claims that there are two further observations that support his case. One is that what appear to be echoes of Pauline passages in Acts 13 and 26 are not true parallels. For example, he disputes use of the title "savior" in Acts 13:23 and Phil 3:20, the former being used of the "earthly Jesus" and the latter of the "returning Lord." He claims there is no parallel in Paul's letters of the adoptionistic sonship of Acts 13:33. The phrase "first to rise from the dead" (Acts 26:23) inaugurates the missionary endeavor, but does not establish Christ's dominion (Col 1:18) or instigate the resurrection of the dead (1 Cor 15:20).[35] The limited usage of "savior" in the Pauline letters (only Phil 3:20 and Eph 5:23, apart from the Pastoral Epistles) and Acts (only 5:31 and 23:23), however, makes it very difficult to establish an author's precise usage. The sample is simply too small to speak as definitively as Vielhauer does. Even so, one might well wonder whether Vielhauer has again drawn the disjunction too firmly. Since "savior" language is probably based in the New Testament upon language of the developing emperor cult,[36] it is

---

[33] See S.E. Porter, "Images of Christ in Paul's Letters," in S.E. Porter, M.A. Hayes, and D. Tombs (eds.), *Images of Christ: Ancient and Modern* (RILP 2; Sheffield: Sheffield Academic Press, 1997) 97–100.

[34] See E. Norden, *Agnostos Theos: Untersuchungen zur Formengeschichte Religiöser Rede* (Stuttgart: Teubner, 1913; repr. Darmstadt: Wissenschaftliche Buchgesellschaft, 1956) 143–263; E. Käsemann, "A Primitive Christian Baptismal Liturgy," in *Essays on New Testament Themes* (trans. J. Montague: London: SCM Press, 1964) 149–168; cf. S. Fowl, *The Story of Christ in the Ethics of Paul: An Analysis of the Function of the Hymnic Material in the Pauline Corpus* (JSNTSup 36; Sheffield: JSOT Press, 1990) esp. 31–45.

[35] Vielhauer, "Paulinism," 44.

[36] See S.E. Porter, "Literary Approaches to the New Testament: From Formalism to Deconstruction and Back," in S.E. Porter and D. Tombs (eds.), *Approaches to New*

difficult to draw a distinction between the physical and spiritual, or rather to see the spiritual without a basis in the physical. Regarding the adoptionistic sonship, Vielhauer has apparently overlooked here the highly disputed language of Rom 1:4 (since he has already decided that it is pre-Pauline) and certain interpretations of Phil 2:6–11, with the man Adam being elevated to exalted Lord.[37] Lastly, regarding the resurrection, the passage in Col 1:18, in fact, is very much in harmony with Acts 26:23, since the resurrection is seen as an inaugurating earthly event, even if it does ultimately result in pre-eminence.

The second feature Vielhauer marshals in support of his hypothesis concerns the structure and content of the speech in Acts 13, claiming that it is closest in structure to Peter's and Stephen's speeches in Acts. The major difference in content concerns what Christ accomplished on the cross. According to Vielhauer, for Paul the cross marks God's judgment on humanity and its reconciliation, the turning of the eras, with the one who believes becoming a new creation; in other words, "salvation is wholly realized."[38] For Acts, the cross marks a miscarriage of justice for which the Jews are held accountable, although their error resulted in the fulfillment of Scripture. The Messiah demonstrates his power in the Church, awaiting his return. Despite the elegance of Vielhauer's summaries, there are a number of factors that he has apparently overlooked. One is that comparison of a Pauline speech of Acts with a Pauline speech outside of Acts is an impossibility. It seems clear, as demonstrated in Chapters Six and Seven, that the author of Acts has had an important role in formulating the speeches, regardless of what one thinks of their historical reliability (e.g. they are too short to be anything more than summaries in most instances). So, how can one say that this, or any, speech is more or less like a Pauline speech elsewhere? Vielhauer states that Paul's speech in Acts 13 is more like Peter's speeches in Acts.[39] Does this mean that the other speeches are a consistent group of "Pauline" speeches? If so, then Vielhauer has apparently compromised his own argument, and perhaps given the clue to accounting for supposed differences

---

Testament Study (Sheffield: Sheffield Academic Press, 1995) 121–122; cf. C.A. Evans, "The Historical Jesus and the Deified Christ: How Did the One Lead to the Other?" in S.E. Porter (ed.), *The Nature of Religious Language: A Colloquium* (RILP 1; Sheffield: Sheffield Academic Press, 1996) 48–57.

[37] See, for example, J.D.G. Dunn, *Christology in the Making: A New Testament Inquiry into the Origins of the Doctrine of the Incarnation* (Grand Rapids: Eerdmans, 2nd edn, 1989) 98–128, although he has been highly criticized for this position. He summarizes (and responds to) his critics in the foreword to the second edition, pp. xi–xxxix, esp. xxii–xxiii.

[38] Vielhauer, "Paulinism," 45.

[39] Vielhauer, "Paulinism," 45.

in the conception of the work of Christ in Acts and in the letters. Vielhauer notes that the speech in Acts 13 and the short one in Acts 26 are the only christological ones,[40] and they are addressed to Jews. Therefore, it makes sense that, being addressed to Jews, they are closest to the speeches of Peter, who in his speeches virtually always addresses Jews (except Acts 10 before Cornelius). If the other Pauline speeches are not christological (according to Vielhauer), it is also understandable that they would have differences in content and, quite possibly, structure from those that do. Furthermore, it also makes sense that the Pauline emphases in the letters are different from those of the speeches, since the letters are all addressed to churches that are predominantly Gentile, including especially Romans and the Corinthian letters (although this is true of all of them, I believe). Vielhauer also neglects the chronological factor, that is, the speech in Acts 13, if it was delivered in Pisidian Antioch as purported, would have been given much earlier than the writing of any of Paul's letters, since the writing of the earliest did not probably take place until just before the Jerusalem Council.[41] There are further difficulties with Vielhauer's analysis, however. The major one is that his summaries are stereotypes, focusing on various things that the Paul of Acts does not say. If one does not say something, that does not mean that one does not know or think it. All of the elements that he contends are typical of Acts, however, are to be found in various forms in Paul's letters, including, for example, the fulfillment of Scripture (see above), the crucial role of the Spirit in the Church (e.g. 1 Corinthians 12 and 14), and even hints of Jewish involvement in the death of Christ (Rom 2:1–16; 9:3–5).

Vielhauer wishes to conclude that "Luke himself is closer to the Christology of the earliest congregation, which is set forth in the speeches of Peter, than he is to the Christology of Paul, which is indicated only in hints."[42] To the contrary, the evidence that he provides, when re-assessed, indicates that there are many distinct points of correlation between the Christology of Acts and of Paul's letters. At the least, they may well rely on common sources, which, of course, cannot provide the basis for distinguishing them, but may well indicate common early Christian belief shared by the two authors.

2. *Eschatology*. Vielhauer believes that the eschatology of the Paul of Acts "disappears" to the periphery "as a hope in the resurrection and as faith in the

---

[40] Vielhauer, "Paulinism," 44.

[41] See Riesner, *Paul's Early Period*, esp. 318–326 but *passim*; and McDonald and Porter, *Early Christianity and its Sacred Literature*, chap. 9, on Pauline chronology.

[42] Vielhauer, "Paulinism," 45.

return of Christ as the judge of the world (17:30 f.), and in this aspect as a motivation of the exhortation to repentance. Eschatology has been removed from the center of Pauline faith to the end and has become a 'section on the last things.'"[43] This is, according to Vielhauer, distinctly Lukan theology, rather than that of even the early Church, and certainly that of Paul, who expected the imminent return of Christ, in light of the already inaugurated new age that looks forward to the conversion of Israel, the redemption of "creation," and the conquest of death (the "already" and "not yet" eschatology, but not thought of quantitatively or in terms of a temporal process). Vielhauer admits that there is a point of contact between Luke and Paul over shared belief that the new age has begun (Acts 2:16–35), but that Luke understands the ages quantitatively and in temporal terms, that is, there is pre-Christian time (Acts 13:16–22) and the new age of Christ that has "broken in." Therefore, the "expectation of the imminent end has disappeared and the failure of the parousia is no longer a problem."[44] This uneschatological perspective is revealed most clearly in the fact that we have the book of Acts. Acts serves two purposes – one of edifying believers through stories about the faithful, and the other of giving a historical report of the apostolic age, written after the event and much more like the account of Eusebius than of Paul (this also accounts for the relationship between Luke and Acts, according to Vielhauer).

Let us assume, with Vielhauer, that both Acts and Paul depict the inauguration of the new age. Is it accurate to say that Paul simply believed in the imminent expectation of the return of Christ and that the author of Acts, writing later, had no concern for this event, but saw the relation of the ages in terms of distinct chronological epochs? Again, too many unproven assumptions seem to have influenced this formulation. The first is that Paul had an unqualified belief in the imminent return of Christ. This is perhaps the case in 1 Thess 4:15, but it is far from certain even there. Too much emphasis has been placed on Paul's use of the present tense-form participle to establish this position.[45] The second participle, περιλειπόμενοι, clearly qualifies any sense of what it means to be alive at this event. The imminent expectation is far less readily apparent in Philippians (e.g. 1:20–24; 2:16–17; 3:11–14),

---

[43] Vielhauer, "Paulinism," 45.

[44] Vielhauer, "Paulinism," 47.

[45] From early in this century, many of the major Greek grammarians have concluded that the participles are not time-based – and for good reasons – regardless of what one thinks about the temporal values of other tense and mood forms. See the summary in S.E. Porter, *Verbal Aspect in the Greek of the New Testament, with Reference to Tense and Mood* (SBG 1; New York: Lang, 1989) 377–380.

which Vielhauer includes in his discussion as being genuinely Pauline. The second assumption is that Luke had Conzelmann's view of the structure of Christian history in mind, since it seems that this is the model that Vielhauer has adopted.[46] There is much to question about this model, including the temporal or quantitative view of eschatology (if such a distinction is even appropriate).

Regarding the historical nature of Acts, Vielhauer in a footnote perhaps reveals most clearly how his set of presuppositions has apparently skewed his analysis. There does not, to my mind, seem to be any necessary contradiction between belief in the imminent parousia and the writing of documents to edify the Church, and even of providing example-stories of early faithful Christians, especially if we use Paul as in some way a model of such writing. Vielhauer's placement of Acts intellectually with Eusebius does not seem to be based on quantifiable evidence so much as his desire to see the book placed there. In footnote 37, placed at the end of his statement about the "historical" purpose of Acts, Vielhauer says this about the classical historian Eduard Meyer: "Ed. Meyer, who approaches Acts with the presuppositions of a historian of antiquity and treats it with the greatest confidence, misunderstands the nature of its accounts and the way in which they are connected..."[47] Has Meyer or has Vielhauer misunderstood the nature of Acts? It seems to me that, when making historical judgments, such as Vielhauer purports to be making, one ought in the first instance to pay attention to historians such as Meyer and their analyses, rather than appealing to questionable theological criteria to arrive at historical conclusions.

3. Conclusion

The conclusions of this chapter are traditional ones.[48] The first is that the standard arguments marshalled in defense of the differences between the Paul of Acts and of the letters regarding his person and work, once analyzed in detail, simply do not point to significant and sustainable contradictions. The second is that the standard arguments marshalled regarding differences in

---

[46] H. Conzelmann, *The Theology of St Luke* (trans. G. Buswell; London: Faber & Faber, 1961 [1957]).

[47] Vielhauer, "Paulinism," 50. He is referring to E. Meyer, *Ursprung und Anfänge des Christentums* (3 vols.; Stuttgart: Cotta, 1921, 1923), a still-valuable, though now widely neglected, resource for the study of the origins of Christianity.

[48] Mattill, "Value of Acts," 77–83, on the One-Paul View of the School of Historical Research.

theology between the Paul of Acts and of the letters, again when scrutinized in detail, are also inconclusive for this hypothesis. There may well be differences of emphasis and focus, but the evidence is far from substantiating contradictions. Even the differences are not so glaring as to lead to the kinds of conclusions posited by Haenchen, Vielhauer and their followers. If the supposed differences are not as clear and telling as often supposed, how does one account for the similarities? One can account for the similarities between the Paul of Acts and of the letters in a number of different ways, none of them necessarily decisive. One of these is that the author of Acts used the Pauline letters so as to sketch a reasonable likeness of Paul. This is probably not sufficient for the depiction of the person of Paul, however, especially since the historical material in the letters is so small in terms of the content of the letters and in comparison with that in Acts. There is the further difficulty that the book of Acts makes no clear reference to knowledge of, and hence use of, Paul's letters. Such a hypothesis of epistolary dependence is clearly not a sufficient explanation for the theological issues raised by Acts, however. The theological situation posited that would elicit Acts, if it were written at a later date and independent of Paul himself, would be significantly different from that of the letters, as Vielhauer attempted to show.[49] Another, and to my mind more likely, explanation is that the author of the book of Acts had some form of close contact with Paul and his beliefs. As Jervell says, "I do not for a moment doubt that the author of Acts knew Paul well, if not personally."[50] There are admittedly some differences between the two authors (some of these have been noted above), but I would contend that these are merely the kinds of differences that one could expect to find between virtually any two different yet accomplished authors when writing about the same events.[51] The possibility of differences would be made more acute by the use of the different genres – narrative versus letter – and their clearly different literary purposes – that of telling the story of early Christianity and that of addressing problems in a local church congregation. At the least, after weighing the arguments as carefully as possible, there does not seem at this point to be any significant argument that would indicate otherwise.

---

[49] J.A. Fitzmyer, *Luke the Theologian: Aspects of his Teaching* (London: Chapman, 1989) 6–7 and 23.

[50] Jervell, "Paul in the Acts of the Apostles," 302.

[51] See F.F. Bruce, "Is the Paul of Acts the Real Paul?" *BJRL* 58 (1976) 282. Cf. J. Knox, "Acts and the Pauline Letter Corpus," in Keck and Martyn (eds.), *Studies in Luke–Acts*, 279–287.

Select Bibliography

Alexander, L., *The Preface to Luke's Gospel: Literary Convention and Social Context in Luke 1.1–4 and Acts 1.1* (SNTSMS 78; Cambridge: Cambridge University Press, 1993).

Aune, D.E., *The New Testament in its Literary Environment* (LEC; Philadelphia: Westminster Press, 1987).

Aune, D.E. (ed.), *Greco-Roman Literature and the New Testament: Selected Forms and Genres* (SBLSBS 21; Atlanta: Scholars Press, 1988).

Balch, D.L., "The Areopagus Speech: An Appeal to the Stoic Historian Posidonius against Later Stoics and the Epicureans," in D.L. Balch *et al.* (eds)., *Greeks, Romans, and Christians: Essays in Honor of A.J. Malherbe* (Minneapolis: Fortress Press, 1990) 52–79.

Barrett, C.K., *A Critical and Exegetical Commentary on the Acts of the Apostles* (2 vols.; ICC; Edinburgh: T. & T. Clark, 1994–).

Bethge, F., *Die Paulinischen Reden der Apostelgeschichte: Historisch-grammatisch und biblisch-theologisch* (Göttingen: Vandenhoeck & Ruprecht, 1887).

Blass, F., and A. Debrunner, *A Greek Grammar of the New Testament and Other Early Christian Literature* (trans. R.W. Funk; Chicago: University of Chicago Press, 1961).

Boismard, M.-E., and A. Lamouille, *Les actes des deux apôtres* (3 vols.; ÉB N.S. 12–14; Paris: Gabalda, 1990).

Bruce, F.F., *The Acts of the Apostles* (Grand Rapids: Eerdmans, 3rd edn, 1990 [2nd edn, 1952]).

Bruce, F.F., *Commentary on the Book of the Acts* (NICNT; Grand Rapids: Eerdmans, 1954).

Cadbury, H.J., *The Making of Luke–Acts* (New York: Macmillan, 2nd edn, 1958 [1927]; repr. London: SPCK, 1961).

Cadbury, H.J., *The Style and Literary Method of Luke* (Cambridge, MA: Harvard University Press, 1920; repr. New York: Klaus, 1969).

Conzelmann, H., *Die Apostelgeschichte* (HNT 7; Tübingen: Mohr–Siebeck, 1963).

Conzelmann, H., and A. Lindemann, *Interpreting the New Testament: An Introduction to the Principles and Methods of N.T. Exegesis* (trans. S.S. Schatzmann; Peabody, MA: Hendrickson, 1988).

Dibelius, M., *Studies in the Acts of the Apostles* (ed. H. Greeven; trans. M. Ling; London: SCM Press, 1956).

Dunn, J.D.G., *Baptism in the Holy Spirit: A Re-Examination of the New Testament Teaching on the Gift of the Spirit in Relation to Pentecostalism Today* (London: SCM Press, 1970).

Dunn, J.D.G., *Jesus and the Spirit: A Study of the Religious and Charismatic Experience of Jesus and the First Christians as Reflected in the New Testament* (London: SCM Press, 1975).

Dunn, J.D.G., *Romans* (2 vols.; WC 38A, B; Waco, TX: Word, 1988).

Dupont, J., *The Sources of Acts: The Present Position* (trans. K. Pond; London: Darton, Longman & Todd, 1964).

Fitzmyer, J.A., *Luke the Theologian: Aspects of his Teaching* (New York: Paulist, 1989).
Fitzmyer, J.A., *Romans* (AB 33; New York: Doubleday, 1993).
Foakes Jackson, F.J., and K. Lake, *The Beginnings of Christianity*. Part I. *The Acts of the Apostles* (5 vols.; London: Macmillan, 1920–1933).
Franklin, E., *Luke: Interpreter of Paul, Critic of Matthew* (JSNTSup 92; Sheffield: JSOT Press, 1994).

Gärtner, B., *The Areopagus Speech and Natural Revelation* (trans. C.H. King; ASNU 21; Uppsala: Gleerup, 1955).
Gasque, W.W., *A History of the Criticism of the Acts of the Apostles* (BGBE 17; Tübingen: Mohr–Siebeck; Grand Rapids: Eerdmans, 1975).
Gasque, W.W., and R.P. Martin (eds.), *Apostolic History and the Gospel: Biblical and Historical Essays Presented to F.F. Bruce on his 60th Birthday* (Exeter: Paternoster, 1970).
Gill, D.W.J., and C. Gempf (eds.), *The Book of Acts in its First Century Setting*. II. *The Book of Acts in its Graeco-Roman Setting* (Grand Rapids: Eerdmans, 1994).
Goulder, M.D., *Type and History in Acts* (London: SPCK, 1964).

Haenchen, E., *The Acts of the Apostles: A Commentary* (trans. B. Noble *et al.*; Philadelphia: Westminster Press, 1971 [1965]).
Harnack, A., *The Acts of the Apostles* (trans. J.R. Wilkinson; London: Williams & Norgate, 1909).
Harnack, A., *Luke the Physician: The Author of the Third Gospel and the Acts of the Apostles* (trans. J.R. Wilkinson; London: Williams & Norgate, 2nd edn, 1909).
Harnack, A., *Neue Untersuchungen zur Apostelgeschichte und zur Abfassungszeit der synoptischen Evangelien* (Leipzig: Hinrichs, 1911).
Hemer, C.J., *The Book of Acts in the Setting of Hellenistic History* (ed. C. Gempf; WUNT 49; Tübingen: Mohr–Siebeck, 1989; repr. Winona Lake, IN: Eisenbrauns, 1990).
Hemer, C.J., "First Person Narrative in Acts 27–28," *TynBul* 36 (1985) 79–109.
Hemer, C.J., "The Speeches of Acts I. The Ephesian Elders at Miletus," *TynBul* 40 (1989) 77–85.
Hengel, M., *Acts and the History of Earliest Christianity* (trans. J. Bowden; London: SCM Press, 1979).
Hengel, M., *Judaism and Hellenism* (trans. J. Bowden; Philadelphia: Fortress Press, 1974).
Horst, P.W. van der, *Hellenism – Judaism – Christianity: Essays on their Interaction* (Leuven: Peeters, 2nd edn, 1998).
Hull, J.H.E., *The Holy Spirit in the Acts of the Apostles* (London: Lutterworth, 1967).

Jervell, J., *The Theology of the Acts of the Apostles* (New Testament Theology; Cambridge: Cambridge University Press, 1996).
Johnson, L.T., *The Acts of the Apostles* (SP 5; Collegeville, MN: Liturgical, 1992).
Johnson, L.T., *The Writings of the New Testament: An Interpretation* (Minneapolis: Fortress Press, 1986).

Keck, L., and J.L. Martyn (eds.), *Studies in Luke–Acts* (Philadelphia: Fortress Press, 1966).
Kee, H.C., *Good News to the Ends of the Earth: The Theology of Acts* (London: SCM Press; Philadelphia: Trinity Press International, 1990).
Kennedy, G.A., *New Testament Interpretation through Rhetorical Criticism* (Chapel Hill: University of North Carolina, 1984).

Knowling, R.J., "The Acts of the Apostles," in W.R. Nicholl (ed.), *The Expositor's Greek New Testament* (vol. 2; repr. Grand Rapids: Eerdmans, 1980).

Kremer, J. (ed.), *Les Actes des Apôtres: Traditions, rédaction, théologie* (BETL 48; Gembloux: Duculot; Leuven: Leuven University Press, 1979).

Kümmel, W.G., *Introduction to the New Testament* (trans. H.C. Kee; Nashville: Abingdon, 17th edn, 1975).

Kurz, W.S., "Narrative Approaches to Luke–Acts," *Bib* 68 (1987) 203–219.

Lampe, G.W.H., "The Holy Spirit in the Writings of St Luke," in D.E. Nineham (ed.), *Studies in the Gospels: Essays in Memory of R.H. Lightfoot* (Oxford: Blackwell, 1957) 159–200.

Lentz, J.C., Jr, *Luke's Portrait of Paul* (SNTSMS 77; Cambridge: Cambridge University Press, 1993).

Longenecker, R.N., "The Acts of the Apostles," in F.E. Gaebelein (ed.), *The Expositor's Bible Commentary* (vol. 9; Grand Rapids: Zondervan, 1981).

Lüdemann, G., *Early Christianity according to the Traditions in Acts: A Commentary* (trans. J. Bowden; Minneapolis: Fortress Press, 1987).

Lüdemann, G., *Opposition to Paul in Jewish Christianity* (trans. M.E. Boring; Minneapolis: Fortress Press, 1989).

Maddox, R., *The Purpose of Luke–Acts* (Edinburgh: T. & T. Clark, 1982).

Marshall, I.H., *The Acts of the Apostles* (NTG; Sheffield: JSOT Press, 1992).

Marshall, I.H., *The Acts of the Apostles* (TNTC; Grand Rapids: Eerdmans, 1980).

Marshall, I.H., *Luke: Historian and Theologian* (Grand Rapids: Zondervan, 1970).

Marshall, I.H., and D. Peterson (eds.), *Witness to the Gospel: The Theology of Acts* (Grand Rapids: Eerdmans, 1998).

Mattill, A.J., Jr, "The Purpose of Acts: Schneckenburger Reconsidered," in W.W. Gasque and R.P. Martin (eds.), *Apostolic History and the Gospel: Biblical and Historical Essays Presented to F.F. Bruce on his 60th Birthday* (Exeter: Paternoster, 1970) 108–122.

Mattill, A.J., Jr, "The Value of Acts as a Source for the Study of Paul," in C.H. Talbert (ed.), *Perspectives on Luke–Acts* (Danville, VA: Association of Baptist Professors of Religion, 1978) 76–98.

McDonald, L.M., and S.E. Porter, *Early Christianity and its Sacred Literature* (Peabody, MA: Hendrickson, forthcoming 1999).

Menzies, R.P., *The Development of Early Christian Pneumatology with Special Reference to Luke–Acts* (JSNTSup 54; Sheffield: JSOT Press, 1991).

Moo, D.J., *The Epistle to the Romans* (NICNT; Grand Rapids: Eerdmans, 1996).

Moulton, J.H., *Prolegomena*, vol. 1 of *A Grammar of New Testament Greek* (Edinburgh: T. & T. Clark, 3rd edn, 1908).

Neil, W., *The Acts of the Apostles* (NCB; London: Marshall, Morgan, Scott, 1977).

Norden, E., *Agnostos Theos: Untersuchungen zur Formengeschichte Religiöser Rede* (Stuttgart: Teubner, 1913; repr. Darmstadt: Wissenschaftliche Buchgesellschaft, 1956).

Page, T.E., *The Acts of the Apostles* (London: Macmillan, 1886).

Pervo, R.I., *Profit with Delight: The Literary Genre of the Acts of the Apostles* (Philadelphia: Fortress Press, 1987).

Pesch, R., *Die Apostelgeschichte* (2 vols.; EKK 5.1, 2; Solothurn: Benziger; Neukirchen-Vluyn: Neukirchener, 1995 [2nd edn], 1986).

Plümacher, E., "Wirklichkeitserfahrung und Geschichtsschreibung bei Lukas: Erwägungen zu den Wir-Stücken der Apostelgeschichte," *ZNW* 68 (1977) 2–22.

Polhill, J.B., *Acts* (NAC 26; Nashville: Broadman, 1992).

Porter, S.E., *Idioms of the Greek New Testament* (BLG 2; Sheffield: JSOT Press, 2nd edn, 1994).

Porter, S.E., "Thucydides 1.22.1 and Speeches in Acts: Is there a Thucydidean View?" *NovT* 32 (1990) 121–142; repr. in S.E. Porter, *Studies in the Greek of the New Testament: Theory and Practice* (SBG 5; New York: Lang, 1996) 173–193.

Porter, S.E., *Verbal Aspect in the Greek of the New Testament, with Reference to Tense and Mood* (SBG 1; New York: Lang, 1989).

Porter, S.E. (ed.), *Handbook of Classical Rhetoric in the Hellenistic Period 330 B.C.–A.D. 400* (Leiden: Brill, 1997).

Porter, S.E. (ed.), *Handbook to Exegesis of the New Testament* (NTTS 25; Leiden: Brill, 1997).

Porter, S.E., and T.H. Olbricht (eds.), *Rhetoric and the New Testament: Essays from the 1992 Heidelberg Conference* (JSNTSup 90; Sheffield: JSOT Press, 1993).

Powell, M.A., *What are They Saying about Acts?* (New York: Paulist, 1991).

Praeder, S.M., "The Problem of First person Narration in Acts," *NovT* 29 (1987) 193–218.

Rackham, R.B., *The Acts of the Apostles* (London: Methuen, 8th edn, 1919).

Robbins, V.K., "By Land and By Sea: The We-Passages and Ancient Sea Voyages," in C.H. Talbert (ed.), *Perspectives on Luke–Acts* (Edinburgh: T. & T. Clark, 1978) 215–242.

Roloff, J., *Die Apostelgeschichte* (NTD 5; Berlin: Evangelische Verlags-Anstalt, 1981).

Rosenblatt, M.-E., *Paul the Accused: His Portrait in the Acts of the Apostles* (Collegeville, MN: Liturgical, 1995).

Schille, G., *Die Apostelgeschichte des Lukas* (THNT 5; Berlin: Evangelische Verlags-Anstalt, 1983).

Schneider, G., *Die Apostelgeschichte* (2 vols.; HTKNT 5.1, 2; Freiburg: Herder, 1980, 1982).

Shepherd, W.H., Jr, *The Narrative Function of the Holy Spirit as a Character in Luke–Acts* (SBLDS 147; Atlanta: Scholars Press, 1994).

Simon, M., "The Apostolic Decree and its Setting in the Ancient Church," *BJRL* 52 (1969) 437–460.

Soards, M.L., *The Speeches in Acts: Their Content, Context, and Concerns* (Louisville: Westminster/John Knox, 1994).

Spencer, F.S., *Acts* (Readings; Sheffield: Sheffield Academic Press, 1997).

Squires, J.T., *The Plan of God in Luke–Acts* (SNTSMS 76; Cambridge: Cambridge University Press, 1993).

Steyn, G.J., *Septuagint Quotations in the Context of the Petrine and Pauline Speeches of the Acta Apostolorum* (Kampen: Kok Pharos, 1995).

Swete, H.B., *The Holy Spirit in the New Testament: A Study of Primitive Christian Teaching* (London: Macmillan, 2nd edn, 1910).

Tajra, H.W., *The Trial of St Paul: A Juridical Exegesis of the Second Half of the Acts of the Apostles* (WUNT 2.35; Tübingen: Mohr–Siebeck, 1989).

Talbert, C.H., *Readings Acts* (New York: Crossroad, 1997).

Tannehill, R.C., *The Narrative Unity of Luke–Acts: A Literary Interpretation. II. The Acts of the Apostles* (FFNT; Minneapolis: Fortress Press, 1990).

Thornton, C.-J., *Der Zeuge des Zeugen: Lukas als Historiker der Paulusreisen* (WUNT 56; Tübingen: Mohr–Siebeck, 1991).

Tuckett, C.M. (ed.), *Luke's Literary Achievement: Collected Essays* (JSNTSup 116; Sheffield: JSOT Press, 1995).

Turner, M., *Power from on High: The Spirit in Israel's Restoration and Witness in Luke–Acts* (JPTSup 9; Sheffield: Sheffield Academic Press, 1996).

Vielhauer, P., "On the 'Paulinism' of Acts," in L.E. Keck and J.L. Martyn (eds.), *Studies in Luke–Acts* (Philadelphia: Fortress Press, 1966) 33–50.

Wallace, R., and W. Williams, *The Acts of the Apostles* (London: Duckworth, 1993).

Watson, D.F., "Paul's Speech to the Ephesian Elders (Acts 20.17–38): Epideictic Rhetoric of Farewell," in D.F. Watson (ed.), *Persuasive Artistry: Studies in New Testament Rhetoric in Honor of George A. Kennedy* (JSNTSup 50; Sheffield: JSOT Press, 1991) 184–208.

Wilcox, M., *The Semitisms of Acts* (Oxford: Clarendon Press, 1965).

Winter, B.W., "In Public and in Private: Early Christian Interactions with Religious Pluralism," in A.D. Clarke and B.W. Winter (eds.), *One God, One Lord in a World of Religious Pluralism* (Cambridge: Tyndale House, 1991) 112–134.

Winter, B.W., and A.D. Clarke (eds.), *The Book of Acts in its First Century Setting.* I. *The Book of Acts in its Ancient Literary Setting* (Grand Rapids: Eerdmans, 1993).

Witherington, B., III, *The Acts of the Apostles: A Socio-Rhetorical Commentary* (Grand Rapids: Eerdmans, 1998).

Witherington, B., III (ed.), *History, Literature and Society in the Book of Acts* (Cambridge: Cambridge University Press, 1996).

Index of Sources

Other Ancient Sources

Index of Names

Index of Subjects